RANDOM
HOUSE
LARGE
PRINT

Additional Praise for Chris Whipple's
THE GATEKEEPERS

"I loved **The Gatekeepers!** The reporting is superb, the writing engaging and wonderfully fair-minded. Unbuttoned at last, these chiefs have wonderful stories to tell. This book serves as a compellingly readable thank-you note to a motley crew of policy nerds, fixers, maniacs, and soon-to-be ex–best friends of the president who have lost sleep—and probably several years off their lives—in the service of the White House, and of their country."

—Alex Beam, author of **The Feud, Gracefully Insane,**
and **American Crucifixion**

"Chris Whipple is one of our era's most accomplished multimedia journalists. Drawing on access to senior officials most reporters can only dream of, his documentary **The Spymasters** brought Americans inside the U.S. intelligence community as never before. Now, Whipple has done it again, exploring the inner workings of the last eight presidencies—from Nixon to Obama—through exclusive interviews with current and former White House chiefs of staff. **The Gatekeepers** is first-rate history, as told by the men who lived it to a man who knows, with supreme assurance, how to write it."

—James Rosen, Fox News chief Washington
correspondent and author of **The Strong Man** and
Cheney One on One

"History, drama, intrigue. Every page is engaging. Required reading for every Washington power player."

—David Friend, **Vanity Fair**, author of **Watching the World Change**

"A vibrant narrative of the real-world West Wing . . . confident and fast-paced . . . In this page-turner of a history, readers will discover new facets of historical events that they felt they already knew."

—**Publishers Weekly**

THE GATEKEEPERS

THE
GATEKEEPERS

How the White House Chiefs of Staff Define Every Presidency

Chris Whipple

RANDOM HOUSE
LARGE PRINT

Cover design by Christopher Brand
Jacket photographs by (top) David Hume Kennerly,
(center) Courtesy Ronald Reagan Library,
(bottom) The White House

The Library of Congress has established a
Cataloging-in-Publication record for this title.

ISBN: 978-1-5247-3629-3

www.randomhouse.com/largeprint

FIRST LARGE PRINT EDITION

Printed in the United States of America

10   9   8   7   6   5   4   3   2   1

This Large Print edition published in accord with the
standards of the N.A.V.H.

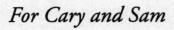

For Cary and Sam

Contents

You have to be the person that says no. You've got to be the son of a bitch who basically tells somebody what the president can't tell him.
—Leon Panetta, chief of staff to Bill Clinton

———

Somebody's got to be in charge. Somebody's got to be the go-to guy who can go into the Oval Office and deliver a very tough message to the president. You can't do that if you got eight or nine guys sitting around saying, "Well, you go tell him."
—Dick Cheney, chief of staff to Gerald Ford

———

If it's between good and bad, somebody else will deal with it. Everything that gets into the Oval Office is between bad and worse.
—Rahm Emanuel, chief of staff to Barack Obama

THE GATEKEEPERS

Introduction

"I Brought My Pillow
and My Blankie"

Rahm Emanuel was so cold he could see his breath as he crossed the White House parking lot and entered the West Wing lobby. It was December 5, 2008, an unusually frigid morning in Washington, D.C. But it wasn't the weather that sent a chill through Emanuel; it was the unbelievably daunting challenge that lay ahead.

In just six weeks Emanuel would become White House chief of staff to Barack Obama, the forty-fourth president of the United States. But for more than a month, he had watched in astonishment as the world they were about to inherit was turned upside down. The U.S. economy was teetering on the edge of another Great Depression. Credit—the lifeblood of the world economy—was frozen. The entire auto industry was on the brink of collapse. Two bloody wars were mired in stalemate. There was more than a little truth, Emanuel thought, to the headline in **The Onion**: "Black Man Given Nation's Worst Job." The stiletto-tongued infighter, former senior adviser to Bill Clinton, and congressman from Illinois felt apprehensive. "I brought my pillow and my blankie," he would later joke, looking back at that dark morning when the fate of the new administration seemed to hang in the balance. The truth was, Rahm Emanuel was scared.

The unannounced gathering at the White House that morning looked like a Cold War–era national security crisis. Black sedans and SUVs rolled up; men in dark suits clambered into the Executive Mansion. Emanuel thought about the elite fraternity that was assembling here: Donald Rumsfeld. Dick Cheney. Leon Panetta. Howard Baker Jr. Jack Watson. Ken Duberstein. John Sununu. Sam Skinner. Mack McLarty. John Podesta. Andrew Card. Joshua Bolten. They were among Washington's most powerful figures of the last half century: secretaries of defense, OMB directors, governor, CIA director, majority leader, and vice president. But they had one thing above all in common. It was a special bond, a shared trial by fire that transcended their political differences: Every one of them had served as White House chief of staff.

As they gathered in the office they had all once

occupied—now home to Joshua Bolten, George W. Bush's current chief—they mingled and swapped stories. It had been Bolten's idea to bring all the former White House chiefs together after the election, to give his successor advice on how to do the job. Bolten guessed that of the thirteen other living chiefs, maybe a half dozen would actually show up. But to his amazement, only Reagan's James Baker and Clinton's Erskine Bowles were no-shows.

"It really was an amazing day," recalls John Podesta, Clinton's final chief, "because it was quite a collection of individuals: from Dick Cheney and Donald Rumsfeld to me and Rahm. The span of ideology and politics, the span of history was all very present. And we all got the chance to give Rahm one piece of advice." Clinton's gregarious former chief Leon Panetta, about to be tapped as Obama's CIA director, was in his element: "All of them were my close friends," he recalls. "And to have them together in that room to wish Rahm Emanuel the best in his entry into that rogues' gallery of chiefs of staff—that was a very special moment."

The ghosts of presidencies past hovered around them. "It's a space where you feel the presence of history," Bolten would recall. "They were all transported back to their time in office."

Dick Cheney, once the thirty-four-year-old chief of staff to President Gerald Ford, pointed to the spot on the floor where Federal Reserve chief Alan Greenspan, immobilized by a bad back, used to lie supine during meetings, declaiming on monetary and fiscal policy. A fire crackled in the corner fireplace below a magnificent oil portrait of Abraham Lincoln. Finally, Bolten called the gathering to order and herded his distinguished guests around a long table.

At opposite ends sat two men whose political fortunes had been linked for a generation: Cheney, who would be vice president for six more weeks; and Rumsfeld, who had resigned under fire as defense secretary. It was Rumsfeld who had taken Cheney under his wing as a young political science grad student in the Nixon White House—and then summoned him to serve as his deputy when he became Gerald Ford's chief of staff. Together they had helped Ford cobble together his "accidental presidency" after the trauma of Watergate; they had also watched helplessly as South Vietnam was overrun by Communist forces, bringing a bloody and ignominious end to the longest war in U.S. history. Thirty years later, during the Iraq War, Cheney, the protégé, would be called upon by George W. Bush to tell his mentor to step down as defense secretary. As the prime architects of another divisive conflict that was ending badly, Cheney and Rumsfeld had come full circle.

Cheney was impressed by the morning's gathering. "This was unique in that you had all or nearly all of the living former chiefs of staff in the room at the same time," he recalls. And the irony of giving advice to Barack Obama's top adviser was not lost on him: "Obama had spent the better part of his campaign trashing us from one end of the country to the other. But he's our president. By that stage he'd won the election. And when you're all sitting around the table and getting ready to say, 'Here are the keys to the men's room,' you really do want to take advantage of the opportunity to say, 'Look, here's a couple of things that you really need to keep in mind.'"

Presidential transitions are awkward, and Cheney had been through his share. "There's always a certain amount of hubris involved for the new crowd coming in: 'Well, if you guys are so smart, why did we beat you?' And so it can get a little tense at times, but you've got to overcome those things, because there aren't very many people who've run the White House. And there are valuable lessons to be learned. You really do want to try to equip the new guy with whatever wisdom you've acquired during the course of your time in office."

It was a moment of bipartisanship that would seem almost inconceivable today, a throwback to a bygone era of civility. "There was a sense in that room," says Podesta, "among Republicans and Democrats, that the country needed people to get together and find some leadership." Even the notoriously partisan Emanuel gave his Republican counterparts the benefit of the doubt. "I think they knew how difficult this moment in time was historically," he recalls. "I think everyone was wishing the administration well." He did something few had ever seen him do before: He pulled out a pen and started to take notes.

Going around the table, one at a time, Bolten asked his guests to give the incoming chief their advice.

Fifty years of presidential history were represented, and no one knew that history better than Ken Duberstein. Cherubic and voluble, with a booming laugh, Brooklyn-born Duberstein had been Ronald Reagan's final chief of staff, and the first Jew to hold the job. "President Reagan didn't hire me for my good looks," he liked to tell people. "He hired me because he knew that I would tell him straight—because that is the Brooklyn way." (After leaving the White House, he set up shop on Pennsylvania Avenue, offering strategic planning to corporate clients.) Technically, Duberstein had been chief for just seven months; in reality, with his mentor Howard Baker preoccupied with a family illness, Duberstein had been Reagan's co-chief for his last two years. Not just companies, but presidents consulted him, hoping the Reagan magic might rub off. And few told more dramatic stories about being a witness to presidential history. At the height of the Cold War, accompanying

Reagan to a speech at West Berlin's Brandenburg Gate, it was Duberstein who urged the president to ignore the objections of his State Department and deliver his iconic challenge to the Soviet Union: "Mr. Gorbachev, tear down this wall!"

Now, in another time of crisis, Duberstein spoke first. "Always remember," he said, looking at Emanuel, "that when you open your mouth, it is not you but **the president** who is speaking." Emanuel stared back at him. "Oh, **shit!**" he said.

The chiefs erupted in laughter. Next up was Jack Watson. Now seventy, square-jawed and handsome, Watson looked like a movie star; that's what Jimmy Carter thought when the charismatic young Atlanta lawyer rode out on his motorcycle to meet the future president at his peanut farm more than forty years ago. As a young marine in an elite special operations unit, Watson had set an obstacle course record at Quantico that stood for more than twenty years; charming, earnest, and silver-tongued, he became a successful trial lawyer, and one of Carter's trusted advisers during his 1976 presidential campaign. "Jack isn't normal," says one of his colleagues. "I mean, he was injected with the perfect serum. If you want to criticize him, he's too good to be true." Watson had been put in charge of Carter's transition, and many believed he was a contender to become his White House chief of staff. But in a fateful decision that would hobble his presidency, Carter refused to appoint a chief.

(Two and a half years later, Carter remedied that but then compounded his mistake by giving the job to a person who was unsuited to it, a brilliant but disorganized political strategist named Hamilton Jordan.) With less than eight months left in his term, Carter finally gave the job to Watson. In that brief period, Watson earned the respect of his peers for his keen grasp of the position—a job he likened to a "javelin catcher." He looked at Rahm and smiled. "Never forget the extraordinary opportunity you've been given to serve, and the privilege and responsibility that it represents," he said. "You are sitting next to the most powerful person in the world. Remember to value and appreciate that fact every single day you're here."

John Podesta, the head of Obama's transition team, was next. Grandson of an Italian immigrant, son of a Chicago factory worker, Podesta had been bitten by the political bug as a college scholarship student back in 1970, when he volunteered for a Connecticut Senate campaign—and met a wonkish Yale Law School student named Bill Clinton. Decades later, in the Clinton White House, Podesta would succeed Erskine Bowles as chief of staff. In the throes of the Monica Lewinsky scandal, Podesta was so well known for his hair-trigger temper that it was said he had an evil twin named "Skippy." But this morning he preached humility and patience. "You've got to slow down, and listen," he said. "You've got a lot of smart people who are in that building with you. And you've got to resist the temptation to always have the answer. Slow down, listen. You'll learn a lot and you'll make better decisions."

Thomas F. "Mack" McLarty, the Arkansas businessman who had been Bill Clinton's first chief of staff, knew better than anyone just how unforgiving the job could be. Courtly and charming, "Mack the Nice," as he was known, was liked by almost everyone in Washington. But he had been a stranger to Capitol Hill and unschooled in its bare-knuckled wars. After a year and a half, with Clinton's agenda stymied and reelection in jeopardy, McLarty had agreed to step down as chief. But everyone in this room could empathize; they had all served at the whim of their presidents, and more than a few had been fired. Some thought McLarty was too kind, too gentlemanly for the job; if pressed, Mack might have agreed. "Try to keep some perspective about what you're doing and try to maintain your humanity," he told Rahm. "You don't always succeed. We're all human and we make mistakes. It starts with recognizing what a privilege it is to serve the president of the United States, but more importantly, the people of this country. Keep that in perspective and don't let it get out of proportion with this regal title of 'chief of staff.'"

McLarty's admonition could have been aimed squarely at another man seated at the table, John

Sununu. George H. W. Bush had picked the combative ex-governor of New Hampshire as his chief, hoping that Sununu's domestic policy chops would complement his own foreign policy expertise. Sununu liked to tell people—with a wink—that he was "just a warm, fuzzy pussycat." In fact, he flaunted his image as the president's son of a bitch like a badge of honor. Arrogant and confrontational, Sununu antagonized Congress, the press corps, and the White House staff alike. Later, when he was caught using government limousines and planes for personal trips, few came to his defense. Sununu would resign under a cloud. "You have to create a firewall between the president and those who are clawing to see the president," he told Rahm. "Even if it creates problems for the chief of staff. I was **very good** at creating problems for the chief of staff."

Leon Panetta was probably the most popular person in the room. The son of Italian immigrants, jovial and outgoing, he was equally at home on his walnut farm in Monterey, California, and in the corridors of the West Wing. But as Bill Clinton's second chief—replacing McLarty—Panetta had wielded an iron fist inside a velvet glove. When he arrived, Clinton's presidency was on the ropes, his ambitious agenda threatened by fights over gays in the military, the Whitewater scandal, and other distractions. The damage was self-inflicted, caused by Clinton's indiscipline and sloppy staff work. Panetta stepped in and brought discipline and focus to the White House—enabling Clinton to regain his traction and go on to win a second term. Now it was Panetta's turn to tutor Obama's incoming chief: "Always, always, be straight and honest with the president of the United States," he said. "Always tell him what he may not want to hear—because frankly, a lot of people in the White House will always tell the president what he **wants** to hear."

Andrew Card, Bolten's predecessor, had set the modern record for longevity as chief: five years and three months under George W. Bush. Yet Card, who had served five presidents, was intimidated, almost awed, by the company this morning. "These were truly historic people who served during phenomenally historic times and it was quite compelling because they're all very wise," he would recall. When it came his turn, Card urged Rahm to protect the office of the presidency: "A lot of people aren't interested in protecting the institution of the presidency, Article 2 in the Constitution. In fact, it's under attack almost all the time from Article 1, which is Congress, and Article 3, the courts. And there really aren't too many people at the White House that pay attention to that."

Next, all eyes turned to Donald Rumsfeld. The pugnacious, suffer-no-fools architect of the Iraq invasion, George Bush's embattled defense secretary had been asked to resign after the bungling of the occupation and the scandals at Abu Ghraib. Bolten, who had brought the chiefs together this morning, had been instrumental in Rumsfeld's firing.

And yet, around this table Rumsfeld was respected for an earlier incarnation—as Gerald R. Ford's remarkably effective chief of staff. In the aftermath of the biggest scandal in American history, with Ford plummeting in the polls after his pardon of Richard Nixon for Watergate crimes, Rumsfeld had put Ford's presidency back on track. He had been a congressman and ambassador—and would become a corporate CEO and defense secretary (twice). But Rumsfeld insisted that being Ford's White House chief was by far the toughest job he'd ever had: "It was like climbing into the cockpit of a crippled plane in flight and trying to land it safely." Rumsfeld had pulled Ford's presidency out of a nosedive.

One of Rumsfeld's first acts as chief had been to appoint Cheney as his deputy. In an episode that would seal their friendship, Rumsfeld had prevented Cheney's career from imploding. Faced with an FBI background check, Cheney confessed a secret: Out West, in his twenties, he had been arrested twice—and jailed—for drunk driving. Rumsfeld (with Ford's blessing) stood by him. For men who decades later would become two of the most powerful and polarizing figures in American history, it was the beginning of a formidable alliance.

Rumsfeld, the wily veteran, turned to Emanuel. "Immediately pick your successor," he told him. "And always remember: You are **not** indispensable." Emanuel could not resist taking a swing at this verbal softball. "Is that true for secretaries of defense?" he cracked. A roar of laughter went around the table. Even Rumsfeld forced a smile.

Finally it was Cheney's turn to speak. Over eight years, the vice president had richly earned his reputation as the Darth Vader of the Far Right, the unapologetic author of the war on terror. But many of the men around this table had known a different Cheney. Decades earlier, succeeding Rumsfeld as chief, he'd been one of the most popular figures in Washington, helping Gerald Ford return from the dead politically and very nearly defeat Jimmy Carter. In that earlier incarnation, Cheney had been known for his humility and uncanny ability to forge consensus; his Secret Service moniker was "Backseat." This supposedly kinder, gentler Cheney also had a wicked sense of humor and a fondness for elaborate practical jokes. The press corps loved him. In the years since, the debate over "What in the world happened to Cheney?" had become almost a parlor game among the chiefs. One theory was that he had been transformed by his experience as the powerful CEO of Halliburton. Others thought he had gone to the dark side in the 1980s, running secret "continuity of government" exercises (war games that simulated nuclear Arma-

geddon). The truth was, Cheney's archconserva-
tive ideology was nothing new; he had always been
"somewhere to the right of Genghis Khan," as one
Ford colleague put it. But Cheney's worldview now
seemed bleaker, his disposition darker. His close
friend and colleague Brent Scowcroft, estranged
from Cheney over the Iraq War, was convinced
that his ex-friend's brushes with mortality had
changed him (Cheney suffered five heart attacks
before his transplant in 2012). "That's what a bad
heart will do to a person," Scowcroft told me. The
Iraq War also triggered fierce arguments between
Cheney and James Baker, his former colleague and
hunting partner. But Cheney's close friend David
Hume Kennerly, Ford's White House photographer, insists that his supposed transformation was
nonsense. He may have a point: Back in the 1970s
Cheney had taken a job aptitude test. His ideal
career match? An undertaker.

Now the most powerful vice president in modern
history, whose nickname was "Big Time," looked
up at Emanuel over his glasses. "At all costs," he
said gravely, "**control** your vice president." The
chiefs erupted in the last round of laughter for
the day. Cheney flashed a crooked smile.

Following the meeting, the chiefs gathered outside Bolten's office. Then they headed down the
hall toward the Oval Office. Leading the way was
Bolten, who would be chief for six more weeks.
At the rear, grasping a cane and clinging to his

ex-deputy Ken Duberstein, was Howard Baker Jr., now eighty-three and hobbled by Parkinson's disease.

Waiting for them was George W. Bush. A presidency that had begun with one cataclysmic crisis, on September 11, 2001, was ending with another: the prospect of worldwide financial collapse. The personal toll it had taken on the president was apparent. A subdued Bush greeted them, with none of his trademark nicknames or quips. "I had seen and met President Bush many times," recalls Podesta. "But I thought to myself that morning how much the wear and tear of that office was lined into his face. He really looked like he was ready to wrap it up." The chiefs said their good-byes to the president and one another and departed.

IT HAD BEEN a singular event, a rare gathering of one of the most remarkable fraternities in Washington. "Every president reveals himself," says historian Richard Norton Smith, "by the presidential portraits he hangs in the Roosevelt Room, and by the person he picks as his chief of staff." Like the commanders in chief who comprise the "Presidents Club," the chiefs are a band of battle-scarred brothers. (There are currently seventeen alive—none of them women, for reasons we will explore.) They have a remarkable mutual respect for their fellow members. "There is no secret handshake, but it is a special bond," says Sununu. Fierce partisans, the chiefs can be ruthless in pursuit of their presidents' agendas: H. R. Haldeman went to prison for perjuring himself in Richard Nixon's Watergate scandal. But they are bound together by the shared experience of having survived what may be the toughest job in Washington—so arduous that the average tenure is a little more than eighteen months. James A. Baker III, the Republican consigliere who served as chief of staff, Treasury secretary, and secretary of state, says: "You can very well make the argument that the White House chief of staff is the second-most-powerful job in government." In fact, the fate of every presidency arguably hinges on this little-understood position.

The White House chief translates the president's agenda into reality. When government works, it is usually because the chief understands the fabric of power, threading the needle where policy and politics converge. Without Jim Baker's deft touch at managing the White House, the press and Capitol Hill—and the president's warring advisers—there would have been no Reagan Revolution. Similarly, Bill Clinton almost surely would have been a one-term president if Leon Panetta had not stepped in as chief of staff and brought discipline and order—not to mention record budget surpluses—to his White House. "Without a great chief of staff, a president frankly doesn't know what he is doing," says Robert Reich, Clinton's secretary of labor. During the last days of his presidency, Barack Obama observed: "One of the things I've learned is that the big breakthroughs are typically the result of a lot of grunt work—just a whole lot of blocking and tackling." Grunt work is what chiefs of staff do.

Conversely, when government fails, it can often be traced to the shortcomings of the chief. The stakes that come with the job could not be higher. "All our presidents select for various positions cronies or political hangers-on or whatever," observed Theodore "Ted" Sorensen, John F. Kennedy's confidant. "But every president knows when he's picking his chief of staff, my God, he'd better get the right man in that job or he'll be ruined." Some of the great blunders of modern history have happened because a chief of staff failed to tell the president what he did not want to hear. Paying hush money to burglars to cover up the Watergate break-in, trading weapons to Iran for hostages, launching the Iraq War on dubious evidence, even bungling the online rollout of health care—all might have been avoided if the chiefs of staff had put these decisions through the rigors of a system designed to avoid disasters.

Few chiefs have come through the experience unbloodied. "None of us is six four anymore," jokes five-foot-nine Duberstein, "even if we started out that way." "People ask me if it's like that television show **The West Wing**," says Erskine Bowles, Bill Clinton's second chief. "But that doesn't begin to capture the velocity. In an average day you would deal with Bosnia, Northern Ireland, the budget, taxation, the environment—and then you'd have lunch! And then on Friday you would say, 'Thank God—only two more working days until Monday.'" Cheney blames the job for causing his first heart attack. After he left the White House, Obama's Bill Daley came down with shingles—caused, he believes, by the stress. The man considered the gold standard in the job, James Baker, found the experience so emotionally grueling and deeply painful that he went to Ronald Reagan and tried, unsuccessfully, to quit.

Emanuel would discover just how relentless the job can be. Over the next twenty months, he would later tell me, there were no moments of peace: "You're on the phone on the way home. You're on the phone during dinner, you're on the phone reading bedtime stories to your kids—and you fall asleep before the book ends. And then you're woken up around three in the morning with something bad happening somewhere around the world." And yet Emanuel would not have traded the experience for any other. "Was it challenging? Was it brutal? Was it really tough?" he asks. "Would I have done it again? Absolutely. These experiences are gifts. They're to be cherished. And I guarantee you, every one of the chiefs would say, 'I would do it again if asked.'"

This book is the story of men who define the

presidencies they serve. It is the story of how Bob Haldeman, Nixon's self-proclaimed "son of a bitch," was widely blamed for causing Watergate. And indeed, Haldeman's failure to speak hard truths to Nixon allowed the scandal to take root. And yet Haldeman's successors credit him with creating the model for the modern White House chief. There is no one-size-fits-all template; every president has different needs. But the "staff system" conceived by Haldeman is a model of governance designed to prevent calamity. Time and again, presidencies that have failed to follow it have paid a heavy price.

It is the story of how two ambitious chiefs, Donald Rumsfeld and Dick Cheney, managed to bring Gerald Ford back from political oblivion to the brink of victory over Jimmy Carter. It is the story of how Carter, the quintessential outsider and among the most intelligent presidents ever elected, thought he could act as his own chief, thereby crippling his presidency. It tells how James Baker redefined the job, mastered its nuances, and—despite being the target of vicious infighting—made bipartisan government work; and how his successors Howard Baker and Ken Duberstein rescued Reagan from the Iran-Contra scandal. It explains how Leon Panetta (along with his deputies Bowles and Podesta) repaired Bill Clinton's broken presidency, fixing a dysfunctional White House and setting the stage for reelection.

It is also the story of how George W. Bush,

the politically gifted son of a president, overestimated his ability to govern—with disastrous consequences. The president who called himself "the decider" did not empower a chief of staff who could tell him what he did not want to hear or rein in his powerful advisers. Andy Card, his longserving chief, would be no match for Cheney, who had mastered the levers of power decades earlier. This would have devastating results when it came to the Iraq War. The bitter internecine struggle among Bush's principal advisers would lead to a Shakespearean drama before the invasion in early 2003—one that revealed an unspoken rift between the president and his father.

Barack Obama's fortunes would also be profoundly affected by his chiefs of staff. A neophyte at governing, the first senator to become president since Kennedy, Obama understood the significance of the position—he went out of his way to convene a secret meeting of Bill Clinton's former chiefs before he was elected. And indeed, with Emanuel at his side, Obama succeeded in staving off another Great Depression, saving the auto industry, and passing his landmark Affordable Care Act. But Emanuel's successors were less assertive. Obama's inability to pass legislation, his failure to get a grand bargain on the budget, and the bungled health-care rollout—all these debacles can be attributed not just to political gridlock, but to his chiefs. And yet Obama's final, and longest-serving, chief, Denis McDonough, would help the president perfect the use of executive power to achieve seminal breakthroughs with the Paris Climate Accord, the Iran Nuclear Agreement, and the diplomatic opening to Cuba. And for better or worse, Obama and McDonough would defy the foreign policy establishment by refusing to strike Syria in retaliation for its use of chemical weapons.

As for Donald Trump, the least qualified person ever elected to the presidency, the fate of his administration may well depend on whether he empowers a chief of staff to be his honest broker— and listens to advice he may not want to hear.

SINCE GEORGE WASHINGTON presidents have depended heavily on the advice and counsel of confidants. But it wasn't until nearly two centuries later that the first White House chief of staff emerged. The framers of the Constitution never envisioned anything like it. Unelected and unconfirmed, the chief serves at the whim of the president, hired and fired by him (or her) alone. And yet, in the modern era, no presidency has functioned effectively without one.

In the winter of 1968, after one of the most bitterly contested election campaigns in American history, Richard Nixon hunkered down in a hotel suite in New York City. He had gone there to plan his presidency, and to get even with his enemies. With him was a man Nixon called his pluperfect son of a bitch, and Lord High Executioner: the man who would become the first truly modern White House chief of staff.

1

"The Lord High Executioner"

H. R. Haldeman and Richard Nixon

On the thirty-ninth floor of New York City's Pierre Hotel, in a suite monitored by closed-circuit cameras and Secret Service agents, Richard M. Nixon looked out over the threadbare landscape of Central Park. It was December 1968, and the president-elect was huddled with his closest adviser, a grave young man in a tweed jacket and a brush haircut. The men were scribbling on yellow legal pads, planning the next presidency of the United States, now just a month away. "The executive branch of the United States is the largest corporation in the world," the adviser, H. R. Haldeman, would reflect years later. "It has the most awesome responsibilities of any corporation in the world, the largest budget of any

23

corporation in the world, and the largest number of employees. Yet the entire senior management structure and team have to be formed in a period of seventy-five days."

Richard Nixon's presidency would be born in the midst of a bloody quagmire and its violent backlash: Americans were dying in the jungles of South Vietnam at a rate of more than three hundred every week; protesters at home clashed with police in riot gear. Promising to end the war, Nixon had won the presidency by a hairsbreadth, the second-closest popular vote margin in history. There was a widespread sense that the center would not hold, the country more bitterly divided than at any time since the Civil War. Presidential chronicler Theodore White wrote: "The United States faced a crisis equal in magnitude to Lincoln's in 1860, or Roosevelt's in 1932. Those crises, however, had been defined—freedom rather than slavery, employment rather than hunger. Richard M. Nixon's crisis was far more complex; it defied definition . . . thus it was graver."

Having served as Dwight Eisenhower's vice president, Nixon knew the presidency could be a "splendid misery," as Jefferson put it, unresponsive even to the commands of the most celebrated general in modern history. "Poor Ike!" his predecessor Harry Truman had quipped upon Eisenhower's election. "He'll sit here and he'll say, 'Do this! Do that!' **And nothing will happen.** It won't be a bit like the Army."

"Presidents need help." That's what the Brownlow Committee, formed by Franklin Roosevelt in 1936, concluded about the burdens of the commander in chief. Eisenhower had found help in the form of an irascible former New Hampshire governor named Sherman Adams. When Ike made his first entrance into the Executive Mansion, the story goes, an usher handed the new president a letter. "Never bring me a sealed envelope!" Ike barked. Nothing, he decreed, should come to the president without first being screened by someone he trusted. Soon Adams was installed as the president's gatekeeper—and the first White House chief of staff was born.

"Possessed of the disposition of a grizzly with a barked shin, often inconsiderate, always demanding," Adams was loyal, selfless, and so fiercely protective of the president that he was called the Abominable No-Man. But Adams was more than a gatekeeper; he was the White House version of Ike's army chief of staff: funneling information, framing decisions, and acting as broker among quarreling cabinet members. He was the first chief—though not the last—who was thought to wield nearly as much power as his boss.

In Nixon's view, the importance of a strong chief of staff was confirmed by the misfortunes of Ike's successors. John Kennedy had rejected Ike's model and decided he did not need a chief; he would be his own gatekeeper. A half-dozen senior aides would have direct access to the Oval Office. But then came calamity: Kennedy was gulled by the Pentagon and CIA into sending a ragtag army of anti-Castro mercenaries onto the beach at Cuba's Bay of Pigs. They were routed, and the new president humiliated. Deceived by his generals, Kennedy concluded that he needed someone he could trust to help him with the big decisions (and to filter conflicting advice). Bobby Kennedy became his de facto chief.

Like Kennedy, Lyndon Johnson resisted concentrating power in a single adviser. Domineering, charming, bullying, LBJ would be his own chief—setting domestic and foreign priorities, reading every memo, corralling his cabinet, wrangling votes on Capitol Hill. His senior White House staff would take their marching orders from him alone. But after five years, humbled by a spiraling death toll in Vietnam and plummeting popularity at home, Lyndon Johnson had been driven from office, spent and defeated.

Now, ensconced in his Manhattan headquarters, Richard Nixon was determined to control his fate. His cabinet would be full of strong, idiosyncratic personalities: in domestic affairs, the distinguished economist Arthur Burns, the liberal iconoclast Daniel Patrick Moynihan, and the charismatic former Texas governor John Connally; in foreign affairs, the former attorney general William Rogers, and the gravel-voiced Harvard intellectual Henry Kissinger. But Nixon wanted someone to keep them in line, to ensure that his agenda would be executed, giving him time and space to think. H. R. Haldeman would be that person. As his chief of staff recalled years later, referring to himself in the third person: "Eisenhower had told Nixon that every president has to have his own 'SOB.' Nixon had looked over everyone in his entourage and decided that Haldeman was a pluperfect SOB. And because of that somewhat unflattering appraisal, my career took a rise."

Nixon was determined to do one other thing: exact revenge on his enemies. To that end, he summoned an important visitor: J. Edgar Hoover, the long-serving FBI director. As Haldeman later vividly recalled: "The president asked me to be present when Hoover paid his respects. Hoover, florid, rumpled, came into the suite and quickly got down to business. He said that LBJ had ordered the FBI to wiretap Nixon during the campaign. In fact, he told Nixon, Johnson had directed the FBI to 'bug' Nixon's campaign airplane, and this had been done." In truth, no such bug had been planted on Nixon's plane. Hoover was lying to the president-elect, cleverly exploiting Nixon's suspicions to enhance his own power. But for the man who was about to become the thirty-seventh president of the United States, this was confirmation of his worst fears about his political enemies: LBJ, the Kennedys, the liberals, and the press.

As Hoover departed, Haldeman recalled, "Nixon decided it was an opportune moment for a cup of coffee, while he thought over this new information. 'Want one?' he asked. I said no, and Nixon stared at the cup for a minute. I remember the moment clearly because his next words surprised me. Instead of remarking angrily on the bugging of his plane, Nixon said with some sympathy for Johnson, 'Well, I don't blame him. He's been under such pressure because of the damned war, he'd do anything.' He paused, holding the cup, then said, 'I'm not going to end up like LBJ, Bob, holed up in the White House, afraid to show my face on the street. I'm going to stop that war. Fast. I mean it!'"

H. R. "Bob" Haldeman and Richard M. Nixon were an odd couple, bound by politics and expedience yet worlds apart socially. Haldeman, an advertising agency executive in Los Angeles, was an unlikely candidate for the president's consigliere. "Bob Haldeman would have been a superstar had he never gone to the White House," recalls Larry Higby, who followed him from J. Walter Thompson to the White House at the age of twenty-three. Indeed, Haldeman in the early 1960s was Southern California royalty: regent of the University of California; president of the UCLA alumni association; founding chairman of the California Institute of the Arts: "He was a fairly easygoing guy," says Higby, now sixty-six, still wiry, animated, and intensely loyal to his mentor. "He loved the beach. He'd go sailing almost every afternoon. When he was in his office he would have tea every afternoon at three o'clock." To Nixon, a grocer's son from Whittier, California, raised by a Quaker mother, Haldeman belonged to another, rarefied world. "Los Angeles has a very distinct social hierarchy— with its own schools, fraternities, and status," says Nixon biographer Evan Thomas. "And Nixon was envious of that: 'Haldeman, wow, he's part of the Los Angeles ruling class.'"

Volunteering for the Ike-Nixon race in 1956, Haldeman reveled in the discipline of presidential campaign work: "It turned out, somewhat to my surprise, that I was a born advance man. This is one of the most demanding jobs in politics. It needs organizational ability, a passion for predictability and punctuality, and a strong enough character to counterbalance the demands of different political groups and personalities." Haldeman was tapped to run Nixon's 1960 presidential campaign, and his 1962 race for governor of California—both losing efforts. A promising young local television reporter named Tom Brokaw was struck by Haldeman's buttoned-down civility. "He was the classic kind of '50s UCLA graduate, Ivy League suits, a straight arrow," recalls Brokaw. But working for Nixon transformed him. "He really changed and became much more serious, much more focused, and much more introspective," says Higby. "He was really shaping what he thought was a great cause for the United States and the world." Selflessly dedicated to Nixon, Haldeman seemed driven not by ideology or friendship but by a sense of mission. Years later, John W. Dean, the president's former legal counsel, told me he still puzzles over the bond between Nixon and his chief: "There was no real close personal bond there, but Haldeman's efficiency obviously appealed to Nixon, and Nixon's politics appealed to Haldeman."

Devastated by his defeat in the 1962 governor's race, Nixon retreated to New York City, where he nursed his wounds in a white-shoe law firm run by his friend and mentor John Mitchell. But Haldeman still believed in Nixon's presidential prospects, and in 1967 sent his boss a memo that would become the blueprint for the next year's presidential campaign. "The time has come," Haldeman wrote, "for political campaigning—its techniques and strategies—to come out of the dark ages and into the brave new world of the omnipresent eye." The "eye" was television, an alternative to the exhausting shoe-leather and whistle-stop campaign that Nixon had run and lost against Jack Kennedy in 1960, causing him to "become punchy, mauled by his admirers, jeered and deflated by his opponent's supporters (and paid troublemakers), misled by the super-stimulation of one frenzied rally after another." Haldeman continued: "He has no time to think. To study his opponent's strategy and statements, to develop his own strategy and statements. No wonder the almost inevitable campaign dialogue borders so near the idiot level."

Haldeman proposed a strategy that would spare Nixon that grueling regimen; and the following year, helped by a young TV producer named Roger Ailes, he crafted a carefully focused television marketing campaign. Nixon was packaged and sold to the country in thirty- and sixty-second advertisements. He defeated Hubert Humphrey by a margin of just five hundred thousand votes (though comfortably in the electoral college). And Haldeman, the consummate advance man, would take an important lesson to the White House: The president's time is his most valuable asset.

Holed up at their transition headquarters, Haldeman read everything he could find on how to organize the White House. He devised what he called a staff system, a model and template of White House governance that almost every subsequent administration would follow.

One person was paying particularly close attention: Donald Rumsfeld, the young, ambitious head of Nixon's Office of Economic Opportunity. "There has to be a staff system, and Haldeman was the person who designed it," Rumsfeld would tell me years later. Haldeman, he notes, adapted the lessons Nixon learned from Ike: "It came really out of Eisenhower who had a military background, understanding the importance of communicating out to important elements—logistics and all the different elements in the military."

On December 19, 1968, Haldeman summoned the staff of the nascent administration to a meeting room at the Pierre. Watching from the back of the room, speechwriter William Safire took notes as Nixon's newly anointed chief addressed the troops:

> "Our job is not to do the work of government, but to get the work out to where it belongs— out to the Departments," Haldeman began. He continued: "Nothing goes to the president that is not completely staffed out first, for accuracy and form, for lateral coordination, checked for related material, reviewed by competent staff concerned with that area—and all that is essential for Presidential attention."

Haldeman then warned about what he called end running: "That is the principal occupation of 98 percent of the people in the bureaucracy. Do not permit anyone to end-run you or any of the rest of us. Don't become a source of end-running yourself, or we'll miss you at the White House." (End running, as Haldeman defined it, is what happens when someone with his own agenda meets privately with the president without going through the chief of staff. The result? All too often, a presidential edict that has not been thought through—with unintended consequences.)

He continued:

"The key staff can always communicate with and see the President when necessary. The priorities will be weighed on the basis of what visit will accomplish most. We've got to preserve his time for the things that matter. Now, that does not mean that everything will be reduced for him to the lowest common denominator. The President wants to make decisions himself, not preside over decisions made by the staff. How we decide what is major and what is minor is the key to whether this is a good White House staff or a lousy one."

He concluded by reading from the Brownlow Committee Report to FDR, describing the ideal qualities of a White House aide. He (or she) "would remain in the background, issue no orders, make no decisions, emit no public statements . . . should be possessed of a high competence, great physical vigor and a passion for anonymity."

It was a pitch-perfect description of Nixon's chief of staff, whose sole interest was to engrave the president's place in history. For the next five years, on everything from walking King Timahoe, the president's Irish setter, to mining North Vietnam's Haiphong Harbor, Haldeman would be Nixon's confidant.

Their relationship was intimate but strangely distant. "I think Haldeman viewed President Nixon as a close working colleague but not a friend," Higby says. "Nixon saw Haldeman, Ehrlichman, and Kissinger as a level below him. This was in contrast to people like John Connally or John Mitchell, whom Nixon viewed as equals and friends." The president and his chief shared the single-minded focus of loners. Physically awkward and socially inept, Nixon was most comfortable brooding in his private study; Haldeman, a tee-totaling Christian Scientist, was so devoted to his work that family and friends were an afterthought. Safire wrote that Haldeman and Nixon were "similar in a way to Cathy and Heathcliff in **Wuthering Heights**—Cathy insisted she was not so much in love with Heathcliff as she **was** Heathcliff—so too did Haldeman see his identity merged with Nixon's."

As chief of staff, Haldeman would be the first person Nixon saw in the Oval Office in the morning and the last on his way to the residence at night. Only three other people were cleared to see the president alone: Ehrlichman, Kissinger, and Connally. (Over time others would gain direct access to Nixon, with dire results.) Haldeman practiced his "passion for anonymity." At cabinet meetings, recalls Higby, "you'd always see him sitting against the wall. He never sat at the table, which other chiefs of staff have done. On the helicopter he and I would often sit toward the back unless he was brought up because the president wanted to talk to him about something."

No nuance of statecraft or image making escaped Haldeman's attention. "He really grasped everything—because he had grown up watching the shift from campaign stops to speeches to television: You know, 'You don't want the platform to be over here because the camera angle will be better,'" recalls Higby. The former advance man was always scanning the horizon for threats. "Haldeman was known for his caution," wrote Safire. "When asked what books the president was currently reading, he would answer with another question, what books did I recommend the president read?" When Safire told Haldeman he was writing a memoir, and was looking for personal sketches, the chief replied: "The president does not doodle." Safire wrote: "Haldeman nibbled his pencil for a moment. Then he looked at me with a humorously evil expression that spoke volumes about his understanding of image merchants in the throes of manipulation: '**Should** the president doodle?'"

Newsweek wrote: "Harry Robbins Haldeman is Richard Nixon's son of a bitch, glowering out at the world under a crew cut that would flatter a drill instructor with a gaze that would freeze Medusa."

John Dean never forgot a car ride from San Clemente to Newport, with the chief and two aides in the backseat. "Haldeman absolutely reamed both of them," says Dean. "I mean, just gave them a tongue lashing—and I'm thinking if he ever did that to me I would not stay in the job. I don't know if he sensed that. He never did that to me, but he did that to a lot of people, and Nixon liked that." Haldeman's memos to the staff were equally unforgiving. As when he took aim at Jeb Magruder, a young assistant, for failing to carry out an assignment:

July 7, 1970

MEMORANDUM FOR: MR. MAGRUDER

I am reluctantly and regretfully sending the attached memorandum to the President.

I never intend to send another memorandum like this to the President and I don't intend to tolerate this kind of total failure on the part of our staff ever again.

I'm not interested in any explanation, excuse, or discussion of this one, and I'm especially not interested in any more B.S. in the form of reports that tell me something has been done when in fact, it hasn't. . . .

H. R. Haldeman

Nothing was exempt from Haldeman's "zero defect" policy, recalls Terry O'Donnell, a White House veteran who became a Nixon aide in 1972. "He expected perfection. He said, 'This White House is the president's house and it should be the best in the world.' So if he walked through the West Wing and saw a paper askance, he'd make note of it. And if he went, literally, into the john at Camp David—because this really happened—and the toilet paper roll was almost run down, he made a note of it and said, 'Terry, that's not as it should be. Fix it.'"

Nixon shared his chief's obsession with the minutiae of White House management; alone in his private office, he would scribble on yellow legal pads (later typed up by his secretary Rose Mary Woods) his thoughts on everything from the modern art in U.S. embassies ("it's godawful and must be removed") to the unacceptable guest list for the annual Gridiron dinner. A single day, March 16, 1970, illustrates the range of subjects that preoccupied the president:

FOR H. R. HALDEMAN, FROM THE PRESIDENT

I would like for you to get. . . . a complete rundown on any comments on news stories, columns, or on television, with regard to my

Gridiron appearance on Saturday. . . . I recall that when each time [sic] Kennedy appeared before the Gridiron there were reams of columns with regard to the effectiveness of the appearance, even though on at least one occasion I recall it was somewhat of a bomb. . . . Give me a full report by the end of this week.

FROM: THE PRESIDENT
TO: H. R. HALDEMAN

Would you have the BORDEAUX years checked? I know that '59 is an excellent year, even with my unsophisticated taste; but my recollection is that '66 is one of the years. The reason I ask is that we seem to have a huge stock of '66 on hand and I wondered why.

Haldeman and Nixon's chief domestic adviser, John Ehrlichman—with their Germanic names— were dubbed by the media "the Berlin Wall." The narrative took root of Haldeman as the leader of a Praetorian Guard that isolated the president, building a wall between Nixon and his cabinet, and the diverse views he needed to make informed decisions.

Yet the narrative was not true. "It was just the opposite," says Higby. "Contrary to what people think, Haldeman worked to get **more** people in to see the president. He was, most of the time, the guy who was trying to break down the wall." It was Nixon who demanded isolation, preferring memos to meetings, retreating to his private hideaway in the Old Executive Office Building. Nixon was "pathologically shy," according to Stephen Bull, a young presidential assistant at the time. Haldeman knew that Nixon functioned best when given private space to make decisions. "The most important thing the president has is time," says Bull. "And the chief's job is to reserve as much of it for him as he can—even if it's just for going over to the Old Executive Office Building to sit there and think and make notes on a yellow pad."

When it came to setting policy, Nixon's White House staff would theoretically defer to the departments: State, Defense, Commerce, Treasury, HEW, Labor. ("Our job is not to do the work of government," Haldeman had vowed.) But in practice, actual governing and all real decisions would take place in the West Wing. (This has been true of every administration since.) William Rogers might have been secretary of state, but Kissinger, the national security adviser, was in charge of foreign policy. Ehrlichman, Nixon's senior aide, decided domestic policy. Nixon saw the White House as a Fortune 500 company, with the Oval Office as the corner office, and Haldeman as chief operating officer. "Policy was going to be decided in the White House," says Higby. "And it was the job of the cabinet to execute. And there were mechanisms put in place to make sure that follow-up and execution did take place."

One of those mechanisms was a "tickler system." Staffers were assigned to follow up on presidential edicts at specific intervals to be sure they were being carried out. John Dean says he ran afoul of the tickler system when he dragged his feet on Nixon's so-called enemies program—a plan to punish opponents with IRS tax audits. "I almost got in deep trouble because I wouldn't implement the enemies program," he says. "I found in the files all these memos back and forth on how they've got to get Haldeman to fire me because I'm not doing anything on it."

On June 29, 1971, exasperated by a series of leaks of classified information, Nixon called a cabinet meeting. "Down in the government," he announced, "are a bunch of sons of bitches. Some of those you've appointed may be well intentioned sons of bitches, but . . . many are out to get us. . . . We have yet to fire any of these people. From now on, Haldeman is the Lord High Executioner. Don't come whining to me when he tells you to do something. He will do it because I asked him to and you're to carry it out! We've checked and found that 96 percent of the bureaucracy are against us; they're bastards who are here to screw us."

The president's tone turned mawkish. "Haldeman has the worst job anybody can have in the White House. I remember poor old Bedell Smith

[Ike's assistant], who had to carry out a lot of tough decisions for Eisenhower. In his later years he started to drink a lot, probably to try and forget the things he had to do in his early years. He was at my house one night and he started to cry, and he said, 'All my life I have just been Ike's prat boy, doing his dirty work.' Well, Haldeman is my prat boy. . . . When he talks, it's me talking, and don't think it'll do you any good to come and talk to me, because I'll be tougher than he is. That's the way it's going to be."

In his diary that night, remarkably, Haldeman recounted with approval this petulant, almost unhinged presidential outburst: "It was pretty impressive, for all of them. I walked out right after Nixon did. They seemed to be very much impressed, so I think it had its effect."

If he misjudged Nixon's cabinet (who were outraged by the episode), Haldeman was better at reading other outsized personalities and egos. Kissinger, egocentric and paranoid, was constantly threatening to resign. The chief of staff became adept at talking him off the ledge. (Except when, with Nixon's blessing, he dared Kissinger to go ahead and quit.) Haldeman was also a sounding board for Kissinger's rants about his enemies, real and imagined. "Henry clearly had a lot of insecurities, as did Nixon," says Higby. "The president always felt inferior to the East Coast press and the Ivy Leaguers. And Henry also saw bogeymen like

Nixon did. His bogeyman happened to be the State Department."

Tolerating ethnic and religious slurs was the price of admission to Nixon's inner circle. "Haldeman's anti-Semitism is one of his fatal flaws," says biographer Thomas. "You can feel it, he's blinded by it. Haldeman is an enabler in Nixon's anti-Semitism, and it brings out the president's raw blind side." A presidential memo, casually dictated to aide Peter Flanigan, conveys the utter banality of Nixon's prejudice: "I have still not had a report that I consider to be adequate on meat prices," Nixon wrote. "I think you will find that chain stores who generally control these prices nationwide are primarily dominated by Jewish interests. These boys, of course, have every right to make all the money they want, but they have a notorious reputation in the trade for conspiracy."

In Nixon's mind, enemies had infiltrated government from top to bottom. Four decades later, over tea at his home in McLean, Virginia, Fred Malek, head of White House personnel then, describes a remarkable order he received from the president in 1971. "He calls me in and he says, 'I think there's a cabal of Democrats, and most of them are Jewish, at the Bureau of Labor Statistics—they're twisting the statistics to make me look bad, the monthly jobs reports. And I want you to find out how many of those people are Democrats, and how many are Jewish, and who are these people?' So I got a list and sent it to him, saying the top fifteen are Democrats—whatever it was. And he said, 'Well, how many are Jewish?' And I said, 'Well, f*ck, how do I know that?'" Afterward, Malek went to Haldeman. "Bob was always the voice of reason in this stuff. He knew how to take things off the table that represented Nixon's darker spirits. And I said, 'Bob, I don't know how to do that; it seems strange, is this a good idea?' And Haldeman said, 'Well, just look at their names and just send him **something**. Just give him something, and get him off it.' So I did. And nothing happened except we took the commissioner—he was a WASP—and we replaced him with this commissioner who was **Jewish**!"

Haldeman often acted as a brake on presidential orders he considered unwise or even illegal. "Presidents are like everybody else," explains Higby. "They have moments of pique—moments when they're really furious or really upset. Not only would Haldeman talk Nixon out of crazy ideas, but they had an understanding that the stuff he [Haldeman] felt was really bad and really wrong, he wouldn't do." Better to let the president cool off, and return another day. "Now, he would always go back to the president, a day or two later, and say, 'I didn't do that,'" says Higby. "'Remember you wanted me to do that? I didn't do that. Here's why.'" Long after he'd left the White House, at a conference in San Diego of former chiefs of staff in 1986, Haldeman was asked: "Did you ever have to talk the president out of a boneheaded idea?" He replied:

I was ordered by the president unequivocally and immediately to commence lie detector tests of every employee of the State Department because there had been a series of leaks which were seriously damaging our negotiations in Vietnam. This was an easy order not to carry out because it was physically impossible to do. It couldn't have been done anyway. But we didn't do it and the president said the next day, "Have you gotten a lie detector program started?" And I said no, and he said, "Aren't you going to?" And I said, "I don't intend to," and he again ordered that it be done.

I again didn't do it on the first round that time, then went back to him later that day . . . and said, "Mr. President, this really is a mistake. There are other ways of dealing with this problem at this point, and we will be back to you with a plan for doing that." We came back with a plan, and he said at that point, "I didn't think you would do it." But it was fairly clear at the time that I was supposed to.

The White House tapes capture countless instances of Nixon doing a slow burn as Haldeman tries to tamp down the president's anger. In the

summer of 1971, Nixon was convinced that classified documents had been spirited out of the State
Department and locked up at the Brookings Institution, a liberal think tank. He demanded action.

**JUNE 30, 1971: THE PRESIDENT,
HALDEMAN, MITCHELL, KISSINGER, AND
MELVIN LAIRD, 5:17–6:23 PM, OVAL OFFICE**

PRESIDENT NIXON: . . . I want Brookings, I
want them just to break in and take it out. Do
you understand?

HALDEMAN: Yeah. But you have to have somebody to do it.

NIXON: That's what I'm talking about. Don't
discuss it here . . . I want the break-in. Hell,
they do that. You're to break into the place,
rifle the files, and bring 'em out.

HALDEMAN: I don't have any problem with
breaking in. It's a Defense Department–
approved security. . . .

NIXON: Just go in and take it. Go in around
8:00 or 9:00 o'clock.

HALDEMAN: Make an inspection of the safe.

NIXON: That's right. You go in to inspect the
safe. I mean, clean it up.

**JULY 1, 1971: THE PRESIDENT, HALDEMAN,
AND KISSINGER. 8:45–9:52 AM, OVAL OFFICE**

PRESIDENT NIXON: . . . Do you think, for
Christ's sakes, that the **New York Times** is wor-

ried about all the legal niceties? Those sons of bitches are killing me. . . . We're up against an enemy, a conspiracy. They're using any means. We are going to use any means. Is that clear?

Did they get the Brookings Institute raided last night? No. Get it done. I want it done. I want the Brookings Institute safe cleaned out and I want it cleaned out in such a way that it makes somebody else [look responsible].

Haldeman managed to shelve the break-in plan, but before long the harebrained plot would come to life again.

For all his paranoia, of course, Nixon had real opposition. He faced a hostile press corps, and a bitterly antagonistic Congress, controlled by Democrats. And yet, with Haldeman cracking the whip, Nixon forged bipartisan success in domestic and foreign affairs. He was ideologically closer to his Democratic opposition than many supposed. Welfare reform (or "workfare") was first conceived by Pat Moynihan under Nixon. And as Evan Thomas points out: "Nixon began the march, and his administration was an active player in other traditionally liberal realms like health care, consumer and job safety, and the environment. He embraced the mid-twentieth-century ethos that government existed to solve problems, and he kept at them until he was swallowed by Watergate." Among Nixon's major domestic achievements, denounced by the

Republican Party ever since, was the establishment of the Environmental Protection Agency.

The crowning success of Nixon's first term was the grand diplomatic opening to China. The landmark thawing of relations between the United States and the People's Republic was executed by Kissinger, but it was conceived by Richard Nixon and produced by Haldeman. Higby recalls a flight on **Air Force One**, returning from India and Pakistan: "And you could see China in the distance out the window. And the president mentioned to Henry, 'We need to bring those people into the world.'" While credit would go to Nixon and Kissinger, the historic trip to China—a master stroke of diplomacy and publicity—was a Haldeman production. "I think that the importance of the pictures that came back, of the meetings, the dinners and the events, were what the breakthrough was all about," says Higby. "And all of that was choreographed by Haldeman."

But Nixon's fate turned on ending the Vietnam War; his inability to do so triggered a pattern of destructive behavior that would end his presidency. The intractable conflict threatened to devour him as it had LBJ. Nixon could not force the North Vietnamese to negotiate a "peace with honor." Nothing worked: not even pretending, as a negotiating bluff, that Nixon might have lost his mind. "I call it the Madman Theory, Bob," he told his chief. "I want the North Vietnamese to believe

I've reached the point where I might do anything to stop the war. We'll just slip the word to them that, 'For God's sake, you know Nixon is obsessed with Communists. We can't restrain him when he's angry—and he has his hand on the nuclear button!' And Ho Chi Minh himself will be in Paris in two days begging for peace."

But the war raged on. More than fifty-seven thousand Americans, and hundreds of thousands of Vietnamese, had been killed, including civilians. Nixon and his inner circle blamed domestic opposition; agitators who were pawns of Moscow; traitors who were leaking national security secrets. The White House was literally surrounded by antiwar protesters.

Besieged, Nixon and his chief would unwittingly give their enemies the keys to the fortress. In February of 1971, Nixon had posed to Haldeman a seemingly mundane question: How could they preserve the president's conversations for posterity? As Bill Safire wryly put it years later, Haldeman "had an eye for history, which was good; but he would come up with a method of preserving everything the president said, which was no good."

On inauguration day, LBJ told Nixon about the manual taping system he had installed in the Oval Office. Nixon ordered it removed. "I want it out," he commanded. But over time, his attitude changed. "The motivation for the taping system was quite straightforward," recalls Higby. "He wanted it for his own personal use when he was going to write his memoirs, the true story of what actually had happened, particularly surrounding Vietnam, the SALT Treaty, and China. And he felt that Henry [Kissinger] would come in and say one thing to him but then would go out and present a different picture to the press."

Haldeman suggested installing a manual recorder, which the president could turn on and off, recording selectively. But Nixon was utterly incapable of operating even the simplest mechanical device. "He just lacked natural grace," recalls Higby, laughing at the memory of "this tremendously clumsy guy. We tried over and over again. He would erase half the memo that he just dictated and then get all frustrated. So we finally had IBM make a special machine that only had 'on' and 'off.' And that was an utter failure once again. He'd forget to turn it on. He wouldn't turn it on right." As Higby recalls: "So eventually Haldeman said, 'Well, the only other thing you can do is do a voice-activated system.' And that is when we put in the system that later became the tapes." The decision to automatically record **every word** spoken in the Oval Office meant that, when scandal struck, nothing would be off-limits to congressional investigators. As one Nixon staffer would later note ruefully, "For want of a toggle switch, the presidency was lost."

On June 13, 1971, the **New York Times** began

publishing the **Pentagon Papers,** a secret history of the U.S. in Vietnam from 1945 to 1967, drawn from classified documents. The sensational leak, by a former Pentagon aide named Daniel Ellsberg, enraged Nixon. In his diary, Haldeman noted: "He feels strongly that we've got to get Ellsberg nailed hard." Nixon's determination to "get" Ellsberg would set in motion what Attorney General John Mitchell called the "White House horrors"— the ill-conceived intelligence operations that would doom his presidency. For Nixon's chief of staff, managing this crisis would be the ultimate test. H. R. Haldeman would fail it spectacularly.

With the tapes silently turning, Nixon demanded dirt on his enemies, and on Ellsberg in particular; a chain of events was set in motion that would spiral out of Haldeman's control. The chief had become adept at ignoring or shelving orders that were beyond the pale. But other Nixon confidants were less squeamish. Charles Colson, a ruthless political hatchet man and Nixon favorite, became the president's go-to person for dubious if not flagrantly illegal commands. Colson came and went from the Oval Office, meeting privately with Nixon. This was the kind of "end run" that Haldeman had feared and warned against. As John Dean recalls, "What happens is, the president goes to Colson, who was never a brake—who would click his heels, stiffen his back, salute, and go do it!!"

And it wasn't just Colson; Ehrlichman was another person Nixon would turn to for dubious missions. Haldeman thought Nixon's order to "blow the safe" at Brookings had been safely shelved. But Dean learned that Jack Caulfield, a private investigator hired by the White House, was about to carry out the plot—with Ehrlichman's approval.

The Brookings break-in was called off after Dean confronted Ehrlichman. But Ehrlichman had set up an under-the-radar intelligence unit within the White House itself. "The Plumbers," as they were known, were born of Nixon's frustration with his own FBI. Nixon was convinced that J. Edgar Hoover was refusing to do for him what he had done for his predecessors: off-the-shelf— that is, illegal—political espionage. "This is a constant theme in Nixon," says John Dean, "where he can find a precedent for everything he does because some other president has done it. He said the Kennedys were even nastier. For a long time I thought, well, maybe there's actually some truth to this. But when you actually look, other presidents didn't make it standard operating procedure."

On September 3, 1971, burglars ransacked the office of Daniel Ellsberg's psychiatrist in Los Angeles. Among them were ex-CIA operatives Howard Hunt and G. Gordon Liddy, cartoonish characters who would soon become famous for their roles in the Watergate break-in. The Ellsberg affair was a fiasco, a Monty Python sketch come to life: Not only did the intruders find nothing to incriminate or embarrass Ellsberg, they trashed the office and snapped photographs of the damage, with Liddy even posing in front of the building. Haldeman appears to have known nothing about this operation in advance. But the sorry episode had been okayed by Ehrlichman in a handwritten note: "If done under your assurance that it's not traceable back to the White House." Not only was it traceable, the bungled break-in threatened to scuttle the prosecution of Ellsberg for national security leaks. And Liddy and his gang were just getting started.

The origin of the illegal break-in at the Democratic National Committee on June 17, 1972, remains a mystery, debated for forty years. There is still no evidence that Haldeman or Nixon specifically approved the plot. But one thing is clear: With winks and nods and looks-the-other-way, the White House gave the green light to an intelligence apparatus that had become a criminal enterprise. Even after the debacle of the Ellsberg break-in, Gordon Liddy was assigned to the Committee to Re-elect the President, a kind of promotion for a thug who was clearly a loose cannon, careening around the deck. "They never said a **word** to Liddy that he'd done anything egregious," says Dean. "Not a **word**. And it's clear Liddy is somebody who, if you gave him an inch he took a mile. He thinks this is the kind of stuff they **want**."

How could the break-in and the other White

House "horrors" have happened on Haldeman's watch? "This is the big mystery about Haldeman," says Evan Thomas. "Most people seem to think he was the best chief of staff ever in many ways. The paperwork was good, the **quality** of the paper was good, the chain of command. And Haldeman enforced that. So he runs this incredibly tight ship. But he just misses the danger of Watergate." For Terry O'Donnell, who worked closely with him, the idea of Haldeman approving tawdry second-story jobs makes no sense: "He had a very keen sense of where the line politically and otherwise was about what you can do. I don't think he ever would have bought into any of the illegal activities—and he would have driven a spike into the Watergate break-in, the stupidest damn thing."

And yet, Haldeman had received repeated warnings. In January of 1972, Liddy met with Attorney General John Mitchell, Dean, and others in Mitchell's office and pitched an intelligence plan that involved kidnapping antiwar leaders, illegal wiretapping, and intercepting ground-to-air communications. It was, Dean says, a "phenomenal, out-of-sight, crazy plan." Puffing on his pipe as he listened to it, Mitchell looked over at Dean and winked. Afterward, Dean went straight to Haldeman: "I tell him what I've heard and how insane it is and he tells me—and it was so intense I've never forgotten it—'**You** shouldn't have anything to do with this.'" A month later Dean walked into Mitchell's office and found (Committee to Re-elect Deputy) Jeb Magruder and Liddy "kind of hunched around Mitchell's desk, and they're talking about bugging and wiretapping. And I know Haldeman's going to back me up on this, so I jump in and I say, 'Listen, I don't know what else has been talked about, but what I'm hearing is the kind of conversation that should never take place in the office of the attorney general.' " Dean walked out and reported back to Haldeman **again**: "I said, 'Bob, they're still talking about this stuff.' And he said, 'Don't worry about it. I'll handle it.' "

But, fatefully, he didn't. Saturday, June 17, 1972, was a beautiful day at the presidential compound in San Clemente, California. Working by the pool, Higby and Haldeman looked up to see Press Secretary Ron Ziegler hurrying toward them. He brought a strange news clipping: Five men, wearing rubber surgical gloves, had been arrested while trying to plant electronic surveillance devices at the Democratic National Committee Headquarters at the Watergate. "We couldn't figure out what the hell that was about," says Higby. "I mean, it didn't make any sense." In his memoir, Haldeman writes: "The news item was jarring, almost comical to me. . . . My immediate reaction was to smile. Wiretap the Democratic Committee? For what? The idea was ludicrous." But Haldeman's claim that he was surprised is as dubious as Captain Renault being shocked that there was gambling going on at Rick's. More persuasive is Haldeman's next entry: "Not that I was all that horrified of wiretapping or bugging in general: Ever since a conversation with J. Edgar Hoover at New York's Pierre Hotel in 1968, which revealed the extent of the political wiretapping by President Lyndon B. Johnson, I had felt no instinctive aversion to such bugging by Republicans." And he goes on: "I tried to visualize the scene: a darkened political office, burglars prowling, flashlights wavering. Whose operation did that sound like? This led me to my second reaction: 'Good Lord,' I thought. 'They've caught Chuck Colson!'"

The cover-up began that weekend. "They have the full story within hours," says Dean. Colson denied involvement, but Haldeman learned that one of the burglars was James McCord, the security coordinator for the Committee to Re-elect the President. Another was "a guy named Howard Hunt, who was the guy Colson was using on some of his **Pentagon Papers** and other research-type stuff. It is decided that they're just going to tough it out," says Dean. "No one's going to admit anything. And in fact they put out a press release that's approved by both Haldeman and Ehrlichman that exonerates the reelection committee. And it's a secret plan to make a crime go away, and disappear."

Within days, Nixon and his chief of staff were neck deep in the cover-up: They discussed everything from paying hush money to the burglars to ordering the CIA to stop the FBI from pursuing its investigation. As Evan Thomas observes: "Haldeman says, 'Well, gee, I didn't think of it as obstruction of justice; I thought of it as containment.' But, boy, his radar sure is failing him." Dean points out that Haldeman "withholds a lot of information from Nixon. . . . He uses a kind of code language and code signals in those early conversations— alerting him to the fact that there are some problems. It was just too ugly to face so that's why it went forward."

Despite the **Washington Post**'s best efforts, the scandal was slow to affect public opinion. By late fall of 1972, Nixon and his chief were on top of the world, basking in the glow of a landslide reelection victory over George McGovern.

H. R. HALDEMAN: There are a lot of good stories from the first term.

PRESIDENT NIXON: A book should be written, called **1972**.

HALDEMAN: Yeah.

NIXON: That would be a helluva book. . . . You get in China, you get in Russia, you get in May 8 [the president's decision to bomb Hanoi, and mine Haiphong Harbor, just before a summit in Moscow], and you get in the election. And it's a helluva damn year. That's what I would write as a book. **1972**, period.

But everything would unravel quickly. By April of 1973, as congressional investigators and prosecutors closed in, the pressure grew for Nixon to save himself by firing his two top aides. But the president could not stomach losing Haldeman. "Haldeman is more important to me than Adams was to Ike," the president told Ehrlichman. "For example, the K [Kissinger] situation, which only he can handle. I can handle the rest, probably, but I can't do that. So protecting Haldeman . . . is a major consideration. He is the P's closest confidant . . . and we can't let him be tarred as a dirty SOB." In his diary Haldeman noted hopefully that Kissinger had spoken up on his behalf: "If the P does let me down or does let the situation develop to the point where I have to get out, he [Kissinger] too will leave because he would refuse to serve in a White House that would permit such a thing to happen."

As he recalled in his diary, Haldeman was having coffee at home with his wife when the phone rang.

A nervous Nixon was on the phone.

"Uh, Bob, we have to make a decision on this, and I've thought it through all the way. It's got to be a resignation."

My lawyer's voice in my mind telling me: **Not resignation. Not resignation. That's a**

clear-cut statement to the public that says "Guilty." . . .

I said, "You know my views on it. But if that's your decision, I'll go with it."

Nixon told his chief a helicopter would bring him and Ehrlichman to Camp David that afternoon, where the president awaited them. Haldeman's fourteen-year-old daughter was at home, but his other children (two sons and another daughter) were scattered around the country. His wife, Jo, got each of them on the phone, but Haldeman could not bear to tell them the truth.

A few hours later, at the Pentagon, Haldeman and Ehrlichman lifted off toward Camp David. "I knew I needed to talk to Ehrlichman," Haldeman later wrote. "But for a few moments I just enjoyed that spectacular view as the helicopter swung low over the River. . . . The chopper flew north toward Maryland where Larry Higby lived."

Years later, Higby described the scene: "It was a cold winter day. It was gray. And my wife and I, with our new baby—and she was now pregnant with our second child—went for a walk. And as we were walking she saw the helicopters go, and I said, 'That's Haldeman and Ehrlichman going up to Camp David. And they're going to resign.' And I must tell you it was quite frightening for a guy, twenty-seven at that point, trying to figure out what we were going to do for the rest of our lives. I figured that if I ever had to go to jail, I had enough money that my wife could live somewhere for a year, and then I would try to pick up the pieces."

At Camp David, Haldeman went straight to Aspen Lodge, where Nixon was waiting for him. As Haldeman later recounted, they stepped out on the terrace, overlooking the Maryland countryside. Nixon said in a hushed voice: " 'You know, Bob . . . last night before I went to bed, I knelt down and . . . prayed that I wouldn't wake up in the morning. I just couldn't face going on.'

" 'Mr. President,' I said, 'you can't indulge yourself in that kind of feeling. You've got to go on.' " Haldeman was deeply touched, but later learned that Nixon had used the same words in his meeting with Ehrlichman, just minutes later: "This hurt me. I had believed that what Nixon said to me was a personal emotional baring of the soul to me alone of the sort he was not often wont to do. Now I see that this was just a conversational ploy—a debater's way of slipping into a difficult subject— used on both of us." As he left, the president patted his chief on the shoulder. Then he reached out. It was the first time, after twenty years by his side, that Nixon had ever shaken Haldeman's hand.

That night, in a televised address from the Oval Office, Nixon announced the resignations of "two of the finest public servants it has been my privilege to know." An hour later, Haldeman called the president—who was inebriated, slurring his words.

PRESIDENT NIXON: Hello?

HALDEMAN: Hi.

NIXON: I hope I didn't let you down.

HALDEMAN: No, sir. . . . You got your points over. . . .

NIXON: Well, it's a tough thing, Bob, for you and for John and the rest, but, goddamn it, I'm never going to discuss the son-of-a-bitching Watergate thing again—never, never, never, never! Don't you agree?

HALDEMAN: Yes, sir. You've done it now, and you've laid out your position. . . .

NIXON: An interesting thing. You know, we haven't heard a—the only cabinet officer that has called—and this is fifty minutes after the thing is over—is Cap Weinberger, bless his soul.

HALDEMAN: Hmm.

NIXON: . . . But let me say you're a strong man, goddamn it, and I love you.

HALDEMAN: Well . . .

NIXON: . . . by God, keep the faith. Keep the faith. You're going to win this son of a bitch.

HALDEMAN: Absolutely. . . .

NIXON: . . . I don't know whether you can call and get any reactions and call me back—like the old style. Would you mind?

HALDEMAN: I don't think I can. I don't—

NIXON: No, I agree.

HALDEMAN: I'm in kind of an odd spot to try and do that.

NIXON: Don't call a goddamn soul. The hell with it. . . . God bless you, boy. God bless you.

HALDEMAN: Okay.

NIXON: I love you, as you know.

HALDEMAN: Okay.

NIXON: Like my brother.

HALDEMAN: Well, we'll go on and up from here.

NIXON: All right, boy. Keep the faith.

HALDEMAN: Right.

"Haldeman is graciously helping the guy who has just canned him and humiliated him and ended his life basically," observes Evan Thomas. "It's a revealing moment—of Haldeman's forbearance, and Nixon's sickness."

Haldeman wasn't finished doing the president's bidding. At the Senate Watergate Hearings, John Dean, who had turned against Nixon, testified that he had warned the president of "a cancer growing on the presidency." Nixon now wondered if the secret White House tapes could be used to his advantage—to discredit Dean's version of events, and that conversation in particular. He asked Haldeman to listen to the tape and give him an assessment. Inexplicably, Haldeman reported back that the conversation posed no problem. In fact, the tape was damning—with Nixon approving hush money payments to the burglars—corroborating Dean's story. Higby says, "The only explanation I ever got from him [Haldeman] on that was: 'I was trying to put the best face on it that I could for the president.' Number two: I think that in his wildest dreams he never thought that the tapes would become public."

On July 16, 1973, on national television, Nixon aide Alexander Butterfield was asked: "Are you aware of the installation of any listening devices in the Oval Office?" Butterfield replied, "I was aware of listening devices, yes, sir." The startling disclosure came as Nixon was hospitalized with pneumonia; two days later, Alexander Haig, Haldeman's successor as chief of staff, ordered the tapes secured and the system removed.

Richard Nixon now faced a momentous decision. Should he order the tapes destroyed? In his memoirs, he wrote: ". . . it would be a highly controversial move to destroy them. [Al] Haig made the telling point that, apart from the legal problems it might create, destruction of the tapes would forever seal an impression of guilt in the public mind. When [Vice President Spiro] Ted Agnew came to the hospital to visit, he told me I should destroy them. . . . Haldeman said that the tapes were still our best defense, and he recommended that they not be destroyed."

Nixon's chief believed the recordings would

somehow exonerate them. "Haldeman said to me, on a number of occasions, I think the tapes will really be the thing that at the end saves the president," says Higby. The truth was just the opposite. The discovery of the tapes—hard evidence of the president's immersion in the cover-up—meant the Nixon presidency was finished.

As their defenses collapsed around them, Nixon and his chief of staff behaved less like seasoned Machiavellis than befuddled amateurs. "The only point of disagreement I've ever had with Bob [Woodward] and Carl [Bernstein] is that they want Nixon to be the Godfather," Dean told me. "And they want the White House to be a criminal enterprise. And it's just not the way it worked." Thomas also paints a picture of a president and his chief careening through a crisis that baffled them at every turn. "Nixon has been portrayed as the **master** criminal—he knows where all the pieces are," says Thomas. "That's not the Nixon in my view. The Nixon in my view is afraid; he's a bumbler at this kind of thing; he's running a clown operation; the only reason he's into political espionage is because Hoover won't do it anymore."

Haldeman would defend Richard Nixon to the end. Before the Senate Watergate Committee, the president's ever-dutiful chief insisted that Nixon had no knowledge of the cover-up and never authorized giving hush money to the burglars. For those untruths, H. R. Haldeman would be convicted of perjury, conspiracy, and obstruction of justice and sent to prison at the federal minimum security facility in Lompoc, California, where he served a sentence of eighteen months.

"Son of Nixonstein" read the caption on a magazine cartoon, depicting the fallen chief as the president's monster. To the press, and to most Americans, Haldeman seemed proof that too much power invested in the White House chief leads to calamity. But that's not the way Haldeman's successors saw him. Years later, in January of 1986, Nixon's ill-starred chief would emerge publicly again. The occasion was a symposium in San Diego, California, of former White House senior aides and chiefs of staff: Dwight Eisenhower's Andrew Goodpaster; John Kennedy's Theodore Sorensen; Lyndon Johnson's Harry McPherson; and three chiefs who followed Haldeman—Gerald Ford's Donald Rumsfeld and Dick Cheney, and Jimmy Carter's Jack Watson.

Haldeman struck these savvy White House veterans as serene, charming, and in total command of his subject. Cheney was bowled over by his mastery of the nuances of the chief's job. "After about two days together, it was clear Haldeman knew more about it than anybody else," Cheney says. "There was a conventional wisdom that Watergate occurred because there had been a very tightly organized White House chief of staff system under Haldeman. That wasn't true. But everybody believed it for a while. The truth is, sooner or later nearly every president, no matter what he thinks when he arrives, ends up following the Haldeman system."

At the conference, Nixon's ex-chief was asked how the Watergate scandal had come about. "The thing that went wrong is that the system was not followed," Haldeman replied. "Had we dealt with [Watergate] in the way we set up from the out-set . . . we would have resolved that matter satis-factorily, probably unfortunately for some people, but that was necessary and should have been done. It wasn't done, and that was what led to the ulti-mate crisis."

"That's exactly what happened," said Dean, when I recounted Haldeman's explanation. (It's a rare point of agreement between Haldeman and his nemesis, still regarded by Nixon loyalists as their Judas.)

Faced with the ultimate crisis, Haldeman failed to execute his own model of White House gover-nance. "Haldeman is at the center of it," says Evan Thomas. "Because he's the guy in the room who should have been able to go: 'STOP! STOP!'" Richard Nixon's chief of staff would eventually confess his failure: "If I had it to do over, I would do so differently. I would take the bad guy in Nixon on frontally, at least some of the time."

Was Nixon's Lord High Executioner unable to confront the president with the unpleasant truth?

Sitting in his Washington, D.C., office more than forty years later, I put that question to Donald Rumsfeld. "I don't doubt for a minute that Haldeman executed the president's desires well—maybe too well," he replied. "I don't think Haldeman ever said, 'No, you're wrong.'" Rumsfeld paused and smiled. "He was dutiful. I was less so."

2

"Beware the Spokes of the Wheel"

Donald Rumsfeld, Dick Cheney, and Gerald Ford

Donald Rumsfeld was at a dinner party in the resort town of Grimaud, on the French Riviera, when he received an urgent message; the White House switchboard was calling. It was August 8, 1974, and Rumsfeld, forty-two, was thousands of miles and an ocean away as the worst scandal in American political history enveloped Richard Nixon's presidency. Now, facing the certain prospect of impeachment and conviction in the Watergate scandal, Nixon was on the verge of resigning in disgrace. And Rumsfeld, former Nixon aide and now U.S. ambassador to NATO, was about to be summoned back from his voluntary exile.

Even in a White House full of sharp-elbowed

strivers, Rumsfeld stood out; on the Oval Office tapes, the president had called him, in Nixon's highest form of flattery, "a ruthless little bastard." Whip-smart, combative, and politically savvy, Rumsfeld was known for his organizational skill and his suffer-no-fools discipline. He had been a college wrestler, a naval aviator, four-term congressman, and head of Nixon's Office of Economic Opportunity and Cost of Living Council. But it was clear to everyone who knew him that Rumsfeld's sights were set much higher. A close friend of fifty years says, "From the moment his feet touched the carpet in the morning to the instant his head hit the pillow at night, Don Rumsfeld thought about one thing—how to become president."

Now, in the waning hours of Nixon's presidency, came news from the White House: Vice President Gerald Ford wanted him to come to Washington right away. But Rumsfeld was a step ahead; sensing the political upheaval that was taking place, he had already booked a flight back to Washington the next day. Rumsfeld called his Brussels office and told them to summon his close friend and protégé to meet him at Dulles Airport. That friend was thirty-three-year-old Dick Cheney.

Rumsfeld and Cheney had met five years earlier: an ambitious congressman and earnest graduate student whose friendship was destined to shape Republican politics for a generation. In the summer of 1968, Richard Cheney had arrived on a bus in

Washington, D.C., a self-described "fuzzy-headed academic" from the University of Wisconsin. "I was about as green as they come," Cheney recalls. "I owned one suit. It was good for Wyoming or Wisconsin. It was a little warm in Washington in the summertime."

Impressed by a Rumsfeld speech, Cheney applied at his office for an internship. "I was taken into his office, sat down, and he started asking me about myself," recalls Cheney of that first encounter. "And I explained how I was an academic and I was working on my PhD. And after about ten minutes, he threw me out."

Undaunted, Cheney went to work for Congressman William Steiger of Wisconsin. When Rumsfeld became head of the antipoverty program in Nixon's Office of Economic Opportunity, Cheney sent him a memo, offering political advice. A second meeting was arranged, and this time Rumsfeld was more impressed. "He looked up at me," says Cheney, "and said, 'You—congressional relations. Now get the hell out of here.'"

Rumsfeld and Cheney had much in common—politically, intuitively, and geographically. "He came from the West, I came from the Midwest," says Rumsfeld. "Our high school and college circumstances were not dissimilar. I liked to work hard, he liked to work hard. He has a nice, quiet sense of humor and the tougher things got, the better he got." When Rumsfeld left the Nixon White

House to become ambassador to NATO in Brussels, Cheney left, too—but he stayed in Washington, working for a lobbying firm. Still, there was little doubt that if Rumsfeld needed him again, Cheney would answer the call.

At 1:55 p.m. on August 9, 1974, Rumsfeld landed at Dulles Airport—less than two hours after the presidency had passed to Gerald R. Ford. Waiting for him was Cheney and one other person. A courier handed Rumsfeld a note, instructing him to report for duty as head of the new president's transition team. Rumsfeld and his young protégé drove into Washington, and Cheney brought him up to speed on the political earthquake that had shaken the country in his absence.

It was a unique moment in American history. No president had ever resigned, and no vice president seemed less prepared to succeed him. Gerald Ford was a gregarious Michigan congressman who had risen to minority leader largely because he had made few enemies (Rumsfeld had spearheaded his campaign for the position). When Nixon's vice president, Spiro Agnew, resigned in a bribery scandal, Ford was not even on Nixon's list to replace him; John Connally, his Treasury secretary, was the clear favorite. But Nixon needed someone who could be confirmed without a fight. Jerry Ford, popular and uncontroversial, was the safe choice, and the House and Senate confirmed him by an overwhelming vote. That was how, on August 9,

1974, as Nixon climbed onto **Air Force One** to begin his flight into exile, Gerald Ford became the "accidental president."

Ford faced daunting challenges: a faltering economy; inflation so severe it was called **stagflation**; a nuclear-armed adversary, the Soviet Union, inciting communist insurgencies around the world; a hostile Congress; an emboldened and cynical press corps; and the imminent collapse of South Vietnam, where the United States had suffered a humiliating defeat in the longest war in the country's history. To confront all of these problems, Gerald Ford would now have to rely on a team of virtual strangers. "He stepped into the pilot seat of an airliner that was going five hundred miles an hour," recalls Rumsfeld. "It was headed straight for the ground. And he didn't even know the crew."

Worried that the world would think he was out of his depth, Ford quickly announced that Kissinger, Nixon's cerebral architect of foreign policy, would continue as both secretary of state and national security adviser. The cabinet would also stay on. Nixon's chief of staff, H. R. Haldeman, was gone—on his way to prison. But Haldeman's successor, General Alexander Haig, would remain as chief—for now. Haig, scheming and mercurial, acted as though **he** was the president, and Ford his understudy.

From the start, Gerald Ford's White House resembled a kids' soccer game, everyone running toward the ball. Ford had announced that he would govern with eight or nine principal advisers reporting directly to the president—a circle, with Ford at the center. He called it "the spokes of the wheel." But the result was chaos and dysfunction. The old Nixon guard, suspicious and embattled, collided with Ford's new team: a colorful cast of collegial, pipe-smoking characters who were used to having the run of his congressional office. Ford's speechwriter and former chief of staff, Robert Hartmann, a gruff, hard-drinking midwesterner, considered himself **primus inter pares**; within hours of Ford's swearing in, he had carted his belongings into a cubbyhole that opened right into the Oval Office. Hartmann and a half-dozen other colleagues expected unlimited access to the thirty-eighth president.

The freewheeling, anything-goes informality was personified by Ford's official photographer, David Hume Kennerly. A Pulitzer Prize winner for his Vietnam coverage at the age of twenty-five, Kennerly, an extroverted Oregonian, was fearless, opinionated, and outspoken. Assigned by **TIME** to photograph the VP, he had struck up a close relationship with Ford, who enjoyed Kennerly's flippant wit. (When a would-be assassin's bullet barely missed the president on a West Coast trip, Kennerly quipped: "Other than that, Mr. President, how did you like San Francisco?") To Gerald and Betty Ford, Kennerly was practically a son.

"At first, his brash manner and irreverence for the office took me by surprise," the president wrote years later. "Soon I began to depend [on] and draw strength from it."

In the West Wing, Kennerly had carte blanche, and the ear of the president. "I would say to my secretary, 'Get me David Kennerly,'" recalls Dick Cheney. "And an hour would go by. And then she would come back and say, 'I'm sorry, sir, but Mr. Kennerly is having cocktails with the president.'" Ford's photographer reveled in the perception that he was the president's confidant, advising him on policy. "I was every political adviser's worst nightmare, but nobody could ever prove it," he says. "But one of the things the president liked about me was that I didn't have any dogs in the fight. I wasn't pushing any agenda."

Ford's loyalists treated the Nixon holdovers, including Chief of Staff Haig, with undisguised contempt. Hartmann called Haig and his staff "the Praetorians" and proceeded to end-run them. Memos from Hartmann would appear in the president's in-box, be signed by Ford, and then vanish— with Haig out of the loop. Terry O'Donnell, personal assistant to both Nixon and Ford, remembers getting a phone call from an exasperated Haig: "He said, 'We've got some people coming in with an in-box under their arm, papers falling out, and getting in there and we have no record of what was discussed or decided or anything else. We can't run the White House this way!'" The free-for-all extended to Ford's cabinet secretaries, who came and went from the Oval Office as they pleased. And meetings with the president and his senior advisers were routinely delayed while everyone waited for Kissinger to show up.

Rumsfeld, still running the transition, did not mince words with the president about his philosophy of White House management. "I told Ford that his approach—known as the spokes of the wheel, where everyone would report to him—was fine for a minority leader in the House of Representatives," said Rumsfeld. "But it would prove to be totally dysfunctional as president of the United States. It would not work. And I would not be a party to anything like it." But Ford was adamant. First, it was the way he had run his congressional office. Second, he wanted a clean break from the tarnished image of Nixon and his imperial presidency, personified by the glowering Haldeman. The humble, plain-spoken president, a vivid contrast to the conniving Nixon, enjoyed an approval rating of 71 percent. He would run the White House his way.

Rumsfeld decided it was time to go. Just a few weeks after the inauguration, he flew back to Brussels to resume his post as ambassador to NATO. Once again, Rumsfeld would be thousands of miles away when a political earthquake struck, an upheaval that would rattle Ford's presidency to its foundation.

At eleven on a Sunday morning, September 8, 1974, Gerald Ford sat at his desk in the Oval Office and stared into a television camera. "Ladies and gentlemen, I have come to a decision which I felt I should tell you and all of my fellow citizens as soon as I was certain in my own mind that it is the right thing to do," he began. Then he made a stunning announcement: "I, Gerald R. Ford, President of the United States, pursuant to the pardon power conferred upon me by Article II, Section 2, of the Constitution, have granted and by these presents do grant a full, free and absolute pardon unto Richard Nixon for all offenses against the United States."

The unexpected announcement set off a political tsunami. "Americans weren't just dumbstruck; they were outraged," wrote White House counselor David Gergen. Ford's surprise decision "reeked of Nixonian secrecy and backroom political treachery." Ford's press secretary, Jerry terHorst, resigned in protest. Rumors spread that Ford had cut a secret deal with Nixon. Blindsided by the announcement, wanting vengeance against Nixon, Americans vented their fury. Calls to the White House switchboard ran eight to one against the pardon; almost overnight, Ford's approval rating plunged to 49 percent.

Just weeks after his inauguration, there had been

more bad news. During a routine checkup, Betty Ford learned that she had breast cancer and would have to undergo a radical mastectomy. When he got the news, Ford was alone with Bob Hartmann in the Oval Office. The president broke down and wept.

It would prove to be the tipping point of Ford's presidency. His popularity was in free fall, the White House in disarray, the first lady's health in jeopardy. Shunned by the president's inner circle, Haig was ineffective and would have to go. Ford himself was drowning in paperwork, awash in the relentless demands on his time. "The president, who did not have executive experience, was learning by fire hose," recalls Terry O'Donnell. Ford decided his only hope was to appoint a new chief of staff. He had one person in mind: Donald Rumsfeld.

Rumsfeld was attending his father's funeral in Illinois, and the president called him there. The next day they met alone in the Oval Office. Rumsfeld was wary. "I'm not the guy to do it, and I don't have any desire to do it," Rumsfeld protested. Ambitious as ever, he knew the chief's job could be a career ender—or worse, in the case of Haldeman. Most important, Rumsfeld knew that Ford was reluctant to give him the authority that he needed. "You don't have the time to run the White House yourself," he told the president. "I know you don't want a Haldeman-type chief of staff, but someone has to fill that role, and unless I can have that authority, I won't be able to serve you effectively." In a memo afterward, Rumsfeld warned Ford that governing without a chief "is your quickest way to lose your credibility because even though you are honest the fact that you don't know what you are doing misleads people and once you lose your credibility, you can't govern, so there has to be order, and . . . I would consider it my job to see that there was order."

Rumsfeld's argument prevailed. As Ford wrote later: "I concluded he was right. The 'spokes of the wheel' approach wasn't working. Without a strong decision-maker who could help me set my priorities, I'd be hounded to death by gnats and fleas. I wouldn't have time to reflect on basic strategy or the fundamental direction of my presidency."

"The president pushed me hard," Rumsfeld recalls. "He told me that Betty had breast cancer. And this wonderful man was getting pounded for the pardon. I felt badly for him. I wanted him to succeed." But Rumsfeld wanted one more thing: a promise that when a cabinet position became available, he would get it. In a memo after the meeting, Rumsfeld noted, referring to himself in the third person: "We talked about how long I would stay in the job, and he said it would be until an opening that Rumsfeld feels is appealing and interesting comes up." The president was impatient. Finally, Ford said, "Come on, Rummy, I've got a golf game! Say 'yes.'" Rumsfeld replied, "OK, I'll do it."

There remained the problem of what to do with the president's erstwhile chief, Al Haig. Over cocktails in the residence, Ford posed the question to Kennerly. Was there a face-saving job the president could offer the ambitious Nixon holdover? Army chief of staff was one option—but Haig had ruffled feathers there when he leapfrogged to four-star general over more senior colleagues.

Suddenly Kennerly had an idea. "What about supreme commander at NATO?" Ford immediately brightened, adding, "It'll get Al out of town." Soon Haig would depart for Brussels, and Rumsfeld would return from Europe to become Gerald Ford's chief of staff.

Rumsfeld moved into the large West Wing office once occupied by Haldeman and Haig. One of his first acts was to evict Hartmann, Ford's trusted speechwriter, from his perch next to the Oval Office; Rumsfeld turned the space into the president's study and sent Hartmann packing down the hall. Henceforth only Ford's two favorite cabinet members—Kissinger and Alan Greenspan, chairman of the Council of Economic Advisers—would be permitted to see Ford alone. There would be no Colsons or Ehrlichmans performing end runs. And Rumsfeld made it clear that the White House trains would run on time. When the notoriously tardy Kissinger kept the president waiting yet again, Rumsfeld called him up with an edict: From now on, the secretary of state would come on time—or not at all.

Donald Rumsfeld was a man in a hurry: all throttle, no brake. Emerging from the Oval Office, he would bark notes into a Dictaphone, resulting in a blizzard of memos (sometimes dozens a day) that were called "yellow perils." To keep meetings moving, he installed a standing desk in his office. Greenspan, plagued by a bad back, lay flat on the carpet. Everyone else stayed on their feet. "You could have a lot of meetings standing up that don't last very long," Rumsfeld explains. "Once you sit down, have a cup of coffee, let people get comfortable, then time goes. When you're White House chief of staff, you don't have a lot of leisure time that you can just be visiting."

"The workload was horrendous," Rumsfeld recalls. "There was the struggle to get a Ford presidency moving and the continuing drumbeat of Watergate." Rumsfeld needed a deputy, and he had someone in mind. "I had tested Dick Cheney in a dozen ways, over the better part of three years, and I knew exactly what I was getting. I had seen him do all kinds of tough jobs and handle them with great skill and sensitivity. And the tougher the job was, the better he got."

There was just one problem: Cheney's background check. Rumsfeld was aware of his protégé's less-than-stellar academic record. Admitted to Yale on a scholarship, Cheney had distinguished himself as a first-class partier and a fourth-rate student. After three failed semesters, the university told him to take a year off; Cheney went back to Wyoming, where he got a job on a road crew stringing power cables. But upon his return to New Haven, Cheney recalls, "frankly, my attitude really hadn't changed at all." After another dismal academic performance, he was told to leave Yale for good.

There was worse to come. Back in Wyoming, Cheney had been arrested twice for drunk driving; after one debauched evening in the summer of 1963, he woke up facedown on the floor of a jail cell. Now, eleven years later, as he awaited his vetting by the FBI, Cheney raised a red flag. "Dick said, 'Well, wait a minute,'" recalls Rumsfeld. "He had a couple of arrests on his record, and he said, 'I'd told you about it, but coming into the White House it might very well be a problem.' Rumsfeld, who had known about Cheney's DWIs when he joined the Nixon White House, said he would tell the president.

A White House aide with an arrest record would give any other president pause. But as Rumsfeld knew, Gerald Ford was not any other president: "So I went to President Ford and I said, 'Look, here's his FBI report, and he's had a couple of DWI incidents. And I want him as my assistant in the White House.' And Ford said, 'If he's good enough for you, he's good enough for me.'"

That Sunday, Cheney was in his West Wing cubicle when the president, puffing on his pipe, came strolling down the corridor to greet him. "There was no reason in the world," Cheney recalled, "why he should reach down and take this guy with a quasi-sordid past and who's been kicked out of Yale and pull me up by my bootstraps and give me a job that a lot of people would have killed for." Of all the presidents Cheney would serve, none could match this gracious gesture by Ford. "When you get that kind of response from somebody, when they are willing to stand up and take the heat during a controversy, rather than chuck you over the side and go with someone less controversial, you never forget that."

Rumsfeld had done a career-changing favor for his friend; in the years to come, during the darkest days of the George W. Bush administration, Cheney would repay him.

WITH HIS DEPUTY in place, Ford's new chief set out to execute the president's agenda. In Rumsfeld's view, decisions were dead on arrival unless they were translated to every relevant department. "There are very few problems in the federal government that are solely the jurisdiction of a single department," he explains. "They almost always have legal implications, so the justice system has to be involved. They almost always have congressional implications, so that part has to be connected. They almost always are blurred between defense and intelligence and diplomacy, so that has to be done.

"Well, who does all of that connecting? It has to be the chief of staff."

It was the chief's job to make sure that every cabinet member got a hearing. Ford could not stand to be in the same room with James Schlesinger, his secretary of defense. Condescending and professorial, brandishing his pipe, Schlesinger spoke to the president as though he were a dim-witted undergraduate. It was Rumsfeld's job to make sure that Ford kept Schlesinger in the loop. "I would find that there would be a meeting being held," Rumsfeld recalls, "and Kissinger and Ford would be deciding something that clearly needed the involvement of the secretary of defense. And I kept trying to get the president to agree to bring Schlesinger into the meetings."

Cabinet members, senior advisers—even friends—could be influential with the president, but Rumsfeld believed the chief of staff was unique. "You've got other people who see the president once a week, once a month, once a year," he explains. "Even though they may have been good friends before, they don't have the ability to pick the right moment to talk to him and tell him what he does not want to hear. Because the chief of staff is with him day in and day out, he has the ability to select moments when he can look at a president and tell him something with the bark off. He is the one person besides his wife who can do that—who can look him right in the eye and say, 'This is not right. You simply can't go down that road. Believe me, it's not going to work, it's a mistake.'"

Genial and outgoing, Gerald Ford saw the best in everybody; it was Rumsfeld's job to suspect the worst. When the president was invited to a birthday party for an old pal, House majority leader Tip O'Neill, his chief of staff sensed trouble. "I found out that the party was being hosted by a lobbyist from Korea, who was under investigation," Rumsfeld recalls. "And I went back and said to the president, 'You're not going to be able to go to Tip's birthday party.' And Ford said, 'I'm going to my friend's birthday party. I've told him I'm coming and I'm coming.' And I said, 'Fine. I'll go back and look at it again.' And sure enough he did not belong at a birthday party being hosted by this guy. And I went back in to the president and said, 'You're not going to go. You can't go. It's just not presidential.' And he said, 'Dammit, Rummy, I'm going to go!' And I said, 'Fine. You're going to walk. There won't be a limousine for you. There won't be any security people for you. You're going to be embarrassed. And you're going to have to get there on your own.'"

Gerald Ford ended up sending his regrets to his friend Tip O'Neill. The lobbyist, Tongsun Park, was later indicted on thirty-six counts, including bribery, mail fraud, and racketeering. He admitted to making illegal cash payments to congressmen, three of whom were reprimanded.

Not everyone welcomed Rumsfeld's ironfisted style. "There's some hostility when you have a tough guy who is not dancing around issues and is returning a paper and saying, 'This is not presidential, this is not ready for the big leagues,'" says Terry O'Donnell. "But Rumsfeld was firm and did not mince words. That was what Ford needed and he delivered it."

Rumsfeld was also skilled at delivering bad news to cabinet members, a task he described as being the president's "heat shield." "You have a secretary of Treasury who doesn't get invited to a state dinner," Rumsfeld explains. "And so you go in to the president and you say, 'Look, he's complaining. He feels he's got to be at the dinner. It weakens him if he's not at the dinner.' And the president says, 'Darn it, he's been at the last three and I've got other people I want to include. Tell him no.' So you go tell him no. Now who's he going to be mad at? He goes away mad at the chief of staff. And that happens a hundred times a day!"

Rumsfeld's aggressive personality, and tightening grip on the president's agenda, did not please Ford's soft-spoken deputy national security adviser, Brent Scowcroft. "Rumsfeld was chief of staff in the Haldeman mode—tough, demanding, obnoxious," Scowcroft told me years later. "He was full of himself. Standup desk, **navy** guy." (Scowcroft served in the air force.) The abrasive chief also collided with the new vice president of the United States, Nelson Aldrich Rockefeller. The larger-than-life scion of America's wealthiest family, a three-time candidate for president, Rockefeller had arrived in the West Wing after a lengthy confirmation battle. Ford assured him that he would not suffer the fate of previous vice presidents. (FDR's VP John Nance Garner had once likened the vice presidency to a "warm bucket of piss.") The president promised Rockefeller he would be in charge of domestic policy.

But the promise was hollow, and Rumsfeld knew it. For one thing, Ford and Rockefeller were ideological opposites. The president, a fiscal conservative, had ruled out any new federal spending initiatives. Rockefeller loved to throw money at problems. The vice president was about to get a master class in bureaucratic infighting from the chief of staff.

"President Ford would say, 'Gee, Nelson, why don't you come in with some ideas on energy?'" recalls Rumsfeld. "And Rockefeller would take a group of people, fashion a major program, take it to the president, and expect him to send it up to the Hill. So the president would say to me, 'Well, what should I do with it?' And I said, 'You have to staff it out: give it to the Department of Energy, the Office of Management and Budget, economic advisers, secretary of the Treasury, and the like.'" Staffing out his proposals was an almost certain way to kill Rockefeller's big-spending agenda. And sure enough, nearly all the vice president's plans were DOA.

Rockefeller and Rumsfeld loathed each other. The rift was generational and ideological, observes historian Richard Norton Smith. "Rockefeller was a Roosevelt Republican. Don Rumsfeld cut his teeth trying to dismantle the New Deal." It fell to Rumsfeld to explain to Rockefeller, twenty-three years his senior, just how the White House works. "The vice president got it in his mind that Henry Kissinger was in charge of foreign policy and Nelson Rockefeller was in charge of domestic policy, which means we didn't need the president," Rumsfeld recalls. "I can remember explaining to him that 'heading up' domestic policy did not mean overriding cabinet officers who had statutory responsibilities on those subjects. And in that stage of his career he didn't take advice—or no—graciously."

At one point, the vice president reportedly stuck his head in the chief's office door and snapped, "Rummy, you're never going to be president!" In truth, Rockefeller was uncomfortable playing second fiddle to anyone, including the president. "He was not designed to be vice president," says Rumsfeld. "He was used to ordering people around, he was used to hiring people and having them do exactly what he wanted. People who disagreed with him? He didn't like people who disagreed with him."

Unable to be everywhere at once, Rumsfeld delegated many of his duties to his young deputy. "I wanted Dick Cheney to get to know the president because I certainly couldn't work seven days a week or be in every meeting," recalls Rumsfeld. "And I had to alternate sometimes and it had to be Dick." In a kind of shakedown cruise, Rumsfeld sent Cheney on a presidential trip to Mexico, where he impressed Ford with his low-key, no-drama efficiency. "I said, 'How did he do?'" recalls Rumsfeld. "And the president said, 'Terrific. He comes in, has his business to talk about, talks about it, and gets out. And goes about it and takes care of the business. He's a fine person and I'm happy to work with him, so rotate him in whenever you want.'"

In temperament, Gerald Ford's deputy chief was the opposite of his mentor. "Rumsfeld did not take advice or even think about anybody else," recalled Gail Raiman, a White House secretary. "Frankly, he was going to do X, Y, or Z, and just do it. And not in the kindest way." By contrast, Cheney was collegial, collaborative, and considerate—the antithesis of the Darth Vader character he would become decades later as George W. Bush's vice president. "Cheney was **very** different," recalls Scowcroft. "The difference between Rumsfeld and Cheney was the difference between night and day. Cheney was very relaxed, not uptight, not overbearing. His attitude was 'We all have to pull together to make the presidency work.'"

Genial and self-effacing, Cheney was a good listener with a gift for defusing outsized egos; his Secret Service name was "Backseat." Tom Brokaw, by now a White House correspondent, found Cheney much more agreeable to work with than Rumsfeld. "I remember one time we were going to Ford's first NATO meeting. And they sent Rummy back to brief us and it was absolutely insulting. He did a kind of **Reader's Digest** explanation of what NATO was. We knew what the hell NATO was; we needed to know what the president's priorities were. But he could not have been more condescending and useless. It could not have been more different from Dick Cheney. He understood what our needs were. He also had a wonderful, kind of quirky sense of humor."

Cheney wielded that wry sense of humor like a scalpel; the press corps loved his penchant for practical jokes. A favorite target of Cheney's mischief was **New York Times** reporter James Naughton. At the end of a long week, Cheney informed Naughton, a renowned practical joker, that he had been granted an exclusive interview with the president, and to report early Saturday morning to Camp David. "The next morning I was sitting in my office in the White House with some of the press corps waiting," recalls Cheney. "And of course, Naughton showed up at the gate. And the marine guard didn't know anything about it, no one had cleared him in, and the president wasn't even at Camp David. He was relaxing and playing golf. Naughton got on the phone and was greeted with raucous laughter. He knew he had been had."

One hundred days into his term, with Rumsfeld and Cheney blocking and tackling, Ford, the ex–college football player, was gaining confidence and running room. "He was just absorbing information and becoming better as president every day," says Terry O'Donnell. "We got it down to a schedule and we got time for him to think, and do some of the things that Haldeman found so very important. Papers were organized, scheduling issues were carefully thought out before they were put on his plate. Rumsfeld and Cheney strengthened that framework, making sure that the president was well served by the staff."

One of their biggest challenges was the cartoonish public image of Gerald Ford. Arriving in Austria for a state visit, Ford had slipped on the rain-soaked steps of **Air Force One** and fallen in a heap on the tarmac; ever since, he had been skewered mercilessly on a new television program, **Saturday Night Live**. Ford had been an All-American football player at Michigan; but in the public mind, he was a pratfalling clown who, reaching for the phone, would staple his ear to his head. The president's homespun amiability was interpreted as stupidity; he could not "walk and chew gum at the same time." Lyndon Johnson quipped that he had played too much football without a helmet.

In Washington, D.C., perception is reality—and Rumsfeld and Cheney sought to change it. Ford's knowledge of the federal budget was encyclopedic; they arranged for him to conduct the annual press briefing on it (a subject so arcane that JFK, LBJ, and Nixon never attempted it). Cheney insisted that few presidents had a better grasp of the workings of government: "He knew it cold. This is a guy who spent twenty-five years on the Appropriations Committee and on the Defense Appropriation Subcommittee. I can remember him correcting a budget analyst on how many park rangers were in the National Park Service. He knew **all** that stuff." But their efforts to overhaul Ford's image were mixed.

Rumsfeld bristled at the perception that Kissinger, and not the president, was running America's foreign policy. After a lunch with **New York Times** editors, in January of 1975, Rumsfeld urged Ford to take more credit: "I told him that in talking about his relationship with Kissinger today, he had undersold his role in my judgement. . . . What Kissinger needs to be great is a strong president—a president who is deeply involved in those issues. . . . He is by virtue of his Congres-

sional background, his Midwestern roots, his political nature, his knowledge on defense matters,
in a position to, if he is strong, if he is forceful, to
make Kissinger great and foreign policy great. . . .
I wanted [President Ford] to know how critical it
was for the country for him to be deeply involved
in that and guiding and directing Kissinger . . .
that Kissinger needed that."

Ford and his chief were about to confront Kissinger over the last dark chapter of America's war
in Vietnam. The bloody quagmire had destroyed
two presidents, at a cost of $150 billion and fifty-
eight thousand American lives. Less than two years
after the withdrawal of U.S. combat forces, North
Vietnamese troops were closing in on Saigon. The
end game would unfold on Gerald Ford's watch.

Scrambling to keep South Vietnam afloat, Ford
asked Congress for $300 million in emergency
military aid. The United States, the president declared, had promised its ally "the means to defend
themselves." Congress rejected his plea. Still, Ford
would not give up. In March of 1975, the president ordered his army chief of staff, four-star general Frederick Weyand, a veteran of several tours
in South Vietnam, to return to the country and
assess its prospects for survival. After the meeting,
David Kennerly, who had been snapping photographs, persuaded Ford to let him go along.

In Saigon, Weyand met with U.S. military and
South Vietnamese officials, while Kennerly set out

to capture a grunt's-eye view of the conflict. The president's photographer headed first to Cambodia, then to Nha Trang, arriving as South Vietnamese troops were fleeing, and then to the former American military base at Cam Ranh Bay, now inundated with refugees. Upon their return to the United States, with Rumsfeld present, Weyand gave Ford his official briefing. "The situation is dire but salvageable," the general reported. But the regime would require $722 million in military equipment and another $300 million in economic aid. Next it was Kennerly's turn. Ford's confidant offered a typically blunt assessment. "Mr. President," he said, "Vietnam has no more than three or four weeks left, and anyone who tells you different is bullshitting."

Two weeks later, Cambodia had fallen, and South Vietnam's capital, Saigon, was on the verge of collapse, besieged by North Vietnamese troops. Even Kissinger, who had railed against abandoning an American ally, saw that the end was at hand. "Kissinger said the Vietnam situation was hopeless as a military matter," Rumsfeld noted in a memo. "U.S. goal is to control evacuation of U.S. and South Vietnamese to whom we have a moral commitment." Ford met with his advisers to discuss airlifting the remaining Americans and their close allies to safety.

But the Saigon evacuation quickly turned into a hellish rout, much of it unfolding on television.

Ford and Rumsfeld spent "that long sad day" watching U.S. forces beat a chaotic and humiliating retreat. Desperate Vietnamese clambered onto overloaded helicopters. (Weeks earlier, a rescue plane full of orphans had crashed, killing nearly all aboard.) In the panic, sailors on U.S. aircraft carriers shoved helicopters over the side into the sea.

As the end neared, Rumsfeld would inflict a final indignity on Ford's secretary of state. Informed that the U.S. ambassador had been airlifted to safety, Kissinger had summoned the Washington press corps for a momentous announcement. "Our ambassador has left," he proclaimed, "and the evacuation can be said to be completed." But it wasn't true; the evacuation was continuing.

Eleven U.S. Marines were still on the roof. What if they were overrun and unable to escape? Sensing a public relations disaster, Rumsfeld ordered Press Secretary Ron Nessen to retract the secretary's statement. Kissinger was livid. But Rumsfeld felt he had done the right thing, later writing, "The war has been marked by so many lies and evasions that it is not right to have the war end with one last lie." A few hours later, the marines were airlifted to safety.

Rumsfeld and Cheney, who would launch another divisive and bloody conflict in Iraq decades later, had watched the Vietnam War end in dishonorable defeat. If they were scarred by the experience, they didn't show it. Each insists he was a hard-eyed realist when it came to Vietnam. "I was heartsick; I felt very much the way Gerald Ford felt," says Rumsfeld. "But there was nothing that anyone could do except to try to see it done with the least loss of life possible."

"You could be angry at watching us having to evacuate out of Southeast Asia," recalls Cheney. "But there was also a sense of relief. It was over. It might have ended badly but the decision had been made. My own personal view on what ought to be done wasn't a factor. I didn't think of it in those terms. I was there to help the president do whatever he needed to have done."

Cheney, who was young enough to have fought in the war himself, had avoided being drafted as a graduate student with multiple deferments. "Though I didn't go and I hadn't been drafted, I was supportive of the troops," he says. "You can look at the enormous cost and conclude that something went wrong. Maybe it was the original commitment or maybe the way it was carried out or the strategy was flawed."

Despite the Vietnam debacle, Gerald Ford's political fortunes were improving in the summer of 1975. "He had climbed out of the debris left by Nixon and was looking ahead," wrote Jim Cannon, a White House aide. "His presidency was going well. He was gaining confidence every day. In the White House, Rumsfeld had imposed order and efficiency."

But storm clouds were gathering. In June of 1975, Ronald Reagan, the former movie actor and governor of California, declared that he would challenge Ford for the Republican nomination. After initially dismissing Reagan as a dilettante, Ford now faced a grueling fight against a formidable challenger for his party's nomination.

By the fall, Rumsfeld was anxious. The unpopularity of Ford's Nixon pardon, the struggling economy, soaring inflation, and foreign crises all threatened to weaken him against Reagan in a race that might go down to the wire. (A peanut farmer and former Georgia governor named Jimmy Carter had not yet emerged as the Democratic presidential nominee.)

And the White House was still suffering from self-inflicted wounds. One problem was the president's public appearances. Stuart Spencer, Ford's reelection campaign manager, recalls that every time the president gave a speech his poll numbers plunged. "Ford would go out on the road and the tracking data would go like this," he says, pointing his thumb to the floor. "We'd stay in the White House playing president, and his tracking data would go like **this**," he says, pointing his thumb up. "So I go to Cheney and say, 'We gotta change our strategy.'"

"He was giving these very dull, terrible speeches," recalls Cannon. "And one day they wrote a line in a speech and the sentence was, 'And I say to you,

this is nonsense." And they made a note in the speech: **with emphasis.** And Ford read it aloud: 'And I say to you this is nonsense—with emphasis.' And Cheney says, 'Well, that's another thing we can't do—write instructions in the speech text.'"

Ford wanted to mimic his hero, "Give-'em-hell Harry" Truman, with an old-fashioned whistle-stop speaking campaign. Rumsfeld and Cheney were aghast. In desperation they called in Spencer, Ford's old friend, to talk him out of it. "So the night I had to sell it to Ford, we were both beat up and tired," recalls Spencer. "And I'm telling him this. Cheney is sitting there—the world wouldn't believe how quiet Cheney was in those days, the little mouse in the corner, but bright and loyal. And finally Ford asks me, 'Well, why not?' And I said, 'Because you're a **lousy f*cking** candidate.' Well, Cheney quits breathing and the old man looks at me like this," Spencer says, grimacing. "'And then he says 'Oh, okay.'"

Another continuing headache was Hartmann. A gifted wordsmith (he had written the iconic line "our long national nightmare is over"), Hartmann hoarded drafts of presidential speeches until the last moment, making staff input impossible. After months of this, Rumsfeld blew a gasket: "This has got to be the dummest [**sic**] operation known to man," he wrote in a memo. "The president of the United States is capable of hiring superior speechwriters. We haven't. Instead, each time we go through this hassle at the end, with a big group. Hartmann making snotty remarks to everyone else. The president pacifying and coddling Hartmann, and getting madder by the minute, and getting at it with other people. He shouldn't tolerate it . . . I told DICK to prepare a memo for the president."

By late October of 1975, Rumsfeld was convinced that Ford's reelection was in jeopardy. He decided to confront the president, citing his fears in writing. On October 24, the chief of staff composed a memo, marked "ACTION." He showed a draft to Cheney—who added his own thoughts, and his signature. To make sure they got the president's attention, Rumsfeld and Cheney added something else: their letters of resignation.

Unflinching, even by Rumsfeld's standards, the memo must rank as one of the most scathing missives ever sent to a president. Under FUNDAMENTAL PROBLEMS, he wrote:

Among the public-at-large, the President is perceived as decent and honest. They like you as an individual, but have doubts about your performance as president. . . . Morale is low, the Administration doesn't function as a team and too often various individuals criticize one another in the press . . . it contributes to the impression that the president is not a leader, and raises questions of competence. . . . Sloppy staff work, press leaks, and public disagreements with the President's position on key issues never result in disciplinary action of any kind. . . . the bulk of the problems involve Hartmann, the Vice President or Kissinger. Bob [Hartmann] is an unusual human being. He simply seems not to work well with other people. The Vice President is in the office that has historically had problems. Henry [Kissinger] seems to have had those problems in whatever he was doing. That is just Henry.

Another heading was labeled GOALS AND OBJECTIVES, with more damning words for the administration:

Our actions should portray the President as the President. He must be perceived as a leader; strong (sometimes tough), but fair . . . it is all well and good to have Americans "like" their president—but it is even more important that they <u>respect</u> him. . . . Every day that we delay action is a day lost forever . . . we only have so many competent people and a limited amount of time. We can't do everything. And shouldn't try.

- Speeches should be sent back when they aren't good.
- Deadlines should be set.

- People who don't perform well should be told so or fired.
- There should be some pain for screwing up; not rewards.
- When people bring minutia to you, you should say it is crap and shove it away.

A final section was titled EFFECTIVENESS:

- Your Administration has to be seen as having sensible answers for the questions Americans are asking. . . .
- That you are focusing on three to five big things. It shows purposefulness—the economy, morality, freedom of choice, energy—whatever—items that are directed toward your constituency.

Finally, decide that you want to win in 1976, decide that it is truly important that there be a Republican President, decide that you do want to do everything possible to achieve it and to effectively govern the American people and provide sound world leadership. . . . The sacrifices a President must make to be a great President are enormous, but they make the difference.

PS: If you can take this load and still smile, you are indeed a President.

Three days later, the president summoned Rumsfeld and Kissinger to the Oval Office. If Ford had read the broadside from his chiefs, he did not mention it. Instead he dropped a bombshell. First, he was asking Rockefeller to step aside as the vice presidential candidate in the upcoming election, replacing him with Senator Bob Dole. William Colby would step down as CIA director, to be replaced by George H. W. Bush (then Ford's envoy to the People's Republic of China). Elliot Richardson would take over from Rogers Morton at Commerce. Kissinger would give up his post as national security adviser to Scowcroft (though he would remain as secretary of state).

Finally, Ford proposed a shakeup in his White House ranks: Rumsfeld would go to the Pentagon to replace Schlesinger as defense secretary. And Dick Cheney would become White House chief of staff.

Ford's dramatic bloodletting—later dubbed the "Halloween Massacre"—left Kissinger and Rumsfeld momentarily speechless. When he recovered, Kissinger protested vehemently. The world would regard his new status as a demotion, he insisted, rendering him powerless. Rumsfeld was conflicted by the news. On the one hand, Ford's chief had long argued that the president should fire Nixon holdovers in order to demonstrate his independence; on the other, this political purging appeared too late, and too desperate, to make a difference. And while Rumsfeld now had a cabinet position, which he had coveted, the Pentagon would take him out of the loop as Ford's reelection battle loomed.

But Ford had not asked for their permission. After forty-eight hours of grumbling, Kissinger accepted his demotion. Rumsfeld continued to resist his new Pentagon assignment even as Ford departed for Florida; it took a phone call from **Air Force One** by Cheney—with Ford hovering over him—to finally bring Rumsfeld around.

Rumors spread that the shakeup had been a Byzantine plot devised by Rumsfeld. Many, including George H. W. Bush himself, became convinced that sending Bush to the CIA had been a Machiavellian ploy by Rumsfeld to sideline Bush as a political rival and keep him out of the running for Ford's vice presidency—all with the Kansas City Republican Convention approaching.

As Bush would later write, "I might be considered by some as a leading contender for the number two spot in Kansas City, but not if I spent the next six months serving as point man for a controversial agency being investigated by two Congressional committees. The scars left by that experience would put me out of contention, leaving the spot open for others."

According to this theory, "others"—the contenders to replace Rockefeller as VP—would include Rumsfeld. (The VP's powers might amount to a warm bucket of piss, but he was next in line for the presidency.)

Rumsfeld insists the plot is fiction, and he makes a compelling case. In March of 1989, he wrote Ford: "As you know, I had nothing to do with your decision to send George Bush to CIA. The first I heard of your decision to change Defense and CIA was when you called me into your office with Henry Kissinger and told us of your plans."

Ford replied in a letter, "It was my sole decision to send George Bush to the CIA. . . . I thought he would be a good choice to straighten out the problems there."

Rumsfeld's defense is also bolstered by the memos he wrote at the time, ranking Bush no higher than other candidates for the CIA job. And Cheney says that Ford's first choice for the agency was actually Elliot Richardson, but Richardson was anathema to Kissinger, and so Bush was a last-minute substitute.

About one thing there was little debate: Dick Cheney's promotion to White House chief of staff was almost universally welcomed. Scowcroft, who would become one of his closest friends, describes this era's Cheney as "relaxed, low-key, trying to get the job done, trying to get things to work smoothly, not let things fall between the cracks. He was just a very regular, down-to-earth guy." Bob Schieffer, the CBS News correspondent, thought Cheney was superb. "He was the best staff man I ever dealt with," he says. "Totally straight. Totally nonpartisan. He clearly knew what was going on, and he never told you any dirty laundry, but he would tell you, 'No, that's not right; that **is** right—or that's something I can't talk to you about.'"

"Cheney was every bit as firm as Don," says Terry O'Donnell, "but he was not as curt, or short. His was a softer management style. They were both equally committed to getting the result—but Cheney would approach it with a little more sugar."

The White House under Cheney was firing on every cylinder. David Gergen, the young Ford speechwriter who would work for four presidents, thought it outperformed any other he had served. "I was so pleased when we made that shift and Dick moved in," he says. "I think the place really hummed then, because we had a president who had really grown into the job, we had a staff that was clicking, we had people who liked each other." Ford was more effective on Capitol Hill, and his poll numbers were climbing. His reelection prospects now depended in no small part on a thirty-three-year-old who had once been thrown out of college and woke up drunk on a jail cell floor.

The tougher the race with Reagan got, the more Ford relied on Cheney. "Once Reagan got his voice and started whipping us, it got rough and tumble," recalls Gergen. "Dick not only won his confidence, but the president realized 'I've got to have a strong chief of staff to make this work.' And he gave Dick a lot more authority. And Dick Cheney, in those days, was a very substantial chief of staff. There were a number of us who thought he'd be a great national candidate one day."

There was one other key player in Ford's campaign, a striving, up-and-coming Houston lawyer named James A. Baker III. Charming, good-looking, and articulate, he had impressed everyone with his uncanny organizational skills and country club manners. In the battle to secure the nomination, Baker was put in charge of counting delegates.

Arriving at the Republican Convention in Kansas City on August 15, 1976, Ford had 1,135 delegates—just five more than he needed to win. But Baker warned that some of the pledges were "soft" and could shift allegiance to Ronald Reagan. After an ugly battle in which Ford was forced to repudiate his own foreign policy, the president finally prevailed.

WHEN FORD FINALLY left Kansas City as his party's nominee, he was down 33 points in the polls. A month earlier, Jimmy Carter had won the Democratic nomination. Carter wasted no time pounding Ford for pardoning Nixon, and hanging Watergate around his neck. The pious outsider who promised that he would "never lie" was the overwhelming favorite to win the presidency in November.

There was more trouble ahead. During his second presidential debate with Carter, in reply to a question about Poland from the **New York Times**'s Max Frankel, Ford declared: "There is no Soviet domination of Eastern Europe, and there never will be under a Ford administration." Incredulous, Frankel gave Ford a chance to correct himself, pointing out that the Soviet Union was "occupying most of the countries there." But Ford stubbornly insisted that "each of these countries is independent, autonomous."

Pressured by Cheney and Spencer, Ford corrected his gaffe a few days later. And after a solid performance in the third debate with Carter, he began to hit his stride. Covering fifteen thousand miles and seventeen states in the final weeks of the campaign, Ford trumpeted his gains in employment, economic recovery, reduced inflation, and peace. Crowds were growing. Ford spoke confidently about his plans for a second term: an arms control agreement with the Soviets; a Middle East peace settlement; middle income tax relief; and a balanced budget by 1980. On the eve of the election—exhausted, hoarse, but excited about his prospects—Ford landed in Grand Rapids, his hometown. The final Gallup poll put him ahead, 47 to 46 percent.

The next morning, Ford cast his vote at a high school polling place; he and Cheney flew back to Washington that afternoon and settled in to watch the election coverage. In the White House that evening, around six television sets scattered throughout the residence, Ford gathered family and friends, including David Kennerly, Bob and Elizabeth Dole, and of course, Cheney.

The early returns were grim. Before midnight, eleven states had gone into Carter's column. When Ford won California, the president recalled, "It was still close enough that there was a real potential for us." Ford retired for the night, leaving the outcome in doubt. But at 1:30 a.m., Ohio put Carter over the top; Press Secretary Ron Nessen climbed the stairs to the residence to break the news to the president.

"I'll never forget the look on his face," recalls Nessen. "He had lost to a tiny, one-term governor of Georgia. And he was just absolutely devastated." Later that morning, his voice reduced to a raspy whisper, Ford dialed Carter's number. He handed the phone to Cheney, who made the concession. "If Jimmy Carter ever enjoyed the sound of my voice, that would have been the time," Cheney wrote later. "I didn't care for the task."

Carter's victory was the closest in the electoral college since Woodrow Wilson's in 1916. A little more than nine thousand votes in Ohio and Hawaii would have changed the outcome. Decades later, you can still hear the disappointment in Cheney's voice. "We came awful close," he says. "I think if we'd had another week, we might have pulled it off."

O'Donnell, the veteran White House aide, says the performance of Rumsfeld and Cheney after the Nixon disgrace nearly won Ford reelection, against all odds. "When Don got in there with the president's trust and confidence, and then later Dick, they strengthened and built a better White House. Both led the president back to a point where despite the pardon and Watergate and the political poison in the country, the president damn near came back and won."

"You had this institution that had been blemished, tarnished, beaten up, considered to be in disrepute—called the White House," says Rumsfeld. "We had a president who hadn't run for vice president or president. We had an economy that was in the tank. A terrible war ending in a difficult way." Forty years later, Rumsfeld would insist that being Gerald Ford's chief of staff was "unquestionably the toughest job I ever had."

By contrast, Cheney reveled in it. He'd made the most of a second chance. "I found myself going from the Rock Springs Jail to White House chief of staff," he reflects. "That's a pretty big chasm to bridge. I loved all of it. I loved Jerry Ford and working with him. I had great people working for me. Those relationships from that first exposure to the political wars have lasted a lifetime."

Cheney looked forward to getting into the arena himself, in elected office—where there would be many more wars to come.

On January 20, 1977, Cheney went to work in his West Wing office for the last time. At a farewell party, his staff presented him with a gift: a beaten-up car seat—a nod to his Secret Service code name. And there was one other thing.

"It was a big piece of plywood with a bicycle wheel mounted on it," Cheney recalls, "and every single spoke between the wheel and the hub had been busted except for one. And they put a tag on the bottom of it." It said:

The spokes of the wheel, a rare form of management artistry as conceived by Gerald Ford and modified by Dick Cheney.

Cheney treasured the gift. But he thought the mangled wheel should do more than gather dust on his garage shelf. Cheney had been giving advice to Carter's transition team, including his top aide, Hamilton Jordan. "As we were getting ready to leave," Cheney recalls, "I heard Jimmy Carter being interviewed. Asked about managing the White House, he said, well, he believed in the concept of the spokes of the wheel—the same phrase Ford had used, the same exact wording."

Cheney propped up the broken wheel in the chief of staff's office, where Hamilton Jordan would be moving in later that day. He pinned a note to it:

Dear Hamilton,

Beware the spokes of the wheel.

Regards,
Dick Cheney

3

"The Smartest Man in the Room"

Hamilton Jordan, Jack Watson, and Jimmy Carter

Jimmy Carter squeezed himself into the small prop plane on the tarmac of Atlanta's Fulton County Airport. It was June 10, 1976, just five months before Americans would elect the next president of the United States. Wedged into the seat facing him was a young attorney with matinee-idol looks named Jack Watson. They had reason to be pleased: Carter, a peanut farmer and one-term Georgia governor, had run a quixotic, against-all-odds campaign that had brought him from obscurity to the brink of the presidency. But Watson was worried. "I thought he might be the most intelligent man elected president in the twentieth century," Watson recalls years later, of the man he would follow to the White House. "I am not saying that lightly. I was keeping in mind Woodrow Wilson and Theodore Roosevelt and FDR. But he'd never held federal office, never been in the Congress, never been a cabinet secretary, was not a prominent figure in the national party. He lacked all the ordinary and customary preparation of networks over the years that most presidents had coming into the office."

Watson, one of Carter's trusted advisers, had sounded the alarm a few months earlier—right after the unlikely candidate had won the crucial Pennsylvania primary: "I sort of had an epiphany: 'My goodness gracious, this guy's got a great shot at being president of the United States.' And talk about someone coming in from the outside, Carter was the pluperfect example of that." Watson began furiously drafting memos to Carter, posing questions he would face as president-elect. "What decisions are going to be forced upon him, what decisions is he going to inherit that he needs to be informed about, what initiatives does he want to take right out of the batter's box—and in order to do that, what does he need to know? What information does he need to have?"

On the day of the flight, Carter had summoned Watson to talk about preparing for the presidency. "It's just Jimmy and me and the pilot," Watson recalls. "And we are on the runway, before taking off, and the single engine is revving loud; we can hardly hear each other. He is speaking very loudly and he said, 'I want to do it. I want to do the transition and follow the outline that you've given me for this work.'" Watson was thrilled that his advice had been heeded. But what Carter said next jolted him. "Looking at me, no smile, those blue eyes staring me down," Watson recalled, "he said, 'I want **you** to do it.'"

Watson was flummoxed; caught off guard. It wasn't that he didn't feel up to the challenge of running a presidential transition; but Watson was convinced that Carter, the quintessential outsider, would be much better off with an insider—someone who knew the ropes of Washington. (Watson even had a candidate in mind: John Gardner, the former head of Health, Education, and Welfare.) "Oh, no, no—I'm not the right person for this, I don't know enough, I'm not **known** enough," Watson protested. "I have no reputation." But Carter was adamant: "'No, you'll **be** that person. They don't know me. And I don't know them. And you do know me. You know my approach. You know my mind. You have a sense for my goals. And I trust you implicitly to do this in the right spirit and in the right way." Watson knew when Carter's mind was made up: "This was an order; it was not, 'Let's talk about this.'"

Carter had good reason to put such faith in his adviser. A Harvard Law School graduate and rising star at a blue chip Atlanta law firm, Watson, then thirty-eight, was charming, charismatic, and focused—he was also the protégé of Carter's close friend and mentor, Democratic State Party chairman Charles Kirbo. Carter had never forgotten his first encounter with Watson: 1966, when the young attorney rode his motorcycle down to Carter's peanut farm in Plains, Georgia. "He was very eloquent, obviously handsome, like a movie star," Carter recalls. "I was very pleased and overwhelmed with pleasure—politically speaking and personally—to have Jack as a new friend and a supporter."

Watson was fascinated by Carter's steely determination and eclectic intellect: trained in the navy on nuclear submarines, he could talk knowledgeably about the throw weights of intercontinental missiles and the political theories of Reinhold Niebuhr: "He was the most supremely self-confident person I had ever encountered," Watson says. "He had an amazing capacity to absorb and assimilate information on a wide range of subjects and to pull the information out in an organized way, and apply it."

Watson set out to prepare the ultimate outsider to become the thirty-ninth president of the United States. "He said, 'Carter has asked me to organize the transition planning effort,'" recalls Alan Novak, who met Watson on one of his early visits to D.C. Novak, a blunt-talking Brooklyn lawyer who had graduated at the top of his class at Yale Law School, says Watson seemed so infallible it was laughable. "The thing about Jack, more than his intellect, was his discipline," he says. "We used to joke about his desk. He would **polish** it. The desk was always shiny and there was nothing on it." Watson, who had been part of an elite U.S. Marines special operations unit, made it all look effortless.

Watson became Carter's ambassador to Washington, D.C., a place so exotic to the Georgia governor that it could have been the Khyber Pass. Yet no one was better suited than Watson to reach out to the doyennes of Georgetown and the mandarins of Foggy Bottom and Capitol Hill. As Novak recalls: "Carter was certainly a jolt, a social jolt to Washington—like when Andrew Jackson took over the White House: shoeless rubes and a lot of jokes like that. All this stuff about Carter being this hick from Georgia. Jack was the antithesis of all that. It was Jack's job to have lunch with the Clark Cliffords and the powers-that-be. He's smart, he's humble, he lets you talk, he's charming. And all those guys loved him: 'Well, OK, if **this** is what Jimmy Carter is like!'"

But battle lines would soon be drawn between Watson's transition team and the campaign staff—a tight-knit group of stalwarts who had worked relentlessly for their candidate for almost two years. It was perhaps the youngest and most devoted inner circle ever assembled for a presidential candidate. (Until Barack Obama's even younger group in 2008.) Jody Powell, thirty-two, savvy and sharp tongued, a political science grad student from Vienna, Georgia, had become close to Carter while serving as his driver; he fiercely guarded their relationship against interlopers. Stuart Eizenstat, also thirty-two, an Atlanta lawyer, was a cerebral, bespectacled expert on domestic affairs. But first among equals was thirty-one-year-old Hamilton Jordan.

Ham Jordan and Jimmy Carter had met and bonded ten years earlier, when Carter was launching his first, ill-fated campaign for governor and Jordan was a brash, ambitious frat boy at the University of Georgia. After attending a Carter speech, Jordan gave up his summer job spraying mosquitos and never looked back. At twenty-six, he ran Carter's successful 1970 campaign for governor; the next year he became his executive secretary, or chief of staff. In contrast to the urbane Watson, Jordan was an unabashedly good old Georgia boy. As Peter Bourne, Carter's biographer, puts it: "He not only lacked the polish that Carter had acquired but pointedly eschewed any inclinations in that direction."

Jordan was a precociously brilliant political strategist, and a perfect complement to the pious, high-minded candidate. "Carter, who wanted to be simultaneously above and a part of politics, saw it only as a means to an end," writes Bourne. "Jordan . . . enjoyed politics and had little compunction about doing what was necessary to win." In

1972, two years before Carter launched his almost laughable campaign for president, Jordan composed a fifty-nine-page memo, spelling out how and why he would win, a blueprint that would become legendary:

> I believe that you should attempt to develop the image of a highly successful and concerned former Governor of Georgia and peanut farmer living in a small rural town, speaking out on the pertinent issues of the day. Once your name begins to be mentioned in the national press, you will not lack for invitations and opportunities to speak to major groups and conventions.

"He had the most brilliant strategic mind I ever encountered," says Gerald Rafshoon, who would join the Carter White House as communications director. Irreverent, self-deprecating, and rakish, Jordan had a loyal following. James Fallows, Carter's twenty-five-year-old speechwriter at the time, says Jordan's dirt-behind-the-ears persona was appealing. "He was often portrayed as being the undisciplined rube, sort of the Burt Reynolds or Dogpatch figure. But he was a genuinely nice person."

While Jordan and his campaign staff barnstormed the country, Watson assembled a transition team; over the next four months they compiled detailed briefing books on everything

Carter would need to know upon taking office—from energy policy to foreign affairs. For advice, Watson sought out Truman wise man Clark Clifford, in addition to other Washington icons: JFK's Ted Sorensen; LBJ's Bill Moyers and Joseph Califano; Nixon's Fred Malek; and presidential scholars Richard Neustadt and Stephen Hess. He drew up lists of talented candidates for jobs in the new administration. Watson's transition effort would become a model for future administrations. "No president-elect before or since had ever been prepared so comprehensively in preparation for taking over the office," writes Bourne.

But word of Watson's activities in Washington landed like a bombshell in Carter's Atlanta campaign headquarters. Just days after Carter's election, a bitter internecine struggle began: pitting Watson and his team against Jordan and the campaign staff. The rupture between the camps was bitter, cultural, and generational. "Watson was just old enough that he would have seemed to Ham and Jody like a grown-up," says Fallows. "Watson was handsome and scrubbed and polished and well organized. Hamilton was shambling and you couldn't even see his desk when you came into his office and you couldn't find him. And Ham and Jody's attitude was, 'Okay, get out there, you try getting up in the Best Western in Americus, Georgia, at 3 a.m. and see how you feel, see how neat you look.'"

"We were all slogging away eighteen hours a day on the campaign, including on policy issues," recalls Eizenstat, looking back forty years later. "Unbenownst to us, Carter had set up—and you could say wisely perhaps—a transition-in-waiting operation that included some very good people. And then Jack was named the transition head. The problem was not Jack's doing—but it looked, from the campaign staff side, like he was aggrandizing power and becoming the chief of staff and bringing his own people over."

Jordan and Eizenstat reacted with alarm, convinced that Watson was making a power grab. "Carter had these true believers and they had given their life to the campaign: Jody, Hamilton, people like that," says David Rubenstein, who was a young White House aide at the time. "In their eyes, Watson was saying, 'Okay, I'm in charge of the transition—and campaign people, thank you very much and good-bye.'"

In truth, Watson was simply doing Carter's bidding. "He's the dutiful public servant working for his president in Washington, plotting nothing," says Novak. "Meanwhile the political operatives in Plains meet with Carter with their knives out and are telling the president blah, blah, blah—Iago-like." Indeed, Jordan and Rafshoon went to Carter, with their knives sharpened. "Ham and I told Jimmy that Jack Watson would be a bad choice as chief of staff," says Rafshoon.

Carter, who hated staff squabbles, got the message: Jordan would be first among equals. "Jimmy called me and said, 'I want Ham to take the lead on staffing issues,'" recalls Watson. Watson would no longer be in charge of hiring, or, in the eyes of the press, the presumptive chief of staff. One columnist dubbed him a "walking dead man." "It had to be a stunning blow to Jack," says Novak. "He never said anything—just 'This is what Jimmy wants.'" "I don't think of myself as a naive guy," says Watson, "but I wasn't prepared for what happened; it was like a bombshell." He dutifully continued to prepare Carter for the presidency. But his relations with Jordan and his camp had been poisoned. Later, Watson quipped: "It was two months into the transition before I felt safe starting my own car."

Watson's demotion would have enormous implications for Carter's presidency. Fundamentally, the rift was philosophical. To Jordan, Carter's victory meant one thing: The outsiders had won; the Establishment had lost. The new administration would answer to the American people—not to Capitol Hill's powers that be. "Carter and the people around him had the view, 'We're not going to be corrupted by your imperial ways,'" says Fallows at age sixty-six. "You can see its modern incarnation in the Tea Party Republicans—thinking they had been elected as a widespread repudiation of business as usual. And that was the sense that people on the campaign had. This was a guy whom everybody had dismissed, a governor of Georgia—and so there was that sense of looking down on the court of the Sun King."

Watson, Carter's emissary to Washington's elite, was thought by the campaign staff to be too cozy with the status quo. "The people that Jack hired had Harvard and Yale credentials, and Hamilton wasn't a Harvard and Yale credentials type of person," says Rubenstein. In case anyone missed the point, in an interview with **Playboy**, Jordan threw down a gauntlet. "If Cyrus Vance is named secretary of state and Zbigniew Brzezinski head of national security in the Carter administration," Jordan warned, "then I would say we failed, and I would quit. But that's not going to happen." (In fact, those appointments **did** happen—and Jordan did not quit. Still, the warning summed up Jordan's torch-and-pitchfork attitude.)

Many years later, Rafshoon, a Jordan ally, recalls the intensity of the feud. "Jack was a Boy Scout," he says dismissively, the old animosities still raw. "He was getting cozy with all the people who ran against us—and that was all of Washington. I think his head was turned. Everybody was kissing his ass."

Looking back, Watson says: "I was trying my very best to be sensitive and collaborative and cooperative—and not self-promoting. I did everything that I knew how to do to avoid that. My limited experience in that rarefied realm did not prepare me for the turf consciousness, the long knives." But he says the conflict was foreordained, not personal. "It was almost like a Greek tragedy— the forces into which we were thrust had their own life; they didn't really emanate from **us**."

Watson knew that in a contest for Jimmy Carter's soul, he could not compete with Jordan. "The bond that developed between Carter and Ham and Jody, those two very young men, from when they were just barely out of college, became almost filial," he says. "Close as I was to Carter, mine wasn't that kind of relationship, spending the night on the road with him. Compared to Ham and Jody, both of whom I liked and respected, I was an outsider. Ham was a brilliant strategic thinker and writer, and Jody was the best press secretary any president ever had."

Attention now turned to the key question: Should Carter have a chief of staff? In December of 1976, Dick Cheney met regularly with Carter's transition team to give the new administration his advice. He was unequivocal: Giving advisers equal access to the president was a nonstarter; without a strong gatekeeper, Carter would be overwhelmed. Rumsfeld had given Watson the same warning. "Cheney and Rumsfeld said, 'This spokes-of-the-wheel thing is bullshit,'" recalls Watson. "'**Read my lips.** Don't do that.'"

But some of Carter's advisers—particularly those

from academia—argued for a return to the old
JFK and LBJ model: a White House without a
chief. The fact that the approach had been tried
and found unworkable did not discourage them.
Neustadt, the Harvard scholar, argued that a chief
of staff would isolate the president from diverse
viewpoints. "He was saying, 'No—you don't want
a deputy president, you want to have a group of talented, triple-threat, flexible people,'" recalls Watson. "But he was talking about historical times, not
current times."

Carter instinctively opposed anything that
smacked of Nixon's "imperial presidency." And
advice from Ford's chiefs was considered suspect.
"Remember Carter was elected in part because
he ran against 'Nixon-Ford.' And when someone
gives you advice who's your political enemy, what
do you say? 'Oh, thank you very much'?" says
Rubenstein. "Or 'If you guys were so smart, you
would have got reelected'?"

Carter's advisers at the time knew it was futile
to argue the point. "I think it was 75 percent the
Watergate thing, and 25 percent personal hubris,"
observes Eizenstat. Overconfidence is an occupa-
tional hazard for incoming presidents—perhaps
especially for Carter. "He'd been manager of the
campaign, why wouldn't he be manager of the
White House staff too?" says Fallows. "It would
be natural for anyone having won the presidency
to think that it's mainly about him or her. That

it is me and my qualities and my judgment and my goodness. And that was especially the case for Carter after Watergate. There is that fallibility of thinking you're the smartest person in the room. So I think he probably thought that he could figure it out. He'd done everything else in an unusual way. So why not this?"

On the night of the election, Carter's close friend (and Watson's mentor) Charles Kirbo had urged the nominee to make Watson his chief. But Carter did not budge, finally snapping: "I can guarantee, Charlie, there will be a role for Jack in the White House, but I don't want to talk about it anymore."

The day after the election, Watson gave a memo to the president-elect, titled "Some Thoughts on Organizing the Executive Office of the President."

At the beginning at least, I think your five to eight top aides should be equal in their status, salaries and access to you. In effect, you should act as your own chief of staff. There is no way for you to predict how your choices for the top jobs will cope with the unique challenges of the White House. If a "first among equals" naturally emerges later, and you decide that designation of a chief of staff would help you, you can name him then.

Watson would later admit that he had trimmed his convictions to match Carter's. "What I believed was that the chief of staff was imperative for a smoothly functioning White House, but that was not going to happen." Moreover, Watson's rival, Jordan, did not want the title, or the responsibilities. He hated administrative duties and was thoroughly disorganized. "Ham's thing was, 'Let me think of a great idea, and I'll give a memo to Carter,'" says Rubenstein. "That's what he was good at. He wasn't good at managing people; he had no skill set in that."

So Carter's White House would revolve around the president—with access shared by Jordan, Powell, Eizenstat, and Watson. National Security Adviser Zbigniew Brzezinski and congressional liaison Frank Moore were the other spokes of the wheel. Eizenstat would be chief domestic policy adviser; Powell, press secretary; and Watson, head of intergovernmental affairs and cabinet secretary. His power diminished, Watson would become Carter's secretary to the cabinet, liaison to the governors, and presidential troubleshooter, crisis manager, and surrogate speech giver.

On January 20, 1977, Ham Jordan moved into Cheney's West Wing office. He soon learned that his proximity to the president brought responsibilities: Like it or not, he was the de facto chief of staff. Jordan's response was to make himself invisible. "He had this chief of staff office, but he was hardly ever there because he didn't want people calling him to make decisions," says Rubenstein.

"So he would go hide out in other offices in the EOB [Executive Office Building] or elsewhere so people couldn't get access to him." Jordan continued doing what he did best: writing memos to the president. Jordan's deputy, Landon Butler, recalls Cheney's advice to his boss: "'Ham, the chief of staff cannot write in this office. You can't sit down for three days and work on a memo. Because everything backs up if you do that.' And that struck me as being damn good advice. Ham never took it."

Jordan also rejected Washington's codes—sartorial and otherwise. "In those days it was novel for people not to wear ties," says Rubenstein. "Hamilton would come to work in chino pants with construction boots or cowboy boots and no tie." Stuart Spencer, the veteran campaign manager, was not impressed by Jordan's casual style. "I remember walking in once to that corner office where the chiefs of staff are—it smelled like a gymnasium. There was crap in the room, all over the floor."

"It fed an overall perception that a bunch of Georgia guys were coming up here, not playing by the rules," says Eizenstat. "Ham had a chip on his shoulder—'We'll show these guys.' It was harmful." It was, recalls a White House staffer, "a sort of personal thumb-your-nose style. 'They don't like me, and I don't like them, they're a bunch of jerks. F*ck 'em!'"

To underscore the point, Jordan refused to take

phone calls from congressmen or senators. "Chuck Percy [the powerful Illinois senator] would call— and Chuck Percy wanted his phone calls returned by the chief of staff," says Butler. "Instead Ham would give them to me." Butler chuckles, still incredulous. "Or he might call back in three or four days." The disgruntled powers that be took out their frustration on the president. "People would sometimes call Carter and say, 'I can't get Hamilton to call me back, but I can get **you** to call me back,'" recalls Rubenstein.

"I loved Ham," says Eizenstat. "He had the greatest political mind of anybody I ever met. But Ham was not interested in the nitty-gritty of policy." He found Jordan's contempt for basic protocol incomprehensible. "The demands from the Hill are incessant," he says. "And the notion that the chief of staff won't respond to them—that's the most basic thing for the office. It's touching base and realizing how other people see things. The Hill **hates** to be surprised, because it makes them look impotent and not in the loop."

Jordan made matters worse by gratuitously offending the Hill's high and mighty. Before the inaugural, Massachusetts congressman Thomas P. "Tip" O'Neill asked for tickets to a gala at the Kennedy Center. O'Neill told friends that Jordan given seats in the nosebleed section—the last row of the second balcony. Jordan denied it, but the powerful Democratic Speaker of the House—

the key to passing Carter's legislation—never forgave him. From that day forward, O'Neill called the president's top adviser "Hannibal Jerkin."

While his chief aide antagonized Congress, Carter was occupied preparing a sweeping legislative agenda. In his diary just a week after taking office, the president noted: "Everybody has warned me not to take on too many projects so early in the administration, but it's almost impossible for me to delay something that I see needs to be done." Carter wanted to do everything at once: transform energy policy; reform the civil service; pass a Panama Canal treaty (relinquishing U.S. ownership); revamp the tax code; reorganize the government; create an agency for consumer affairs; contain hospital costs; cut inflation; reform Social Security and welfare.

In the fall of 2011, the thirty-ninth president spoke with me at the Carter Center in Atlanta. Eighty-six years old, frail and stooped, he had lost none of his determination, intensity, or certainty. As president, Carter was determined to pursue what he thought was noble and right. The truth was, there was hardly a political bone in his body. "I was not a natural-born politician," he says. "I never thought about running for office until I was thirty-eight years old. When I got to be president, while most of my advisers were saying, 'Let's postpone the unpleasant and unpopular things,' I just didn't do it. My problem in life or my success in life—whatever you want to call it—was to figure out how I could make a goal be realized, without adequate thought to the political aspects of it."

The president was unable to prioritize. "Pretty soon there were so many things going on—far more than we imagined," says Butler. "The initiatives were either forced on the president—like the Panama Canal, and the SALT talks—or the things we took up; there were forty or fifty initiatives that were bouncing around!" Eizenstat sensed that their agenda was spinning out of control: "It doesn't take but about twenty-four hours in the White House for all the problems to converge—to know that you've got to have someone to sort through this thicket, to try to make sense of it. What priority do you set—when you're trying to get your energy policy done, when you're trying to get your stimulus package passed, when you've got tax reform coming up at the very same time? Everything in Washington is connected. **Everything**. You step on their toes on one thing, they're going to remember on the next thing."

Carter plunged ahead, stepping on toes. His success in passing the Panama Canal Treaty, relinquishing American ownership of the waterway, was a pivotal achievement, ending a legacy of American colonialism. But it came at a heavy political price, alienating conservative Democrats. Another self-inflicted wound involved domestic water projects. Gerald Ford's budget had contemplated building

320 dams across the country; Carter, convinced that these were examples of corrupt pork-barrel extravagance, decided to ax all but 19—at a savings of $5.1 billion. When the plan was revealed at the end of February, Congress rebelled. The president's congressional team had failed to warn him that key senators and congressmen would cry foul, and Carter was forced to accept a compromise plan.

The former one-term governor was learning by total immersion. "I'll never forget one time I was talking to Brzezinski about Carter," recalls Brent Scowcroft. "And he said, 'He's wonderful. I can give him 150 pages to read at night—and he **reads** it. He makes marginal comments.' And I said, 'Zbig, that's a **terrible** thing for you to do. Because he doesn't have **time** for that.'" No detail of governing was too trivial for the president's attention. "We were at a reunion one day," recalls Arnie Miller, a former White House aide, "and I said to Carter, 'Thank you for empowering us to do things.' And he said, 'I didn't do anything. I just read your memos.' I said, 'You didn't just read them, you corrected the typos!' That's the level of detail he got into, which the chief of staff should have been doing." Instead, the president personally signed off on everything from typos in memos to requests to play on the White House tennis court.

Carter could not perform his presidential duties and also run the White House staff. Since the days of Haldeman the chief of staff had presided over an early morning meeting. "The chief is also organizing what **the staff** is doing," explains Eizenstat. "You've got the OMB people; you've got the congressional relations people; you've got the legal advisers office; you've got the National Security Council and domestic policy office—and everybody's got their own things; it's important that they understand what the other is doing." The staff meetings took place, but Jordan rarely attended.

Initially Carter chalked up some successes: domestically, he deregulated natural gas, established a new Department of Energy, and passed a government reorganization bill. In foreign affairs, in addition to the Panama Canal Treaty, he negotiated a SALT II accord; restored relations with the People's Republic of China; and laid the groundwork for the extraordinary Camp David Accords between Israel and Egypt. Respect for human rights around the world was recognized as a bedrock principle of U.S. foreign policy.

But as the end of his first year approached, Carter was in trouble. He had declared a national energy policy to be "the moral equivalent of war." (The press ridiculed it with the acronym MEOW.) But the bill that he delegated to Energy secretary James Schlesinger was hopelessly complex and bogged down in Congress. Carter had antagonized many conservative Democrats, and alienated the party's liberals, with his opposition to new spending. His approval rate had plummeted to 34 percent. The president looked haggard and aged. "It's become obvious to me," Carter wrote in his diaries, "that we've had too much of my own involvement in different matters simultaneously. I need to concentrate on energy and fight for passage of an acceptable plan." But instead of focusing, Carter's response was to work harder across the board. "We probably had two hundred people and all of them horses, all of 'em passionate, all of 'em hardworking," says Butler. "So somebody had to set an agenda. Somebody had to set the tone and say, this is important, and this isn't. And that wasn't easy to do." At the urging of Eizenstat, Vice President Walter Mondale was drafted to prioritize issues according to the level of attention required: presidential, vice presidential, cabinet. But even this did not solve the problem. As Eizenstat points out, "You needed to have someone to execute them. And that couldn't be the vice president."

There was worse to come. First, OMB director Bert Lance, perhaps Carter's closest friend and confidant, became embroiled in scandal, accused of allowing cronies improper overdrafts when he was president of the National Bank of Georgia. Lance would twist in the wind for months (with Carter stubbornly sticking by him), until finally resigning. The economy had slowed dramatically, and inflation was soaring; wholesale prices jumped 14 percent. Then came the most dramatic shock: OPEC (the Organization of the Petroleum Exporting Countries) announced an increase in the price of oil of 50 percent.

As Carter's challenges mounted, his de facto chief of staff was undergoing a personal crisis. Jordan's after-hours behavior was becoming erratic, if not reckless. "He had a couple of friends, fraternity brothers from Georgia, who would come up and he'd go out and get in trouble," Butler recalls. "His personal life was a wreck—I mean, he literally lived out of his car for a while." Jordan's marriage was coming apart. Even when he had a bed to go home to, Butler had to make sure Jordan got there in one piece. "There was more than one night when I had to help him into his car—into **my** car, not his car."

It's hard to shock the Washington press corps, but Jordan's gallivanting was so much at odds with Carter's rectitude that it fed their natural cynicism. Behavior that had seemed harmless during the campaign was different now that they were in the White House. As biographer Bourne delicately puts it: "The irreverence, the lusting, the drinking . . . often facilitated the rapport between the staff and the traveling press corps who were not always averse to many of those vices themselves. What it did not engender was respect."

Disrespect flowed both ways: Jordan and Powell shunned invitations to the Georgetown parties where the press held court. "We failed to appreciate until too late the repercussions of our failure to socialize," Powell would later write. "Part of Washington felt that we were arrogant and interpreted each regret as a snub. Others [thought] the White House had been taken over by the Visigoths." Powell was especially thin-skinned in response to critical stories and excoriated reporters who he believed were gossip peddlers. So when the Washington press corps took dead aim at rumors swirling around Jordan, the results were explosive.

On December 18, 1977, Sally Quinn of the **Washington Post** reported that Jordan had attended a party, where he met the wife of the Egyptian ambassador. As Quinn memorably related it, Jordan "gazed at her ample front, pulled at her elasticized bodice and was prompted to say, loudly enough for several others to hear, 'I've always wanted to see the pyramids.'" The story, pounced on by the wire services, spread around the world, along with the White House denial that any such thing had taken place. Jordan also vehemently denied it. But the "pyramids story" was just the beginning of a narrative that would cause lasting damage to Jordan and the administration.

On January 10, 1978, Jordan and his wife, Nancy, announced their separation. A month later, the **Washington Post Sunday Magazine** ran another story about Carter's chief, which Powell later described as "the trashiest piece of journalism I have ever seen." At a Washington singles bar, Jordan had supposedly been rebuffed by a young woman; he responded by spitting his drink down the front of her dress. The alleged "amaretto and cream" incident so outraged Powell that he launched an investigation of the **Post**'s story and then distributed a thirty-three-page rebuttal to the press corps. "I had underreacted to the pyramids story," writes Powell. "I was determined not to make the same mistake again. I did not. I made exactly the opposite mistake, with even more disastrous consequences." Powell's overblown response kept the story alive for weeks, generating coverage usually reserved for superpower summits or natural disasters. As a result, Powell writes, "Hamilton had come to be viewed . . . as a politically astute ne'er-do-well."

By the summer of 1979 the Carter presidency was besieged by crises. OPEC's dramatic price increases caused severe shortages and mile-long gas lines, where motorists seethed, and fistfights broke out. Inflation continued to spike. Most alarming of all, the shah of Iran, America's longtime ally, had been overthrown in a coup by radical Iranian mullahs, an uprising that took the CIA completely by surprise.

As Kevin Mattson wrote, in **"What the Heck Are You Up To, Mr. President?"**:

1979. A good year to pronounce the American century dead. . . . Just as in Vietnam, America felt defeated by a third world country. Except here the damage was harsher for those at home. . . . The age of limitless, low-price gas—what better symbol of American power than that?—had ended. As gas supplies dwindled, prices rose, and so would the general inflation rate up, up, up into double digits. The prosperity of the 1960s—when economic abundance raised tides and floated most boats—had collapsed . . . Americans looked like citizens occupying an empire in its final days.

Exhausted, Carter returned from a marathon foreign trip to an urgent warning from Jordan: He must immediately address Americans' anger over the energy crisis. A prime-time televised address was scheduled; but after reading a draft of the proposed speech, Carter called Jordan and his top aides from Camp David. He had said it all before, he told his stunned advisers: "I am not going to bullshit the American people." Carter was canceling the speech. When Jordan and the others argued, the president hung up on them.

Holed up in his cabin at Camp David, Carter embarked on one of the strangest episodes in presidential history. Months earlier, Patrick Caddell, Carter's pollster, had sent the president a memo arguing that Americans were no longer listening to him; the only way to reach them was to address their fundamental anxieties and fears. Spurred on by Caddell, Carter was determined to confront his own failure of leadership, and what he believed was America's underlying spiritual crisis.

Over the next eight days, summoned by Carter, more than 150 people made a pilgrimage to Camp David: members of Congress, mayors, governors, religious leaders, philosophers, journalists, economists, "wise men" from previous administrations. As the president sat on the floor, cross-legged, taking notes, all weighed in on America's existential crisis and opined on how to fix it. It was a kind of corporate retreat and consciousness-raising session that would leave millions of Americans baffled. When Carter returned to the White House, as one writer put it, "he had created expectations akin to Moses's descent from Mount Sinai."

The president unburdened himself in a televised address:

I want to talk to you about a fundamental threat to American democracy. . . . It is a crisis of confidence. It is a crisis that strikes at the very heart and soul and spirit of our national will. We can see this crisis in the growing doubt about the meaning of our own lives and in the loss of a unity of purpose for our nation. . . .

Carter went on to describe the symptoms of America's ills:

What you see too often in Washington and elsewhere around the country is a system of government that seems incapable of action. You see a Congress twisted and pulled in every direction by hundreds of well-financed and powerful special interests. You see every extreme position defended to the last vote, almost to the last breath, by one unyielding group or another . . . you see paralysis and stagnation and drift. You don't like it, and neither do I. What can we do?

His solution was to exhort Americans to face the truth—both practically and spiritually: "On the battlefield of energy we can win for our nation a new confidence, and we can seize control again of our common destiny. . . . We simply must have faith in each other, faith in our ability to govern ourselves, and faith in the future of this nation."

When Carter finished his jeremiad, the White House phones lit up; the response was overwhelmingly positive, with 84 percent of callers supporting the president. Overnight his approval rating shot up eleven percentage points. Carter's bold rhetorical gamble seemed to have paid off. (Even though Ronald Reagan and Ted Kennedy would later turn the so-called malaise speech against him to devastating effect.)

But whatever goodwill Carter had earned was about to be squandered. Just two days later, the president announced a dramatic shakeup: He asked his entire cabinet to resign. The move was meant to be pro forma: Carter planned to replace just three cabinet officials. But the unexpected announcement gave the impression of a presidency careening out of control.

In the commotion, another presidential decision had gone almost unnoticed. During his discussions at Camp David, the wise men—John Gardner, Clark Clifford, and others—had given Carter unanimous advice: The "spokes of the wheel" approach was not working and had to be scrapped.

Reluctantly, two and a half years into his presidency, Carter agreed to give Ham Jordan the duties, and the title, of chief of staff. But it was obvious that Carter had gone all in on a bad bet: He had chosen the wrong person for the job.

True believers were beginning to desert the administration. In May of 1979, Carter's speechwriter James Fallows—who had recently resigned—wrote a cover story for **The Atlantic Monthly**. In "The Passionless Presidency," three years of frustration came spilling out: "Jimmy Carter tells us that he is a good man. His positions are correct, his values sound. . . . This is not an inconsiderable gift; his performance in office shows us why it's not enough."

The problem, Fallows argued, was fundamental:

Carter and those closest to him to him took office in profound ignorance of their jobs. They were ignorant of the possibilities and the most likely pitfalls. They fell prey to predictable dangers and squandered precious time. . . .

Carter often seemed more concerned with taking the correct position than with learning how to turn that position into results. He seethed with frustration when plans were rejected, but felt no compulsion to do better next time. He did not devour history for its lessons, surround himself with people who could do what he could not, or learn from others that fire was painful before he plunged his hand into the flame.

Fallows was not the first of the Carter faithful to become disillusioned. Alan Novak, who had worked with Watson on the transition, had thought Carter's obstinate refusal to appoint a chief was fatal from the start. He turned down Watson's offer of a job in the White House: "My reaction was, if the president is this much of a numbskull, I'm not going to go into government. If he literally can't tell shit from shinola, God save the Republic! I mean, it was as simple as that."

In late October of 1979, a crisis that would put the Carter presidency to its ultimate test was about to unfold. The exiled shah of Iran, on the run since being forced to flee his country, had asked for permission to enter the United States. The longtime American ally, reviled by the Iranian mullahs, suffered from lymphoma and needed advanced medical treatment. Reluctantly, Carter told his national security adviser, Brzezinski, "to permit the shah to go to New York . . . and just inform our embassy in Tehran that this would occur." The shah was admitted to Manhattan's New York Hospital.

Two weeks later, on November 4, an angry mob of Iranian militants overran the U.S. embassy in Tehran, seizing sixty-six Americans as hostages. "Initially I expected the Iranian students to release the hostages quickly," Carter wrote in his diary. "It was inconceivable to us that militants would hold our embassy personnel for any length of time." But it was the beginning of a siege that would last 444 days. Blindfolded and paraded before television cameras, the traumatized hostages would become a symbol of American helplessness.

That Sunday night, CBS aired a special report: an hour-long interview, conducted by correspondent Roger Mudd, with the man poised to run against Carter for the Democratic presidential nomination: Edward M. Kennedy. Since August it had been clear that Kennedy would challenge the beleaguered Carter; when he announced his candidacy on November 6 in Boston's Faneuil Hall, the last surviving Kennedy brother was a two-to-one favorite. But his appearance with Mudd was disastrous: When asked why he wanted to be president, Kennedy was almost incoherent.

Watching from the White House, Carter noted: "Despite his popularity, I remained confident that we could beat him." Jack Watson was also watching with his friend Novak, who had once worked for the Massachusetts senator. "And of course Ted didn't have a good night," Novak recalls. "We're watching, and at a certain point, Jack says to me, half jokingly, 'And you worked for **that** guy?' I said, 'Jack, at least Kennedy would never choose Ham Jordan as chief of staff.'"

In light of the hostage crisis, Carter decided to suspend all his campaign appearances. "That was one of the decisions the president made with which I personally disagreed," recalls Watson. "Every night on the **CBS Evening News,** Walter Cronkite would say, 'It is Day 109, or Day 110 since the hostages were taken.' I did not think the president needed to add to that by sequestering himself in the White House. I informed him of the costs—the political costs—that were being paid by his staying off the trail." But Carter rejected Watson's advice and stuck to his so-called Rose Garden strategy.

In April of 1980, Carter decided on a daring gambit to end the siege: he would launch a covert military mission to rescue the hostages; helicopter-borne commandos would sweep into Tehran under cover of darkness, free the American captives, and spirit them to safety. But Operation Eagle Claw (as it was called) was a spectacular failure. Carter vividly remembers the ill-fated mission: "So we sent two extra helicopters, never anticipating that **three** out of eight would fail," he acknowledges. "One turned around and went back to the aircraft carrier completely. Another got caught in a sandstorm in the desert. And a third one, as we were getting ready to move toward the rescue operation itself, developed a hydraulic leak and crashed." The disaster left eight Americans dead in the Iranian desert. "I think it was the right thing to attempt," Carter says. "Obviously, I regret that we didn't send nine helicopters instead of eight."

Kennedy's bid to wrest the nomination from Carter would ultimately fail. But as the general election loomed, it was clear that the president instead faced a serious threat from a Republican opponent he once dismissed as laughable: Ronald Reagan. The unlikely Republican presidential nominee from California, a former B-movie actor, had a formidable ally: James Baker (the onetime Ford delegate counter and manager of George H. W. Bush's 1980 presidential primary campaign) was now in charge of preparing Reagan for his televised debates with Carter.

With the general election looming, Carter needed his top political strategist at the helm of his campaign. So on June 11, 1980, Ham Jordan resigned as chief of staff to become chairman of the campaign committee. Carter's new chief would be the man who was passed over at the start: Jack Watson. It was almost four years to the day since Carter had asked him to run his transition. Over the previous three years, Watson had deftly navigated the emergency involving the near meltdown of the nuclear reactor at Pennsylvania's Three Mile Island; a nationwide truckers' strike that had turned violent; and the chaotic Mariel Boat Lift, which sent thousands of Cuban refugees swarming ashore in Florida. Watson had also tended Carter's relationships with governors across the country: As a result, he got a unanimous resolution from the Democratic governors supporting Carter over his rival Kennedy.

As Reagan sharpened his attacks, Carter's poll numbers kept slipping. Unemployment worsened; interest rates spiked to 20 percent. And efforts to free the hostages were unavailing. "Disillusionment grew rapidly after my failure to gain their freedom," Carter wrote. "My standing in the public opinion polls fell. Only 20 percent of those interviewed approved of my handling of the presidency."

Yet by the fall the race had tightened dramatically. Reagan had emerged from the Republican Convention in July with a substantial lead over his opponent. By October—thanks in part to fears that Reagan was a reckless cowboy—Carter had narrowed the gap to just four percentage points.

On October 28, the candidates squared off in their first and only televised debate, which did not go well for Carter. Trying to connect with parents, Carter talked about his twelve-year-old daughter Amy's fear of nuclear war. It "made her the most famous antinuclear advocate in America because of the ridicule it aroused from Governor Reagan and the news reporters," Carter wrote. Moreover, Reagan defused the wonkish president with homespun charm. "There you go again," Reagan protested gently, waving off a Carter attack. "Reagan was, 'Aw, shucks, this and that, I'm a grandfather and . . . I love peace,' etc.," wrote Carter dismissively. But he knew the damage was done.

With the election approaching, "there were two White Houses—one working on the hostages, the other working on everything else," as Jordan observed. Carter, Jordan, and his national security team—Brzezinski; Secretary of State Cyrus Vance; his deputy, Warren Christopher; and others— furiously pursued every avenue to resolve the crisis. There were promising signs that the Iranians might be willing to negotiate. And one dead end followed after another. "It was out of my hands," Carter wrote. His reelection depended on "irrational people on the other side of the world over whom I had no control."

Meanwhile Watson set out to make the White House function. "When he asked me to be chief, I was surprised," recalls Watson. "I regretted I didn't have more time. There was time to start making a difference—but just a start." In eight months on the job, despite white-knuckle, round-the-clock hostage negotiations, Watson brought order and efficiency to the West Wing and mended relationships with the powers that be on Capitol Hill, who were astonished to suddenly have their phone calls returned. "Jack knew what to do, knew how to get it done," says Jay Beck, Jordan's deputy and close friend. "I think throughout that last year, when Carter was so focused on the hostages, Kennedy, and all, Jack was there to make the trains run." Indeed, an article in **Presidential Studies Quarterly**, published in 1993, would cite Watson as one of the three best chiefs in modern history.

But a functioning White House, however belated, could not change the harsh reality: inflation, unemployment, sky-high interest rates, foreign crises—and the lingering Iranian crisis. The day before the election, Caddell relayed to Carter "very disturbing poll results, showing a massive slippage as people realized the hostages were not coming home. . . . almost all the undecided voters moved to Reagan." Reagan won the election by 51 percent to Carter's 41 percent in the popular vote, 489 votes to Carter's 49 in the electoral college. An agreement to release the hostages arrived, but only at the very last moment: twenty minutes after Reagan's inauguration; they left Iranian airspace on a flight to Germany, and home to freedom.

On Watson's last day as chief of staff, during the inauguration ceremony, he stayed behind to look after the White House. The reality of leaving it had not dawned on Watson until that moment. "I'm walking to the Southwest Gate, which I had come into and out of hundreds of times," he recalls. "And suddenly I realized that the moment I stepped through the gate, I couldn't get back in. I was **finished**. And I felt I was in one of those old western movies, where the disgraced officer is called out on the parade field in front of everybody. And I had this mental image of my epaulets being stripped off my shoulders, and my sword broken."

He goes on, "I was disappointed that we weren't going to have the opportunity to continue. I felt that we'd learned a lot. Carter is a supremely educable man. And I knew that he had learned important things. He was still going to be a president firmly dedicated to his policies—and politics be damned. But I believed that a second term of the Carter presidency would've given to the country some important things. And I regretted profoundly that we weren't going to have that chance."

Carter's presidency was by some measures successful: On energy, deregulation, the Middle East, and a host of other issues, his legislative batting average was higher than any president since Lyndon Johnson. "You'd be hard-pressed," says Eizenstat, "to say that this president was anything other than successful in terms of achieving major policy goals." Ironically, Carter's appointment of Paul Volcker to head the Federal Reserve may have been decisive in slaying inflation—which would happen on Reagan's watch. But Carter never mastered an overarching message for his presidency. As Fallows put it, "I came to believe Carter believes fifty things, but no one thing."

"A second term would have been excellent," insists Eizenstat. "This is the shame of it. Carter had learned his game. And with Jack, we would have had fewer priorities, more focused priorities, the hostage crisis settled. . . ."

The drama of Ham Jordan's personal life was not over. In the summer of 1980, threatened with prosecution for tax evasion, a co-owner of New York City's notorious disco Studio 54 made a startling allegation: Jordan had been a frequent visitor to the club and had snorted cocaine there. After a lengthy and expensive FBI investigation, Jordan was exonerated of the bogus charge. But under the headline: "Unfair Battering Taken by Hamilton Jordan," Richard Cohen wrote in the **Washington Post**:

If he is known for anything, it is not for being the president's close friend, his chief of staff and, at the end, the chairman of his campaign committee, but as the guy who spit Amaretto down some woman's blouse. . . . Hamilton Jordan, after all, leaves Washington in debt to lawyers, bruised and battered and slightly soiled, but with few of us having a firm idea if he was good or bad at what he did. All we really know for sure is that he does not use cocaine. It cost both us and him a bundle to find out.

One reader was paying close attention. James Baker, Reagan's incoming chief of staff, wrote a note on Cohen's column: "Clip and Save."

In December, President-elect Reagan made one of his first visits to Washington, D.C., for a reception in his honor at the home of Kay Graham, the publisher of the **Washington Post**. Graham had called Watson and asked him to come over early. Arriving with Nancy, Reagan spotted Carter's outgoing chief across the room. He strode over to him and stuck out his hand. "Hello, Jack, it's so nice to see you again," the president-elect said: "You know, Jack, my people tell me that if you'd been chief of staff from the beginning, I wouldn't be here." Reagan may have just been practicing his legendary flattery. Or perhaps he genuinely believed what some others suspected: that Carter might have fared differently had Jack Watson been his chief from the outset.

"We shouldn't think that putting one person in a position changes everything," says Eizenstat. "It wouldn't have eliminated inflation; it wouldn't have made the hostage situation go away. But it would have created an initial impression of more organization, of a clearer sense of priorities, of a more professional operation. So, yes, I think it would have made a difference." Carter's stubborn belief that he could be his own chief had cost him dearly. Eizenstat concludes: "It was a terrible idea. It was a disastrous idea. Because presidents have too many things to do. They need someone to organize issues for them, to organize decisions, to bring the politics and the policy together, to have outreach to interest groups, to make sure that relations with Congress are going as smoothly as possible, to make sure the scheduling is done in the most logical way, to set priorities. That can't be done by the president himself—however smart or wise he is."

"The baseline rules of the job are pretty simple," Watson says. "Knowing your president, and being loyal to him in the broadest sense. Wanting him to be a great president—and therefore telling him when you don't think he is. Being tough enough to make hard decisions and to take a lot of criticism for them. Being a real hard-ass—firing somebody who needs to be fired. Telling someone on Capitol Hill: 'We're not going to do that—and here's why.' And sometimes you're being as gentle as a butterfly. You have to be tough and you have to be gentle and you have to be sensitive—a lot of the qualities of a good Marine officer."

"In retrospect," says Fallows of Carter's White House, "there should have been some way to empower Ham as the confidant, as the trusted truth teller. And somebody else would be the one asking, 'Okay, where should we be six months from now? Where should we be two years from now?' Every president is destined to fail in some way, because the job involves a wider range of talents than any person has. And so, yes, every president should have a chief of staff who makes a complete whole. And few of them do."

And yet Jimmy Carter himself is unrepentant. "I think that the White House mechanism worked quite well in the first couple of years," he insists. "I had studied the recent history of the White House, and most certainly the relationship between the president and his chief of staff. And I really hadn't gleaned anything that would make it a particularly attractive position." Had he learned anything from the chiefs of staff who served his predecessors? I ask him. "I don't really look back on Cheney or Rumsfeld or Haldeman," he replies, "as having performed in a sterling way that enhanced the success or the reputation of their president. I don't think an officially designated chief of staff would have changed anything."

"I have great respect for President Carter, but as I look back on it, I would say that was a mistake," says John Podesta, Bill Clinton's final chief. "I'm sure he still feels like it was the right call, but as I look at the results of his presidency, and certainly the fact that he was a one-term president, if you're looking for an organizational model, you wouldn't start there."

"Every president looks fifty years older when leaving office," says Fallows, "because even somebody who figures out how to win the office can't really imagine the demands it brings and the complexity. And so it's difficult to have the tragic imagination of how hard it's going to be—especially if, like Carter, he had had a high estimate of his own abilities."

Fallows pauses, as he considers Carter's successor. "And maybe that's the strength of presidents like Reagan—who don't think they're the smartest person around."

4

"One **Hell** of a Chief of Staff"

James A. Baker III and Ronald Reagan

In the Pacific Palisades neighborhood of Los Angeles, James Baker stood on the porch of Ronald Reagan's home, peering through the window. It was November 6, 1980, just two days after Reagan had been elected president of the United States. A few months earlier, Baker had been the campaign manager for his bitter rival. Now he was the newly anointed White House chief of staff.

Reagan had summoned Baker to his home this morning to meet his inner circle. "That was a traumatic thing for me," Baker recalls. "I go up there and look through the window—and there are all the people I've been fightin'! **All** of 'em!"

Gathered inside were Reagan's closest advisers: Edwin Meese, his top aide and chief of staff during his governorship; William Casey, an old friend who would become his CIA director; Michael Deaver, the Reagan family confidant; Lyn Nofziger, his loyal political strategist. Suddenly Baker, the consummate Washington insider, felt like an outsider—trapped behind enemy lines. He froze, afraid to knock on the door. Moments later the door swung open, and Reagan appeared, beaming. "Jim, what are you doing out **here**?" the president-elect asked. Still grinning, he waved Baker inside.

Baker would never forget the sunny reception he received from the fortieth president, or the dark days that followed—when the battle for the soul of the Reagan presidency began. For Baker, that struggle would be more emotionally grueling and deeply painful than almost anyone around him knew.

Almost thirty years later, a former Reagan staffer got a rare glimpse of his inner turmoil. Accompanying him on Baker's chartered plane to a speaking engagement, she and Reagan's former chief reminisced about their White House days. "Jim Baker spoke emotionally of what a good man Reagan was. And how people didn't really understand the depth of his sweetness and goodness and loyalty," she recalls. But then came a startling moment. "Baker's eyes filled with tears. He told me what it had been like for him to be chief of staff in a White House riven by different philosophies and ideological outlooks. And every day various people would try to take Jim Baker out."

She continues: "He **hated** it. He hated the tension. He hated the pointless animosity. And his eyes **really** filled with tears when he said that he tried, under the stress and strain, to quit." The moment was a revelation. "I had simply never known, having seen Mr. Baker walk through the halls—coolly, in his tall gray suit, smiling at everybody and being very soft-voiced, as only a killer could be—I just never knew what it took out of him."

James A. Baker III was an improbable choice to become Reagan's closest adviser. "One of the most amazing things that ever happened to me in life," he says, "was when Ronald Reagan asked me to be his White House chief of staff." After all, Baker, a former marine and Texas lawyer, was the good friend of Reagan's political opponent George H. W. Bush. Baker and Bush had met in 1959 at Houston Country Club, where they became tennis doubles partners (neither could serve well, but Baker's ground strokes complemented Bush's volleys). Almost a decade later, when Baker's wife, Mary Stuart, died of breast cancer—leaving him with four boys, aged seven to fifteen—Bush was at his side. When his friend proposed that Baker work on his senatorial campaign to take his mind off his grief, Baker replied: "Number one, I don't know anything about politics, and number two, I'm a Democrat." Bush laughed. "We can take care of that second problem," he said. They did, and though Bush lost that Senate race, it was the beginning of a close friendship, and a formidable political team.

To Baker, Ronald Reagan had seemed equally unacceptable. Only a few months before he was chosen as his chief, Baker had privately dismissed the Republican candidate as "a grade B movie actor, **Bedtime for Bonzo**; he was gonna get us in a nuclear war, he was dangerous, he was terrible."

As election day in 1980 approached, the overwhelming favorite to become Reagan's chief was Meese, the affable attorney who had served as the California governor's loyal confidant—as close to Reagan as Ham Jordan was to Jimmy Carter. Yet the idea of Meese as White House chief troubled some of Reagan's friends and family. Meese was adept at framing issues for his boss but famously disorganized; his briefcase was known as the "black hole": Papers went in and never came out. Stuart Spencer, Reagan's old friend and campaign manager, thought Meese was a nonstarter. "Ed couldn't organize a two-car funeral," he says.

Spencer was convinced that Reagan, the ex–Hollywood actor, needed Washington's equivalent of a great director. Carter and Reagan were opposites: the former a compulsive micromanager, the latter a gifted performer trained at hitting marks set by others. "Not because Reagan didn't have any skills or anything, but I watched him as governor," says Spencer. "Reagan was, 'I've got a role to play, I've got a script to learn—and you're a producer, you're a director, and you're a cameraman: Now you do your job and I'm gonna do mine.' What does that mean? You've got to have one **hell** of a chief of staff!"

Trusted as he was by Reagan, Spencer was even closer to Nancy—"the personnel director," as he called her. Just weeks before the election, he had dinner with the Reagans in their hotel suite. "I said, 'You know, Governor, you're gonna win this thing. . . . We gotta start talking about a chief of staff—because all over the street I hear it's going to be Ed Meese. That is not good news.'" To Spencer's surprise, the Reagans readily agreed. "They said—**both** of 'em—'oh no, no, not Ed Meese.' And I went phewwwwww."

Spencer had been watching Baker since he'd been Ford's delegate hunter in 1976: "I thought, number one, he's organized. Number two, he's upwardly mobile—he didn't want to look bad." Deaver, too, had been impressed by Baker's cool efficiency and shared the doubts about Meese. Moreover, Baker had something none of Reagan's men could offer: He knew his way around Capitol Hill—the key to governing in Washington.

"I said to Reagan, 'I think the guy you want to look at is Jim Baker,'" says Spencer. "'Do you have feelings about him?' And Reagan said, 'Well, he ran the Bush campaign.' And I said, 'That's right.'

So we just had a discussion, and at the end of it Nancy—this was why she was so good—she says, 'Stu, will you commit to me that he will work for Ronnie's agenda and not his own?' And I said, 'I'll **guarantee** ya.'"

So the Reagans invited Baker to join them on their next campaign flight, and they were disarmed by his smooth manner and self-possession. It did not hurt that the tall, courtly Texas lawyer looked every bit the part. "Nancy would eye his dress, his style, his presence," says Spencer. And Baker could turn on the charm. "I think part of choosing Baker was that Nancy thought he was good-looking," says Lesley Stahl, the CBS News correspondent. "Did Lesley really say that?" Baker asks me, without missing a beat. "Well, you tell Lesley: I think **she's** good-looking!"

Two days before the election, recalls Spencer, Reagan called him into their hotel suite. "'We're gonna go with Jimmy Baker.'" Margaret Tutwiler, a savvy thirty-year-old campaign staffer who would follow Baker into the White House, was impressed by the president-elect's clear-eyed call. "Ultimately Reagan had to make a very tough decision," she says today. "Not easy—and Reagan was not a mean person. This wasn't someone pulling something over on somebody. I give Reagan enormous credit for seeing the logic in it."

Carter was arguably the most intelligent president of the twentieth century, whereas Reagan had once been called, unfairly, "an amiable dunce." Yet in choosing Baker, Reagan had intuited something his predecessor did not grasp. As Reagan's biographer Lou Cannon wrote: "He did not know one missile system from another and could not explain the simplest procedures of the federal government, but he understood that the political process of his presidency would be closely linked to his acceptance in Washington. In this he was the opposite of Jimmy Carter, who knew far more and understood far less."

When Reagan announced Baker's appointment, the day after the election, it set off a firestorm among the Californians. "Meese was down. Meese was very down," says Baker. According to Spencer, he wasn't just down . . . he "went **ape shit**." It wasn't merely losing out on the job; Meese and his allies saw Baker's arrival as a call to arms. "Conservatives who greeted Reagan's election as the triumph of an ideological revolution were dismayed at the Baker selection," wrote Cannon. "It was inconceivable to them that Reagan would want a political pragmatist as his top aide."

The war between the pragmatists, led by Baker, and the ideologues, or "true believers," had begun. Characteristically, Reagan's response to his friend Meese's disappointment was to tell his new chief to patch things up. "I want you to make it right with Ed," he told Baker.

Baker's next move would speak volumes about

his mastery of White House governance, and his ability to outsmart his rivals. The next morning, he invited Meese to breakfast. It was a shame about all this fuss, Baker told him, pulling out a yellow legal pad. Why don't you and I just divide up our duties, lawyer to lawyer?

Baker proposed that Meese should be "counselor to the president"; he would be in charge of policy, supervise the domestic and national security councils, preside over cabinet meetings, and have cabinet rank. Baker, as chief of staff, would control access to the president, paperwork, speechwriting, and the White House staff. Meese readily agreed, and Baker had a memo typed up for their signatures. "The way I made it right with Ed worked," says Baker. "It worked for the Gipper, it worked for the country, it worked for me."

The truth was, Baker had cleverly seized the levers of power. While Meese was technically in charge of "policy," Baker was in charge of executing it; the chief also controlled information to and from the president, and the daily message. Meese was left, as one observer put it, "with a nice title and a fancy office and little else." Baker states it more diplomatically. "I worked it out in a way that Ed could handle—and I was still in a position to run everything."

"It takes most chiefs of staff four years or more to figure out how to run the place," says Richard Norton Smith. "Baker knew it immediately." To help him manage the first family, Baker had made an indispensable ally: Mike Deaver. A gifted advance man with a genius for staging events, Deaver choreographed Reagan's public appearances in ways that conveyed patriotic optimism to American viewers. He was also like a son to Nancy Reagan. Baker could rely on Deaver to keep the first lady in the loop, and to relay Nancy's updates on how "Ronnie" was feeling—delivered every morning just before the president arrived at the Oval Office.

Baker, Meese, and Deaver now constituted Reagan's "troika."

They inherited a country in crisis. At home, inflation was soaring, interest rates had topped 20 percent, gas prices kept rising, and unemployment was headed toward double digits. Overseas, the Soviet Union occupied Afghanistan and seemed poised to keep going to the Persian Gulf, threatening the world's oil supplies. Moreover, Reagan was taking office after a succession of failed presidents, done in by assassination, war, scandal, and economic crisis.

On a legal pad, Baker noted: "About to inherit worst economic mess of any Pres. in 50 years. So first order of business—get a handle on the economy! Second: Our international position has deteriorated badly. (1) defenses weak (2) Our word is no longer trusted—because our diplomacy has been uncertain. RR [Ronald Reagan] wants to see flag of liberty flying once again around the world. Thinks U.S. has a special mission in lifting that banner."

As the inauguration approached, Baker met with his predecessor, Jack Watson, and took hand-written notes on his advice.

Roles of C of S (acc to Jack Watson)

1) <u>Resolve disputes</u> that don't need to go to the Pres.

2) <u>Be an HONEST BROKER.</u> Make sure everything completely staffed out.

3) C of S is place where policy and politics come together. (make sure the <u>political</u> aspect—the p.r. aspect—is looked at.)

4) <u>Administer</u> the place. Run it.

Next Baker met with Dick Cheney. His notes from Ford's former chief filled four yellow legal pages.

****** **Central Theme we ought to push**
Pres. seriously weakened in recent years
Restore power & auth to Exec Branch—
Need strong leadership

Get rid of War Powers Act—restore impound-ment rights

2) Strong Cabinet & strong staff in WH Not "either or" proposition.

Have to have both.

3) Orderly schedule & orderly paper flow is way you protect the Pres.

Well designed system. Got to be brutal in scheduling decisions.

Most valuable asset in D.C. is time of RR

Need to have discipline & order & be discriminating

*DON'T USE THE POLICY PROCESS TO IMPOSE YOUR POLICY VIEWS ON PRES.

Baker recruited a high-powered staff that knew its way around the White House. "One thing I believed was to surround yourself with really good people," he says. "A lot of people were afraid to do that for fear it would take the sheen off them." At fifty, Baker had nothing to prove. "I'll tell you this," says Margaret Tutwiler, "and I believe it about Baker and I believe it about Reagan: The most successful managers are those that are secure enough to surround themselves with extremely strong-willed, talented people."

In addition to Tutwiler, Baker brought in David Stockman, widely regarded as an economic genius, as director of OMB; John Rogers, a capable administrator; Fred Fielding, a seasoned White House counselor; David Gergen, a shrewd communications veteran; and Richard Darman, a brilliant expert in governmental affairs.

It was Darman's idea to create a governing body that Baker called "a key to my success": the Legislative Strategy Group. The LSG, chaired by Baker, would decide what was doable and what was not on Capitol Hill—with input from congressional liaison Max Friedersdorf and his capable young deputy, Ken Duberstein. "You could do all the policy studying in the world and come up with papers and options," explains Baker. "But in terms of actually getting things enacted into law, it was the LSG where the decisions were made."

Reagan cared about a few deeply held beliefs: reducing government, projecting military strength, and cutting taxes. The details of how to achieve these goals . . . not so much. "Reagan really needed a chief of staff," says Brent Scowcroft. "He wasn't interested in much of the work of the president. So Baker really was a copresident in a way."

A reporter who covered the Reagan White House recalls, "There were times when the president would arrive in the morning and say, 'Well, boys, what do you have for me?' And Baker would organize an agenda and an objective for the president. . . . They initiated programs that they knew he would like—and Reagan was grateful for that."

Baker assigned Gergen to do a study of the first one hundred days of five previous presidents—and, drawing from their track record, draft an "Early Action Plan" for Reagan. "Carter's experience convinced us that focus is essential for a new president," Gergen wrote. "He had tried to emulate Roosevelt by sending up stacks of legislative proposals in his early months. But his ideas had no internal coherence." By contrast, Reagan's agenda would be coherent: "We ought to have three goals, and all three of them are the economy," said Baker.

Part of the chief's job was to be a "javelin catcher," as Jack Watson had put it, and it did not take long for the spears to start flying. Just a few hours after Reagan's swearing-in, still dressed in their formal clothes, Baker, Deaver, and Meese were in the West Wing, when Al Haig came barging in. The former chief of staff to Nixon and Ford, now Reagan's secretary of state, was clutching a memo, ready for the president's signature, which would put Haig in charge of crisis management. He and Reagan had agreed to the arrangement, Haig insisted. This was news to Baker and the troika. They explained that the arrangement would have to be cleared with the secretary of defense, the CIA director, and the national security adviser. Haig was livid and stormed away.

It was the first of many times Baker would clip the wings of the self-described foreign policy "vicar." Early in 1981 Haig boasted privately to Reagan and his advisers that he could "turn Cuba into a parking lot"; publicly, he wanted to "lay down a marker" with the Soviets over Central America. To that end, Haig had scheduled television appearances to warn the Soviets against meddling in El Salvador. Baker was incensed: Central America was a thorny problem that would cost Reagan political capital and detract from their focus on the economy. So Baker went to Reagan and got permission to rein Haig in. Then he called the secretary of state and told him to "get the hell off television."

"You do not serve your president well if you are just a yes man," explains Baker. "That's not what presidents need; that's not what presidents want. One of the things I am most proud of is that all of the presidents I have worked for have said, 'Jim Baker was able to tell me what he really thought, whether I wanted to hear it or not.' You have to be willing to do that. You have to be willing to speak truth to power."

Reagan's hard-core followers heard not truth but betrayal. "We had a lot of tension in that first term between the so-called true believers and my side of the White House, the get-the-job-done, pragmatic type," says Baker. To the true believers, every Reagan compromise was a capitulation. "I had to deal with Meese, and he would not want to make the kind of compromises that were necessary to get something enacted into law," says Baker. "And that was debilitating. We used to call it a rat f*ck. That first term was a rat f*ck: people stabbing you in the back, always fighting."

In this ideological and philosophical knife fight, Baker was outnumbered. Arrayed against him were not just Haig and Meese, but CIA director Bill Casey, Defense secretary Caspar Weinberger, and UN ambassador Jeane Kirkpatrick. Bill Clark, who would become Reagan's national security adviser, had drawn a target on Baker's back. Clark was "not the brightest bulb in the chandelier," says Baker, "but, boy, you talk about somebody who tried to appeal to the dark side of the old man, that was Bill, and he was extraordinarily difficult. Reagan liked him, so when you had him teaming up with Meese and Casey and Weinberger and Kirkpatrick, that was fairly formidable opposition."

Baker fought back by keeping friends like Deaver and Nancy close—and by cultivating the White House press corps. Meese bitterly accused Baker of leaking negative stories about him. Baker pleaded guilty to spinning, not leaking. "There's a difference," he says. "Leaking is when you put something out to drive policy in one way or another, or to scratch your own back or promote yourself at the expense of somebody else. But it's **your job** as the chief of staff to spin the president's position."

Baker charmed the jaded press corps by telling them everything he could on "background"; he warned them off half-baked stories and was always accessible, day or night. (Though he rarely agreed to be quoted directly.) "He understood that the press corps was part and parcel of governing," says Tutwiler. "He always treated them with respect— even if he couldn't stand the individual he was dealing with."

The CBS News White House producer Susan Zirinsky knew a maestro when she saw one. Zirinsky, the model for the hard-charging, elfin character played by Holly Hunter in the movie **Broadcast News**, enjoyed matching wits with Baker. "He had this zen quality," she says. "He was put together and he just exuded this air of calm and cool and above it all. He was the one with the secret sauce. He was the one who you thought knew everything; he was giving context and perspective—without spin; whether you agree or disagree, you know he was a straight shooter. That's what everybody felt. He was a straight shooter. And **extremely** bright."

The week before she started at the White House, Peggy Noonan, the speechwriter, bumped into Baker at the White House Correspondents Dinner. "Remember," he told her, "if they start shooting at you, just duck—and let them hit me." "He was grounded in reality like a tough Texan," she says. "He was a lawyer. He was a guy who didn't seem to move forward with a lot of illusions about life or people or organizations or systems."

Tutwiler thought Reagan, the cowboy, and Baker, the outdoorsman, had something in common. "Reagan was very secure in his own skin," she says. "I feel the same way about Jim Baker—that they're fine being alone. Reagan loves to go out there and ride that horse, chop that wood. Baker loves to sit in his turkey blinds—they're people who can spend time with **themselves**."

In the gospel according to Baker, preparation was the first commandment. "Day in and day out, he's focused. He does not wing it. He thinks before he speaks," says Tutwiler of the man she called Mr. Cautious. "He has that yellow legal pad, and he writes everything down." Baker logged sixteen-hour days and personally returned every phone call, no matter the hour. "I'm driving down Pennsylvania Avenue one night with Reagan," says Stu Spencer. "And all the lights were on in the West Wing. And Reagan says, 'What's with all the lights on?' I say, 'Well, they're working.' And he goes, 'Oh my God, tell Baker to go home.'" But for all his preparation, Baker could never have anticipated the crisis that would soon unfold, which would come within a hairsbreadth of ending the Reagan presidency.

March 30, 1981, was a warm and blustery day in Washington; Reagan had been in office just over two months. Baker was in his West Wing office when David Gergen burst in with shocking news: Shots had been fired at the president. Reagan had been rushed to George Washington University Hospital. Deaver was with him and called Baker

H. R. "Bob" Haldeman in his office. Richard Nixon's "Lord High Executioner" created the model for the modern White House chief of staff.

Photo Courtesy Richard M. Nixon Presidential Library

Haldeman briefs Richard Nixon. The Watergate cover-up, the biggest scandal in American political history, took place because Haldeman could not tell the president the unpleasant truth. *Photo Courtesy Richard M. Nixon Presidential Library*

Donald Rumsfeld unwinds riding a unicycle during a visit with friends in Maryland circa 1975. When it came to governing, he and Dick Cheney warned Gerald Ford, "Beware the spokes of the wheel."

Photo by Dick Swanson

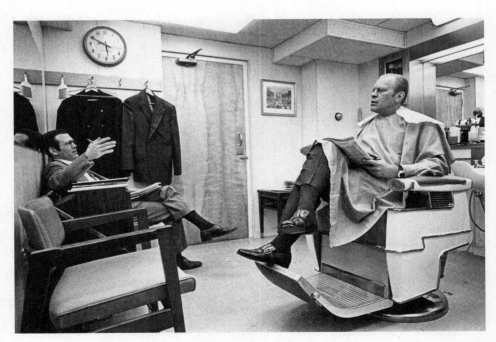

Gerald Ford gets a trim in the White House barbershop, and a briefing by his chief of staff Rumsfeld. *Photo by David Hume Kennerly, Gerald R. Ford Presidential Library*

Rumsfeld observes a briefing in the White House press room. *Photo by David Hume Kennerly, Gerald R. Ford Presidential Library*

Rumsfeld and his deputy Cheney with Betty Ford. The first lady was a popular and outspoken figure in the White House, and nationwide. *Photo by David Hume Kennerly, Gerald R. Ford Presidential Library*

In a cabin at Camp David, Cheney, just thirty-four years old when he became chief, confers with Gerald Ford. *Photo by David Hume Kennerly, Gerald R. Ford Presidential Library*

Jody Powell (*left*) and Hamilton Jordan. The bond between Carter and his two closest advisers was almost filial. *Photo Courtesy Jimmy Carter Presidential Library*

Hamilton Jordan in his White House office. He did not want the title, or the responsibilities, of chief of staff. *Photo Courtesy Jimmy Carter Presidential Library*

Carter and Jordan on the White House tennis court. The president scheduled play himself. According to a May 26, 1977, memo: "You must have personal permission from the President each time you would like to use the tennis court." *Photo Courtesy Jimmy Carter Presidential Library*

Jack Watson in his White House office. Once a contender to become Carter's first chief of staff, Watson was pushed aside in favor of Jordan, a decision that would hobble the Carter presidency. *Photo Courtesy Jimmy Carter Presidential Library*

Carter and Watson confer on *Air Force One*. During the final year of Carter's presidency, Watson would become his highly effective chief of staff.

Photo Courtesy Jimmy Carter Presidential Library

Ronald Reagan and his chief of staff James A. Baker III at a cabinet meeting. The president who ran as an outsider understood he needed a Washington insider to help him govern. *Photo Courtesy Ronald Reagan Presidential Library*

Left to right: Baker, Edwin Meese, and Michael Deaver. The "troika" divided the responsibilities of running the White House—but Baker was first among equals. *Photo by David Hume Kennerly, Getty Images*

Reagan's consummate chief returned every phone call, no matter how late at night. *Photo Courtesy Ronald Reagan Presidential Library*

Baker prided himself on telling Reagan the unvarnished truth. "You have to be able to tell the president what he does not want to hear." *Photo Courtesy Ronald Reagan Presidential Library*

Baker with his top lieutenants (*left to right*): Larry Speakes, Richard Darman, Ken Duberstein, David Stockman, and David Gergen. The "pragmatists," as they were called, won more than their share of battles with the right-wing Reagan ideologues, or "true believers." *Photo Courtesy Ronald Reagan Presidential Library*

Nancy Reagan and Chief of Staff Donald Regan. Regan lost his job after he hung up the phone on the first lady. "That's not just a firing offense," said James Baker. "That may be a hanging offense!" *Photo Courtesy Ronald Reagan Presidential Library*

Ken Duberstein and Howard H. Baker Jr. in the Oval Office. Baker and his deputy made a secret pact: If they concluded that Reagan was lying about the Iran-Contra scandal, they would resign. *Photo Courtesy Ronald Reagan Presidential Library*

Duberstein with the president. Reagan's final chief described his role as being the president's "reality therapist." *Photo Courtesy Ronald Reagan Presidential Library*

President George H. W. Bush with Chief of Staff John H. Sununu on *Air Force One*. An acerbic former New Hampshire governor, Sununu was forced out as chief after he was caught using military transportation for personal trips. *Photo by David Valdez, Courtesy of George Bush Presidential Library*

with details: The president had been walking to his motorcade from a Washington hotel when a gunman opened fire. Press Secretary James Brady and a Secret Service agent had been wounded, perhaps mortally. Reagan had been hit—but no one knew how serious the wound was.

"We'd only been there for two months," recalls Baker, "and the president is shot. And you're wondering, this is the beginning, but is it also the **end**?" Meese appeared in Baker's doorway, and the two advisers departed for the hospital.

Moments later, a manic figure, wearing a trench coat with shoulder pads and epaulets, came rushing into Baker's office. It was Haig. Wide-eyed, he grabbed a phone and demanded to be connected with the vice president, who was returning to Washington on **Air Force Two**. "I thought, this guy's off his rocker," says a staffer who witnessed the scene. "He's screaming on the phone to Bush, saying, 'Reagan's been **shot in the back, shot in the back**!' And I'm, like, how do you know that? The guy was making this up! This is just **wild**."

Meanwhile, Baker and Meese arrived at the hospital just as the president was being wheeled down the hall. A bullet had lodged in his chest, and he was on his way to surgery. "Who's minding the store?" Reagan quipped as he rolled by. Baker and Meese ducked into a janitor's closet to discuss a key question: With the president about to be incapacitated, his prognosis uncertain, should they invoke the Twenty-fifth Amendment and transfer power to the vice president?

Baker worried that empowering Bush might look like a coup on his part: After all, he was the vice president's best friend and ex–campaign manager. On the spot, he and Meese agreed that invoking the amendment would be premature.

While the troika held down the fort at the hospital, another emergency meeting was taking place. Gathered in the White House Situation Room were Weinberger, Treasury secretary Donald Regan, National Security Adviser Richard Allen, Attorney General William French Smith, Fielding, Darman, and Haig, who had rushed there after calling the vice president.

Baker had given Haig the job of coordinating White House public statements with the troika at the hospital. But this was not enough for Haig. "The helm is **right here in this chair**," he barked. "No one seemed to pay much serious attention," wrote Darman later. "Mentally, I dismissed Haig's statement as utterly absurd."

Larry Speakes, the deputy press secretary (pressed into service for the wounded Brady), was holding forth on national television in the press room a floor above. The group watched on a monitor as Speakes foundered when asked who was in charge at the White House. "Jesus Christ, Almighty," shouted Haig. "Why's he doing that?" He jumped out of his chair and bolted out the door. Moments later, he appeared on television—perspiring, red-faced—before the eyes of the world.

"The **Crisis Management** is in effect," Haig proclaimed gravely. (Whatever that was, it sounded unsettling.) But he wasn't finished. "Constitutionally, gentlemen," Haig stammered, "you have the president, the vice president, and the secretary of state in that order. . . . As of now, **I am in control** here in the White House."

Watching the bizarre scene, as the secretary of state mangled the order of presidential succession, Don Regan exclaimed: "What's this all about? Is he **mad**?"

Already on edge before Haig's outburst, tempers were now flaring in the Situation Room. At issue was how to show the world—friends and foes alike—that everything was under control. A large number of Soviet submarines had been spotted unusually close to the eastern United States. The discussion turned to American military readiness, and the whereabouts of the suitcase with the secret codes for launching U.S. nuclear missiles, known as the "football." Weinberger, as defense secretary, had "national command authority"; as a precaution against enemy mischief he had raised the alert level of U.S. bombers.

"What kind of alert, Cap?" interjected Haig, who had returned, perspiring, from the press room.

"It's a standby alert," said Weinberger. "Just a standby alert."

"You're not raising readiness?" asked Haig.

"No, no, no . . . they'll probably put themselves on alert, but I just want to be sure."

"Do we have a football in here, do we?" asked Haig.

"Right there," Allen said.

Allen raised his hand and thumped a suitcase that was sitting at his feet. Suddenly Don Regan chimed in.

"Al, don't elevate it—be careful," he cautioned.

"Absolutely," Haig said. "Absolutely."

Elevating the so-called DEFCON level of U.S. military forces could start an escalation on both sides that might lead to nuclear war. (DEFCON 1 is the highest level, signaling an imminent attack; DEFCON 5 is the lowest, indicating the world is at peace.) Now Weinberger said something that suggested he lacked a basic understanding of U.S. military readiness. Asked what level U.S. forces were at, he replied: "It's probably DEFCON 2."

Haig blew up. The secretary of defense had just declared that U.S. military forces were poised one level short of nuclear war. (Weinberger had meant to say DEFCON 4, not 2.) As if that weren't enough, Fielding, Haig, and the vice president's chief of staff were huddled over documents that, when signed by a majority of the cabinet, would invoke the Twenty-fifth Amendment—the option Baker and Meese had already rejected. Darman was worried. "One quick pass around the room and the group might have begun the effective removal of the president of the United States." Darman stepped out of the room and called Baker, who readily agreed with his trusted aide's next move: Darman gathered the documents, took them to his office, and locked them in his personal safe. Baker left the hospital and returned to the White House.

At 6:15 p.m., the chief of staff walked into the Situation Room. The squabbling stopped as Baker pulled up a chair. As Darman recalled, "The power-sensitive sit. room group showed a little extra gravitational pull in his direction." Baker told the group that the president's surgery had been successful, and his prognosis was good. There was "no need to get involved in questions of succession. By tomorrow the president will be able to make a decision."

"Baker is not perfect," says Tutwiler. "But he can handle pressure. He's a Steady Eddie. And he's a realist. It's almost clinical. He doesn't lead with emotion. He can handle a whole lot of incoming and just not get rattled." Baker's version is that he simply delivered a dose of reality. "My message when I got back to the Situation Room was calming, because I relayed the doctors' message. And the doctors' message was that the surgery had been successful. They expected the president to gain a full recovery."

Minutes later, the vice president's plane landed at Andrews Air Force Base. At 6:59 p.m. Bush walked into the Situation Room, where cooler heads were finally prevailing. "The sense of crisis passed," wrote Darman. "A calmer reality returned. And the Reagan Revolution, which less than a day before looked as if it might suddenly be over, was left to follow what course it could."

In truth, the Reagan Revolution was stalled, its bold economic agenda gridlocked. But after the shooting, as public affection for the president soared, Baker sensed an opportunity to change Reagan's fortunes. For the president's first public appearance since the shooting, Baker and Deaver proposed a special joint session of Congress. On April 28, Reagan, accompanied by the head of his Secret Service detail, strode into the House chamber triumphantly, to a raucous ovation. Reagan thanked the American people for their prayers and their flowers. Then he seized the occasion to tout his budget bill, reducing taxes and cutting spending by $36.6 billion. "The people want us to act, and not in half measures," he declared. "It's a little ironic," says Baker. "But the event that almost cost him his presidency and his life ended up strengthening him politically. And it may have helped us accomplish his signature policy goal, which was to [cut taxes] and to do it with Democratic votes."

And Reagan **was** prepared to cut taxes, by making deals with Congress. Unlike many of his followers, the president was more interested in putting points on the board than in toeing some ideological line. "He knew when to hold 'em; he knew when to fold 'em," says Baker. "He was a great negotiator. Reagan always said, 'I'll take eighty percent of what I want, and come back later for more.' He never understood the diehards who would go off the cliff with their flags flying."

Baker and his team went to work on the Democratic Speaker of the House, Thomas P. "Tip" O'Neill. "The president and Tip O'Neill were bitter policy enemies," says Baker. "But they both understood that your political adversary didn't have to be your political enemy. And that's why they were able to achieve a heck of a lot of good for this country." The legislative deals between the two Irishmen were "baked ahead of time," by the staff, as Duberstein put it. But that was fine with the president and the Speaker. "They would fight all day long over policy and after five o'clock they'd get together, drink whiskey, and tell Irish stories," Baker remembers.

Baker wasn't Irish and rarely drank, but he shared Reagan's love of a good joke—the more off-color the better. "Baker has a wicked sense of humor. Reagan did. George H. W. Bush does," says Tutwiler. "And humor was a serious part of all three of those guys." Reagan's humor was a powerful part of his political appeal. (It was also, of course, a potent weapon during a televised debate, as Jimmy Carter and Walter Mondale discovered.) "I think the president halfway expected us to show up every morning at the nine o'clock briefing with new material, a new joke," says Baker.

Reagan had a ready supply of canned anecdotes for almost every occasion. But he could also ad-lib when required. On a state visit to England, Baker and Deaver arranged for the president to go horseback riding with Queen Elizabeth at Windsor Castle. When the time came, the queen's horse took off at a gallop—farting uncontrollably. Reagan and his horse rode just behind. Upon their return, the queen stammered, "Mr. President, I am so **terribly** sorry." Reagan smiled and cocked his head. "That's funny," he responded. "I thought it was the horse."

Nine days after his triumphant address to Congress, Reagan's landmark budget bill passed, with sixty-three Democrats joining the GOP. ("The tired but happy LSG had expected about forty Democrats," Baker noted.) Despite the victory, there was trouble ahead—the Reagan Revolution was on a collision course with the "third rail" of American politics.

Reagan could be passionate—even obstinate—about his favorite causes, and for years he had advocated making Social Security voluntary. Stockman and Richard Schweiker, Reagan's secretary of health and human services, wanted to tackle that sacrosanct entitlement program head-on. But Baker knew that touching the third rail could be fatal.

"It was my view that going up to the Hill with a bill to reform Social Security was really dangerous from a political standpoint," Baker recalls. "If you touched it, you got electrocuted." It fell to the chief of staff to explain such realities of political life to Reagan. "I argued fairly vigorously with the president that we ought not to do it."

Reagan didn't want to hear that advice. But when Baker enlisted the first lady's support, the president heard it, and ultimately accepted it. ("Nancy was Baker's partner in crime on that," confirms Spencer.) Months later, when Stockman wanted to revive the issue, Baker called in the Republican leaders of the House and persuaded Reagan to set up a bipartisan blue-ribbon committee, providing political cover for any unpopular cuts. Consequently, the Greenspan Commission would succeed in reforming Social Security in 1983.

The Reagan Revolution was based on an article of faith: cutting taxes would stimulate the economy and generate so much growth that tax revenues would actually increase. Stockman was the Robespierre in green eyeshade who would lead them to the ramparts. During the primary campaign, George H. W. Bush had called this idea "voodoo economics." Republican majority leader Howard Baker Jr. called it a "riverboat gamble." Yet on August 13, 1981, Reagan signed into law the most dramatic tax cut in U.S. history, the Economic Recovery Tax Act.

Unfortunately, the bill for those cuts soon came due. The tax cut amounted to a staggering $750 billion. A stubborn recession choked off economic growth. Stockman's projections of a balanced budget had counted on "future savings"—drastic spending cuts that had yet to be realized (and never would be). Suddenly Reagan's beloved tax cuts seemed unsustainable. Stockman warned of disrupted markets, sky-high interest rates, and a deficit of as much as $100 billion for each of the next four years.

The only solution was to raise taxes—an unthinkable prospect to Reagan, who could detect a tax increase no matter how well disguised. "I'm not one of those who thinks Reagan was stupid," says Tutwiler. "And I watched Baker and Stockman inside the West Wing. Reagan couldn't do this detail stuff, that wasn't him. But this guy can't be fooled. They had charts, they had all this crap. And Reagan said, basically: 'Well, fellas, that's a tax.'"

Again, it was Baker's job to sell it to Reagan, to avert fiscal disaster. "The president was adamant about not raising taxes," he says. "It was something that he felt viscerally about." With support from Meese and Deaver (and, once again, Nancy), Baker warned the president of the consequences of failing to act. Reagan finally acquiesced. "I never will forget him taking his glasses off, throwing them on the desk, and saying, 'OK, dammit, I'm going to do it—but it's the **wrong** thing to do.'"

"Baker delivers bad news in a most respectful way," says Tutwiler. "It's not that he's sycophantic; he's not at all—but he has a lot of patience. He has an enormous amount of personal security because he was somebody before he came here." Spencer adds, "Jimmy was good at sayin', 'Hey, boss, you're wrong.' He learned one thing from me: You can stand up to a president who is a secure individual in his own right."

THE REAGAN REVOLUTION was about to face another existential crisis; one arguably more dangerous than the deficit. In December 1981, **The Atlantic** published an article that set off shock waves. Based on months of conversations with Stockman, the story was a devastating indictment of Reaganomics by its own architect. Reagan's budget director was quoted as saying the tax cuts were a "Trojan horse." The whole idea of supply-side economics, Stockman suggested, was unworkable, mission impossible.

Meese, Deaver, and Nancy were appalled. They wanted Stockman fired. Immediately. Baker called the budget director into his office. As Stockman recalls, "his eyes were steely and cold."

"My friend, I want you to listen up good. Your

ass is in a sling. All of the rest of them want you shit-canned right now. Immediately. This afternoon. If it weren't for me, you'd be a goner already."

Baker continued: "You're going to have lunch with the president. The menu is humble pie. You're going to eat every last motherf*cking spoonful of it. You're going to be the most contrite son of a bitch this world has ever seen. . . . When you go through the Oval Office door, I want to see that sorry ass of yours dragging on the carpet."

Stockman did as Baker instructed. His lunch with the president—or visit to the "woodshed"—was portrayed in the press as a moment of truth: Would the president fire him on the spot, or accept his apology? In fact, Baker had convinced Reagan in advance that Stockman was essential to their economic agenda; no purpose would be served by canning him.

Baker wasn't being kind—just clear-eyed about his interests and the president's. "He wasn't some milquetoast doughboy—oh, let's all sit around the campfire and sing 'Kumbaya,'" says Tutwiler. "But he understood the politics of serving—you cut somebody out, they can pay you back." As for Reagan, when it came to firing people, he was a marshmallow; the president believed in second, third, and often fourth chances.

It would not be long before the true believers struck again. In September of 1983, Baker was in a car on his way to lunch at Washington's Madison Hotel when his office called. Was Baker aware that, in order to investigate a leak, the president had approved the use of polygraphs on everyone who had attended a recent National Security Council meeting? No, Baker was **not** aware. The plan had Bill Clark's name written all over it. Baker told his driver to head back to the White House.

"So we turned the car around, and I went busting into the Oval Office and the president was having lunch with Vice President Bush and Secretary of State George Shultz," Baker recalls. "I stood at the table, and I said, 'Now, Mr. President . . . this would be a **terrible** thing in my view for your administration—you can't strap up to a polygraph the vice president of the United States. He was elected. He's a constitutional officer.'"

Shultz, who was also unaware of the plan, spoke up bluntly. If the president wanted his secretary of state to take a polygraph, okay—but it would be the last thing he did before resigning. "Well, President Reagan realized of course that he'd made a terrible mistake," says Baker. "I got that turned around in a half a day or less. The president rescinded everything he'd done—which is exactly of course what he should've done."

When he had agreed to the position as chief, Baker had told Reagan it was a job done best in "two-year increments"; after that, he would move on. Baker was now well into his third year. He was exhausted, restless, and eager to take his next step toward a cabinet position. In November 1983 an opportunity suddenly arose: Baker's nemesis, Bill Clark, left his position as national security adviser.

Baker and Deaver hatched an audacious plan—one that they believed would not only serve their personal advancement but would also address a festering problem. Unlike the domestic shop, the national security side of the White House was a mess: a snake pit of dysfunction and warring egos. Baker thought he could change that by becoming national security adviser. Deaver would become chief of staff, and there would be seamless coordination of domestic and foreign affairs. "Deaver was the closest aide to the Reagans personally—and would have been a very fine chief of staff," says Baker. "And I would have been a good, if I may say so, national security adviser."

If the true believers got wind of their plan, they would pull out all the stops to kill it. So Baker and Deaver got the blessing of Bush, Shultz, Spencer, and Nancy before pitching the idea privately to Reagan. The president agreed. A press release, prepared by Tutwiler, was ready to go. The shakeup, as Baker would say, was a "done deal."

But Baker had not counted on the horse getting out of the barn. On his way to a meeting of the National Security Planning Group right before the scheduled announcement, Reagan casually mentioned the new plan to Clark. Baker's nemesis betrayed no surprise but asked the president to delay an announcement. During the meeting, Clark scribbled handwritten notes and slipped them to Meese, Casey, and Weinberger, asking them to meet him and the president afterward.

"Timing is everything, and our timing failed us," Baker wrote later. "Mike and I did not know that the president was meeting with the four horsemen of our apocalypse." The four horsemen were joined by Kirkpatrick, who was also opposed to the plan. Casey told Reagan that he could not give the NSC job to Baker, a man he considered to be the "biggest leaker in Washington." So Reagan told Baker and Deaver that he wanted to think about it over the weekend. "Mr. President, I don't want to be a problem for you," said Baker. "If there's that much opposition, let's forget it." Deaver, who knew the plan was dead, took the news hard.

Reagan's decision not to move Baker to the NSC would have profound and unintended consequences. As the president would later write: "My decision not to appoint Jim Baker as national security adviser . . . was a turning point . . . although I had no idea at the time how significant it would prove to be."

But for the time being, as his reelection approached, Reagan's political fortunes were improving. The recession had loosened its grip. Jobs were coming back, and inflation was under control. The president was scoring points as a decisive leader. When the Air Traffic Controllers Union called an illegal strike, Reagan fired them. And when American students were threatened by a communist insurgency on the tiny island of Grenada, Reagan sent in an invading force to rescue them. For better or worse, the so-called Vietnam syndrome, and the paralysis of the Carter years, had been banished. Baker and Deaver commissioned an all-star team from Madison Avenue to work on a televised reelection ad campaign: They called it "Morning in America."

The Democrats countered that the Reagan Revolution had left millions behind. (At their San Francisco convention, New York governor Mario Cuomo turned one of Reagan's favorite images, the "shining city on a hill," against him: "There's another part to the shining city: the part where some people can't pay their mortgages, and most young people can't afford one.") Walter Mondale, the Democrats' presidential nominee, painted the president as an empty suit, presiding over cruel cuts to American's safety net and producing dangerous deficits.

Two televised presidential debates were scheduled, and Darman (who did an uncanny impression of Mondale) was assigned to get Reagan ready. But at the first debate, the president's performance was disastrous. His answers were muddled, and he looked aged and confused.

Failing to prepare for debates is a form of hubris shared by presidents who run for a second term.

"It's not that they get rusty," says Tutwiler. "It's an attitude. 'I'm president of the United States—what are you talking about? I've got **Air Force One**, I've got **Marine One**, I've got all this **stuff**. I'm not gonna put up with this.'" But while Reagan admitted that he was to blame for his dismal performance, Nancy and the president's closest friends insisted it was his staff's fault: Reagan had been **over**prepared. "The man was absolutely smothered by facts and figures," said Paul Laxalt, the Nevada senator. "He was brutalized by a briefing process that didn't make sense." Reagan's inner circle blamed Dick Darman, the debate coach—and, by extension, Baker.

The first lady, Meese, and Deaver all agreed: Darman would have to go. "Deaver came to see me and said we gotta get rid of him," says Baker. "And I said, 'Let me tell you something, I am not about to fire Dick Darman over this. We prepared the president the exact same way we prepared him before [in 1980]. I'm not gonna do that.'" Baker stood his ground, and Darman stayed. His defense of his deputy had been both loyal and pragmatic: Darman was the guy who made the trains run at the White House.

But these battles had taken a heavy toll on Baker. He was burned out. "It's a goddamn difficult job in the best of circumstances," he says. "And because I had to deal with Meese and the ideologues shootin' at me all the time, that made it even tougher. Four

185

years and two weeks was longer than anybody else had ever held that job and not gone to jail!" Baker was bone tired from working around the clock; his wife, Susan, was fed up; and he didn't think he could endure the internecine warfare much longer.

"Debate-gate," as he derisively called it, was the last straw. Baker decided to go to the president and offer to resign. "I said, 'Mr. President, one thing I know for sure, and that is the staff should never be the story. Here's what happened, and if you want me to step down, I'd be happy to.'" Reagan fixed his chief of staff with a look of bafflement. "The president said to me, 'Absolutely not. I don't want you to.'"

So Baker stayed on, but with an eye for an exit ramp. By one account, the criticism from the Reagans had hurt him deeply. "Baker is less of a hard-bitten person than he pretends to be," wrote biographer Cannon. "The public scapegoating of the debate coaches . . . reinforced his feeling that the Reagans, especially the First Lady, were 'takers' who lacked any real appreciation for what was done for them."

"No, that's overwritten," responds Baker. "Was I disappointed? Sure. But it wasn't the president. It was not the Reagans." His voice becomes softer. "Yes, it was Nancy, Laxalt, Stu, and Deaver. They wanted to find a scapegoat. And I wasn't gonna do that."

I ask Spencer, confidant of both Baker and the Reagans, if their chief of staff felt unappreciated by them. He thinks for a moment, then replies, "I can see it happening. I don't know—but they never sent out a lot of thank-you notes." He raises an eyebrow. "You know?"

"It wasn't a fun time," says Tutwiler. "I mean, this isn't bean bag, as you know. I think that politics, generically speaking, is a user business. And if you want to get into it to be thanked all day long for your great contributions, you're in the wrong business. Whether it's Jim Baker or somebody at my level, that just doesn't exist."

In the second televised debate, Reagan recovered his easygoing confidence, including a good-natured ad-lib: "I will not make age an issue in this campaign. I am not going to exploit for political purposes my opponent's youth and inexperience." The line knocked Mondale on his heels. Reagan won reelection in a landslide, carrying 49 states and amassing 525 electoral votes.

For Baker, the celebration was short-lived. Ten days later, Don Regan, enraged by a negative story in the **Washington Post**, called the chief of staff to complain that Baker's people had leaked it. Baker denied it, but Regan was unmoved. Never known for subtlety, Regan shouted: "F*ck yourself and the horse you rode in on!" Then he slammed the phone down. Baker went over to see Regan, and "we quickly resolved the matter—ex-Marine to ex-Marine." Then Regan made Baker an offer. "We should swap jobs," he said.

"Do you really mean that?" asked Baker.

"I guess I do."

"Well, watch out. I may just take you up on it."

"When you're ready to talk, I'll be here."

Baker went back to the White House "to consult with my own troika—Susan Baker, Dick Darman, and Margaret Tutwiler." He and Darman got out their yellow pads and made a list of pluses and minuses—starting with the downside of staying as chief of staff:

Stay

Downside

1. **totally exposed/accountable for any and all "failures."**

2. **defense???**

 soc. sec. reversal perhaps

3. **have to re-staff with people won't really favor**

4. **everything a repeat, somewhat boring**

5. **Senate losses in '86**

6. **possibility of counter-coup or unfavorable terms if things go sour**

Then Baker and his deputy enumerated the pluses of staying on:

Upside

1. poss. longest c.o.s. in modern period.

2. poss. Sec State

(query this??)

3. "responsible" thing to do

Darman summarized the downside and upside of going to Treasury:

Treas

Downside

1. will be in middle of revenue fight (true also if stay [as COS])

2. "leaving a sinking ship" stories (mitigated somewhat by DTR apt.)

3. not as good as State (but: bird in hand vs. bush)

Upside

1. helps RR bld momentum (while JAB still centrally involved as chief ec. spokesman)

2. serious, substantive job

- back to professional image (not just pol.)
- better positioning for later:
  a) public life
  b) private life

3. can make own agenda—and stay a "winner"

Did the notation "poss. Sec State" mean that he hoped Reagan would appoint him to the position? I asked Baker.

"No, what it's saying is maybe in a Bush presidency," he replies. "What was in my mind was getting out of that rat f*ck, okay? Number one. And number two, getting a substantive, very important cabinet position."

The job swap with Regan "was a done deal in those two men's minds," recalls Tutwiler. "Obviously they had to go talk to Reagan—and get his buy-in, and Nancy's. But I don't think there was a huge gap before they said, 'Okay.' And then: BAM, it was announced and it was done." She laughs, recalling the earlier NSC job fiasco. "Because Baker knew, once you announce something, it's done!"

Baker had set a modern record for longevity in the job; more important, he had redefined the position. "I find myself thirty-four years after the fact saying, 'Do things the way James A. Baker III did them,'" says Mary Matalin, who served three Republican presidents. "You gotta have nerves of steel, you have to have endless energy, you gotta know how to pace yourself—because it is not just the most important job, it's the hardest job: You have to be like three people. But none of that would matter if your skill set doesn't complement the president's. James Baker complemented, he augmented, he meshed—he was a leader."

John Podesta, the fiercely competitive Democrat, says Baker transcended party differences: "I think if you asked any of us who have served in the role, name two or three of the best White House chiefs of staff, James Baker would be on everyone's list."

Ken Duberstein was also watching Baker closely. "Presidents sometimes make the mistake of hiring for the White House chief of staff somebody who brought them to the dance, rather than the person who needs to be the dance partner once you're governing," he says. "In campaigning, you try to demonize your opponent. In governing, you make love to your opponent. That's how you put coalitions together. Jim Baker understood campaigning, but he was a real pro at governing."

If some viewed Baker as copresident, he didn't see it that way. "You are extraordinarily powerful when you are White House chief of staff," he says. "You may be the second-most-powerful person in Washington. But the minute you forget that your power is all vicarious from the president—then you're in trouble. Your job is to make sure the president gets to hear all sides of every issue. But that doesn't mean that you don't make your case."

Stu Spencer, who still fondly calls Ronald Reagan "my guy," says: "Without Jimmy, my guy would never have become the legend he was."

On February 3, 1985, Baker submitted a letter to Ronald Reagan.

Dear Mr. President,

I respectfully submit this letter of resignation as Chief of Staff and Assistant to the President. . . .

You have accorded me the greatest privilege of my life: the honor of serving as your Chief of Staff over the past four years—years which historians will undoubtedly view as a period of much-needed and striking accomplishment. I know that you are fond of saying that such achievements are a team effort, but if that is so, it is also true that rarely in our nation's history has a team been so ably led and inspired . . . by your success and personal example you have restored the potency, purpose and effectiveness of the Presidency.

The next day, Donald T. Regan moved into Baker's old office. The blunt-talking Irishman, an ex-chairman of Merrill Lynch, had been an effective Treasury secretary, and was Reagan's favorite cabinet member. But it was evident to some that Regan portended trouble. "He was ill-cast," says Peggy Noonan. "He was a Wall Street CEO. Other people with egos as big as Don Regan's know to hide it, to put it aside, to not show it until you lose your temper with your wife. Don Regan couldn't do that."

5

"Don't Hang Up on the First Lady"

**Donald Regan, Howard H. Baker Jr.,
Kenneth Duberstein, and Ronald Reagan**

Donald Regan waited nervously in the corridor outside the Oval Office. It was January 7, 1985, and Reagan's secretary of the Treasury, accompanied by James Baker and Michael Deaver, was mentally rehearsing the pitch he had prepared for the president of the United States. As they were waved inside, Deaver broke the ice: "Mr. President, I've finally brought you someone your own age to play with." Ronald Reagan, smiling, stood up and came around his desk.

"Don has something he wants to discuss with you that he's talked to me and Jim about," Deaver said. "We'd like to know what you think about it." It was a pivotal moment for the Reagan presidency. Within months, the men who had run the Reagan

White House—the troika—would be gone: Baker would vacate his job as chief of staff to become secretary of the Treasury; Meese would give up his post as counselor to the president to become attorney general; Deaver would leave to become a lobbyist. And Donald Regan would become Reagan's new chief of staff. But before such a seismic shift at the highest levels of his administration could take place, Reagan would have to give his okay.

Regan would never forget making his case to become chief of staff, and the president's demeanor in response. "[Reagan] seemed equable, relaxed—almost incurious," Regan recalled in his memoir, **For the Record**. "This seemed odd under the circumstances. . . . In the president's place, I would have put many questions to the applicant. How will you be different from Jim Baker? How will you handle Congress? What do you know about defense and foreign affairs? Who will you bring with you and who will you get rid of? What practices will you want to change? How will you handle the press? Why do you want this job?"

But the president simply listened, nodding affably. "Reagan made no inquiries. I did not know what to make of his passivity," Regan wrote. "He looked at Deaver and Baker as if to check the expressions on their faces, but asked them no questions either." When he had finished, Reagan simply said, 'Yes, I'll go for it.'"

Regan found the president's apparent indifference startling. He and Reagan had enjoyed each other's company—swapping stories and Irish jokes—but Regan had never spent more than a few minutes with him. "The president's easy acceptance of this wholly novel idea of switching his chief of staff and his secretary of the Treasury, and of the consequent changes in his own daily life and in his administration, surprised me," he wrote. "He seemed to be absorbing a **fait accompli** rather than making a decision. One might have thought that the matter had already been settled by some absent party."

In fact, the matter **had** been settled. Days before the Oval Office meeting, Baker and Deaver had sought approval for the plan from the "personnel director"—the first lady. Nancy Reagan was a fierce guardian of her husband's best interests. "She could smell a situation where somebody was grinding their own ax in a heartbeat," says Baker. The first lady's antennae reminded Ken Duberstein of her husband's favorite Russian phrase: "You remember that expression: 'trust but verify'? Well, he was trust. She was verify."

Yet remarkably, in the case of Don Regan, Nancy Reagan's radar failed her. If the prospect of losing all three of the president's closest advisers at once had given her pause, she evidently did not say so—to the troika, nor to her husband. It was only in retrospect that Nancy Reagan saw what a grave mistake it had been to allow Baker and Regan to swap jobs. "If by some miracle I could take back one decision in Ronnie's presidency," she wrote, "it would be [this one]." The new arrangement, she conceded, led to a political disaster.

Donald Thomas Regan had come a long way from the working-class Irish Catholic neighborhood of his upbringing. The son of a Boston policeman, he won a partial scholarship to Harvard. Upon graduation, he enlisted in the U.S. Marines, and, after a tour in the South Pacific, headed to Wall Street and a job as a trainee at Merrill Lynch. Ambitious and driven, Regan worked his way up to chairman—leaving more than a few bodies in his wake. He boasted about being "hated" on Wall Street, which he regarded as a clubby cartel. Reagan admired his up-by-the-bootstraps success and enjoyed his bawdy locker-room humor.

"He looked like George Raft, the 1930s movie star with gray hair and hooded eyes and a beautiful suit," recalls Peggy Noonan. "He struck me as an Irish rogue—but from Wall Street, which was a different kind of Irish rogue." Indeed, Regan was accustomed to doing things **his** way, barking out orders and gathering the trappings of power. It wasn't just the thousand-dollar suits, cuff links, and pocket squares, or the government limo with flashing lights and his own Secret Service detail. On one of his first trips with the president, Regan added a new protocol—Before entering a room, his arrival would be announced: "Ladies and gentlemen, the chief of staff to the president of the United States!" (When word got back to Baker and Deaver, they were appalled.)

Regan's imperious airs were reinforced by the people he brought with him to the West Wing. Gone were Baker's talented lieutenants Darman, Tutwiler, Stockman, and Gergen, who not only knew the White House staff system, but also policy and politics—and who were unafraid to challenge their boss. In their place came a coterie of Regan sycophants who, as Spencer put it, "spent all their time saluting."

Obsequious with Regan, they were clueless in the ways of White House governance. "I had the immediate sense: This will not work," recalls Noonan. "They were just second-rate, and they didn't know what they didn't know. That's going to cause problems in a White House that is already well-oiled and functioning: You don't have to strip all the gears." Early on, she corralled Press Secretary Marlin Fitzwater: " 'Marlin, you know these guys, what's with them?' And he started flapping his arms. He said, 'They're flappers; they just flap around.' It was true; they were like pigeons hitting the building walls with their wings." But the term that stuck was the one coined by Noonan. "I nicknamed them the mice. Because they were always running across the floor."

Lesley Stahl would later write:

It is fair to say that the day Reagan agreed to the Baker-Regan switch was the day his White House lost its magic. The first-term team of Baker, Darman, Deaver and Gergen understood what the president could and could not do. They knew Reagan had a great store of common sense, but they also knew he was ill-informed. Issues had to be explained to him at a simple level. . . . Don Regan knew none of this. And there was no one left to explain it to him.

As chief of staff, Baker had been emphatic: "The most important word in the title is **staff**." Regan had other ideas. "He wanted the job because he thought it would serve **him** well: that he would be the star," recalls Tom Brokaw. "He was frustrated [at Treasury] because he was on the outside looking in. And he didn't appreciate that the reason Jim was so successful was the discretion he used in how he ran the White House. It was a complete misreading on Regan's part of what the chief of staff's job meant." Ideally, the chief is the COO to the president's CEO. "Regan thought he was the CEO," says Duberstein, "and Ronald Reagan was the retired chairman of the board."

Watching from afar, at his ranch house in California, Stu Spencer was troubled: "I'd look at all these pictures on the wire. And there's the president of the United States—and there's Don

Regan. Regan was in every photograph; that's when I started to get nervous." Spencer tried to give the new chief advice: "Every time I was in Washington I would sit down with Regan. And I'd go through this exercise—the care and feeding of the Reagans. 'Cause every president and family is unique. 'This is how you handle it, and so on'— and he dismissed me." Spencer waves his hand as though swatting a fly. "So after about the fourth or fifth time, I said, 'Screw him.'"

Regan immediately marked his territory. In an interview with the **Washington Post**, the new chief expressed amazement that his predecessor Baker had wasted time talking to the press: He would have more important things to do. And Regan vowed that no detail would escape his attention: "A sparrow will not land on the White House lawn without my knowing about it."

But the first major crisis of Reagan's second term would catch his new chief of staff off guard. German chancellor Helmut Kohl had invited the president to participate in a ceremony marking the fortieth anniversary of World War II. As part of the remembrance, Kohl asked Reagan to join him in laying a wreath in a cemetery of German war dead.

Choreographing the trip would be Deaver's last major assignment before departing the White House. In February, he and his advance team

chose a site at a place called Bitburg. "The cemetery I reviewed was ideal," he recalled, "beautifully
coated with a long winter's snowfall." But unbeknownst to Deaver, hidden under the fresh snow
were not just the graves of German soldiers, but
stones marked ss WAFFEN—"all the proof needed
that these dead soldiers had been responsible for
unspeakably ghoulish acts during the war."

The White House announced that during his
trip to Germany, Reagan would visit a World
War II military cemetery "in a spirit of reconcilia-
tion." The news was greeted with outrage. Jewish
and veterans' groups were appalled. Congress was
in an uproar.

But Reagan had made a promise to his friend
Kohl and dug in his heels. "I think that there's
nothing wrong with visiting that cemetery," he
insisted to a group of broadcasters. "Those young
men are victims of Nazism also, even though they
were fighting in the German uniform, drafted into
service to carry out the hateful wishes of the Nazis.
They were victims, just as surely as the victims in
the concentration camps."

The president's dubious comparison triggered
more protests. Rabbi Alexander Schindler of the
Union of American Hebrew Congregations de-
cried the president's remarks: "To equate the fate
of members of the German army bent on world
conquest with that of six million Jewish civilians,

including one million innocent children, is a distortion of history, a perversion of language and a callous offense to the Jewish community."

When word got out that the cemetery had SS gravesites, Nancy Reagan urged her husband to cancel the visit. Deaver and other senior staff realized they had made a blunder; and so did Regan (although at first he was so furious at Jewish attacks on Reagan that he favored going ahead to spite them). During the first term, the combined forces of Baker, Deaver, and Nancy (with an assist from Spencer) would have brought the president around. But this time Reagan would not budge—even after Holocaust survivor Elie Wiesel, during a White House visit, delivered an eloquent plea: "May I, Mr. President, if it's possible at all, implore you to do something else, to find a way, to find another way, another site. That place, Mr. President, is not your place. Your place is with the victims of the SS."

"My life became a living hell, so I can only imagine what Ronald Reagan was going through," Deaver wrote later. Crushed by his failure to become chief of staff during his abortive palace coup with Baker, Deaver was depressed and drinking heavily. His friendship with Nancy Reagan was coming apart. "She was convinced I had literally ruined her husband's presidency, and perhaps the rest of his life," he wrote. "We had a very painful, emotional confrontation. I was already a wreck because I had let Ronald Reagan down. Disappointing my friend Nancy added to the devastation I felt."

As the scope of the debacle became clear, the chief of staff tried to duck responsibility. Regan blamed Deaver for not knowing in advance about the SS soldiers' graves. "How the hell did **that** happen?" he demanded. (Regan later accused Deaver of "drinking a quart of Scotch whiskey a day and masking his breath with mints.") Reagan appeared to take the acrimony in stride, blaming it all on a hostile media. But he was emotionally wounded.

For Nancy the affair was deadly serious, and the buck did not stop with Deaver. As H. W. Brands wrote in **Reagan: The Life**, "She blamed Don Regan for putting her husband in such an embarrassing position, and she mildly blamed her husband for permitting Regan to be where he could do such harm."

Don Regan's problems were just beginning. In the spring of 1985, the president had a colonoscopy that revealed a polyp; his doctors scheduled surgery to remove it in July. During that procedure, they discovered a golf-ball-sized mass on the side of the colon; it would have to be removed in another operation. Nancy, who had worried obsessively about her husband's health since the shooting, was distraught. "I felt as if I had been hit by a ten-ton truck," she said.

"Nancy Reagan stammers slightly when she is

upset," recalled Regan. "And her voice was unsteady when she called me from Bethesda Naval Hospital. In [an] illness of this kind speedy treatment is essential, and so I was concerned—apprehensive would be a better word—when she told me that the operation might be delayed for a day and a half. 'I'm reading something into this,' I said, speaking cautiously because we were on the telephone. 'Am I on firm ground in doing it?'

" 'Yes, possibly,' the first lady replied."

Nancy would later insist she meant that "Ronnie's condition was probably more serious" than she was willing to say on the phone. But according to Regan, the "delay" was due to the best-kept secret of the Reagan presidency: the first lady was consulting an astrologer.

Nancy had dabbled in astrology since 1965, encouraged by her friend the Hollywood talk-show host Merv Griffin; but after the assassination attempt in March of 1981, she started leaning more heavily on her "friend," a psychic named Joan Quigley. It fell to Mike Deaver, in consultation with Nancy, to make sure that Reagan's schedule was in favorable alignment with the planets. During the first term, the secret was so closely held that not even Jim Baker's staff was aware of it. Until one day, when the White House press corps rebelled over the itinerary for an overseas trip. "The press were saying, 'Why the hell are you making us leave from Andrews [Air Force Base] at 3 a.m.?' " says a

Baker aide. "And I kept harping on Baker: 'Why in God's name are we dragging all these people out there at that hour?' So he said, 'Why don't you go talk to Mike about this.'" The aide went to see if Deaver could help. "And I remember him telling me about the astrologer. It was **insane**. And I never told a living soul. Not one soul. Not my family. **Nobody.** I went back to Baker's office. And I remember him turning around and saying, 'Do you understand **now**?'"

While Reagan was in the hospital, Regan indulged his imperial instincts. He was not above planting leaks in the press to let the world know who was in charge. On July 15, the **New York Times** reported: "President Reagan's chief of staff, Donald T. Regan, is the dominant figure in the White House. . . . With each passing day, Regan's grip on the machinery of the administration grows firmer. 'Everyone works for Regan,' one unnamed White House aide said." The self-serving quotes displeased Nancy. But even worse was another line: "Nancy Reagan, the president's wife, has come to rely increasingly on Mr. Regan, a factor that further solidifies his position."

It was wishful thinking on Regan's part. He was getting under her skin. For one thing, the first lady looked askance at the chief's frequent use of the president's helicopter, **Marine One**, for visits to the hospital. "I must have had some inkling, even then, of what increasingly bothered me about Don

Regan," she wrote, "which was that he often acted as if **he** were the president." Worse, from Nancy's point of view, was Regan's haste to put the president back to work after his operation. Impressed by Reagan's quick recovery, Regan thought the president was well enough for bedside visitors. Nancy went ballistic. "Within forty-eight hours of the surgery, Don wanted to bring in George Bush and Bud McFarlane to meet with the president," she complained. "I thought that was much too soon—"

She called Regan. "Why are you doing this?" she demanded. "It's too much. He needs rest."

There would be more angry phone calls to come.

THE BITBURG AFFAIR, and the run-ins with Nancy, were just a prelude to a full-blown crisis. Soon Regan and the White House would become embroiled in a scandal that would shake Americans' trust in Reagan and threaten to end his presidency.

On November 3, 1986, a Lebanese newspaper, **Ash-Shiraa**, published a story so bizarre it almost defied belief. According to the report, a U.S. national security official had flown to Tehran on a daring clandestine mission. Despite a strict embargo against trading weapons with Iran, the C-130 plane was loaded with military spare parts. In a surreal touch, the official—Bud McFarlane, the national security adviser—brought along gifts for his Iranian hosts: a hollowed-out cake in the shape of a key, with a Bible inside it. The affair, which would become the Iran-Contra scandal, is Exhibit A in the argument that the White House chief of staff can change the course of history. Reagan himself concluded that the scandal would not have happened on James Baker's watch.

The report of the Tehran visit came as Reagan was presiding over a White House ceremony welcoming home David Jacobsen, an American who had been recently released by Iranian-backed militants after a year of captivity in Lebanon.

At first, the White House stonewalled. Confronted by a shouting scrum of reporters, Reagan responded peevishly. "There's no way we can answer questions having anything to do with this without endangering the people we're trying to rescue," he snapped.

"Why not dispel the speculation by telling us exactly what happened, sir?"

"Because it has to happen again and again and again until we have them all back," the president replied.

In his diary, Reagan noted the press was chasing "an unfounded story originating in Beirut that we've bought hostage Jacobsen's freedom with weapons to Iran. Our message will be we can't and won't answer any Q's on this subject because to do so will endanger the lives of those we want to help."

Answering those questions would also have revealed the truth: The administration had been trading arms to its sworn enemy Iran in return for American hostages.

The plight of American hostages in Lebanon—there were seven being held by Hezbollah militants—weighed heavily on Reagan. Tip O'Neill noted that while the president could not grasp abstractions such as the number of people living in poverty, he could be moved to tears by the stories of individuals. The hostages were flesh and blood to Reagan, and he could not bear the idea that nothing could be done to free them. He was tormented by the suffering of William Buckley, the CIA Beirut station chief kidnapped in March of 1984—who was undergoing torture by his captors.

The Iran-Contra affair was hatched in Reagan's National Security Council, a dysfunctional group of characters who—with Baker and Meese gone—lacked adult supervision. Robert "Bud" McFarlane, who had replaced Bill Clark as national security adviser, was ambitious and insecure, with a penchant for secrecy. Admiral John Poindexter, who would succeed McFarlane, was a pipe-smoking introvert with no political or legal acumen. Oliver North, an army lieutenant colonel, was an overzealous cowboy. Along with Casey, whose speech was so incomprehensible he was nicknamed "Mumbles," they would bring Reagan to the verge of impeachment.

The primary author of the plan was McFarlane. With the Soviet Union threatening the Middle East, he believed the United States should pursue every opportunity to regain its influence with Iran. Casey shared that goal but was consumed by another objective: obtaining the release of his station chief, Buckley—who, under torture, might reveal the identities of CIA agents throughout the Middle East.

McFarlane had been approached by an Israeli official who told him there were moderates within the Iranian leadership who wanted better relations with the United States. They would prove it by obtaining the release of Buckley, and perhaps other hostages—if the United States would permit the shipment of U.S. antitank weapons to Iran.

Reagan learned of the plan when he entered the hospital for his cancer operation in July of 1985. In his diary he noted: "Some strange soundings are coming from the Iranians. Bud M. [McFarlane] will be here tomorrow to talk about it. It could be a breakthrough on getting our 7 kidnap victims back."

The next day, with Don Regan at his side, McFarlane briefed the president on the covert initiative. As the chief of staff later told investigators, "The president after asking quite a few questions . . . assented and said yes, go ahead. Open it up."

Reagan was well aware that he had approved trading arms for hostages. In his diary, he noted: "Only thing waiting was N.S.C. wanting decisions on our effort to get our 5 hostages out of Lebanon. Involves selling TOW anti-tank missiles to Iran. I gave a go-ahead."

As biographer Lou Cannon wrote:

That Reagan approved the arms sales is not a matter of dispute. Nor is it disputed that Reagan and other White House officials deliberately concealed knowledge of these sales from Congress, keeping them secret until American hostage David Jacobsen was released.

Yet with the cat out of the bag, and the press clamoring for explanations, Reagan seemed unable to admit to himself what he had done. Ten days after the story broke, Reagan addressed the American people on television. "The charge has been made that the United States has shipped weapons to Iran as ransom payments for the release of American hostages in Lebanon," he said. "Those charges are utterly false. The United States has not made concessions to those who hold our people in Lebanon. And we will not." The president conceded that he had authorized the transfer to Iran of small amounts of defensive weapons.

But "these modest deliveries, taken together, could easily fit into a single cargo plane."

The problem was, that wasn't true. And neither the chief of staff nor anyone else in the White House knew exactly what the facts were.

Despite his protestations of ignorance, Regan had been in favor of the Iran initiative. As Cannon wrote: "Regan thought that sending thousands of missiles to Iran in return for two hostages was comparable to Nixon's secret 1972 decision to re-establish relations with China. . . . At no time during the crisis did he recognize the depth of public and congressional feelings about covert dealings with Iran."

On November 20, 1986, the president swatted away questions in a televised press conference. "What would be wrong," asked a reporter, "in saying that a mistake was made on a very high-risk gamble so that you can get on with the next two years?"

"Because I don't think a mistake was made," Reagan insisted. "It was a gamble that, as I've said, I think the circumstances warranted."

Five days later, Ed Meese, now the attorney general, who had been conducting his own investigation, told Regan that he had to see the president right away. Regan recalled the president's reaction to the stunning news Meese delivered. "The color drained from [Reagan's] face, leaving his skin pasty white. . . . The president wore a stern, drawn expression that was new to me—and just as new, I suspect, to Meese, who has known him for twenty years."

Reagan recorded the news in his diary that night: "On one of the arms shipments the Iranians paid Israel a higher price than we were getting. The Israelis put the difference in a secret bank account. Then our Col. North (NSC) gave the money to the contras."

The Contras, a ragtag band of mercenaries fighting the Sandinistas in Nicaragua, were strictly prohibited by Congress from receiving U.S. funds. The so-called Iran-Contra affair was about to become a full-blown scandal.

When Reagan recovered his composure, he told Meese: "Get to the bottom of this, Ed. We have to go public with what we already know as soon as we can." The next day, stepping up to the lectern in the White House press room, the president made a brief statement. Then he turned the proceedings over to Meese. "Certain monies . . . were made available to the forces in Central America which are opposing the Sandinista government there," the attorney general announced.

Nancy Reagan was aghast. "If Ronnie was incredulous, I was furious," she recalled. "I called Don Regan from my office to let him know how upset I was. I felt very strongly that Ronnie had been badly served, and I wanted Don to know. . . . He was chief of staff, and if he didn't know, he should have. A good chief of staff has sources ev-erywhere. He should practically be able to smell what's going on."

From his post at Treasury, James Baker observed Regan's troubles with a dose of schadenfreude. "Regan said there is not going to be a sparrow that lands on the White House lawn that I don't know about," Baker recalls. "And then Iran-Contra broke. And there were stories in the press quot-ing Don Regan saying, 'Iran what? Iran-Contra? Who me?'"

During the first term, Nancy wrote, "If anything devious had been going on in the West Wing base-ment it would have come to light—and certainly to Ronnie's attention. But now all the power of the troika was concentrated in one man."

The official investigation into the scandal, the **Tower Commission Report**, confirmed Nancy's suspicions about the chief of staff. "Regan . . . was personally active in national security affairs and attended almost all the relevant meetings," it concluded. "He must bear primary responsibil-ity for the chaos that descended upon the White House. . . ."

But the Reagans bore responsibility for having put Regan where he was. The Iran-Contra affair would never have happened if they had granted Baker's wish to become national security adviser. And it's almost impossible to imagine the scandal taking place while Baker was chief. He kept a close

213

eye on national security matters; a plot to sell arms to Iran through shady middlemen with Swiss bank accounts would never have passed Baker's sniff test. "McFarlane and Poindexter would have been afraid to have secret channels, and a guy like Ollie North would never have been allowed to roam free," says Noonan. McFarlane deferred to Baker; by contrast, McFarlane and Regan barely spoke to each other. Under the troika, even Casey was kept on a leash: Whenever the CIA director met with Reagan, Deaver would pop in afterward and ask the president what they had discussed. As for the diversion of money to the Contras, Baker had argued against **any** third-party funding for them; he surely would have opposed diverting profits from dubious arms sales. Like Nancy, "Mr. Cautious" was always scanning the horizon for risks. "Baker was an established and admired Texas lawyer," says Noonan. "They don't do Bibles hidden in cakes." Dick Cheney is emphatic. "Iran-Contra never would have happened on James Baker's watch."

By December of 1986, Don Regan knew the sharks were circling. At the press conference where the diversion to the Contras was revealed, he wrote, "Everyone seemed to be thinking a single thought: another presidency was about to destroy itself. The blood was in the water." Regan tried to distance himself from the scandal. When pressed to accept responsibility, he conjured up a new metaphor:

"Does a bank president know whether a bank teller is fiddling around with the books? No."

Regan was headed for a reckoning with Nancy Reagan. In January of 1987, the president was in the hospital recovering from a prostate operation. Regan was eager to schedule a presidential press conference as soon as possible. During a phone call with Reagan's chief, Nancy objected—then finally relented, snapping: "Okay, have your damn press conference!" Regan replied, "You bet I will!" Then he slammed down the phone.

When Baker heard about the incident, he knew Regan was finished. "He hung up on the first lady!" Baker recalls, still incredulous, thirty years later. "That's not just a firing offense. That may be a **hanging** offense!"

Nancy set out to apply the coup de grâce. To help persuade her husband to get rid of Regan, she summoned two veteran Washington hands to the White House residence: former secretary of state Bill Rogers and Democratic elder Robert Strauss. As Regan later reconstructed it in his book:

The President was told the press hates and mistrusts Regan and believes he has mishandled the crisis. The impression was being created that I bore major responsibility for the disaster that was engulfing the Presidency. . . . I was going down fast and the President's friends were afraid I would drag him down with me. If his popularity was destroyed, his ability to govern would be destroyed too. The President's place in history was at stake.

Ronald Reagan had to get rid of me. . . . "You don't have to do it yourself," he was told, in effect. "Someone can approach Don and appeal to his loyalty."

Persuading Regan to resign would not be easy. "The only guy left in the complex still on speaking terms with Regan was Vice President Bush," says Spencer. "I went to see him and he did the deed." On February 23, the vice president called Regan into his office. He said, "Don, why don't you stick your head into the Oval Office and talk to the president about your situation?" As Regan recalled:

I went into the Oval Office and took my usual chair at the side of his desk.

"I think it's about time, Don," said Reagan.

I felt drained but combative. "All right, Mr. President," I said. "Why don't you tell me? Where's your head on this? What do you think I should do?"

"I think it would be appropriate for you to bow out now," he said.

His words shocked me. I said heatedly, "What do you mean, 'now'? You can't do that to me, Mr. President. If I go before the [Tower] report is out, you throw me to the wolves. I deserve better than that."

I could see that he was shaken and not quite sure what to say or do next. Finally he said, "Well, what do you think would be right?"

"The first part of next week," I replied.

Reagan hoped to appoint his old friend Paul Laxalt as Regan's replacement. But Laxalt declined—and recommended Howard Baker Jr., the senator from Tennessee. "It's not a bad idea," Reagan noted in his diary. "He thinks Howard is looking for a graceful way of getting out of running for Pres. I'd probably take some bumps from our right wingers but I can handle that."

Events soon overtook Regan's plan for a dignified exit. On Friday, February 27, CNN reported that Regan had been fired and replaced by Baker. Regan was furious. He dictated a letter on the spot.

Dear Mr. President:

I hereby resign as Chief of Staff to the President of the United States.

Respectfully yours,
DONALD T. REGAN

The phone rang, and Regan picked it up. It was the president.

"Don, I'm terribly sorry about what's happened. I didn't mean for this to happen." The CNN report was true, Reagan said. "Howard will be the new chief of staff. He's looking forward to talking with you."

"I'm sorry, Mr. President," Regan replied, "but I won't be in anymore. This is my last day."

Don Regan stormed out of the White House. He and Reagan never spoke again. In his diary the president noted: "My prayers have really been answered." Nancy wrote: "That night, for the first time in weeks, I slept well."

Joy Baker, the wife of Howard Baker Jr., was at their summer home in Florida when the phone rang. "It was the president, and he said he'd like to speak to Howard," she recalled. "I told him that Howard was at the zoo with his grandchildren. And the president said, 'Well, wait until he sees the zoo I have in mind.'"

HOWARD H. BAKER JR., the former Senate majority leader, and vice chairman of the Senate Watergate Committee, could not have been more different from the domineering Regan. Courtly and self-effacing, "the great conciliator" was a political animal and team player, with many close friends on Capitol Hill. He would need those friends in the months to come, as the drumbeat of the Iran-Contra scandal grew deafening.

When Baker returned from Florida, on a plane sent by the White House, he was worried. For months, badgered by the press about Iran-Contra, the president had seemed befuddled and confused in his public appearances. Rumor had it that he was losing his mental faculties—perhaps even going senile. If true, Baker feared he might have to take the drastic step that was rejected when the president was shot: invoke the Twenty-fifth Amendment. "After I went to the White House the first day, I told people from my staff that I was aware of the rumors that President Reagan was not competent, and we might have to consider his replacement. That was a **terrible** thing to consider."

After meeting with Reagan, Baker concluded that the president was mentally capable. "I had a long meeting with him and discussed many issues in depth. And I came away from it totally reassured. And went back to the staff and said, 'We will not talk about [replacing the president] anymore.'"

For his deputy, Baker reached out to Ken Duberstein, the amiable but tough wrangler of votes on the Hill for Jim Baker's Legislative Strategy Group. Duberstein, who had left after the reelection, was reluctant. "I said, 'Howard, this is a real bad time for me,'" he recalls. "'I'm making money for the first time in my life. I just moved into a new house. And my wife is pregnant.'" After a phone call from the president, Duberstein went to see Reagan in the Oval Office. "Reagan got up from behind his desk. And he walked over to greet me, and said, 'Howard's told me all the reasons why you can't come back. I just want you to know one thing. Nancy and I want you to come home for the last two years of my administration.' Well, that was it—a done deal!" Duberstein says with a laugh.

Ronald Reagan was in deep trouble. Politically, the Iran-Contra scandal had wounded him severely, perhaps even fatally. His approval rating had dropped from 63 percent after the assassination attempt to 47 percent. Duberstein says he and Baker made a secret pact: They would sit down with the president and ask him everything he knew about the scandal. "Howard and I shook hands on the idea that if we found out that the president had been lying, we would resign."

Accompanied by an aide, A. B. Culvahouse, they met with the president in the Oval Office. At the end of the conversation, it wasn't at all clear what Reagan knew, or when he knew it (to use the phrase Baker made famous during Watergate). But they were confident he was not lying. "We became convinced that Reagan was absolutely telling the truth," says Duberstein, "and wouldn't have known Ollie North but for photographs he saw in the newspapers. And what we realized was that under Regan nobody was minding the store. It was a bunch of cowboys out there."

Howard Baker was eager to demonstrate that

he was no Don Regan. "You can't be a president's chief of staff if you think you are president consciously or unconsciously," he said. "You've got to realize, as much as it bruises your ego perhaps, that you're working for him, and carrying out his policies. You're free to argue with him, to debate with him, to disagree with him—but you can't ever substitute your judgment for his." Or hers. Baker quickly learned that Nancy was also a force to be reckoned with. One day Jim Cannon ran into Baker—red-faced, flustered, and clearly shaken, having just come from a one-on-one meeting with the first lady. The new chief blurted out: "Don't let anyone tell you that there has never been a woman president of the United States!"

With the **Tower Commission Report** about to be released, and the extent of the president's involvement still unknown, the Reagan presidency hung in the balance. Congressional investigators were circling, and there was a real prospect of impeachment. As far as Congress was concerned, "Reagan wasn't just a lame duck, he was a dead duck," recalls Duberstein. He and Baker became convinced there was only one way to survive Iran-Contra: Reagan must go on national television, acknowledge his role in the scandal, and apologize.

But the president's stubbornness once again kicked in: Reagan did not believe (a) that the United States had traded arms for hostages or (b) that he had done anything wrong. In his mind, the administration had never dealt with terrorists who held the hostages—only with Iranian "moderates." And he did not consider the arms shipments to be part of any quid pro quo.

In desperation, Baker and Duberstein reached out to Stu Spencer. Reagan's old friend said he would help—but he would do it **his** way.

Spencer wanted the president to hear directly from the head of the investigative commission, John Tower, the retired Republican senator from Texas. "I said, 'I'm going to get Tower over here,'" he recalls. "And Howard Baker nearly had a heart attack. And he says, 'If you do that, you'll interfere with the [investigative] process.' And I said, 'F*ck the process.'"

Spencer sneaked Tower through the Treasury Building and up the stairs to the White House residence. Speechwriter Landon Parvin came along. Reagan and Nancy listened as Tower laid out the litany of wrongdoing, and Reagan's knowledge of it. "Tower was a drinker, and of course he'd been drinking that night," says Spencer. "He started to tell the Iran-Contra story, and he started crying, he got emotional as hell—Jesus, God, it was a mess."

When Tower was finished, Spencer walked him to the elevator and then returned to the residence. "Reagan kept saying, 'I didn't know any of this,'" Spencer says. "And I still didn't know what the hell happened. So finally I said, 'Mr. President, whatever you did, **mea culpa** this. You can survive it. That's all I can tell you.'"

"Reagan came to the conclusion that it was the only way he could turn the chapter," says Duberstein. Parvin went to work on a speech, and Reagan agreed to consider it.

On March 4, 1987, Reagan sat at his desk in the Oval Office and looked into the camera. "I wasn't sure he was going to do it until he stood up to the TV," recalls Howard Baker. Then Reagan addressed the nation.

A few months ago I told the American people I did not trade arms for hostages. My heart and my best intentions still tell me that's true, but the facts and the evidence tell me it is not. As the Tower board reported, what began as a strategic opening to Iran deteriorated, in its implementation, into trading arms for hostages. . . . There are reasons why it happened, but no excuses. It was a mistake.

Reagan confessed that his lax "management style" had permitted the NSC to spin out of control. And he concluded:

By the time you reach my age, you've made plenty of mistakes. And if you've lived your life properly—so, you learn. You put things in perspective. You pull your energies together. You change. You go forward.

My fellow Americans, I have a great deal that I want to accomplish with you and for you over the next two years. And the Lord willing, that's exactly what I intend to do.

Good night, and God bless you.

Afterward the president noted in his diary: "The speech was exceptionally well received & phone calls (more than any other speech) ran 93 percent favorable." It was indeed a tipping point for the presidency. Ronald Reagan's credibility would never completely recover. But within a month, most Americans had forgiven him.

Nancy was relieved by the change in White House management. Howard Baker, she noted, was "a wonderful choice. He was calm, easygoing, congenial, self-effacing. He was politically astute. He had credibility with the media. . . . Howard was a complete change from what we had, and he gave us a chance to restore some morale to the office."

But Baker needed help: his wife, Joy, had been diagnosed with cancer, and he shuttled frequently to Tennessee to be at her side. In his absence, Duberstein ran the White House. Just as Dick Cheney had been with Don Rumsfeld, Duberstein was now a virtual co–chief of staff.

With her friend Deaver gone, Nancy dealt directly with Duberstein. "Reagan was always in the Oval at 9 a.m.," he says. "She would call me at five minutes of nine and give me a heads-up about something they had just talked about, or they had read in the newspaper that morning. It was so I could start my mind thinking, or people working—so that I could anticipate and help him out and guide him. If he didn't sleep well the night before, sometimes she would tell me that—so that I could adjust his calendar a little bit. 'Did he need **all** of those meetings?' Or 'Give Ronnie a little bit of a break here.'"

Duberstein understood that Reagan needed more human interaction. "One of the problems with Don Regan was that he shut the door to the Oval Office. My attitude was, instead of having Reagan reading all the material, open the door and let him see people. He's an actor. He likes to look at people. He learns that way—whether it was congressmen or White House staff or cabinet officers."

But that did not mean abdicating his role as gatekeeper. "So many people walk into the Oval Office with an agenda and say, 'Mr. President, this is in your best interest,'" Duberstein explains. "And your job is to figure out why it's in **their** best interest first and the president's second."

He had learned from Jim Baker the importance of telling Reagan no: "Look, it's never easy telling a president, 'It doesn't add up. It doesn't make sense.' But you have to do it in a way that the president says, 'I get it. You're looking out for my best interests, you're looking out for what's right.' The White House chief of staff is the person who is the reality therapist so that the president can let down his hair and say, 'Okay, I'm frustrated. I can't figure this one out.' Or 'Help me walk through this.' And if you're a good chief of staff, you say, 'Okay, think about this and think about that.'"

IF REAGAN'S FIRST term had been focused on domestic policy, the second would revolve around the issue that had made him famous: the Cold War. For all his passion to reduce government and cut taxes, Reagan's overriding goal was to defeat Communism. "With welfare, taxation, and everything else he went through the motions," says Spencer. "What Ronald Reagan ate, slept, and breathed was what to do about the Soviet Union."

For almost forty years, the fierce Cold Warrior had thought of the U.S.-Soviet struggle in Manichean terms: "We win—and they lose." But after surviving the assassination attempt, Reagan decided that he had been spared for a larger, divine purpose. "He believed in Armageddon," says Spencer. "The Cold War meant one thing: a nuclear holocaust that would destroy America and most everyplace else." Reagan's insistence on victory over the Evil Empire had softened. "A nuclear war cannot be won and must never be fought," he proclaimed. He would devote the remainder of his presidency to averting Armageddon—with a new Soviet leader: Mikhail Gorbachev.

Since their first summit in Geneva in November 1985 Reagan, introverted and intuitive, and Gorbachev, extroverted and intellectual, had developed a grudging mutual respect. At the showdown in Reykjavik, Iceland, in October 1986, Gorbachev had very nearly talked Reagan into abolishing nuclear weapons; the bold gambit had been dashed by Reagan's stubborn refusal to give up research on his Strategic Defense Initiative (SDI), the missile-defense system known as "Star Wars." But the failed Reykjavik summit turned out to be a watershed: Faced with the prospect of trying to match U.S. military spending, the Soviets had come back to the negotiating table.

In late 1987, Gorbachev was prepared to cut a deal with Reagan to eliminate all intermediate-range and short-range missiles. Soviet foreign minister Eduard Shevardnadze and Secretary Shultz announced that Gorbachev would come to Washington for a summit, where he and Reagan would sign the so-called INF (Intermediate-Range Nuclear Forces) Treaty. But at first the summit did not go well for Reagan. Arriving in Washington, Gorbachev was received like a rock star; climbing out of his limousine on Connecticut Avenue, the Soviet leader was greeted with applause from a startled but enthusiastic crowd, and he shook hands and held babies like a conquering American politician.

After the ceremonial signing of the treaty, Reagan and Gorbachev and their national security advisers went to the Cabinet Room for a plenary session. But Reagan was disoriented and uncertain. "There were too many people and Gorbachev did very well and Reagan was more passive than usual," says Duberstein. While Gorbachev waxed eloquent off the cuff about his government's reform program **perestroika**, Reagan could not think of anything to say. Finally, he trotted out a hackneyed joke about a Soviet taxi driver.

"We went back to the Oval Office and the president was distraught," says Duberstein. "He had let everybody down. So we focused that night and early the next morning on how does he come back and take the lead?"

The president arrived at the Oval Office the next morning with an unexpected prop. "It was a gift he had gotten the night before: a baseball autographed by Joe DiMaggio." Duberstein and Reagan improvised a plan to put the president and his guest at ease. When Gorbachev arrived, Reagan led him—accompanied only by their interpreters—into the small study off the Oval Office. "We can keep our rigid ideological positions," Reagan told the Soviet leader. "Or we can play ball. What would you like to do, Mister General Secretary?" As Duberstein tells it, "Gorbachev replied, 'Let's play ball.' And we went back in to the Oval Office. And that's where most of the major progress was made."

If he was often uncomfortable without a script, Reagan was unsurpassed as an orator and personally wrote some of his best material. In June of 1987, over the objections of his foreign policy advisers, he would deliver a defiant speech that came to symbolize his presidency.

As part of a ten-day European trip, Reagan was invited to visit West Berlin to celebrate the city's 750th anniversary. The stakes for his speech, at the iconic Brandenburg Gate, were enormous: Twenty years earlier, Jack Kennedy had set the bar with his ringing declaration, **Ich bin ein Berliner**.

With an advance team, speechwriter Peter Robinson flew to Berlin to research ideas for Reagan's address. He was met by the city's ranking American diplomat. Berliners were used to the wall, he told Robinson. "No chest-thumping. No Soviet-bashing," he warned him. "And no inflammatory statements about the Berlin Wall." Robinson was desperate, uninspired—until, shortly before leaving the city, he accepted an invitation to dinner from a family of West Berliners. The conversation was animated and gloomy, dominated by the plight of families torn apart by the East-West divide. Before departing, Robinson asked his hosts, "Is it true? Have you gotten used to the Wall?" His hostess, a gracious woman, suddenly grew angry, red-faced. "If this man is serious with his talk of **glasnost** and **perestroika**," she snapped, "he can prove it. He can get rid of this wall!"

Robinson believed he had stumbled upon the central passage of Reagan's speech: After some false starts—including "Herr Gorbachev, bring down this wall"—he finished his draft and sent it through White House channels. "The speech came to my desk because I had the final chop before it went to the Oval," recalls Duberstein. "And it was flagged by the State Department because they objected to a paragraph in the speech. And I gave it to the president with the understanding that the State Department objected. And the president said, 'Well, what do you think, Ken?' And I said, 'I think it's a hell of a speech, it's a hell of a paragraph. You are the president. You get to decide.'"

He continues: "The next day I get a call from George Shultz, telling me that he wanted me to convey to the president that he shared the department's objection to that paragraph in the speech. And 'would I please tell the president?'" Duberstein pauses and smiles. "And I knew at that moment that the speech was okay with George Shultz. Why? Because if he had really objected, he would have asked me for ten minutes of the president's time to argue his case in person."

On June 12, 1987, as Reagan and Duberstein rode in the presidential motorcade toward the

Brandenburg Gate, the president rehearsed the speech aloud, as he always did—even when using a teleprompter. "And he turned to me and said, 'It's going to drive the State Department boys crazy but I'm going to leave it in,'" says Duberstein.

Twenty minutes later, Reagan stepped up to the podium, with the massive gate looming behind him. Right up to the last moment, the State Department and National Security Council tried to block what he was about to say, submitting alternate drafts by fax. Reagan had been told that East Berliners might be able to hear him from the other side of the wall. He was angered to learn that East German police had herded listeners away.

Reagan began, getting angrier as he reached his crescendo:

> There is one sign the Soviets can make that would be unmistakable, that would advance dramatically the cause of freedom and peace.
>
> General Secretary Gorbachev, if you seek peace, if you seek prosperity for the Soviet Union and Eastern Europe, if you seek liberalization: Come here to this gate! Mr. Gorbachev, open this gate! Mr. Gorbachev, tear down this wall!

"I was standing off on the side," Duberstein recalls, "and I remember looking out at the audience of hundreds of thousands of people and having chills up and down my spine. It was one of those moments that defined history. We did not know when Germany would be reunited. But standing there you had a sense that the wall was going to come down, and Reagan and America would prevail."

With help from his chiefs of staff, Reagan had played his starring role in a revolution. On his watch, the United States embarked on a military spending spree that the Soviets could not match. Two years later, the Berlin Wall would indeed come down, and the Soviet Union would crumble. "He knew what he wanted to accomplish and he went and accomplished it," says Duberstein. "As he would say in his farewell address, not bad, not bad at all for a B-movie actor."

DAVID STOCKMAN, whom Baker had taken to the woodshed over his apostasy in **The Atlantic**, later wrote that Reaganomics had been a cruel trick; it had been all smoke and mirrors—with the lasting price of sky-high deficits. For historians, he wrote in his memoir, **The Triumph of Politics**, "The secret of the Reagan era's fabulous free lunch will be beyond dispute. The record will show that within the span of a few short years the United States flung itself into massive hock with the rest of the world."

James Baker rejected that view. In a 1998 interview he observed: "There was a revolution, and it began with tax reform. Tip O'Neill would never have wanted to see that 70 percent tax rate go down, and we did it. Tax reductions, the impetus to the economy, free trade, the elimination of a lot of regulations, downsizing of government—you don't hear anybody out there arguing to go back."

With help from an empowered White House staff, Reagan, more than any modern president, wore the burdens of the office lightly. He might have lost his mental sharpness, but his hair was still jet-black, his jaunty confidence intact. For Reagan, the presidency was never, in Jefferson's phrase, a "splendid misery." It was instead, as Lou Cannon wrote, "the role of a lifetime."

On the morning of January 20, 1989, Duberstein and Colin Powell rode together to the West Wing for their last day at work. On the way, Duberstein fielded calls from senators pleading—to no avail—for a presidential pardon for Oliver North. "I had several senators calling me an idiot in the car," he recalls. "We showed up in the Oval and to my horror, I had not realized that all his things were gone! The White House was barren! No personal effects, nothing."

Duberstein braced himself for the president's arrival. "Reagan walked in from the colonnade, and you could see him look. He turned to Colin and me and reached into his pocket, and said, 'Well, boys, I guess I don't need **this** anymore.' It was the nuclear codes card. And we said, 'No, put it back in your pocket! It's still active until noon!'" An hour later, the presidency passed from Ronald Reagan to George Herbert Walker Bush.

After the inaugural ceremony, the Reagans walked from the east side of the Capitol toward the helicopter that would take them to Andrews Air Force Base, and home to California. Duberstein went with them. "We did the ceremonial flight over Washington as the presidents are accustomed to taking," he says. "And we get over the White House and Reagan looked down and tapped Nancy on her knee and said, 'Look, dear, there's our little bungalow.' And that was the moment that every-body teared up. That was the end of the Reagan presidency."

James Baker, Reagan's former chief, watched as the helicopter disappeared. Now that his friend George H. W. Bush was president, he would soon have the cabinet job he coveted, as the nation's top diplomat. He had no way of knowing that he would be forced to give it up—for a role he thought he had seen the last of.

6

"The Prime Minister"

John Sununu, Samuel Skinner,
James A. Baker III, and George H. W. Bush

In a suite at the Houstonian Hotel in Houston, Texas, Vice President George H. W. Bush was having coffee with his closest adviser, an earnest thirty-seven-year-old Californian named Craig Fuller. It was election day, November 8, 1988, and soon Bush would learn whether he would become the forty-first president of the United States. Over breakfast, Fuller wondered when Bush would bring up a subject that had been lingering for months: Who would be his White House chief of staff?

Fuller had spent the last four years as the vice president's chief after a stint as Reagan's cabinet secretary. Months earlier, when the vice president had asked Fuller what job he might want in a Bush presidency, Fuller had been noncommittal, saying

235

that he might be ready to leave government. In his heart of hearts Fuller would have leapt at the prospect of becoming the president's chief of staff. But Bush had not offered him that job—and now he was asking again about Fuller's future. "Do you still feel the same way about leaving government?" Fuller felt a sinking sensation. Once again Bush had not offered him the job he really wanted, and he would never be presumptuous enough to ask for it. Fuller answered, "I do."

The conversation turned to Bush's options for his White House staff. "This is going to be difficult, but I want someone from outside Washington," he said. "I'm thinking about John Sununu as chief of staff." Fuller was surprised, even startled. But he knew there was no point in telling Bush what he really thought. Not yet. "I had a reaction, but I just held it," Fuller says.

John H. Sununu, the pugnacious Republican governor of New Hampshire, had struck up a friendship with the vice president during trips to Washington after his election in 1982. Born in Cuba to parents of Lebanese and Greek descent, sharp tongued and acerbic, Sununu had a PhD from MIT and was a member of the Mega Society, an obscure high-IQ organization. His bond with the Bush family deepened during visits to their compound at Walker's Point in Kennebunkport, Maine, where they debated politics and policy and went for white-knuckle ocean rides on Bush's speedboat **Fidelity**. That bond would pay off for both men when Bush faced the biggest test of his political career—the February 1988 New Hampshire presidential primary.

Just a week earlier, Bush had suffered a devastating defeat in the Iowa caucuses, finishing a distant third behind Republican majority leader Bob Dole and the right-wing televangelist Pat Robertson. Bush was dejected, but he refused to spend the night in Iowa licking his wounds; instead the Bush family and their key staffers boarded a late-night flight to New Hampshire—whose primary would be his last stand. If he were to have any chance of stopping Dole's momentum and securing the nomination, he needed to win it. As Barbara Bush stepped off the plane, she was met by Sununu and treated to a bold prediction.

In Sununu's version of the story, he confidently assures her that Bush will win—and even predicts the margin of victory. "I was very comfortable with what New Hampshire was going to do for them," Sununu says. "We had worked hard. We understood who was going to vote for him and not vote for him. I told her we were going to win between nine and ten points—and we won between nine and ten points. It's sometimes nice to be right!"

That's not quite the way Barbara remembers it. "John greeted us when we got off the plane, having lost Iowa," she recalls. "I said, 'Oh, John, it looks terrible.' And he said, 'No, no, we're going to win.'

But in Mrs. Bush's telling, Sununu's promise was pure bluster. About a year later, Mrs. Bush says, "He told me, 'I lied. I didn't think we were going to win.'"

Bush ended up defeating Dole in New Hampshire with 38 percent of the vote to Dole's 29; afterward, Bush swept the southern primaries and rolled to the nomination. But the turning point had been New Hampshire. And Sununu's promise of victory—founded or not—had earned him the eternal affection of the Bush family. His brash persona and cutting sense of humor seduced Barbara. "I loved him," she says. "I thought he was wonderful. And if I didn't, I would have told George."

But Fuller and others had their doubts about Sununu as chief. Fuller thought the opinionated governor had strong views on energy and foreign policy and wondered if he could be an honest broker for the president. Bush's close friend Jim Baker also had qualms. In his view, Sununu had two strikes against him as a would-be chief: The governor not only had been a "principal," as Don Regan had been, but he was also an outsider to Washington. Finally, Sununu could be insufferable—sometimes wrong but never in doubt. Even Barbara had to admit, "He did not suffer what he considered 'fools' gladly. So I think it made John occasionally seem arrogant. But you know, people are so afraid of **me** too!"

Everybody had a theory about why Bush had

picked Sununu. "The president-elect was really looking for someone who had been an elected official," says Tim McBride, Bush's personal aide at the time, "someone who understood the intersection between elective politics and governing." David Bates, then a White House assistant, thought Bush, with his expertise in foreign affairs, "probably thought that having a governor would bring a lot of knowledge of domestic affairs. He would be a good complement to him."

At College Station, Texas, in 2012, the former president sat down with me for a rare interview. "I'd seen him in action up in New Hampshire," says Bush of Sununu. "He's a very bright man, very bright. He was a strong, principled man, and I just thought he'd be very good." Eighty-eight years old, wheelchair-bound due to a form of Parkinson's disease, Bush was as lucid as ever, but struggled to complete his sentences. I asked him how he would grade his good friend Jim Baker as Reagan's chief. "I would give him an A-1," he said. "He did what Reagan wanted but he also was not afraid to lead or just say, 'Mr. President, let's try this.' He was outstanding. Outstanding in every way."

And yet, as George H. W. Bush assumed the presidency, he wanted a chief in a different mold from Baker. As vice president, Bush had watched as Reagan's every move and utterance was scripted. He understood Reagan's need for direction but found it unseemly, beneath the dignity of the office. Moreover, Bush had taken a pounding from the press for his supposed spinelessness. George Will dubbed him Reagan's "lap dog," and cartoonist Garry Trudeau eviscerated him as a political eunuch—he'd "put his manhood in a blind trust." Even **Newsweek** ran a Bush cover titled "Fighting the 'Wimp Factor.'" The slights had wounded him deeply (and enraged his son George W.). Bush knew that he needed a chief of staff—but he, the president, would call the shots.

Bush even took pains to assert his independence from his close friend Baker. On the eve of the 1988 Republican Convention, Baker—who had left his job as Treasury secretary to run Bush's campaign—had been kept in the dark until the last minute about his vice presidential pick: Dan Quayle. (Partly as a result, Quayle was poorly prepared for his first press conference, and his performance was widely panned.) Bush's convention acceptance speech had also made it clear that he would be his own man. "I have seen modest decisions made with anguish, and crucial decisions made with dispatch," he intoned, reaching his crescendo, "and so I know what it all comes down to . . . after all the shouting and the cheers—is the man at the desk. My friends, I am that man."

While he presented himself as a successor to Reagan in many respects, Bush also sought a shift in ideology and tone. At the convention he had whipped up the hard-right faithful by vowing,

"Read my lips, no new taxes!" But now that the ugly election campaign was over, he would pitch a bigger tent, welcoming moderates into the party. In speechwriter Peggy Noonan's words, he had called for a kinder, gentler nation, inspiring "a thousand points of light."

Kinder and gentler did not, however, describe the new White House chief of staff. "John would be characterized as irascible: 'Oh my God, what shit storm are we going to walk into today?'" says McBride. "He was tough—'You'd better have your arguments lined up, you'd better be well prepared.' Could that hurt someone's feelings if they weren't prepared? Probably."

Just days after the inauguration, Sununu displayed his hair-trigger temperament when he summoned the administration's energy experts to his office. Sununu listened as they went around the table, giving policy recommendations. After a few minutes, the chief had had enough. "Stop!" he barked. "None of you know what the **f*ck** you are talking about! Go back to your offices, get your acts together and come back when you know what the **f*ck** you're talking about!"

After they filed out of his office, Sununu turned to his mild-mannered deputy, Andy Card. "You know what's going to happen now, don't you?" he said. "They're going to go back to their offices and tell everyone, 'That Sununu is a tough son of a bitch!'" Card, whose wife is a minister and who rarely swears, looked at Sununu. "No, they're not," he replied. "They're going to go back to their offices and tell everyone, 'That Sununu is a f*cking asshole!'"

Card was right; the White House staff recoiled. "A lot of people including myself would go to Andy on things if we didn't have to go to Sununu," admits Bates, "because we all liked Andy. He was always in a good mood." Sununu was unrepentant. He was fond of saying, "If people don't like you—and love your boss—then you've done your job." But as his predecessors Baker, Cheney, and Watson tried to tell him, the chief's job is much more than being the president's son of a bitch. The trouble was, Sununu wasn't listening.

Every incoming chief seeks advice from those who came before; the first phone call usually goes to Jim Baker ("Congratulations," he often begins, "you've got the worst f*cking job in Washington"). It's a kind of listening tour, where the new kid on the block soaks up wisdom from his elders. But Dick Cheney says his advice for Sununu fell on deaf ears. "Sununu comes over to my office and as I was talking, he sat back, looked at the ceiling, and twirled his thumbs," Cheney says. "He wasn't the least bit interested. I think somebody told him he should do it."

Later on, when Sununu's troubles began, allies would be in short supply.

Sununu was better at managing the boss than

the staff, and Bush welcomed his whip-cracking efficiency as a gatekeeper. The president appreciated his intelligence and wit. "There was never a sense that John was trying to limit access to the president in a way the president wasn't comfortable with," says McBride. "It was a very buttoned-up place, access to the president was controlled, and I think that's an important part of the chief of staff job."

Sununu's control did not extend to Bush's national security team. National Security Adviser Brent Scowcroft, Defense Secretary Cheney, Chairman of the Joint Chiefs of Staff Colin Powell, and Secretary of State Jim Baker inhabited their own fiefdom, with its own rules. "Sununu wanted to be the prime minister," says Scowcroft dismissively. "I thought he was too overbearing—in the Haldeman mode." Scowcroft warned the chief not to tread on his turf. "We sat down before the administration began, and I said, 'Here is what I want. I will keep you informed as to what I'm doing.'"

Unlike their bickering predecessors under Reagan, Bush's foreign policy advisers worked together harmoniously. "We were the exception to the rule," says Baker. "We didn't backbite and leak on each other and backstab each other. We had all worked together in other iterations for Ford and Reagan— and so we were friends and we operated that way."

Baker was first among equals, as close to Bush as a brother, and his principal confidant. "Everybody knew I was speaking for the president," he says. "It was a seamless relationship that had existed for forty-five years. And nobody in Washington who wanted to get into foreign policy turf was going to get between me and my president. That was the most important element of my success as secretary of state."

The forty-first president was determined to finish what Reagan had started: negotiating reductions in nuclear weapons—and, with the unwitting help of Gorbachev, dismantling the Communist bloc. As the Soviet empire began to unravel, unleashed by the forces of **glasnost** and **perestroika**, Bush's team responded with remarkable nuance and restraint. Thanks in no small part to their diplomacy, the Soviet Union would end with a whimper and not a bang.

THE BEGINNING OF the end for the Soviet empire would not be long in coming. On November 9, 1989, two years after Reagan had stood at the Brandenburg Gate, Scowcroft brought Bush startling news: "The Wall has been opened," he said. They stepped into the small study off the Oval Office and turned on the television.

What Bush and his adviser saw was almost unimaginable: Residents of East and West Berlin, forcibly separated for decades, were now together, dangling from the despised barrier of concrete and barbed wire, joyfully chipping away at it with homemade knives and sledgehammers. The East–West divide that had stood since 1961 was disintegrating.

Bush refused to celebrate. "We had serious concerns through that whole process that if we gloated, it might give the hawks in the Soviet Union an excuse to stop the process," recalls Sununu. "And so the president was very careful about not over-rejoicing." Still, with the whole world watching, the United States could not ignore the seminal event—so Sununu helped convince the president to invite a small group of reporters into the Oval. "And I remember one of the reporters almost obnoxiously accusing the president of not showing enough emotion," he recalls. "President Bush was smart enough to understand that the right thing for America and the world was to show a little bit of discipline."

Sununu brought his own discipline when it came to pushing the president's domestic agenda. "He is an incredibly quick study, an extremely smart guy; and one of the prerequisites for that job is to know politics and policy," says Bates. "To be able to size up an issue quickly. He was able to do that and understood the political ramifications. Something may be a good policy but does it have a chance of passing? He had a good grasp of that. He seemed loyal to the president. I saw him go toe to toe with some greats from industry and he would defend the president vocally and adamantly and seemed to enjoy sparring with them."

While he preferred foreign policy, Bush had many friends in Congress, and he didn't hesitate to work the phones when he needed their support on domestic legislation. "This was a very involved president, a very agenda-driven president, a very goal-oriented president," says Sununu. Bush's combative chief relished the intellectual combat and arm-twisting with Capitol Hill. With Sununu's help, Bush succeeded in enacting a legislative agenda that would seem liberal today: strengthening the Clean Air Act and the Civil Rights Act, and passing the landmark Americans with Disabilities Act (ADA). Sununu deserved credit for advancing the president's environmental agenda. "We had done acid rain legislation in New Hampshire when I was governor," he says. "The president felt very comfortable letting us push that approach for the legislation. It turned out to be one of George Bush's great accomplishments—major environmental legislation that defined the way you can deal with complicated problems and still come up with a package that had great bipartisan support."

But the president and his chief would have less success fulfilling his brash pledge never to impose new taxes. Bush was determined to balance his budget, and as the deficit mushroomed, it became clear that his vow had been foolish. Bush signed a bill that raised marginal tax rates from 28 to 31 percent. "I knew this might well mean that I would be defeated for reelection," the president recalls. "But I think we had to do that. We had to control spending and have more revenue. So I took a big hit on it, you might say."

ON AUGUST 2, 1990, the president's daily intelligence brief indicated almost nothing out of the ordinary. But the crisis that would define George H. W. Bush's presidency was already unfolding.

That evening Powell learned that Iraqi troops, poised on the border with tiny, oil-rich Kuwait, were invading. "My guys came in and they said to me, 'It's not only their troops in the front line, it's oil tankers, gas tankers, you name it—they're bringing forward a logistics train,'" recalls Powell. "'It isn't an exercise; it's an invasion.'" The crisis caught both the CIA and the Soviet KGB completely by surprise.

The next day, at a meeting on the crisis, Powell says, "I was, essentially, well, 'What is the mission? What are we going to do? Are we interested in making sure they don't go into Saudi Arabia? Or are we ready to say we're going to kick them out of Kuwait?'" Bush was leading with his head, not his gut. "It was clear to me in discussions with the president and Brent and Jimmy that everybody was trying to work through this without a preconceived decision and come at a decision as a result of logic, not of an emotional reaction," says Sununu.

The most urgent priority was stopping Saddam's army short of the oil fields of Saudi Arabia. But as Bush's team would soon learn, the president would not stop there.

Stepping off **Marine One** on the South Lawn, returning from a conference in Aspen, he was met by a crush of television reporters. "This will not stand, this aggression against Kuwait," Bush declared. Powell was watching at home on CNN. "And I said to myself, 'Ah! That gives me a lot of guidance!'"

The president "made the decision, early on, that he was going to reverse Iraq's invasion of Kuwait," recalls Baker. "But he felt a very, very solemn responsibility when the time came to order America's young men and women into combat." On October 12, 1990, Bush noted in his diary: "Had lunch with Sununu, Scowcroft and Baker. . . . The thing that weighs on me is sending kids into battle and lives being lost." Estimates of U.S. casualties were sobering. "All the experts were running around saying, 'Oh, we're going to sustain 2,000, 5,000, 10,000 casualties,'" recalls Powell.

The predictions took an emotional toll on Bush, according to Baker. For all his upper-crust, New England reserve, the president could be reduced to tears by the prospect of young Americans losing their lives. "One of the tough times was when a dear friend of the president, an Episcopal bishop, came in and tried to lecture him on not sending American men and women into conflict on a moral basis," recalls Sununu. "It was tough on the president to be accused by somebody of that, of considering an immoral act—when he understood the immorality of allowing people in a country that was invaded to suffer under the throes of that invasion."

Baker recalls getting a call from the president right before the launch of Operation Desert Storm. "He said, 'Come on over and have lunch with me.' And just the two of us had lunch in the residence quarters of the White House, and he said, 'I know I'm doing the right thing but I still worry about the Americans, the brave Americans that are going to die.' That was a very anxious moment for him."

Twenty-five years later, I asked the former president if he could recall that decision. "I remember when we did commit American troops into battle," he says softly. "You just feel a personal burden. Because you know you're alone, under no committee. You alone were responsible for putting them in harm's way."

For all his trepidation, Desert Storm would turn out to be a rout. On January 16, 1991, the assault began: U.S. bombers pummeled Iraqi forces from the air, and more than 540,000 American troops, bolstered by forces from thirty-three other nations, rolled over the Iraqi military, achieving a crushing, decisive victory. One hundred forty-six allied troops were killed. (There were 145 noncombat-related deaths.) Even the **New York Times** editorial page, initially wary of the invasion, saluted Bush, and the obliteration of Saddam's army:

> American and allied forces suffered dozens of casualties, not thousands, in winning their lightning victory over Iraq's sadistic blusterer. It's a glowing moment for the soldiers and pilots of many nations. . . . The world that overestimated Saddam Hussein also underestimated George Bush. This page, and others who agreed with the president's goals but thought he was pressing too fast, have to acknowledge that his choices at treacherous junctures proved as successful as they were bold.

"That was a textbook case of how you fight a war," says Baker. "You get in, you do what you said you're going to do, and you get out. And you have overwhelming force to get the job done." The first Gulf War's strategy of winning with decisive force would become known as the "Powell doctrine." (In a bitter irony, Powell would later be remembered for his prominent part in promoting another, ill-fated American war in Iraq—one in which the forces sent would be far from decisive.) As the Iraq Republican Guards fled along the so-called highway of death, a debate erupted in the media. Should the U.S. military go all the way to Baghdad and topple Saddam Hussein?

Powell says that during the first Gulf War, the idea was so untenable it was never talked about. "We were never going to Baghdad," he says. "It was never discussed. It never was anything that entered the president's mind. He had no desire to occupy an Arab state, and he wanted to accomplish what the UN resolution called for, and to restore the legitimate government of Kuwait. And that's what we did." That opinion was unanimous among the president's advisers, including Cheney. It would be less unanimous just over a decade later—when some of the same advisers debated whether to invade and occupy Iraq during the presidency of Bush's son, George W.

The success of Desert Storm transformed the perception of George H. W. Bush. One poll reported his approval rating at 90 percent. But the euphoria would be fleeting. At home, a stubborn recession had taken hold. Bush realized that in a tough reelection battle, his credentials as a war hero would mean less than the state of the economy.

AS THE PRESIDENT turned his focus to domestic affairs, his chief of staff was becoming a liability. Sununu's scorched-earth attitude toward his staff was catching up with him. Yet far from regretting his tirades, Sununu cited them as proof of his managerial genius. "I guarantee you that contrary to the legend, any strong statements on my part are both controlled, deliberate and designed to achieve an effect," he boasted. "There is no random outburst. It is all designed for a purpose."

Capitol Hill's power brokers were not amused. After tangling with Sununu at the 1990 Budget Summit, the distinguished West Virginia senator Robert Byrd erupted: "I have never in my life observed such outrageous conduct as that displayed by the representative of the president of the United States. Your conduct is arrogant. It is rude. It is intolerable."

Sununu was also shirking his role as honest broker. His penchant for playing prime minister led him to screen out policy proposals he didn't like. Cabinet secretaries complained so bitterly that the president set up a post office box at his home in Kennebunkport—a back channel for messages that would otherwise get spiked by the chief.

Bush's chief also displayed what some called the "Don Regan syndrome," elbowing his way into every photo—and blaming the president for the staff's mistakes. After Reagan's summit at Reykjavik was initially perceived as a failure, Regan had compared himself to the guy with the broom who follows the circus elephants, cleaning up the mess. Similarly, when Bush misspoke about credit card interest rates in a campaign speech, Sununu falsely told the press the president had "ad-libbed." His suggestion that the mistake was the fault of a president who had blundered off script had to be corrected by Press Secretary Marlin Fitzwater. "Sununu just didn't know how to play the role," says Reagan's old friend Stu Spencer. "He didn't know when to come forward and when to stay in the background—like Jimmy [Baker] did and Cheney did and Ken [Duberstein] did."

In a scholarly article published in **Presidential Studies Quarterly** in 1993, "The President's Chief of Staff: Lessons Learned," James Pfiffner put Sununu in the company of Sherman Adams, H. R. Haldeman, and Donald Regan—each of them proof that "a domineering chief of staff will almost certainly lead to trouble":

> . . . strong chiefs have learned the hard way that serving the president means being able to cultivate other constituencies for his use. Sununu did not recognize this, and thus felt free to alienate Congress, the Cabinet, the press, and interest groups as well as his White House subordinates. It is as if his attitude were "I am so powerful that I do not have to be nice, or even minimally civil, to other people." In this he was ignoring the old Lebanese proverb that holds, "one kisses the hand that one cannot

yet bite." When Sununu got into trouble those who previously had to kiss his hand turned to bite it.

Yet Sununu was oblivious to the enemies who were circling. "I'm going to say something that most chiefs of staff will think [is] crazy," he says. "I think being chief of staff was the easiest job I ever had. It's the job where I had all the resources that were necessary in order to do the job. I was never in doubt as to what the president wanted. And so I was able to go home every night with virtually everything quite tidy."

It turned out that Sununu had all the resources he needed, and then some. Evidently deciding that military transportation should be at his disposal, the chief began taking flights home to New Hampshire, and other personal trips, from Andrews Air Force Base. One of the first people to notice was the defense secretary. "That was our operation out there at Andrews," Dick Cheney recalls. He learned of the chief's comings and goings from his general counsel, Terry O'Donnell. "Terry came to me and said he'd been informed that Sununu was using official aircraft for flying from his home in New Hampshire—and going to some stamp-collecting thing in New York," Cheney says.

It wasn't just military planes and helicopters; Sununu had commandeered a White House limousine to attend a stamp auction in New York City.

"It was clear it was going to be an embarrassment," says Cheney, "because he couldn't justify what was being done. He was the chief of staff, kind of arrogant, didn't take advice kindly. And there were people who were eager to take a shot at him. If he continued down this road, he was going to get in trouble."

Cheney and O'Donnell went to see Sununu. "I was pretty direct," says Cheney. "I didn't get anybody else involved. I just went straight to John, and laid it out for him, said, 'You're going to create a problem for the president, and it's going to be embarrassing for you if you keep doing this. And you really need to clean it up.'" Sununu's reaction reminded Cheney of the time the new chief twirled his thumbs in his office. "He said, 'Oh, fine, thanks for coming, I really appreciate it,'" says Cheney. "And then he went ahead and kept doing exactly what he was doing."

Soon the press got wind of Sununu's dubious junkets and began a drumbeat of disclosures. The **Washington Post** reported more than seventy trips by Sununu on military aircraft; the flights had been designated official business, but at least twenty-seven appeared to be personal. In his defense, Sununu argued that he was following a Reagan-era directive that top officials must be reachable at all times by the White House. Asked about that argument, Ken Duberstein says: "That is unadulterated bullshit."

As the press kept digging, other improprieties came to light. Sununu was accused of making phone calls to EPA and the U.S. Forest Service to grease the skids for a friend's application to enlarge a ski resort. (The friend had contributed to Sununu's campaigns and let him ski for free.) It was a charge nearly identical to one leveled at Ike's chief, Sherman Adams (who was also, coincidentally, a former New Hampshire governor). Caught in the crosshairs, Sununu proceeded to make himself an even bigger target. At a bill-signing ceremony on the White House lawn, he shouted at a **Washington Post** reporter: "You're a liar. All your stories are lies. Everything you write is a lie!" The press was now in full pursuit of Bush's defiant chief of staff.

For months, the president and Barbara endured the criticism of their good friend. But by the fall of 1991, Bush knew something had to be done. Firing anyone, much less Sununu, was anathema to him. Before taking such a drastic step, Bush wanted someone to sound out his top advisers and come back with a recommendation for "how things should be structured." But whom to entrust with that task? The president turned to his son, forty-five-year-old George W. Bush.

George W. Bush jumped at the assignment. The eldest Bush son, by now comanager of the Texas Rangers baseball team, was living in Houston but could not resist meddling in his father's campaign.

"The last thing any family member should do is burden the President with complaints or concerns, but . . . I told Dad that I was worried about the re-election effort," he writes in **41**, his book about his father's presidency. George W. was fiercely loyal—even ruthless—when it came to his father, his protective instincts as laser-sharp as Nancy Reagan's.

Bush reported back several days before Thanksgiving. As he wrote in his memoir, "People were dissatisfied. . . . Most felt that [Sununu] had denied them access to the Oval Office and limited the flow of information to Dad. I had always liked John, but my job was not to debate the case; it was to report the findings." In **41**, Bush describes his conversation with the president, over dinner, at the White House residence:

> Dad took it all in and didn't say much during the main course. Finally, during dessert, he said that he agreed with the conclusion . . . that he needed a new Chief of Staff. Then he asked, "Who do you think should tell John Sununu?"
>
> I was surprised by the question. "Why don't you talk to him?" I asked.
>
> He said, "I'd rather it be someone else." We ran down a list of possible names, none of whom he wanted to handle it.
>
> Finally, in spite of my misgivings about the awkwardness of a President's son delivering

such a message, I said, "Dad, look, if no one else can do it, I can talk to Sununu anytime you'd like."

To my amazement, after a long pause, he said, "Fine."

Persuading Sununu to quit would be a more daunting task than George W. bargained for. In his memoir, Bush writes: "Dad . . . asked me to notify John, which I did in an awkward conversation. He submitted his resignation shortly thereafter." In fact, when George W. broke the bad news to him, Sununu simply ignored him. The embattled chief walked into the Oval Office and said to the president: "Am I doing a good job?" Allergic to confrontation, Bush replied: "Fine."

That weekend, between tennis games at Camp David, Bush called Andy Card at home and asked him to come to the Oval Office on Monday—with Scowcroft, White House counselor Boyden Gray, and communications director Dorrance Smith. But none volunteered to give Sununu the coup de grâce. "You're close to him," the president pleaded to Card, "why don't **you** tell him?" That afternoon, Card walked into Sununu's office. "You need to do this," the deputy chief told his boss. "The president will accept your letter of resignation." The next morning Sununu came to the White House with a prepared letter. But the beleaguered chief still was not ready to go. He lashed out at enemies real and imagined, blaming the press, the White House staff—even pro-Israeli groups, who, he claimed, had targeted him because of his Lebanese heritage.

A presidential trip was scheduled for that afternoon, and when **Air Force One** took off, Sununu was aboard. It was only after the president and his entourage landed in Hattiesburg, Mississippi, that George H. W. Bush's chief finally submitted his handwritten resignation letter:

December 3, 1991
President George Bush
The White House

Dear Mr. President,

A little over three years ago you asked me to be your chief of staff. I eagerly and appreciatively accepted.

. . . These have been amazing times for the world and the nation; they have been exciting and thrilling times for me. . . . You, the Vice President, Gates, Scowcroft and I proved we could do very serious things well without taking the process or ourselves too seriously.

. . . I have always said I wanted to serve as your Chief of Staff as long as I could contribute to your success and help deal effectively with both the issues and the arrows. But . . . I would never want to not be contributing positively, much less be a drag on your success. Therefore, as we enter the contentious climate of a political campaign, I believe it is in your best interest for me to resign as Chief of Staff to the President of the United States effective December 15, 1991.

. . . I think you know that the responsibility and authority (contrary to the legends out there) never meant as much to me as the opportunity to assist you to be (and to be recognized) a great president. I intend to continue that effort as an ordinary citizen. . . .

I assure you that in the pit bull mode or the pussycat mode (your choice, as always), I am ready to help. . . .

Sincerely and respectfully,
John H. Sununu

Gracious and genuinely fond of his ex-chief, Bush penned a reply.

Governor John H. Sununu
Chief of Staff
The White House

Dear John,

I now have your letter resigning as Chief of Staff effective December 15. It is with reluctance, regret and a sense of personal loss that I accept your resignation as Chief of Staff. . . .

John, I find it difficult to write this letter both for professional and personal reasons.

On the professional side, thanks to your leadership we have made significant accomplishments for which you deserve great credit.

Working with others here in the White House, throughout the administration, and on Capitol Hill, you have played a major role in achieving some of our significant goals.

And yes, from my vantage point and our families' as well, the friendship we treasure is stronger than ever.

I hope you and Nancy, free of the enormous pressures of the office you have served so well, will enjoy life to its fullest. You deserve the best.

Most sincerely from this grateful President,
George Bush

The president wrote separate letters to Sununu's wife, parents, and children, a gesture that touched his outgoing chief. "For chiefs of staff that are the spear catchers, the javelin catchers, it's especially hard on their family," Sununu says. "One of our sons was in the school system in Virginia, and it was particularly tough on him. Some of the teachers in Virginia are horse's asses."

I asked George H. W. Bush if it was hard for him to fire his friend. "I think it is for everybody, most people," he says. "Yes, it is. It was. But it was time to make a change, time for him to make a change. I remember saying to John, 'I think we gotta go our separate ways.' He's a good man, and we remain close friends to this day."

If he had mustered even modest support, Sununu might have held on to his job. But he had few allies: "You can be there to back somebody up, or you can just let it happen," says Tim McBride. "Those who might have risen to his defense sat back—including members of Congress." Pfiffner, author of the study on the White House chiefs, wrote: "In searching for enemies who would have liked to do in John Sununu if they had the chance, one is reminded of the Agatha Christie novel **Murder on the Orient Express** . . . in which many suspects on the train had sufficient motive to have killed the victim. The mystery is solved when it is disclosed that each of the suspects was guilty because each had plunged the same knife into the victim."

Sununu conceded that he had made mistakes. "If I had to do things over as chief of staff," he says, "I might have given a lot more focus to trying to get the president to take the credit for what he accomplished." Another error, he says, "was thinking that not talking to the press was a strong plus, and I did that out of loyalty to the president. I didn't realize that maintaining a better relationship with the press would have been of value to the president."

Perhaps, but Sununu's fundamental problem was his sense of entitlement. Jim Baker's rule—that principals rarely succeed in the job—had proved true again. "The people who don't succeed as White House chief of staff are people who like the **chief** part of the job and not the **staff** part of the job," says Baker. "You've got to remember that you're staff even though you're powerful."

SIX DAYS AFTER Sununu's last day as chief, on Christmas Day 1991, Mikhail Gorbachev, who had tried to save Soviet Communism with his dramatic reforms, called George Bush at Camp David with a stunning announcement: The Soviet Union, which had posed a mortal threat to the West for nearly eighty years, no longer existed. Its nuclear arsenal, he assured the president, was in safe hands. The epochal turn of events was a vindication for the foreign policy of George H. W. Bush and his lieutenants Baker, Scowcroft, Cheney, and Powell.

It was virtually the last good news the forty-first president of the United States would receive. For all his success in foreign affairs, the president was taking a beating in public opinion at home. As Jon Meacham writes in **Destiny and Power**, quoting from the president's diary, just two days after Gorbachev's announcement, Bush received a poll that was discouraging in every way—not only in my own popularity, but the American people are all over the field on what they want to see to fix the economy . . . nobody thinks we're doing a damn thing about the economy . . . even though inflation is better than it's ever been; interest rates are lower than they've been; unemployment is less bad than in a recession, everyone thinks we're on the wrong track, and confidence is at a lower level than even Jimmy Carter's horrible days.

It was a far cry from the heady days following the Persian Gulf War: Over the course of the year, Bush's approval rating would plunge fifty points to a dismal 40 percent. As a tough reelection battle loomed, Bush now had to make two critical appointments: a campaign manager and a chief of staff.

Bush believed that politics and governing should be separate, like church and state; he wanted different people in charge of the White House and the campaign. For campaign chairman he chose his old friend and pollster Bob Teeter. For White House chief, Scowcroft proposed Andy Card, who knew the job intimately but was self-effacing and ego-free. But Bush had someone else in mind: his secretary of transportation, Sam Skinner.

Samuel K. Skinner was the polar opposite of his colorful, larger-than-life predecessor: If Sununu dominated any room he walked into, Skinner became invisible. A Chicago-born businessman and seasoned bureaucrat, Skinner had earned the nickname "Master of Disaster" for his quiet, efficient handling of crises such as the Eastern Airlines strike, Hurricane Hugo, and the **Exxon Valdez** oil spill. "The president said, 'I'd like you to become chief of staff and we are going to do something different,'" recalls Skinner. "'I want to try a system where politics will be outside and the government will be inside—you and Teeter will work together and if there are any problems we will work to resolve them.'"

Skinner should have known he was in for a rough year: On his first day as chief of staff, George Bush threw up on the prime minister of Japan. In Tokyo on a state visit in January 1992, Bush was at a dinner given by Kiichi Miyazawa when he suddenly turned pale and slumped over onto his host. When he regained consciousness, Bush discovered that he had vomited on himself and the prime minister. Skinner, who had not accompanied Bush, watched the bizarre episode on TV.

Nineteen ninety-two would indeed become Bush's **annus horribilis**. The economy continued to lag. Vulnerable from having reneged on his "no new taxes" pledge, Bush now faced a conservative challenge from Pat Buchanan in the Republican primaries. (Bush again won New Hampshire, but Buchanan took a stunning 40.4 percent of the vote.) On the campaign trail, the president seemed tone-deaf, at one point expressing amazement at a demonstration of a supermarket scanner. Bush's Democratic rival, Bill Clinton, had chosen an energetic young southerner, Al Gore, as his running mate and was gaining momentum out of the convention. And Bush also faced a dangerous and unpredictable threat from a third party candidate, the eccentric billionaire Ross Perot. (The cochairman of Perot's campaign was none other than Jimmy Carter's ex–campaign manager and chief of staff, Hamilton Jordan.)

Skinner felt overwhelmed. "You're really at the center of a tornado, so to speak, when you are in a cycle where you are running for reelection and you are not doing well," he says. "It can be the worst job in the world, especially if you are in a losing campaign and what you are doing on behalf of the president and what your campaign is doing isn't resonating with the American people."

Bush was disillusioned with Skinner. He noted in his diary: "I must confess, I miss Sununu and his brilliance and his ability to put things into perspective, and to get up and browbeat the Hill. Yes, there was a lot of china broken, but I'm wondering if we don't need the Chief of Staff to step up his activities, and get control of more."

"Sam's a very able fellow, and he did a good job," says the president. "But he came in at an extraordinarily difficult time. We were facing a perception—

you know, eight years of Reagan, four years of Bush. And Clinton was a charismatic, young challenger. And the economy was bad, and Clinton campaigned on 'the economy, stupid.' And he was right to focus on that!"

With the clock running out on his reelection, Bush needed a strong leader to shake up both the White House and the campaign staff, someone with unquestioned experience and authority. There was only one person he could think of: Jim Baker.

But Baker was deeply invested in his job as secretary of state and would never voluntarily leave it. Persuading his best friend to replace Skinner—and rescue his reelection—would require all of George H. W. Bush's diplomatic skills.

The president and his secretary of state had planned a getaway with their sons—Jeb and Jamie—at Baker's ranch in Wyoming. Baker did not realize he had walked into a trap. "He said, 'I need you back,'" recalls Baker. "I didn't want to go; nobody would want to do that, after having been secretary of state—to get right back into the nitty-gritty of the political centrifuge. I really thought I was doing a lot of good for the country as secretary of state. And there were a lot of things that we could still get done." But Baker knew he didn't have much of a choice. "I never really hesitated to say yes. I'd always said yes to him before, and after all, he had a lot to do with my success in politics and in public service."

Baker returned to Foggy Bottom and prepared to turn over the department to his deputy, Lawrence Eagleburger. On August 13, 1992, he could barely get through his farewell address to the staff: "There were tears in my eyes as I rode the elevator back up to my seventh-floor office as a now-lame-duck Secretary of State," Baker wrote later, "tears of pride mingled with enormous reluctance to relinquish the most personally satisfying of all my government assignments."

Afterward, the president sent his new chief a note:

Jim—

As I listened to that thunderous applause at State just now, I realized just how much you are giving up to come here. I am so very grateful.

Get some rest. I'm glad we will be side by side in the battle ahead—

Your Friend,
George

THE BATTLE WAS joined, but it was too late to affect the outcome. Roaring out of his convention, Clinton led Bush in the polls by 57 to 32 percent. The mercurial populist Perot had withdrawn from the race, only to jump back in before the debates.

"It was tough because we couldn't get traction until about four days before the election," says Baker. "Then we began to see our numbers change. It changed dramatically. And we were really moving maybe five or six days before the election."

On November 2, Bush noted in his diary:

> This is the last day of campaigning in my entire life . . . we have 4 or 5 more rallies to go. It's a joy having George with us—feisty fighter and campaigner if there ever was one—and he and Jim Baker sit up with me in my office on **Air Force One** and we talk about the pollsters and we talk about [the] baseball commissioner, and how the job has changed, and we talk about the last hurrah, the last campaign forever. . . . We even talked about who should be Chief of Staff in the White House after Jim Baker finishes his job, a job that I think will take 120 days.

Baker was first to receive the grim news the next morning. "I think the toughest moment was when I got the exit polls and it was apparent that we were going to lose," he says. "And I had to go tell the president. And he was getting a haircut. We were down in Houston, Texas. And he was in the barber's chair when I had to tell him. And it was tough—very, very tough. And of course, he is my extraordinarily close friend, has been for forty years. He's the godfather of my daughter. He's a guy that I just love. So it was hard, it was hard to see that happening to him."

In his diary, Bush wrote: "It's hard to describe the emotions of something like this . . . but it's hurt, hurt, hurt and I guess it's the pride too . . . I think of the country and the people who are hurting and there is so much we didn't do. There are so many places we tried, and yes, we made progress. But no, the job is not finished and that kills me. . . ."

But for Barbara Bush, who despised the ugliness of the campaign and dreaded fighting with a Democratic Congress, losing was a relief. "Had we won, it would've been miserable," she says.

"I think history is going to treat him very well," says Baker of his old friend. "Like Winston Churchill, who was a war hero for his country and then they turned him out right after that, the same thing happened to George Bush 41. The world changed totally and completely on his watch. It was George Bush that presided over a peaceful end of the Cold War. It didn't have to end peacefully. It could have ended with a bang—that nuclear bang we feared for forty years. He is the one that brought Israel and all of their Arab neighbors to the table for the first time to talk peace at the Madrid Peace Conference; unified Germany in peace and freedom as a member of the North Atlantic

Treaty Organization. We had a lot of unfinished business in the foreign policy field. It made losing tough. Losing is **always** tough."

Baker believed there had been three main reasons for their defeat: After twelve years of Republican rule, voters were ready for a change; Ross Perot, with 19 percent of the vote, had taken just enough Bush votes to ensure Clinton's victory; and, less than a week before the election, Special Prosecutor Lawrence Walsh had indicted Cap Weinberger for his role in the Iran-Contra scandal, unfairly tarring Bush.

But one factor was in the administration's control, according to Baker: "When we went up for the State of the Union address in January of 1992, the president should've said, 'I've just done **Desert Storm**. Now I'm going to do **Domestic Storm**. I'm going to turn my attention to our problems here at home.' But we didn't do that. The president's economic advisers were telling him that the economy was going to come back. Indeed it did—it came back just in time for Bill Clinton to take the oath of office."

Bill Clinton, the gifted forty-six-year-old political force of nature, was so masterful on the campaign trail that he was dubbed "the natural." His tightly disciplined campaign headquarters were justly celebrated in a documentary called **The War Room**.

But some wondered if Clinton would be a natural at governing from the White House. Later, one staffer would sum up the frustration of his first year and a half: "We went from **War Room** to Dorm Room."

7

"An Iron Fist in a Velvet Glove"

**Thomas F. "Mack" McLarty, Leon Panetta,
Erskine Bowles, John Podesta,
and Bill Clinton**

Robert Reich sat in the kitchen of Bill and Hillary Clinton's home in Little Rock, Arkansas. It was November 18, 1992, and Reich, Clinton's confidant since they were Rhodes Scholars at Oxford and classmates at Yale Law School, was celebrating his friend's good fortune. "Bill is going to be president," he had written in his diary. "If the times call for a strong president, he will govern much as Franklin Roosevelt governed—with boundless energy, great charm, and bold initiative. . . . But I worry that his leadership may fail. He'll become unfocused and too eager to please."

William Jefferson Clinton had won the presidency by charming and cajoling his way through a bruising primary battle and a roller-coaster general election against Republican rival George H. W. Bush and independent candidate Ross Perot. But what kind of president would emerge from the crucible of the campaign? James Carville had been Clinton's ostensible campaign manager, rallying his troops with the disciplined message "The economy, stupid." But it had been Clinton—brilliant, undisciplined, and indefatigable—who truly called the shots.

As he prepared for the presidency, Clinton was cramming like the lanky, disheveled Yale law student that he had once been, who rarely cracked a book until the night before the exam and usually got an A. (In the classes they shared, Reich raised his hand a lot and often had the right answer; Hillary raised hers all the time and always had the right answer; Clarence Thomas never raised his hand; and Bill rarely showed up.) The president-elect, six foot one and charismatic, and his friend, four foot eleven and wonkish, made an odd couple then, too. Now, sipping coffee in Clinton's kitchen, just eight weeks before the inauguration, they debated the merits of possible cabinet secretaries. All well and good—except Clinton seemed oblivious to the people who would matter most: his White House staff. "Clinton spent an enormous amount of time picking his cabinet," recalls John Podesta. "And no time picking his White House staff."

The day after the election, in a hasty announcement, Clinton had revealed his choice for chief of staff: Thomas F. "Mack" McLarty. Charming and courtly, a former star quarterback and student council president, Mack had attended kindergarten with Clinton in Hope, Arkansas. Everyone thought he would grow up to become governor. Instead, he made a fortune for Ford in the trucking business, then became head of the Arkansas-Louisiana Gas Company. Clinton's selection of McLarty was a last-minute, seat-of-the-pants decision, but also a telling one: In the White House, Bill and Hillary Clinton would hold their friends close, and their enemies at a distance. McLarty would be one of Clinton's loyal "Arkansas Mafia," a group that would include White House counselor Vincent Foster, and their friends-without-portfolio, television producers Harry and Linda Bloodworth-Thomason.

When Clinton asked him to become his White House chief, McLarty initially demurred. He lacked Washington experience, he warned his friend. And McLarty had one other worry: "I said, 'You know, we've been friends a long time. We've worked together and we're not getting any younger. I would hate to see this impair our friendship and, you know, it has the possibility of doing that.' But Bill smiled and he said, 'Well, I've thought about that. It could make it stronger, you know.'"

Reich, who would become Clinton's secretary of labor, sensed trouble. "The chief of staff cannot be a dear old friend," he remembers thinking when McLarty accepted the job. "It's too difficult for the chief to tell the president no. It's also difficult for the chief of staff and his boss to see and understand clearly their respective roles and not to let the past intrude on the present."

And there were plenty of problems to deal with in the present. Bill Clinton's first days in the Oval Office were like a White House version of the stateroom scene in the Marx Brothers film **A Night at the Opera**. Ten-minute meetings went on for hours, with almost anyone who wanted to participate dropping in. Staffers sprawled on sofas and the floor. Coffee cartons and donut boxes piled up. Erskine Bowles, head of the Small Business Administration, couldn't believe what he saw on visits to the West Wing. "It was a mess. I mean, really a total mess," he says, shaking his head. "People would wander in and out of the Oval Office, the president would get a little bit of information here, a little bit of information there. And so it took him more time to make worse decisions."

Leon Panetta, head of the Office of Management and Budget, was also taken aback. "I would go to a meeting in the Oval Office and every Tom, Dick, and Harry on staff was in that meeting," he says. "There was a lot of talk, and it was very disorganized." It was so bad, Bowles noted, that Hillary Clinton would come down the hall from her West Wing office and try to impose order. "There were plenty of good people, but no accountability," he says. "It drove the first lady crazy; so she would come in and take over meetings."

Things were almost as bad when Clinton ventured outside the Oval; the president lingered at every event and schmoozed on every rope line, running way behind schedule. McLarty admits the transition from campaigning to governing was a steep learning curve. "I think that President Clinton's greatest strengths were in some ways his weaknesses as well," he says. "The fact that on the campaign trail he would linger with people, listen to them attentively, remember what they said—the great empathy, I-feel-your-pain—was absolutely true. But in trying to manage the White House, stay on schedule, move things forward, it may not serve quite so well."

But the problem wasn't just Clinton. "Every fifteen minutes of every day was scheduled," says Bowles. "The president had this reputation for being late. Of course he's late! He lives in a changing world, and if you have every fifteen minutes of every day scheduled, he's gonna be late! So to me that was poor staff work as opposed to the president's fault."

Labor secretary Reich was alarmed but more forgiving toward McLarty. "Mack got a bad rap because the chaos was blamed on him," he says. "He could have been a stronger chief of staff, but Bill Clinton didn't necessarily want a strong chief of staff. Bill Clinton put him in that place because Bill Clinton wanted to run the White House himself and didn't want to be disciplined." Podesta says the president did not fully grasp that the chief of staff is a gatekeeper—and honest broker of his cabinet's views. "He's a governor. His staff were these guys that ran the Highway Department, right? So I think he thought he was going to interact more with his cabinet than you ever do."

McLarty was known to almost everyone in Washington as "Mack the Nice." "Mack was an incredibly kind man, a really bright man, but Washington takes a special type," says a Clinton staffer who had served in a previous administration. "The White House chief of staff, a good one, is everywhere. He's in all the meetings; he has his finger on everything. Mack had no idea what goes on in the White House—he didn't know where to go, who to see. And Mack's not good at reading people. He can't look at anybody and tell who's trouble, who to keep a finger on."

The result was a rugby scrum of ambitious aides jostling for the president's favor. There were the true believers, committed to Clinton's liberal agenda, such as George Stephanopoulos and Paul Begala. There were the Washington insiders, intent on reducing the deficit, like economist Robert Rubin, the ex–Goldman Sachs cochairman, and Harvard's Larry Summers. There were hard-nosed campaign operatives: Harold Ickes and Ira Magaziner. And then there was Rahm Emanuel, one of Clinton's senior advisers.

Emanuel, just thirty-three, was already a legend for his rich vocabulary of four-letter words, and for his willingness to walk over hot coals, broken glass, or worse to get a job done. People who disappointed him could expect the unexpected: like a dead fish, which Emanuel famously sent in a box to a pollster who betrayed him. The Luca-Brasi-sleeps-with-the-fishes treatment was just for openers. Bob McNeely, the White House photographer, marveled at his modus operandi: "He twisted arms. He threatened people. He called 'em names. There was a little bit of the Lyndon Johnson treatment: 'We'll close every post office in your district.'"

The early Clinton presidency was a battle among these various factions, each competing to control the agenda—and often leaking their version of events. "You'd have Bob Reich going out and saying something in one town," explains Bowles, "and then Bob Rubin in another town saying the opposite of what Bob Reich said." And then there were the unscheduled events. "You inevitably were going to have what I called UFOs, that is, unforeseen occurrences," says McLarty. "You have your message of the day. And inevitably something's going to happen, whether it's a tragedy or a national calamity or something on the Hill or whatever, that will throw you off message."

But Clinton didn't need a tragedy to knock him

off message. Just two days after the election, speaking to reporters, the president was asked about his campaign promise to allow gays to serve in the military. "I don't think status alone . . . should disqualify people," Clinton replied. The trouble was, he had not consulted the Pentagon or senators who opposed lifting the ban. The result was a controversy that lasted for almost a month into his administration—until the president finally announced a compromise agreement called "Don't ask, don't tell."

Never had such a serious presidency been perceived to be so unserious. In May, while awaiting takeoff on **Air Force One** at the Los Angeles International Airport, the president was given a haircut by an upscale hairdresser known as Christophe. The episode quickly turned into farce. The **New York Times** reported that Clinton had shut down two of four runways for hours while being pampered by a hairstylist to the stars. (In fact, the haircut caused no delays.) It became a feast for the tabloids, and more fodder for his Republican enemies.

That same month, apparently at the urging of their friend Harry Thomason, the Clintons requested an FBI investigation of the White House Travel Office, which handled flight arrangements for the press corps; the probe revealed financial improprieties, and embezzlement by the supervisor. Within days, McLarty ordered all seven employees fired. Justified or not, the sacking of the Travel Office workers, many of whom had been there for years, needlessly antagonized their friends in the press corps, who were already gunning for the president.

Six months into the presidency, Hillary was at the end of her rope. As Bob Woodward wrote in **The Agenda:**

Over the last months she had reached some conclusions. The burden of carrying out the administration policies was too much on her husband. He was the chief congressional lobbyist, the chief message person, the policy designer, the spokesman—he carried out all the functions. Too many senior people in the administration and on the staff were stopping short of full preparation.

The first lady did not hesitate to sound off to McLarty, whom she'd known for years. "Hillary was direct," he says. "I wouldn't classify it as a riot act, but her message at times was clear: 'We need to allocate more time here. He just can't do this. You've got to tell him on this. I know the president wants to do this, but it's just not going to work.' And I would usually loop back with the president and say, 'Mr. President, I think your wife makes a good case here. She feels strongly about it. Don't you think we ought not to do that event?'"

The first lady's frustrations finally came to a head at a meeting ostensibly called to discuss a gas tax. Instead, it became a day of reckoning. With lawyerly precision, Hillary Clinton delivered a brutal critique of White House management. The economic team and the political team were not communicating. The communications team was ineffective. She was furious. "This is unacceptable and unfair to Bill," she said, according to Woodward:

> The president had become the "mechanic-in-chief," put in the position of tinkering instead of being the president who had a moral voice, who had a vision, who was going to lead them on this journey. The economic plan wasn't about budgets and numbers, she said. It was a values document. It was to help working people and small businesses. . . . That's what we should be talking about, she added. "I want to see a plan." She wanted everybody involved. "As we develop these policies, we have to decide how to explain them."

The first lady wanted to set up the governing equivalent of a War Room—the brutally efficient campaign headquarters run by Carville and Stephanopoulos. As Woodward recounts it, the president then stood up and began yelling: "'I'm leaving and I'm going to Tokyo,' he shouted. He turned to McLarty and the vice president. 'Mack and Al, you two, I want it solved. I want it done before I get home.' Though his eruption carried an emotional punch, it paled compared to Hillary's withering analysis. There was no denying the critique—most pointedly, a scalding indictment of McLarty. At crucial moments like this, Hillary was often the de facto chief of staff."

"It was chaotic," says Podesta, with a laugh. "But to defend Mack a little bit, Clinton got a lot of stuff done in that first year." Indeed, with McLarty at the helm, the president put in place a deficit-reduction plan; passed the North American Free Trade Agreement; and signed into law the Brady Bill, requiring a five-day waiting period for background checks on gun purchases. He also enacted an economic plan that would eventually lead to a balanced budget and a surplus.

But Clinton's signature issues—a middle-class tax cut; a stimulus package; health-care reform— were dead, or languishing. The bad political news was compounded by personal tragedy. On the evening of July 20, 1993, in the White House residence, the president was in the midst of a live interview with CNN's Larry King when McLarty received an urgent message. "Mr. President, I've got some serious news," McLarty told him during a break. "It's not good news. It's not an international incident or national security issue. It's not about Hillary or Chelsea. But we need to talk."

McLarty threw his arm around the president and led him upstairs. Vince Foster, their close mutual friend, had been found dead, he told him, with a bullet wound to his head. "I still can see the pain and shock in the president's eyes and in his face to this moment," says McLarty. "It was more physical and visceral and visual than in words. It was kind of a gasp of, 'Oh no. This can't be true.'"

It was true—Foster had committed suicide. But instead of sympathy, the Clintons received venomous attacks from the right-wing media, who alleged that Foster had been murdered by the Clintons to cover up corruption and skulduggery. A flurry of headlines continued about their investments in a land deal known as "Whitewater"—a bogus scandal that, as Benghazi would become years later, was all smoke and no fire. The relentless assault from conspiracy mongers only reinforced the Clintons' belief that they would never get a fair hearing.

Despite his setbacks, the president thought all his hard work and effort would be appreciated. But when shown opinion polls, he was shocked. "I couldn't believe the American people were seeing me primarily through the prism of the haircut, the Travel Office, and gays in the military," he wrote in his memoir. "Instead of a President fighting to change America for the better, I was being portrayed as a man who had abandoned down-home for uptown, a knee-jerk liberal whose mask of moderation had been removed."

The most painful casualty was health-care reform. Just five days into office, Clinton had put Hillary in charge of achieving a goal that had eluded Democrats since Harry Truman. But the Task Force on National Health Care Reform, run by the first lady and adviser Ira Magaziner, was insular, secretive, and politically tone-deaf; it ended up producing a hopelessly complex plan. "I remember the first time I heard them lay it out," recalls Leon Panetta, head of the Office of Management and Budget. "My reaction was, this is impossibly complicated. The first lady did what she always did—she acted as if anyone who disagreed with her didn't know what they were talking about—and I said to myself, 'Okay, I'm recusing myself from this issue.'" Clinton's plan was savaged by negative advertising from the powerful insurance lobby. It would soon be dead on arrival in Congress.

By the summer of 1994, Bill Clinton was in trouble. He was discouraged, full of contempt for "Washington and Washington people." After a year and a half, the consensus even among his allies was that Clinton would be a one-term president. The administration's agenda was paralyzed. "It was in danger of running aground," says Reich. "Bill Clinton was doing everything, and trying to be everything to everybody. His tendency toward lack of discipline was overwhelming him and overwhelming the White House staff. There was no coordination to speak of, there was no overall control. There was a lot of wasted time and wasted motion."

Reich and a few other cabinet members staged an indirect intervention. "Many of us who were old friends of the president used back channels—both with Hillary and the president—to tell him that he needed to run a tighter ship. I used every back channel I had. I talked with Hillary, with Al Gore, I slipped messages to the president, I talked to other people who were seeing the president daily." The Clintons got the message. "I think he understood completely, and she did too, that the White House was in disarray," says Bowles. "We were going not sideways, we were going down! They saw that, and knew they had to do something quickly."

In June of 1994, Panetta, the OMB director, was aboard **Air Force One**, bound for Europe to commemorate D-Day. After takeoff, Clinton pulled him onto the couch just outside the president's cabin. "The president basically said, 'What would need to be done in order to make the chief of staff job respond in an effective way?'" recalls Panetta. "'How do I better organize the office?'" He did not immediately realize the president was dangling the chief of staff's job. But, Panetta says, "the fact that he wasn't asking me a budget question kind of rang a bell that something was going on."

Leon Edward Panetta, born in Monterey, California, to Italian immigrant parents, was a onetime army intelligence officer. He started his political career as a Republican and, as head of HEW's Civil Rights Section under Richard Nixon, incurred the president's wrath by moving too fast on desegregation; Panetta resigned before Nixon could fire him. A Democrat ever since, he served nine terms as a congressman. Panetta was highly respected and good-natured, a devout Catholic who always carried his rosary beads and punctuated conversations with a booming laugh. Blunt and grounded, Panetta was a hawk on the budget but liberal on social issues, and he rarely pulled his punches.

Later on during the flight, Stephanopoulos, who'd gotten wind of the impending shakeup, corralled Panetta in the empty baggage section. Stephanopoulos had initially welcomed Clinton's choice of McLarty, thinking McLarty's lack of Washington experience would only make **him** more valuable. But now Stephanopoulos had fallen out of favor with the president, blamed for cooperating on Bob Woodward's critical book **The Agenda**. The disgraced aide saw an opportunity to make an ally of Panetta: "I handed him the book I was reading, **The Haldeman Diaries**, with a placemark on page 309," he said. It was Nixon's 1971 address to his cabinet. " 'Here,' I told Leon, 'you need this, this ultimate control' ":

From now on, Haldeman is the Lord High Executioner. Don't you come whining to me when he tells you to do something. He will do it because I asked him to and you're to carry it out. . . . I want discipline. It's up to Haldeman to police it. . . . When he talks, it's me talking, and don't think it'll do you any good to come and talk to me, because I'll be tougher than he is. That's the way it's going to be.

"You need a broader mandate than Mack's," Stephanopoulos told him. "You need the power not to be overridden, not to have to deal with three different White Houses. You need to be a dictator." Panetta thanked him for the advice and took the book.

Back in Washington, Panetta encountered the vice president in the West Wing parking lot. "Al Gore said, 'You know the president wants to make you chief of staff,'" Panetta recalls. "And I said, 'You know, Al, I'm not interested. I'm doing a great job as director of OMB.' I didn't particularly want that job because I felt comfortable doing what I was doing—and also the White House was pretty screwed up! I said, 'I'd really like to stay where I'm at.' And Gore said, 'No, the president is interested in you doing that job.'"

Panetta continues: "The next thing I knew I get a call to go up to Camp David and meet with the president. So I got in a helicopter and flew up with Al Gore and Tipper. And they take me to the president's cabin there. And I'm in a room—it's

Bill Clinton, Hillary Clinton, Al Gore and Tipper Gore, and me. And I knew at once this was not going to be a fair fight!" Panetta lets out a loud laugh. "I said, 'I'm really valuable to you as OMB director. We've got your economic plan in place.' And the president told me something that I'll never forget. He said, 'Leon, you can be the greatest OMB director in the history of the country, but if the White House is falling apart, nobody will remember you.'"

Panetta accepted the job—with a few conditions. "I said it's important (1) that I have the trust of you and the first lady; (2) that you give me the authority to do some reorganization if I think it's necessary in order to make the place work. And (3) that we really be honest with each other—that we tell each other what we feel and what we're thinking."

Unlike some of his predecessors, Mack McLarty would not have to be forced to step down. In fact, by the summer of 1994 he realized it was time for a change, and he recommended Panetta as his replacement. "It's always pretty tricky to give up a job like a chief of staff's position," says McLarty. "It has a public profile to it. And so it's never easy. It's sometimes not very pleasant." But McLarty was realistic. It was time, he thought, "to frankly make some changes because we were moving into a much more partisan time, into midterm elections, a much more hostile environment in terms of the personal attacks—and that does not play to my strength and personality." Instead of going back to Arkansas, McLarty would stay on as counselor to the president, building bridges to moderate Republicans in Congress.

Panetta knew the White House was run informally, but he had no idea how informally. "I went to Mack and said, 'I'd like to see your organizational chart for the White House staff.' And he said, 'You know, Leon, I don't believe we have one of those.' And I said, 'Oh, shit.' That's when I knew I was in deep trouble! I had to basically organize the White House using little boxes. My army training helped me well because I basically established a kind of chain of command on the staff, who reported to who, and built the staff based on that organization chart."

As his deputy, Panetta installed Bowles, who had left a lucrative business as an entrepreneur and investment banker to run the Small Business Administration. Around the West Wing, gossips wondered: How much money had Erskine given up to go into public service? No one knew, but guesses ran in the tens of millions of dollars. "You have to remember that there are no businesspeople in the White House," says Bowles. "So what we had to do was make it simple." Mild-mannered and businesslike, the North Carolina–born Bowles had a missionary zeal for management: His first three commandments were "organization, structure, and focus." Although he had not known Bowles before he became his deputy, Panetta would come to rely heavily on him during the difficult budget negotiations ahead.

Strangers at first, Bowles and Clinton had formed a personal bond during the campaign: Bowles's son suffered from diabetic seizures, and Clinton promised him that he would reverse the ban on fetal stem cell research that might point the way toward a cure. Once in the White House, the president unwound with his deputy chief over rounds of golf at the Army Navy course. "We both were southern guys," says Bowles. "We both liked policy and politics. We both liked playing golf. We married girls at Wellesley—both of 'em Phi Beta Kappa, smart women out of the same class. But I knew I worked for him, and that's the relationship you can't lose. I don't think it's critical to be the president's friend, or even important, but you have to know him. You have to know what he's good at, what he's not good at, where he needs help—and then your job is to do that."

Bowles's first goal as deputy chief was to take control of Clinton himself. "The biggest asset you have is your president's time," he says. To figure out how that asset was being used, Bowles conducted a "time and motion" study of the president. "We went back and took all of the president's old sched-ules and then we got the reality—because people record what the president actually does. We color-coded it: Foreign policy was red, economic policy was blue, and so on. The president wanted to focus on X, Y, and Z. By color-coding just what they had laid out, you could see that he wasn't focusing on X, Y, and Z. And since there was a whole rainbow of colors every day, you could say: 'Hey, how are you going to get a single message out when you're doing six messages every day—or three messages every day? That's **crazy.**'"

The color-coding helped show Clinton just how inefficient his schedule was. From now on, Bowles would ensure that Clinton was using his time effectively—and, in doing so, give him time to think.

The president was no longer pulling all-nighters the way he had during the campaign, but Clinton's method of preparing—for everything from school uniforms to Middle East peace—was unique. "I don't care how important the issue was, you couldn't get him to hit a lick at a snake [read a memo or open a book] till, maximum, two days before," says Bowles. "And then all of a sudden you would see books on the subject from the White House Library stacked that high on his desk." He raises his hand above his head. "And you'd see periodicals on the subject from people—Far Left, Far Right, didn't matter—scattered over in the East Wing of the living quarters. And when I looked at his phone messages, he would've called people on the periphery of the subject to ask them questions.

And he read like that old Evelyn Wood [speed-reading] course. He could take a page and read it just like that and he retains everything in it—and have a full discussion with me at the same time. And how he does it, I'll never know."

While his deputy revamped Clinton's schedule, Panetta took charge as gatekeeper. "The first order of business was obviously to make very clear that I was going to be a chief of staff that would in fact control the staff, and that if they wanted to go to the president, they would have to go through me," he says. Jovial and collegial, Panetta had a humble manner. But few mistook his gregariousness for weakness. There would be no more uninvited guests dropping in on the Oval Office. "Leon has an iron fist in a velvet glove," says Reich. "He's not a disciplinarian for the sake of being a disciplinarian; he's actually a very gentle soul, but he knows when discipline is necessary."

Panetta also knew how to roll with Clinton's famous nocturnal habits. "I remember it was two thirty, three o'clock in the morning, and I get a call from the president and I said, 'Holy cow, what's going on?' And he said, 'Leon, are you watching Fritz Hollings on C-SPAN?' And I said, 'Are you kidding me, Mr. President?' I said, 'Nobody in the country is watching Fritz Hollings on C-SPAN right now. Everybody's asleep, and you should be asleep too.'" Bowles, who got his share of midnight calls, says they were Clinton's way of thinking out loud. "With President Clinton those calls didn't always require an answer. What he was doing was thinking through a problem and he wanted somebody he trusted who wouldn't go blab about it. Just listen."

Panetta continues: "Working for Bill Clinton is a very special experience because you're dealing with somebody who's extremely bright, who's got a mind like a steel trap, gathers all the facts, doesn't forget a thing, and at the same time wants to be able to get input from everybody. And then when he makes a decision, his mind doesn't stop. It keeps churning. He keeps working it, and the toughest part of dealing with him was to say, 'You've made a decision. Now we've got to move on. We've got **other** decisions to make.'"

No one needed to tell Panetta that the president was not his only client. "I knew that it was really important to keep Hillary informed of what was going on," he says. "The reality was that Hillary cared enough about what was happening with the president—if she felt he wasn't being well served, and this goes back to when he was governor, she would play the role of chief of staff, trying to get things done." For the next six months, until he had earned her trust, Panetta went out of his way to give Hillary weekly briefings.

Frustrated, Bill Clinton was lashing out at those around him, but Panetta knew the storm would pass. "The president wanted to get rid of Stephanopoulos, and he wanted to get rid of Rahm—he thought they were both leakers," says Panetta. (Emanuel had also, inevitably, stepped on the toes of powerful figures on Capitol Hill.) "He wanted to get rid of the press secretary, Dee Dee Myers." Panetta stalled for time. "What I did was I said, 'Look, let me look at the operation.'"

While Panetta dragged his heels on firing Emanuel, Clinton turned to Bowles. Not once, but five times the president ordered him to fire Rahm. But Bowles refused. "I told him, 'Hell no, I wasn't going to fire him,'" he says. "The president would say, 'Why not?' And I'd say, 'Because every time you come out of that Oval Office and you've got some new thing you want us to do, and I can't get the bureaucracy to do it, you know what I do? I give it to Rahm. And two days later he comes back and it's done! There are twenty dead people back there—but it's done!'"

Panetta agreed that Rahm was indispensable. And he enjoyed his brash persona. "Are you really Italian?" Panetta needled him, when Emanuel stuck his head in the chief's office door one morning.

"Italian enough to date your daughter!" Rahm replied.

"Not **that** Italian," said Panetta.

"Rahm is a doer, and he gets it done come hell or high water, and sometimes he steps on a lot of people to get it done. But he's gonna take the hill.

And that's a good quality," says Panetta, "but the best way to deal with that is to make sure that you keep your arms around him, so that he doesn't just feel that he can do anything he wants on his own." Panetta also persuaded Clinton to keep Stephanopoulos. "I saw in George the ability to provide some really good political advice." But he also saw the need to keep him in line. Stephanopoulos had a small office adjoining the Oval. "So I said, 'You cannot use that back door. You gotta come to me.' And I would determine when George would go in to the Oval Office."

While he kept aides on a short leash, Panetta knew how to motivate his troops. "Leon is not a bully," says Reich. "He's not an attack dog. He's really a very sweet man. What Leon proves is you don't have to be a bully or an attack dog to be an effective chief of staff. You just have to be very smart. You have to know when to be tough, and also when to let the reins be a little looser. Because the people around you have to have some degree of autonomy or else they're not going to do well."

That attitude would come in handy in late 1994, when Clinton's presidency seemed to hit rock bottom. Health-care reform was officially dead; Congress had launched hearings into the Whitewater scandal; and in the November midterm elections, the Republicans "beat the living daylights out of us," as Clinton put it, winning the House in a landslide, creating the first Republican majority in forty years. The newly anointed speaker was Newt Gingrich, architect of a manifesto called "Contract with America"—a declaration of war on "government that is too big, too intrusive, and too easy with the people's money." Clinton himself was declared irrelevant by Congress and the media. A few months later, when the president called a press conference, only one network televised it. Plaintively, Clinton protested: "The president is relevant. . . . The Constitution gives me relevance; the power of our ideas gives me relevance; the record we have built up over the last two years and the things we're trying to do give me relevance."

Clinton would soon prove just how relevant he still was. On April 19, 1995, an explosion rocked the Alfred P. Murrah Building in Oklahoma City. "We first got the news through CNN and I went to the Oval Office and told the president," recalls Panetta. "He came out into the outer office. There was a television there. And he was watching CNN—and when he saw that tragedy and the number of lives that were lost, you could see it in his eyes what a tragedy this was for the country, and for those families that were impacted by that explosion." Clinton refused to be stampeded into declaring that the attacks had been the act of Muslim terrorists. (It turned out to be the work of a domestic right-wing terrorist named Timothy McVeigh.) At the memorial service at the bombed-out site in Kansas City, Clinton excelled as the nation's consoler in chief. "You have lost too much, but you have not lost everything," he told the victims' families. "And you have certainly not lost America, for we will stand with you for as many tomorrows as it takes."

Clinton had regained his voice—and his swagger. He'd soon call on it to deal with an intractable crisis in the heart of Europe, one that threatened his legacy. Between 1991 and 1995, more than two hundred thousand people had been killed in the former Yugoslavia. Serbian dictator Slobodan Milošević had unleashed "ethnic cleansing" pogroms and civilian massacres. In the fall of 1995, belatedly and reluctantly, the president launched a NATO bombing campaign. "The president made a lot of gutsy calls—and that's what I liked about him," says Bowles. "Lots of people thought, 'God, you know, it may take him a while.' But I thought that was a strength. He wanted to hear all sides of the argument. He didn't subscribe to the 'ready, fire, aim' school. He was 'ready, aim, aim'—and then he fired."

Even in the face of massive bombardment, the Serbian dictator was at first defiant. "Milošević didn't back down as many of his [Clinton's] advisers told him they thought he would," recalls John Podesta, the White House staff secretary. "And I remember distinctly his key security advisers were nervous: Will this work? Did we do it right? Will it succeed? The president was the calmest person in the group. The decision was on him. He knew that if it was wrong, he'd bear the burden, but he was confident that he had made the right decision." The bombing campaign eventually forced Milošević and his opponents to the negotiating table; in November, at an air force base in Ohio, diplomat Richard Holbrooke hammered out the Dayton Accords, bringing the war in Bosnia to an end.

That same month, with Panetta's help, Clinton prepared for a showdown with his domestic enemies in the House. As budget negotiations approached, the president thought he could persuade Newt Gingrich to see things his way. Panetta wasn't so sure. "The president always feels that he can convince anybody, anywhere, anytime, what the right thing is to do," he says. "And he felt he could convince Newt Gingrich." Like Jim Baker, Panetta believed the chief's most important duty was to tell the president what he did not want to hear. "And I said, 'I don't think that's going to happen, Mr. President. I dealt with Newt Gingrich when I was in the Congress. He's not going to do that. And he'll put a knife in your back. He's got a bunch of revolutionaries that just got elected. He's not about to cut a deal with you.'"

Panetta was right. Instead of an olive branch, Gingrich brought a knife: a budget that slashed every program favored by Democrats. But Clinton was prepared to call his bluff. As negotiations reached a climax, Gingrich and Senate majority leader Bob Dole met with Clinton and Panetta in the Oval Office to hear the president's final offer. "And Bob Dole said, 'We'll take it.' And Gingrich said, 'I can't.' And I remember something that Bill Clinton said, which I never forgot. He looked at Gingrich and he said, 'You know, Newt, I just don't believe what you want us to do is right for the country. And I may lose the election based on what I do here, but I honestly believe that what you're recommending is not right for the country.' I never forgot those words because Bill Clinton at that point had drawn a line."

Gingrich did not budge, and Clinton vetoed his draconian budget, leading to a monthlong government shutdown. "The Republicans really didn't believe that the president had the guts to absolutely stand up for his position and say, 'Hell no, we're not going to do it that way,'" says Bowles. "And when he did, they were both surprised and unprepared. And he was prepared. We didn't know who the winner or the loser was going to be. But he was willing to risk his presidency on doing what he felt was the right thing." As it turned out, the shutdown was blamed squarely on the Republicans. After a petulant Gingrich complained about his seating during a trip on **Air Force One**, the **New York Daily News** depicted the House Speaker as a crybaby on its cover. It was a turning point in Clinton's march toward reelection.

Still, the Clintons were taking no chances. Their insecurity about the new Republican Revolution would lead to a bizarre West Wing drama, and a test for Panetta. "There was a growing sense that Bill Clinton would be in real trouble as far as his reelection," says Panetta. "Bill Clinton is not somebody who just simply sits back and assumes that fate is in charge; he basically tries to control fate. And so he decides, 'I gotta find out what's going wrong, what's happening here.'"

Clinton's inner circle knew that someone was advising the president behind the scenes. But that someone was invisible—a phantom. The president arrived at meetings with prebaked decisions. Sitting in the Oval Office, Bowles was thinking, "Where was the real meeting taking place? And it became clear that the real meeting was taking place over in the East Wing with this guy who I had never heard of!" Even Panetta did not know the identity of the mystery adviser, who evidently lurked in the White House residence, whispering in the president's ear at night. "His code name was 'Charlie,'" he recalls. "And it was Harold Ickes who finally nailed who 'Charlie' was."

His name was Dick Morris, one of the strangest characters in American politics, and one of the most despised. An amoral but brilliant political gun for hire, Morris had helped Clinton revive his political career in the 1980s; after being thrown out of the governorship in a devastating reelection defeat, Clinton—with Morris's help—had come back to win the office again. It was Hillary, desperate after the midterm debacle, who reached out to Morris again. "Morris is a guy who has a pretty good sense of where the popular will is, what makes them tick—what it was that Clinton was doing wrong," says Panetta. "And so Morris started doing polling for the president and started providing the president with advice. Harold and George thought he was the devil, and dirt." So did Bowles and Bob Reich. "Dick Morris is not just unscrupulous, he really was as close to a terrible person as I've ever come across," says Reich. "He had a gigantic ego, impossible to deal with, terrible values and dishonest. He turned the White House on its head and made everybody's job much harder."

Morris was a direct challenge to Panetta's authority as chief, if not a slap in the face. "It was amazing to see something planned in Leon's office—and then literally the next day none of that happened," says Bowles. "I couldn't have stood that. And Leon is stronger than I am. But he stood it." Panetta was smart enough to realize that Clinton needed Morris, and he worked out a compromise. "What I could not tolerate as chief of staff was to have somebody who was planting political advice with the president and then trying to implement it through the staff of the White House," he says. "That's where I drew the line and told the president, 'Look, this is unacceptable. I can't have any political person trying to deal with the staff.' And the president to his credit respected that, and we told Morris that he's got to present the information to the president and to me, and then we'll decide what does or does not get done. Morris understood that he was going to have to play by my rules."

Bowles was impressed by the way Panetta lowered the boom on Morris. "Leon had such presence, and he has physical strength, mental strength, a likability and humanity that's contagious," he says. "But you know when you're around Leon that he is the boss."

With Panetta steering the ship, Clinton was picking up speed. At Morris's urging, the president pursued a political strategy called "triangulation"—co-opting traditionally Republican issues; on August 22, 1996, the president signed into law a bill "ending welfare as we know it." The economy was expanding, unemployment was dropping, and government spending was reduced. The 1993 Deficit Reduction Act had set the stage to ultimately turn the largest deficit in history into the largest surplus. On November 5, 1996, Clinton was re-elected with 49 percent of the vote, becoming the first Democrat to win a second term since Franklin Roosevelt. Not only did Panetta deserve much of the credit; it almost surely would not have happened without him.

"Leon put the Clinton presidency back on

track," says Reich. "I think the most effective chiefs are self-effacing like Leon. They know that all of their power and authority derive from the president. They're not there to make headlines. They're not there to assert their own will. They are instruments by which a president can be more effective. And to that extent they are a rarity." When he became Obama's first chief, Emanuel set out to emulate Panetta. "If you ask me who I tried to model myself after, it would be Leon," he says. "I loved Leon. I loved his humanity and his ability to be frank with the president and then execute what the president wanted."

Grueling as the chief's job was, Panetta could be misty-eyed about it. "Sometimes the president would leave for a meeting, and I'd be alone in the Oval Office and I'd say to myself, 'Man, what a great country—where a son of immigrants can be next to the most powerful position on the face of the earth.'" But Panetta had warned Clinton that he would only stay for two years. "I felt that the most important thing you can do is protect your humanity. And the way I thought I could do that was by going back to California. You're like a racehorse in the chief of staff's job—you're constantly up, you're constantly wired, you're constantly running hard. And then suddenly the race is over." A thoroughbred like Panetta would be impossible to replace. The president considered his national security adviser, Sandy Berger. Berger, a slightly disheveled workaholic, had met Clinton back in 1972 on George McGovern's presidential campaign, and they'd been friends ever since. Clinton valued his wisdom and wry sense of humor. He also considered Harold Ickes, the hard-nosed political operative from New York City, grandson of FDR's secretary of the interior. But at the last moment, Clinton turned to the deputy with whom he had formed a close personal bond, in the White House and on the golf course: Erskine Bowles.

Bowles had left the White House before the reelection to return to North Carolina. Since then he had pitched in part-time, helping Clinton prepare for his debates and plan for a second term. But he was not eager to come back. "I flat said no a couple of times," says Bowles. "And I went back for three reasons. One, I really cared deeply about the president. Two, I knew his number one agenda in his second term was to balance the federal budget. I felt he needed somebody to drive it through. And three, he leaned on me really hard."

Bowles was no stranger to the West Wing, but the relentless pace of the job stunned him. "You simply can't get it done in what anybody would call a normal day because you live in a twenty-four-hour news cycle," Bowles says. "When something might not be going on here, something is going on in Europe or Asia or the Middle East. In an average day you would deal with things like Bosnia, Northern Ireland, the budget, taxation, the environment—and then you'd have lunch. And people would always joke, 'Thank God it's Friday, only two more workdays till Monday.'"

The entrepreneur–investment banker defined the job in corporate terms. "I always thought of the president as the CEO," he says. "He's the one that sets the agenda. It's his presidency, not yours. And the job of the chief of staff is to be the chief operating officer—to make sure that if he sets the goals, you set the objectives, the timelines, and the accountability to make sure that what he wants done is done, when he wants it done, and is done right."

Bowles carried around a card with the president's top priorities written on it—and rebelled when Clinton tried to go off script. "One day the president came out of his office and he had another one of his great ideas," he recalls. "And believe me, they were unbelievably great ideas. And I turned to him and said, 'Mr. President, you have got to go back into that Oval Office, right now! You've got to look at this list of things that you and I agreed you wanted to get done. Not that I wanted to get done, but you wanted to get done. If you will stay focused on those three or four things, I can set up the organization and the structure and the focus to make 'em real. But you can't do a thousand things.'"

Clinton sometimes called Bowles his closest friend in the world, but Bowles was determined not to let that interfere with telling the president the truth as he saw it. He had done his homework, consulting his predecessors on both sides of the aisle. "As Don Rumsfeld told me, 'You've got to be prepared to be fired,'" Bowles says. "'Because if you're not, then you're not going to give him the right advice. And the right advice is not always yes.'"

Even good friends were not exempt from the president's famous temper. "Bill Clinton used to go forty feet off the ground," recalls Panetta. "He'd come in in the morning and something had bothered him—and you kind of let him go through it because it was good therapy for him." But Bowles was having none of it: "We were going to have a relationship that was a peer relationship. And I had big boy pants on, and if he acted like that around me, I was gonna leave. And he knew that—and so he didn't."

"The power of the chief of staff is derived," says Bowles. "If you have the trust and the confidence of the president, you have all the power you need to get what you need done. If you've lost the confidence of a president, people smell it, feel it, know it within seconds—and you become an overblown scheduler."

The true test of Bowles's power came in the summer of 1997, when he would square off against Gingrich and Trent Lott, the Senate majority leader, in an effort to produce a balanced budget. "The president really empowered me to negotiate the balanced budget agreement, and those guys knew that when I said, 'We got a deal on this point,' they didn't have to say, 'Erskine, will the president really do this?'" Bowles emerged from the marathon talks with the first balanced federal budget since 1969. And with something else as well: agreement on a State Children's Health Insurance Plan. "I'll never forget it if I live to be a zillion," says Bowles, "when I told the president we'd balanced the budget, brought down the debt—and yet we had invested $27 billion in health care for poor kids. Five million poor kids were going to get health-care insurance! You could have lit the room up with the smile on his face."

It was the high point of Bowles's White House career. But the low point was soon to come.

BOWLES'S DEPUTY, John Podesta, was the first to get the news, startling in its tawdriness, and frighteningly specific: A young White House intern claimed to have had sex with the president, and Special Prosecutor Kenneth Starr had evidence to prove it. No one knew where his investigation might lead. "I got the first phone call from a reporter from the **Washington Post**, who had been tipped that this was going on," recalls Podesta. "And that first twenty-four hours was definitely a sinking feeling of 'What is this? What is going

on? We don't have any idea what's happening here.'
And that kind of loss of control can get to you. You
just feel like you're falling and there's no bottom."

Podesta asked Special Counsel Lanny Davis to
look into it. Davis called back soon afterward. As
he recounted in a memoir:

"John, the **Post** is running a story with three
key facts confirmed, and they want our comment," I began.

"What are they?"

"First, they've confirmed that a White House
intern named Monica Lewinsky claims to have
had an affair with the president, and this is
corroborated by tape recordings between Ms.
Lewinsky and a friend."

An audible intake of breath.

"Second, they've confirmed that Ken Starr
got the tapes, went to the attorney general, and
has received the authority from the three-judge
panel to investigate the president's role, which
includes possible perjury, subornation of perjury, and obstruction of justice."

Another more audible intake of breath.

"Finally, they've confirmed that as a result
of suspicions about this affair someone at the
White House caused Ms. Lewinsky to be trans-
ferred to a job at the Pentagon."

A long silence, another, quieter intake of
breath, and then . . . a sigh.

"You better come down here right away," Podesta said quietly.

For Podesta, the Monica Lewinsky scandal was realpolitik, nothing personal. "I didn't approve of what the president did, but that's not what this really was about," he says. "This wasn't about whether he had a relationship with a young woman; this was about his opponents trying to stop him from doing what he wanted to do because they wanted to do things differently."

But for Bowles, the news of Clinton's behavior was devastating. "He was so disturbed he wouldn't go to meetings about this," says Peter Baker, the reporter who called Podesta that night, and author of **The Breach**, an account of Clinton's impeachment. "At one point, Erskine just burst out: 'I don't want to know a f*cking thing about it. Don't tell me about it!'" Bowles was so nauseated by the affair it literally made him ill. At one meeting, he blurted out, "I think I'm going to throw up." He fled from the room and never returned.

Bill Clinton coped by compartmentalizing, alternately governing and managing the scandal. In **My Life**, the president wrote: "I was compelled as never before to live parallel lives, except that this time the darkest part of my inner life was in full view." I asked Bowles about those parallel lives. "Well, nobody compartmentalizes everything, okay," he says. "It has a big effect on you. Sure, I knew when it was toughest on him and when it wasn't. My job was to know my client, understand him, and also to make sure he didn't lose focus on his agenda. But I had to make sure I left enough time for him to deal with this other matter."

To this day, Bowles can barely talk about "this other matter." At the time, he coped by devising a strategy of containment—walling off the scandal for others to deal with. "It was tough on the president and it was tough on the White House staff," he says. "And I had to figure out how we executed on his goals while dealing with this other crisis on the side. I made the decision—history will argue whether it was right or not—to isolate that in particular cells in the White House with people who would deal with that and deal with that solely."

Bowles's deputy, Podesta, was put in charge of managing the Lewinsky "cells"—staffed by lawyers, communications people, and others—while Bowles kept Clinton focused on governing. "John oversaw all of that operation. I thought he was unbelievably talented in areas where I was unbelievably untalented," says Bowles. "I did not like dealing with the investigations; I just hated it. And John was just great at it." Podesta—who called himself the "secretary of shit"—would be responsible for trying to prevent the looming impeachment and conviction of the president of the United States.

"This was hugely embarrassing to the president,

as it would be to anyone, to have their personal life exposed this way," says Podesta. "So there were ugly days. The day the president did the deposition in the White House—that was an ugly day. But he was able to put it aside, do his job, get to the Oval Office, think about that as a day where he could do what he said he would do for the American people. And when he had to deal with the lawyers, he'd deal with them."

Podesta and Bowles also had to shore up their troops. "It was critical to keep the staff from feeling like the bottom was falling out," says Podesta. "At some level that's being a battlefield commander. You've just got to keep your troops focused on what the goal is on a day-to-day basis. Keep the discipline strong, intimidate when you need to—and let somebody cry on your shoulder when that's appropriate."

For many, the scandal was not just disillusioning, but frightening. "This was really a burden on many young people, the first time they had interacted with a prosecutor or with the criminal justice system, and they were scared," Bowles recalls. "You could always tell a member of the staff who had gotten a subpoena—and everybody got one, down to the very lowest levels."

Americans still approved of Clinton by a large margin. "They were sticking with him," says Podesta. "They wanted him to do the job that they had elected him to do." On August 17, 1998, the day he gave his deposition at the White House to Special Prosecutor Kenneth Starr, Clinton's approval rating was 64 percent. Afterward, on television from the Oval Office, the president admitted that he'd had an inappropriate relationship with Lewinsky, but also delivered an angry, defensive attack on his enemies.

Meanwhile, the world did not stop turning just because Washington was consumed by the Lewinsky affair. Three days after his televised admission, the president was told that the Pentagon had located a terrorism training complex in Afghanistan and a pharmaceutical plant suspected of making chemical weapons in Sudan—both linked to Osama bin Laden. In a surreal coincidence, Hollywood had recently released a movie, **Wag the Dog**, in which a president starts a war to divert attention from a sex scandal. "We knew that since that movie **Wag the Dog** was out there, the next day everybody would be saying, 'Oh, they did it just to draw attention away from this Monica stuff,'" says Bowles. "But President Clinton said, 'Look, it's the right thing to do. We have to do it. We'll bear the political price, but we're going to get this done.'" Clinton ordered cruise missile strikes from ships in the Indian Ocean. "He did it knowing that the newspapers and the Congress would go after him tooth and nail," says Bowles. "And they did. But he did the right thing." (Alas, by the time the missiles struck their targets, bin Laden had vanished.)

The Bowles-Podesta strategy of focusing on governing paid off. In the 1998 midterms, the Republicans were routed—and, as a consequence, Gingrich resigned his speakership. And then Clinton's Republican enemies overplayed their hand. They pursued impeachment, forging ahead even though they lacked the votes for conviction in the Senate. According to Clinton's account in **My Life:** "Newt told Erskine that they were going to go forward with the impeachment despite the election results and the fact that many moderate Republicans didn't want to vote for it. When Erskine asked Newt why . . . the Speaker replied, 'Because we can.'"

On the morning the United States Senate opened its impeachment trial, Clinton, Podesta, aide Doug Sosnik, and the president's dog, Buddy, were in the president's small dining room off the Oval Office. "We were watching television, and the votes coming up," recalls Podesta. "Two articles were voted up, two articles down. That was a sober moment. But I think we felt relatively confident at that point that the Senate would in fact acquit him because these were not impeachable offenses."

He continues: "And when that did occur in the Senate, I was with the president, and with Jesse Jackson in the Oval Office. And Reverend Jackson had been a big, staunch, stalwart supporter through this whole period. And we all held hands and said a prayer. And those two guys were a little bit more used to that. I'm a Catholic, so I tend to wait till Sunday." Podesta laughs. "But I think the prayer was less about what had just happened and more about the future. This had been a struggle, but a struggle worth fighting because we had good things we could still do."

The struggle had taken a toll on the White House staff. From the president's emphatic, televised denial—"I did not have sexual relations with that woman"—until his admission on the day of his White House deposition, they had been kept in the dark for eight months. "Look, the president admitted he lied," says Peter Baker. "There were some on his team who would never believe him at all, which is a terrible thing, because if you can't believe your boss, how can you work for him? And there were some who believed him, because they felt like they had no other choice but to believe. How could they not believe? And they were really devastated to learn later that he didn't tell them the whole truth. So for his staff, this is the worst of all possible worlds."

Bill Clinton had lied not only to his wife, his cabinet, and his aides, but to his close friend and chief of staff, Bowles. "Erskine hated it," says Peter Baker. "It was the worst experience of his life. This was the exact last thing he wanted to do. It troubled him deeply. I think he came to the conclusion that Clinton hadn't been 100 percent honest with him. It made him reassess what he thought was his friendship with Clinton."

"We were all mad at him," says Podesta. "Everybody was mad at him, and most of us, including me, let him know it. It was a sense of disbelief—like, 'How could you be so, mmm, stupid?'" Podesta swallows the adjective. "He swore at me a lot and I swore at him a lot. But I think we all felt a personal bond to him, and loyalty to the project that he was trying to engage in."

Deeply wounded, Bowles left the White House in the fall of 1998. "I wanted to get out," he says. "The president and I talked about it, he talked me out of it a lot of times and I finally convinced him that John Podesta would be the best chief of staff he ever had." In his memoir, Clinton wrote: "Through our trials and triumphs, our golf matches and card games, Erskine and I had become close friends. I would miss him, especially on the golf course." After losing two close races to become senator from North Carolina, Bowles became president of the University of North Carolina, and later cochairman, with Senator Alan Simpson, of the National Commission on Fiscal Responsibility and Reform, better known as the Simpson-Bowles Commission.

ON OCTOBER 20, 1998, Podesta became Clinton's fourth and final chief. He and Clinton had known each other more than a quarter century; they'd met while volunteering for Joseph Duffey's antiwar campaign for senator of Connecticut back in 1970. (Duffey won the Democratic primary in an upset, but lost the general election to Republican Lowell Weicker.) "Wiry, ascetic, profane and relentless," as Peter Baker described him, Podesta looked the part of a hard-bitten presidential consigliere. But he was also a kind of Renaissance man: an avid environmentalist, information technology expert, and amateur historian, he could talk knowledgeably about the hydrofluorocarbon limits in the Montreal Protocol and bombing sites in the Balkans. (He was also passionate about UFOs, and the horror–science fiction drama **The X Files**.) "He had the right personal qualities," wrote Clinton. "A fine mind, a tough hide, a dry wit, and he was a better hearts player than Erskine Bowles."

Podesta was determined to prove that Bill Clinton's presidency was not over yet. He banned staffers from talking about "legacy"—that was a word for lame ducks—and, with the scandal in the rearview mirror, focused on governing. His role model as chief was James Baker. Every morning at seven thirty, Podesta convened his own version of Baker's Legislative Strategy Group, bringing together top advisers to address key challenges: "If there was a bottleneck in Congress, how do we move past that? If there was legislation headed at us that we needed to veto, how do we deal with that? If there were economic crises globally in Asia and other places, you know, how do we manage those big initiatives?"

On top of those policy challenges were electoral ones. "We had the vice president running for president. We had the first lady running for the U.S. Senate, and we had to keep an abnormal number of balls in the air," he recalls. In the course of the bitter impeachment fight, Podesta had developed a bond with Hillary. "She and I became very close during that experience," he says. "And I talked to Hillary routinely. And she would give me advice, or tell me what she thought ought to be a priority that wasn't." At least the Lewinsky drama was no longer keeping him up at night: "Once we stabilized, it was a challenge but I wasn't losing sleep over this—the way I probably lost sleep over whether legislation would be passed, or the Kosovo war would turn out okay."

The Dayton Accords had not ended conflict in the Balkans. In 1999, Serbian dictator Milošević began driving Albanians out of Kosovo. With Podesta at his side, Clinton decided to intervene—ordering a massive bombing campaign. "Those are always really, really tough judgments," says Podesta. "They're tough judgments for the president, tough judgments for the staff. You're putting people's lives on the line. You are unleashing tremendous violence on hopefully the intended target—but there's always collateral issues. At the end of the day, if you're a normal human being, that's got to weigh on you."

On the home front, Podesta believed in the power of small initiatives. "Clinton was criticized sometimes for small stuff—the famous one was school uniforms," he says. In his 1996 State of the Union speech, the president had vowed to support schools in their effort to break a cycle of violence, truancy, and disorder. "And if it means that teenagers will stop killing each other over designer jackets," he vowed, "then our public schools should be able to require their students to wear school uniforms." They were, Podesta admitted, "small ideas, not presidential—the press didn't like it. But for a mom who's sending her kid off to school in a tough environment, that meant a lot. Clinton understood that these cultural things, these smaller things, added up to momentum that created a sense of opportunity in the country. Where there was an opportunity to make someone's life a little bit better, we took it."

In order to do so, the president made ample use of his executive power—a strategy Podesta championed and would later help perfect as an adviser to Barack Obama. "Republicans criticized Clinton for this, but I viewed it as one of his greatest achievements," he says. "He had a lot to do that required the application of executive authority. His power under the Constitution and the laws of the United States took the form of protecting the great spaces in America, eliminating road building in roadless forests, protecting those natural resources for future generations, putting in place the first-ever health privacy rules, cleaning up the air and the water. There was just a very long list of things that the president had the power to do. He had the talent in his cabinet to do it. And of course we had to have a system that could digest and move that stuff forward."

The thick-skinned consigliere of presidential scandals could be strikingly sentimental. On January 11, 2000, standing at the edge of the Grand Canyon, the president and Interior secretary Bruce Babbitt designated three new national monuments and expanded a fourth in Arizona and California, including one million acres and a stretch of thousands of small islands along the California coast. Podesta remembers "standing on the north rim of the Grand Canyon, where we had helicoptered over the narrow canyon. You could see the vista from there. Perhaps it was the majestic setting, but the fact that sitting at a little table that had been set out there, with the stroke of a pen, you could protect that for generation after generation—it was just an amazing experience for me."

Podesta continues: "People always ask me if the TV show **The West Wing** was real; and I always say the set wasn't really like the West Wing"— the actual West Wing is much less grand, the offices smaller. "But the interesting thing is what the show got right: The people there aren't cynical. They're actually trying to do a good job for the country. And they thought they could do it better than the other guys could. John Spencer, the actor who played Leo, the chief of staff, and I became friends—and I always said that to him, you know, these people are not cynical."

Still, Bill Clinton's presidency was nothing if not complicated, noble and compromised, right to the end.

On his last night in office ("exhausted to the point of foolishness," as one writer put it), the president signed 177 presidential pardons and commutations of sentence. Most controversially, he pardoned Marc Rich, a financier who had fled the United States on the eve of being indicted for evading tens of millions of dollars in taxes. Rich's wife Denise had contributed $450,000 to the Clinton Library and $100,000 to Hillary Clinton's Senate campaign. Clinton's pardoning spree was a final paroxysm of bad judgment—and no one was around to talk him out of it. Podesta had gone home for the night.

Once again, some of the shine had come off a presidency that had once seemed so bright. As Joe Klein wrote in **The Natural**:

Clinton appeared to be promising greater things than he could ever deliver—in fact, nothing less than a political renaissance, a return to the days when public affairs seemed central to the life of the republic, when government was seen as a moral force, when politicians were seen to be wise rather than corrupt. If Ronald Reagan had challenged the pessimism of the post-Vietnam era, liberals hoped that Bill Clinton would challenge the cynicism.

In the end, cynicism won—with a major assist from Clinton himself. But amid the dashed hopes and the scandals and the bitterness, a great deal of real work was done.

The next morning, Podesta went to the White House before the inauguration. "The president spent the morning wrapping up the last of his knickknacks that were going to be sent down to Little Rock," he recalls. "And we were feeling a sense of accomplishment, because the country was in a better place than when we started. I remember walking the colonnade with the president, and I said to him, 'We did good, boss.' And we went over to the residence. Vice President–elect Cheney was there and President-elect Bush. It's always slightly awkward at those moments, and of course this was a highly contentious campaign that had been finally settled by the Supreme Court, voting five to four." The incoming and outgoing leaders of the free world sipped coffee and traded small talk, trying to be gracious.

As they were loading up the motorcade to head

for the Capitol, Podesta says, "A member of the Marine Corps band was playing the piano. And Bill Clinton decided he wanted one last song. And he went over and sat with him at the piano, and they played one last song."

Dick Cheney was thinking about the day he arrived in Washington thirty-two years earlier, a grad student, wearing the only suit he owned. His journey was not over yet. "I was riding to Capitol Hill in a limousine as the newly elected vice president, together with George Bush, to be sworn in as the Bush-Cheney administration," he says. "And I couldn't help but be amazed at all that had transpired since."

Dick Cheney and Donald Rumsfeld, protégé and mentor, were coming home again.

8

"The Decider"

Andrew Card, Joshua Bolten,
and George W. Bush

In the living room of Blair House, the nineteenth-century presidential guest quarters on Pennsylvania Avenue, George W. Bush and Andrew Card were planning the forty-third presidency of the United States. It was January 19, 2001, the night before the inauguration, and the president-elect and his incoming chief of staff were keenly aware that they were part of a rare historical moment. Not since John Quincy Adams's administration in the 1820s had the son of a president held the office. (Bush had read "a fair amount about Quincy," he wrote later. "I admired his abolitionist principles, although I wasn't crazy about his campaign to exclude Texas from the Union.") Card considered George H. W. Bush his hero and held

324

James A. Baker III and Barbara Bush in equally high esteem.

The newly anointed chief had thought long and hard about what he wanted to tell George W. before he took the oath of office. Card was known for his meandering anecdotes; Bush, famously impatient, nicknamed him "Tangent Man." But Card—a close friend of the Bush family for almost a quarter century, who had served as deputy chief during George H. W.'s administration—had a story he thought the new president needed to hear. "I told him about watching his dad, as president of the United States, make the very difficult decision to send young men into harm's way," he recalls. "I remember watching as the first President Bush made the decision to send troops into Panama to bring Manuel Noriega to justice. There was a meeting in the Oval Office. And I was bringing in an easel, to put these maps and photographs up, and I remember Secretary of State James A. Baker III, after the presentation, turned to President Bush and said, 'Mr. President, this is your decision. It's not our decision. It's your decision. And I'm going to leave you to your decision.' And he turned and walked out of the room and everybody left with him."

Card was suddenly alone with George H. W. Bush. "And the president was left with a great burden. He went behind his desk, sat down in the chair, and I was folding up the easel when I watched the president fold his hands. I honestly believe that he was praying. And he looked right at me, but the truth is he was looking through me. And he said, 'I'm making a decision that will cost young men their lives.' And he got up from the chair and he walked out the door to the Rose Garden. I folded up the easel, walked out of the Oval Office, and I was shaking."

Card was deeply moved by the way Bush Sr. approached his solemn duty. "I told George W. Bush that story so that he would understand the context in which his father made very difficult decisions," he says. But he could not tell how much attention the younger Bush was paying; the president-elect seemed focused on the next day's inaugural address. "I think he appreciated it," says Card. "I'm sure he got tired of listening to me after a while." Then he adds: "Little did I know that President George W. Bush would be a wartime president."

George Walker Bush's presidency would be transformed on September 11, 2001, when terrorists attacked the World Trade Center and the Pentagon. In the aftermath, Bush and his advisers would rally a wounded nation; launch a daring invasion of Afghanistan, routing al-Qaeda and its host, the Taliban; set up a sweeping new national security infrastructure; and rewrite the rules of surveillance, detention, and interrogation. But in the end, George W. Bush's legacy would be defined by his decision, made with Card at his side, to invade and occupy Iraq.

Andrew Card Jr., who was raised in Brockton, Massachusetts, brought the earnest, wide-eyed enthusiasm of a former Boy Scout to government service. After stints as a state representative and losing candidate for Massachusetts governor, he joined George H. W. Bush's 1980 presidential campaign and eight years later served as his deputy chief of staff and secretary of transportation. Like Mack McLarty, he seemed not to have an enemy in the world. On visits to his father's White House, George W. would often wind up in Card's office, his cowboy boots on Andy's desk, kicking back and shooting the breeze; and it was Card, of course, who successfully completed W's failed mission to persuade his father's chief of staff, John Sununu, to resign.

Card was organized and efficient, and he knew the workings of the White House. So in 2000, as George W. Bush eyed the Republican presidential nomination, Card was asked to run the convention in Philadelphia. Upon arriving for a walk-through, Bush had talked about his plans for the presidency, were he to be elected, and told Card cryptically: "Keep your dance card clear." Later, Bush asked Card to meet him in Florida; but first, he told him to drop in on his parents in Houston. Card had done so—but he found the visit very odd. "They were asking me to take good care of their son, and [saying] that I would understand, and they were really glad I would be at his side," Card recalls. He had no idea what they were talking about. "I'm thinking to myself, 'It doesn't sound like a transition, it sounds like something else.'"

The Thursday before the election, Card finally met with Bush over breakfast in Tampa. "'If you want me to do the transition, I'd be glad to do it,'" Card remembers saying. "I'm not talking about the transition," Bush replied. "I'm talking about the big one." For the first time, Card realized Bush wanted him to be his chief of staff.

Card, who had watched five previous chiefs in action, had a couple of conditions for accepting the job. "'First,'" he told Bush, "'we have to have a very candid relationship. You have to be comfortable with me saying anything to you—and I will be comfortable with you saying anything to me.' The second thing was, 'As long as I'm your chief of staff I can't be your friend.' And then I said, 'If you're looking for more than one chief of staff at the same time, I don't want to be one of them.'"

But first, there was an election to win. On the evening of November 7, Bush and his entourage watched the returns from the Governor's Mansion in Austin, Texas. As the evening wore on, it was clear that the race wouldn't be decided that night. Al Gore, the Democratic nominee, had won the popular vote, but the electoral college hinged on Florida, where the candidates were separated by only a few hundred votes. To take charge of the

battle over the recount, Bush needed to send someone with world-class legal, political, diplomatic,
and communications skills, and the mind-set of a
killer. He chose James Baker.

While the constitutional showdown played out,
Bush and his incoming chief began planning for a
transition they still weren't sure would take place.
"I broke the job down into the care and feeding of
the president; policy formulation; and marketing
and selling," recalls Card. "You have to make sure
that the president is never hungry, angry, lonely, or
tired, and that they're well prepared to make decisions that they never thought they'd have to make.
You have to manage the policy process and make
sure no one is gaming the president. And the last
category is marketing and selling. If the president
makes a decision and nobody knows about it, did
the president make a decision?"

Card continues: "Jim Baker was the role model
and I learned an awful lot from him. I tried to
live up to how he did the job." But the Baker
model could only go so far: Card understood that
George W. Bush—like his father—did not want a
chief who would be perceived as the real power behind the throne, as Baker had been with Reagan.
"I think that Andy probably gave George W. Bush
great comfort that it would be a White House that
was well run," says Peter Baker, author of **Days
of Fire: Bush and Cheney in the White House.**

"And yet Bush did not want a more forceful chief of staff like a John Sununu or a Don Regan. That was clearly something he was trying not to have."

And Card's relationship with Bush was different from Baker's with Reagan. "Andy was pretty close to the president in a way that Baker and Reagan weren't," says Peter Baker. "Bush and Card had a personal relationship. Andy would go biking with him, which is a big deal for Bush. He established a real alter-ego kind of relationship."

And there was one other reason why Andy Card, as chief of staff, would be different from Jim Baker: Dick Cheney.

In the history of the presidency, there had never been a relationship like Bush and Cheney's. For starters, no vice president had ever chosen himself for the position—but that is essentially what Cheney did. He had been leading Bush's personnel search: "I'd walked through this process for a couple of months listening to him describe what he was looking for," recalls Cheney of his talks with Bush about a vice president. "At the end of the process he turned to me and said, 'You're the solution to my problem.' And that's when I knew I had failed as a headhunter." Cheney punctuates his observation with a chuckle.

In Bush's view, Cheney solved several problems: First, he had no presidential ambitions of his own. (Cheney had flirted with running in 1996, but decided against it; he couldn't stand all the fund-raising and glad-handing.) Bush would not have to worry about a vice president with his own political agenda. "Other vice presidencies crater," says Cheney. "And that happens because lots of times the vice president is using it as a stepping-stone for his own campaign; he's worried about how he's going to run in Iowa four years hence. And I didn't carry that baggage."

But Bush was also looking for something else in his VP: someone as seasoned in national security matters as Bush himself was unprepared. "If there was a hole in the operation, it was in national security," says Cheney. "And not only did I work for Ford, but I'd been in Congress, I'd been on the Intelligence Committee, I'd run the Defense Department successfully. I fit the mold of what he was looking for." Although the popular perception of Cheney calling all the shots for Bush was untrue, theirs was an unprecedented sharing of power—almost like the "copresidency" that Ronald Reagan had dangled in front of Gerald Ford at the convention in 1980.

Cheney had always believed that "the chief of staff has more power, if you want to put it in those terms, than the vice president." But that wouldn't be true in George W. Bush's administration. "We had a different kind of arrangement," Cheney admits. "I think it was unique. I don't think it's ever been like that." Cheney would be a primary voice on national security affairs—and many other policy issues. That was the way Bush wanted it. "There was never a contract, and I didn't have to really ask him for anything," says Cheney. "I was going to have the opportunity to get involved in anything I wanted to get involved in."

"Cheney had a big role from the beginning that no previous vice president had," says Peter Baker. "I think Card understood that was the dynamic he was coming into. Cheney had been chief of staff. He knew how to run a White House. So I think he was respectful of Andy Card, but just by dint of his own experience and the force of personality and his strong views, he did in fact play a quasi chief of staff role."

Erskine Bowles watched the Cheney-Card dynamic with amazement. In the Clinton White House, he says, "the vice president was fighting his way in to have **lunch!**" But with Bush, "the decisions flowed through Cheney, and I think Andy was okay with that. He's a really nice guy. But Cheney had the president's ear. Cheney had a ton of power and influence, he had knowledge and experience, he had the total trust of the president, and he was the last guy in the room. In my opinion, Cheney **was** the chief of staff." If so, Cheney was a de facto chief with a difference: He couldn't be fired.

Can the chief of staff do his job when the vice president wields such power? I asked Cheney about that at his house in Jackson Hole, Wyoming, in the spring of 2015. "Yeah, well, I don't think of it as a zero-sum game where there's only so much power," he says. "I think when the two of them are working together, it's more effective. Because Andy's doing X and I'm doing Y. Or Andy's involved in what I'm doing. I liked the way he operated, obviously. Andy and I were good friends. Andy had a good sense for how he wanted to operate. I think Andy saw the wisdom of having me in that job."

Cheney also liked the person he had picked as secretary of defense: Donald Rumsfeld, whose appointment Bush had agreed to despite those old rumors that Rummy had sent Bush's father into exile as CIA director in order to remove him as a VP contender back in 1976. ("Don't forget what he did to your daddy," Jim Baker reportedly reminded the president when he learned of the decision.) But George W. Bush didn't care about those ancient grudges. In fact, he and Cheney had initially planned to give Rumsfeld the job he really wanted: CIA director. But during the transition, Bush hit it off with Clinton's director, George Tenet; and the fact that Tenet had recently named the agency's headquarters after Bush 41 did not hurt the director's chances.

Bush turned to Cheney's old mentor to run the Pentagon. So Rumsfeld, once the youngest defense secretary in history under Ford, would now be the oldest under Bush.

Cheney and Rumsfeld were together again, this time more powerful than ever.

Card at first welcomed the old masters, and valued their advice. "Secretary Rumsfeld treated me very well, appreciating the burden that I carried," he says—though the former chief was not above making Card's life more difficult. "He would say, 'I know you've got a terrible job and, I'm going to make it worse right now.'" Card laughs. "So at least he would telegraph it and give me the heads-up!" And Card says the vice president did not wield his power at his expense. "Cheney understood the job I had, and his office was right next door—and he was terrific at making sure I knew what he was up to. Yes, he had strong opinions and very erudite views on policy, but I was never blindsided by the vice president."

Still, Card had no illusions about Rumsfeld and Cheney. "They knew how to play the game and to participate in the bureaucracies of Washington and the political dynamics of the White House quite well," he says. "So you couldn't pull anything over on them. They knew how to pull strings to manipulate people to do things."

Cheney and Rumsfeld were not the only powerful figures in the White House. Bush's cabinet looked like homecoming week for his father's friends from the Gulf War. Colin Powell, the secretary of state, was regularly named the "most admired" American and had come close to running for president himself. Bush compared him to George Marshall, the iconic secretary of state and architect of the postwar world. Condoleezza Rice, the national security adviser, had been Bush Sr.'s expert on the Soviets. And then there was George W.'s own powerful Texas mafia: Karl Rove, the political director who had engineered his election victory; and Karen Hughes, his communications director and close friend.

Even-keeled and steady-tempered, Card seemed well equipped to juggle all those egos. "The president wanted a guy who could deal with strong personalities like Karen and Karl and Cheney and all the rest of us," says Mary Matalin, Cheney's counselor, "and who could deal with people who wanted to wield power. The more power everybody had, the more effective everybody would be. The Bush model was, 'We're all on the same team and we all need to perform at our highest level.' And he was prescient to choose people who didn't promote their own agendas."

But in truth, not since the Reagan administration had there been such a fractious and contentious national security team, riven by outsized egos, conflicting agendas, and petty bickering. It would become, as Jim Baker once memorably said, another "rat f*ck."

One of the first battles came in early March over global warming. Senator Chuck Hagel wanted to know the president's position on capping carbon emissions, and the Kyoto Protocol, which called on industrialized nations to reduce greenhouse gas emissions by 2012. Cheney drafted a letter for Bush's signature, rejecting both the carbon caps and the Kyoto Protocol. He went directly to Bush and persuaded him to sign it on the spot. The letter made no mention of working with other countries to find alternative solutions. More important, the policy decision had not been cleared with EPA director Christine Todd Whitman—or with Powell. "Condi calls me in the morning and says, 'The vice president wants to answer Chuck Hagel right away,'" recalls Powell. "And I said, 'Why now? We need to take the time to break it to our friends and allies gently.'" Powell said he'd draft some language to soften the letter. "And she called back and said, 'No, that's not working.' I said, 'Well, why not?' 'Well, because it's not working.' I said that I'd be right over."

Powell rushed to his car. "When I got to the White House, I handed the language to Condi and she said, 'Too late. The president signed it. The vice president has already taken it to the Hill.' And I said to the president, 'Mr. President, you're going to pay a big price for this. It didn't need to be done this way, and we know you were going to get out of the Kyoto agreement—but without consulting our friends, without laying the groundwork for it, you're going to pay a price for this.'"

It was a telling instance of the outsized influence of the vice president, and it raised the question: Where was the chief of staff?

Powell would go on to clash with Cheney on multiple fronts. Wrapping up a trip to the Middle East, the secretary of state announced that the United States wanted to convene a conference of foreign ministers to discuss Israeli-Palestinian issues. Cheney was furious and demanded that Bush put Powell on a leash. Similarly, when Powell announced that Bush would "pick up where the Clinton administration left off" on negotiations over North Korea's nuclear capability, Cheney was incensed. No decision had been made, but Powell had evidently used a dirty word—"Clinton."

Powell by no means lost every fight. "Rumsfeld and Cheney and I had disagreements on arms control with the Russians," Powell says. "They didn't want to have a nuclear agreement to reduce nuclear weapons. Guess what? We got a nuclear agreement because the president asked me to do it, and I did it."

But during the first term, Cheney would prevail on the national security issues he cared about. He had a voracious appetite for raw intelligence reports—and indulged it. Early on, the vice president spent hours at CIA headquarters, reading reports and peppering analysts with questions. "I put together a tour," Cheney recalls. "I did virtually the entire intelligence community. I did CIA and NSA and DIA [Defense Intelligence Agency]— and went through the whole schmear. And I loved doing it. It was always an interest of mine anyway, and now this was nirvana." Cheney received the Presidential Daily Brief (PDB) every morning before Bush did, as well as extra raw intelligence "behind the tab." He played referee in disagreements between the agencies. "Sometimes he would insert himself," says Card, "not to change an analysis, but to challenge it." But Card admits that Cheney's intrusion in intelligence matters could cause friction. "I did see some, I wouldn't call it manipulation, but I did see some heavy-handed questions or challenges being raised," he says. "And so that was a source of frustration. I would hear the grumblings within the National Security Council staff."

Powell believed that Cheney was out of bounds. "This was an odd White House arrangement, where the vice president was right in the middle of it all and he would see everything that was going to the president and he was instrumental in monitoring the national security staff," he says. In Powell's view, it was a direct challenge to Card's role as honest broker, and to Rice's authority as head of the NSC. Such intrusions, he says, would have been unfathomable in Reagan's White House (or H. W.'s): "It's not the system that I grew up in. It's not the way I ran the National Security Council. It's not the way I dealt with Ken Duberstein, who was the chief. We all were one team."

Meanwhile, Islamic terrorism was on the rise, and the Bush White House seemed to be looking the other way. In the spring of 2001, alarmed by growing threats against American interests by al-Qaeda, CIA director George Tenet proposed an aggressive plan to destroy the terror group in its homeland. The plan, he said, called for "launching a paramilitary operation, getting into the Afghan sanctuary, creating a bridge with Uzbekistan. We knew exactly what to do. We were ready to do it." But the CIA plan was rejected. "The word back was, 'We're not quite ready to consider this. We don't want the clock to start ticking.'" Tenet says the Bush White House was focused elsewhere. "Because of other agendas, there was not a will to take this final action."

Cheney says he doesn't recall the CIA proposal. "I would think I would have been aware, if they were really pushing that hard," he says. "I was at that point up to my eyeballs trying to get reacquainted with the whole situation, and not focused just on al-Qaeda by any means." And he downplays the quality of the intelligence he was provided. "We did know about bin Laden. The kind of information we would get, it wasn't anything you could act on. Just there's a threat out there—yeah, there's a threat out there."

But the warnings about al-Qaeda would reach an alarming crescendo on July 10, 2001. That morning, at CIA headquarters, the head of the al-Qaeda unit, Richard Blee, burst into the office of Cofer Black, the counterterrorism chief. "The sky's falling," he said. The CIA had reports of imminent threats against American interests—they were multiple-sourced and credible. Director Tenet picked up the phone and called the White House. "I said, 'Condi, I have to come see you. We're comin' to the White House **now**.'" The CIA team briefed Rice on the gathering threat: "There will be significant terrorist attacks against the United States in the coming weeks or months. The attacks will be spectacular. They may be multiple. They could be in the U.S. Al Qaeda's intention is the destruction of the United States." Finally, Black slammed his fist on the table. "We need to go on a war footing **now**!" he said.

The CIA's warning was met mostly with blank stares. Rice later wrote that her memory of the meeting was "not very crisp." The president was traveling in Boston that day, and Cheney does not remember hearing about the CIA alarms. "I do not recall George coming in with his hair on fire saying, 'They're coming! They're coming! They're coming!'" he says. Card, too, insists the nature of the al-Qaeda threat was vague. "The mind-set of the people that I knew, even in the intelligence world, didn't really think of planes as weapons of mass destruction," he says. "So even if we had been told that's what it would be, it would have been very hard to anticipate what kind of reaction we should have. Do you say no one should fly?"

Black, the former CIA counterterrorism chief, believes the Bush White House simply couldn't grasp the nature of the al-Qaeda threat. "I think they were stuck back somewhere when they were last in power," he says. "You know, they thought terrorists were Euro lefties who drink champagne by night, blow stuff up during the day. It's almost incomprehensible to me how you could warn senior people so many times, and nothing actually happens."

A few months later, of course, the threat from al-Qaeda would become terrifyingly concrete— and Andy Card would find himself in a situation he'd never bargained for.

"I WANTED TO be the opposite of **Cheers**, that bar from the television show, where you walked in and they said, 'Everybody knows your name,'" says Card. "I wanted to be the chief of staff where **nobody** knew my name. But that all changed on September eleventh, 2001."

Early that morning, Bush had gone for a run in Sarasota, Florida; Card remembers the stench of rotting fish from a red tide. As they arrived for an education event at Emma Booker Elementary School, a national security aide brought Card a baffling report: A small plane had crashed into one of the World Trade Center towers, she said. Card told the president, who asked to be kept updated— and then strode into the classroom full of second graders.

Card continues: "And then a nanosecond later, that same person came to me and said, 'Oh, my gosh. Another plane hit the other tower at the World Trade Center.' I stood at the door and my first thought was actually, 'UBL.' Usama bin Laden. That's what we called him."

He goes on: "I knew I faced a test that chiefs of staff have to perform: Does the president need to know? Yes. And I made a decision that I would pass on two facts and make one editorial comment, and that I would do nothing to invite a question or start a dialogue." Card walked up to the president, leaned over, and whispered into his right ear, "'A second plane hit the second tower. America is under attack.'"

Bush responded with a look of bafflement, then sat motionless for almost seven minutes. His apparent paralysis was later skewered by Michael Moore in his documentary **Fahrenheit 9/11**. But Card says he was pleased the president stayed put. "First of all, he did nothing to introduce fear to those very young students," he explains. "Second, he did nothing to demonstrate fear to the media that would have translated to the satisfaction of terrorists all over the world. But also it gave me time to say, 'Get the FBI director on the phone. Get a line open to the vice president. Get a line open to the Situation Room.' To the crew of **Air Force One**: 'Get back on **Air Force One**.' And to the Secret Service: 'Turn the motorcade around.'"

When he emerged from the classroom into a makeshift crisis center, Bush consulted by phone with Cheney and his FBI director. Then, clearly shaken, he delivered a hastily drafted statement for the television cameras, vowing to "hunt down and to find those folks who committed this act." He finished with the same phrase his father used to draw a line in the sand after Iraq's invasion of Kuwait: "Terrorism against our nation **will not stand**."

The motorcade raced to the airport, where heavily armed Special Forces skirted the tarmac and the engines of **Air Force One** were already spinning. As the presidential plane took off, Card faced his first real test as chief of staff. Bush was hell-bent on returning to Washington, D.C. But Card knew that was a presidential order he would have to defy. "President Bush was adamant. He even used terms like 'I am the president of the United States,'" Card recalls. "I was trying to be cool, calm, and objective. I had the Secret Service very firm with me. I had the president of the United States very firm with me." Bush was in Card's face, furious, screaming at his chief. Card gently pushed back. "I just said, 'Mr. President. I really can't recommend that. We have to know more about the nature of the attacks and if others are coming.'"

Bush finally acquiesced to a detour, agreeing to head for Barksdale Air Force Base in Louisiana; so began the daylong odyssey that would take the president, Card, and their entourage to Offutt Air Force Base in Nebraska. They finally returned to the capital that evening. "As we're coming in to land at Andrews Air Force Base," Card recalls, "we're all looking out the windows, and you could see the faces of the pilots of the fighter jets that were accompanying **Air Force One**. And then you could see the smoke billowing out of the Pentagon, and I remember the president saying to me, 'That's the face of war in the twenty-first century.'"

At the White House, Cheney, Rice, Matalin, Deputy Chief Joshua Bolten, and others had rushed to the bunker below the East Wing, the Presidential Emergency Operations Center (PEOC). Cheney practically had to be lifted out of his chair by a Secret Service agent when the word came to scramble. But in the PEOC, Cheney was calm and deliberate as he took charge and issued orders—and confronted the urgent question of whether fighter pilots should shoot down commercial airliners, if necessary. In a phone call, Cheney and Bush had agreed to authorize that extreme measure; so when a plane was spotted heading toward the White House, Cheney gave the go-ahead. A few minutes later, at Bolten's suggestion, the vice president called Bush and informed him of the order he had just given. The incoming plane turned out to be a false alarm.

Even after Bush returned to Washington, Cheney remained at the forefront of what would become the war on terror. "We pushed the limits, no question about it," he says. "But we did it very carefully. The week after 9/11, the first few days, Tenet and Michael Hayden came to see me, heads of CIA and NSA. I asked them, 'Could you guys do more than you're doing if you had more authority?' And they said, 'Yes, we could.' And so I went to the president and we had a proposal that he signed off on. And that was expanding the reach of NSA and going beyond anything we'd done before." Two and a half years later, the legality of the warrantless surveillance program—the best-kept secret of Bush's war on terror—would come under attack from his own Justice Department; James Comey, the acting attorney general at the time, threatened to resign unless the president dialed back some of its provisions. Bush backed down and agreed to modify the Internet surveillance part of the program.

Cheney continues: "When we got into enhanced interrogation, same thing. We had a handful of people who could tell us what we needed to know about al-Qaeda, and we weren't going to get it by using just the U.S. Army manual. They are able to take the guy and send him to a black site if we've set it up some place, which we had. Because they're more sophisticated and better equipped at interrogation than the guy who can read the U.S. Army manual and say 'Please, please, pretty please, tell us what you know.' They had a different mind-set, a different way of operating. And I was a great believer."

In the new wartime White House, there were fears of a second wave of attacks, perhaps even a nuclear bomb planted in Washington or New York City. To Bush, Cheney, and CIA director Tenet, the country was in crisis mode, and that required extraordinary measures. And if they didn't always consult with cabinet members before 9/11, they were hardly dotting every "i" and crossing every "t" in its aftermath.

Once again, Powell was incensed. "We did not have a full discussion of circumstances under which the Geneva Convention should apply and we did not have a full discussion on the use of military commissions," he says. "That was decided, and the decision was handed down. It was running directly to the president from the vice president and with advice from his counsel and from the Justice Department. When I heard about it, I said, 'They're in for a shock!' They think they're going to get a kangaroo court of military officers who will hammer anyone that goes before them. They do not understand the military ethic." In fact, Powell points out, military tribunals are just as respectful of defendants' rights, and just as time-consuming, as civilian courts.

Cheney was unapologetic. On **Meet the Press**, the vice president told Tim Russert that the

United States would have to go to "the dark side" if it wanted to best al-Qaeda. "I said, 'We've got to spend time in the shadows in the intelligence world. A lot of what needs to be done here will have to be done quietly, without any discussion, using sources and methods that are available to our intelligence agencies.'" It wasn't long before the architect of the war on terror was being portrayed as Darth Vader. Jon Stewart put on the **Star Wars** villain's helmet to address Cheney as a "kindred spirit" on **The Daily Show**.

Friends, too, noticed a change in Cheney. Brent Scowcroft, his colleague from the Gulf War, had been talking with him constantly since the transition. "In the first six months of the 'W' administration, I was just fine with Cheney," he recalls. "But after 9/11 he just really turned. I think something **really, really happened** to Dick Cheney. A good guy before, low-key, made things work, but not in a big pompous way—and then he just went way, way . . ." Scowcroft's voice trails off. "I don't know whether it was 9/11 that did something to him, or if he's an example of what a bad heart does to people."

"He was different," says Colin Powell. "He had become far more conservative with respect to his views. He was not as appreciative of diplomatic efforts." Bob Schieffer, the CBS correspondent, agrees. "He changed. And he admitted he changed. I went and asked him one time, and he said, 'Well, it's the job—and it's 9/11.'" Schieffer, too, thought Cheney's heart problems might have had something to do with the vice president's dark new outlook.

"I don't think of it as though I changed," says Cheney, almost fifteen years later, at home in Wyoming. "I think of it as this is a different set of problems than we'd had before. I mean, it just was a different era. And what had happened between Desert Storm and 9/11 was we'd had an attack on the United States, and the loss of three thousand lives. We only lost twenty-four hundred in Pearl Harbor. So if we hadn't treated that differently—as a war, not a law enforcement problem—we'd have been derelict in our duties. And to all my friends out there saying Cheney changed, I say, you weren't in the bunker on 9/11."

Cheney loses no sleep over accusations that he overstepped his authority. "The **New York Times** editorialized that I should be prosecuted as a war criminal," he says, arching an eyebrow. "But we had our ducks in a row, did it exactly the right way, and we pushed the envelope as far as we could in order to do what we needed to do. And it worked." While both the legality and effectiveness of enhanced interrogation and NSA surveillance are still a subject of fierce debate, it is true that no more terrorist attacks on the homeland occurred on Bush's watch.

. . .

FOUR DAYS AFTER September 11, Bush convened a meeting of his war cabinet at Camp David to plan a response to the attacks. Cheney, Rumsfeld, Powell, Tenet, Card, and others were briefed by intelligence and military officials and discussed their options. "We had to take military action against those that had done this to us," says Powell, "and it was in Afghanistan that we had to take the action."

But not everyone agreed that Afghanistan should be the target. Out of the blue, Paul Wolfowitz, Rumsfeld's deputy, posed the question: "Shouldn't we go after Iraq? Isn't Iraq a part of this?"

"Iraq had always been in the background before 9/11," says Powell. "It's not as if we ignored Iraq. But there was no intention of doing anything at that point because it wasn't a major crisis for us." Still, Iraq was a preoccupation for some members of Bush's national security team, particularly Wolfowitz.

Wolfowitz "raised that issue frequently during the day," recalls Powell. "And then after lunch, the president said, 'Well, let's see what you all are thinking.' And we went around the table. The consensus was for Afghanistan. The president realized there was no connection to 9/11 with Iraq at this point. No one's given us the intelligence to suggest that." Powell couldn't fathom the detour

Wolfowitz was advocating. "To take that cause cé-lèbre [Afghanistan] and convert it into a reason to go after Iraq made absolutely no sense to me."

On October 7, 2001, the Bush administration launched Operation Enduring Freedom, a CIA-led paramilitary invasion of Afghanistan; in just over nine weeks, U.S. Special Forces routed the Taliban and decimated al-Qaeda. Despite Osama bin Laden's escape at a mountain redoubt called Tora Bora, it was a spectacular victory, achieved with worldwide goodwill. But the CIA's triumph would be followed by one of its darkest chapters.

During the early days of his presidency, Bush had said little about Iraq; there was no public appetite for war, and he had done nothing to make a case for it. But the attacks of 9/11 had changed the equation. Bush had ignored Wolfowitz at Camp David—but in late September, even as the invasion of Afghanistan was under way, he asked Rumsfeld to stay behind after a national security meeting. They were alone in the Oval Office. "I want you to develop a plan to invade Iraq," Bush said. "Do it outside the normal channels. Do it creatively so we don't have to take so much over." Rumsfeld agreed to come up with a plan.

For Bush and his mentor Cheney, it had become an article of faith: after 9/11 it was unacceptable to leave in power an enemy of the United States who might have chemical, biological, or even possibly nuclear weapons.

In the fall of 2002, the CIA issued a National Intelligence Estimate: "Iraq's Continuing Programs for Weapons of Mass Destruction." The administration touted it as evidence that Saddam Hussein was producing chemical and biological weapons and acquiring components for nuclear weapons. According to the estimate, Iraq had acquired uranium "yellowcake" from Niger—a claim that had been debunked internally by the CIA a year earlier, but that Bush would go on to repeat.

The evidence linking Saddam to al-Qaeda was similarly shaky. In making the case against the dictator, the vice president spoke of a link between the plotters of 9/11 and Iraq: an alleged meeting between one of the hijackers and a top Iraqi intelligence official. But CIA director Tenet insists that a grainy photograph of the "meeting" had been discredited. "There were a number of instances where he [Cheney] made speeches where he was going much further than anything that we would ever say," says Tenet. "And I remember once going to the president and saying, 'Look, this has gotta stop. We just can't support this language.'"

But whatever his mix of motivations—strategic, political, personal, psychological—Bush was moving toward war. Card says Saddam got under the president's skin. "President Bush was offended when Saddam Hussein said to the families of suicide bombers, 'We are going to reward you. We'll pay your family two thousand dollars if a member of your family is a suicide bomber.' That was a statement in and of itself at a time when the world was saying we cannot allow terrorism to stand."

For Bush, targeting Saddam was also personal. In 1993, when his father, the ex-president, was on a visit to Kuwait, the Iraqi dictator sent a hit squad in a failed attempt to assassinate him. "Bush said on a couple of occasions that, you know, he tried to kill my daddy," says Peter Baker. "He obviously had a thing about Saddam Hussein from the beginning and wanted at the very least to undercut him, if not find a way to take him out." Wolfowitz and his allies had already drawn a target on the Iraqi dictator's back. "There's no question those guys were very focused on Saddam Hussein long before 9/11," says Baker. "And that they were focused on regime change. They signed on to that as a policy."

As plans for the war began to solidify, Colin Powell was disturbed; it seemed to him that diplomacy had been abandoned. "I said to the president, 'You know, I really need to have a private conversation with you.'"

On August 5, 2002, Powell met with George W. Bush and Condi Rice upstairs in the White House residence. "I said, 'I want to make sure you understand some of the consequences of this,'" Powell told the president. "'Once you take out a regime, you become governor. You're in charge. If you break it, you're the one that's got to put it back together. And if you are going to have to do military action, you need to gather support for that, and identify those who will not support you. So if you're thinking about this, you have to take into consideration a lot of issues besides just the military plan.' And the president said, 'What do you recommend we do?' I said, 'I recommend that we take it to the United Nations. That not only gives you United Nations authority, but it also shows you've made an effort to avoid war.'" Before invading, Bush promised Powell he would go to the UN for a resolution authorizing force.

That wasn't enough for Brent Scowcroft. No one was more respected for geopolitical expertise, or for impeccable judgment, than Bush Sr.'s former national security adviser. Back in the Gulf War days, Cheney had described his colleague to George H. W. Bush: "Scowcroft gets it right. He's absolutely totally loyal to you. He doesn't have any ego. He's an honest broker for all the rest of us to deal with."

In May of 2014, I spoke with Scowcroft in his Washington, D.C., office, surrounded by stacks of books on geopolitics. Eighty-nine years old, the elder statesman of Republican foreign policy, still razor-sharp, speaks softly but with conviction.

To Scowcroft, nothing about the argument for war added up. "They were making the case that simply couldn't be made—because it was just counterfactual," he says. "And that's what gave me the clue. They said that Saddam was working with al-Qaeda. And I thought, not reasonable. Saddam Hussein was a radical, not a conservative. In fact, he wasn't religious at all. And the notion that [al-Qaeda and the Iraqis] had this meeting was just not . . ." He shakes his head, incredulous. "And the part about uranium yellowcake in Africa and so on. I knew that whole story." Scowcroft wasn't buying any of it.

On August 15, 2002, he published an op-ed in the **Wall Street Journal**. Headlined "Don't Attack Saddam," it argued, in the language of realpolitik, that invading Iraq would invite disaster:

> The United States could certainly defeat the Iraqi military and destroy Saddam's regime. But it would not be a cakewalk. On the contrary, it undoubtedly would be very expensive—with serious consequences for the U.S. and global economy—and could as well be bloody . . . a military campaign very likely would have to be followed by a large-scale, longterm military occupation.

Scowcroft's dissection of the Iraq war plan caused a sensation. Many in government and the media assumed he was serving as a proxy for the president's father; he and 41 were, after all, as close as brothers. But Bush Sr. maintained his silence, and Scowcroft insisted, at least in public, that he spoke only for himself.

George W. Bush was furious: He told Rice, Scowcroft's former protégée, to call him at home. "Condi said, 'Why did you do that? Why didn't you come and talk to us?'" recalls Scowcroft. "And I said, 'Condi, I tried and there was nobody to talk to.'" Scowcroft was suddenly persona non grata with George W. "That's how I went off the rails with 43," he says. "Because I said 'Don't do that. You don't need to. It's the wrong thing to do.'" Scowcroft and Cheney, once close friends, would not speak again for years.

I asked Scowcroft: Do you think George H. W. Bush agreed with your view in the **Wall Street Journal**? "Never talked to him about it," he replies. He pauses, then adds: "But, yes, I do." When Scowcroft sent his op-ed to the paper, he simultaneously sent a copy to Bush Sr. "I always kept him abreast of what I was doing when it involved 43," he says. Scowcroft got no response—which he took to mean that Bush Sr. agreed with him.

In his memoir, George W. insists: "Some in Washington speculated that Brent's op-ed was Dad's way of sending me a message on Iraq. That was ridiculous. Of all people, Dad understood the stakes. If he thought I was handling Iraq wrong, he damn sure would have told me himself."

But Scowcroft says, of his close friend Bush Sr.:

"I was doing what he would have done if it hadn't been his son."

"You were saying what he couldn't afford to say?"

"I think so. Yeah, yeah."

"If you're right—that Bush Sr. disagreed with his son's policy on Iraq—how much do you think that troubled him?"

"I think it troubled him a lot. I think he was loyal to his son. He said, 'I've had my time, he has his time.' But I don't think he agreed with him."

"It's one of the great mysteries—like trying to figure out the Clinton marriage," says Peter Baker. More than a dozen years later, Bush Sr. told biographer Jon Meacham that his son was badly served by his "iron-ass" advisers Cheney and Rumsfeld, but he would not confide his personal view about the war. "Any father would probably prefer to say that the son was led into the wrong place than he chose to go there of his own volition," says Baker.

But the truth was that Bush Sr. was deeply worried about the impending invasion from the start. At his ranch house in Palm Desert, California, in April 2016, I suggested to Stu Spencer, the plain-speaking Republican campaign strategist, that 41 would probably take his view about the war to his grave. "No, it'll get out there," he says. "Because a lot of people knew he was against it. [James] Baker heard it every day he saw him. And other guys who were close to him. They heard it all the time. We **all** felt that way. We thought there was a better way to do it. Jimmy and I, we were all good friends of Cheney's, too."

The sharp divide over the war between Bush 41's inner circle and Cheney erupted during a memorable get-together in the Texas countryside, hosted by James Baker. "We went hunting when Cheney was VP down at Jimmy's ranch," says Spencer. Gathered for a weekend of quail hunting, drinking, and camaraderie were Spencer, Baker, Ohio congressman Rob Portman, and journalist Tom Brokaw. "We all agreed that Cheney was off base with this crap," says Spencer. "So we said, 'Let's stick it to him tonight. You're the lead guy, Spencer!' So we're eatin' dove and we're drinkin' and I said, 'Hey, Richard, what's all this **bullshit** about [yellow] cake and blah, blah, blah?' I'm all over him. And God, he got mad. Right back at me. And then Baker jumps on top of him. And poor Portman is sitting there like this." Spencer mimics a wide-eyed spectator, watching a Ping-Pong game. "This guy's talking to **the vice president** like that? And Dick was very touchy about it."

Ten days after Scowcroft fired his shot across W's bow, James Baker published his own op-ed in the **New York Times**. His was a more nuanced argument about the impending war, advocating that Bush seek a UN resolution before invading. But in May of 2016, Baker told me he agreed with Scowcroft's darker view, and so did George H. W. Bush. "The president and I both did," he says. "Where we were was, you better understand this is not going to be like Desert Storm. This is not gonna be like Gulf I. You're talking about invading their homeland. You're talking about doing all this stuff, and if you're gonna do it, you'd better be prepared for the consequences."

Baker continues: "I will tell you this: 41 and I were both very anxious about this deal. And we were both anxious about the way in 43's administration the secretary of state was not on the same page with the vice president or the rest of the administration; that was a matter of some concern to us. And I remember flying from Kennebunkport with 41, and we were talking about it. And he was concerned about it."

More than a year earlier, Baker and Bush 41 had been so alarmed by the way Colin Powell was being undercut in Bush 43's administration that Baker privately urged W's secretary of state to fall on his sword: "I said, 'Colin, you need to go in and say to the president, "This is not what I signed on for." And let him know that if you're not going to be his primary adviser in devising and implementing his foreign policy, that's not what you signed on for.'" But Powell would not threaten to resign. "He wouldn't do it," says Baker. "He never did it."

Colin Powell was not happy when I relayed Baker's version of events. "I don't recall that conversation," he says. "If Jim says he said it, I wouldn't deny it. But I don't ever recall anything as stark as that."

Chief of Staff Thomas F. "Mack" McLarty (hand on Clinton's back), Bill Clinton, and a gaggle of White House officials. Early in his presidency, meetings were disorganized, standing-room-only affairs: "Every Tom, Dick, and Harry" was there, complained Leon Panetta. *Photo by Robert McNeely, Courtesy William J. Clinton Presidential Library*

McLarty in the Oval Office. *Photo by Robert McNeely, Courtesy William J. Clinton Presidential Library*

Clinton's second chief, Leon Panetta, was reluctant to take the job. He accepted only after being flown to Camp David, where he was persuaded by the president, Hillary Clinton, and Vice President Al Gore and his wife, Tipper. *Photo by Barbara Kinney, Courtesy William J. Clinton Presidential Library*

Gregarious but focused, Panetta brought discipline to the White House—and ruled with "an iron fist inside a velvet glove." *Photo Courtesy William J. Clinton Presidential Library*

President Clinton, Panetta, and Deputy Chief Erskine Bowles.
Photo Courtesy William J. Clinton Presidential Library

As Clinton's third chief, Bowles, a multimillion-aire entrepreneur, brought a brisk and efficient corporate style to running the White House. *Photo by Robert McNeely, Courtesy William J. Clinton Presidential Library*

The president and John Podesta on *Air Force One*. When the Monica Lewinsky scandal broke, his final chief shouted at him, "How could you be so, mmm, stupid!" *Photo Courtesy William J. Clinton Presidential Library*

Just after the House voted to impeach Clinton, the president addressed the nation, with (*left to right*) Podesta, House Minority Leader Richard Gephardt, Vice President Al Gore, and Hillary Clinton. *Photo Courtesy William J. Clinton Presidential Library*

George W. Bush and his chief of staff Andrew Card. Like his father, Bush did not want an empowered chief in the mold of James Baker. *Photo by Eric Draper, Courtesy George W. Bush Presidential Library*

Left to right: Secretary of State Colin Powell, Card, and Vice President Dick Cheney. Powell believed that Cheney's outsized influence hindered the chief of staff's role as an honest broker to the president. *Photo by Eric Draper, Courtesy George W. Bush Presidential Library*

The forty-first and forty-third presidents on George W. Bush's first day in office. As the invasion of Iraq loomed, Bush Sr. had grave doubts about the war but would not confront his son directly. *Photo by Eric Draper, Courtesy George W. Bush Presidential Library*

On September 11, 2001, Card whispered
in the president's ear, "A second plane
hit the second tower. America is under
attack." *Photo Courtesy George W. Bush
Presidential Library*

Vice President Dick Cheney
and Defense Secretary
Donald Rumsfeld. As
Gerald Ford's chiefs,
they had watched the
humiliating U.S. retreat
from South Vietnam.
Thirty years later, they
were the prime architects
of another war that was
ending badly. *Photo by David
Hume Kennerly, Getty Images*

In the Presidential Emergency Operations Center (PEOC) on 9/11, Deputy Chief
Joshua Bolten briefs National Security Adviser Condoleezza Rice and Vice President
Cheney. *Photo by David Bohrer, Courtesy George W. Bush Presidential Library*

President Barack Obama and his first chief of staff, Rahm Emanuel. Underneath the brash, profane persona, Emanuel was a true believer.
Official White House Photo by Pete Souza

Press Secretary Robert Gibbs, Emanuel, and Nancy-Ann DeParle, director of the White House Office of Health Reform. DeParle was a contender to become the first female White House chief of staff. *Official White House Photo by Pete Souza*

The president confers with Bill Daley, his second chief of staff. Daley, who replaced Emanuel when he left to run for mayor of Chicago, was an awkward fit among Obama's staff, and departed after a year.
Official White House Photo by Pete Souza

Jack Lew and the president on a trip to Mexico. A former OMB director, Obama's third chief left to become secretary of the Treasury. *Official White House Photo by Pete Souza*

Barack Obama with Denis McDonough, his final chief of staff. McDonough, fiercely competitive and loyal, called himself the president's "staff guy." Others said he was so close to Obama they could be brothers. *Official White House Photo by Pete Souza*

The president, Press Secretary Josh Earnest, McDonough, and Counselor to the President John Podesta. In 2014, with his agenda stalled, Obama hired Podesta to help him pursue climate change reform by executive order. *Official White House Photo by Pete Souza*

Every day at five o'clock, Obama and his chief performed "the Wrap," a walk around the South Lawn. (McDonough usually carried a red folder.) It was after just such a walk, on August 30, 2013, that Obama shocked the world with a declaration: He would not unilaterally strike the Syrian regime despite its use of chemical weapons.

Official White House Photo by Pete Souza

In a historic gathering on December 5, 2008, eleven former White House chiefs of staff (and Bush's Joshua Bolten) gave the incoming chief, Rahm Emanuel, their advice. Afterward, they posed in the Roosevelt Room. *Left to right:* (front row) Jack Watson, Donald Rumsfeld, Dick Cheney, Howard Baker Jr.; (back row) Samuel Skinner, Rahm Emanuel, Thomas F. "Mack" McLarty, Leon Panetta, John Sununu, Joshua Bolten, Kenneth Duberstein, John Podesta, Andrew Card.

Photo by Eric Draper, Courtesy George W. Bush Library

He pauses. "Jim may have said that, but to say I should have resigned, or I should have said . . ." He lets the sentence hang. "I gave the president my best advice on the fifth of August, 2002, and then later that month, when the president accepted my recommendation that he take the issue to the UN. We discussed this with the other members of the team, Cheney and Rumsfeld. They weren't happy about it. But they saw the wisdom of doing it, and so they all agreed to my recommendation to take the issue to the United Nations."

Powell continues: "I got a resolution unanimously from the Security Council, which put demands on Saddam Hussein to turn over all the information about his weapons of mass destruction. He was given a get-out-of-jail card. He did not take that card. And then by the middle of January, the president pretty much decided that conflict was necessary to rid us of Saddam Hussein and also to make sure there were not weapons of mass destruction. The intelligence community, sixteen agencies strong, told us that there were weapons of mass destruction. Every member of the Congress, including Mrs. Clinton, Senator Kerry, and a total of 376 members of Congress, all agreed that this was unacceptable and they voted for conflict, should that become necessary, and Saddam Hussein had not met the UN test. And so that's where we were at the beginning of January, when the president said, 'No good. We're going to continue down a path to get rid of him and weapons of mass destruction if they exist,' and we thought they did. And at that point, once he made his decision, I fully supported that decision."

Powell's anger suddenly boils over. "I'm tired of this shit! If that's what Jim said, then Jim didn't understand everything I was doing in that period and didn't understand how it [came] out. I tried to help the president. I gave him my recommendations. He followed my recommendations. We got the UN resolution. We did everything before going to war."

It was a war that, for all his efforts to give diplomacy a chance, Powell had signed on for. On February 5, 2003, the secretary of state stood before the United Nations Security Council and delivered the administration's case for war in a pivotal speech vetted by CIA director George Tenet. Despite Powell's efforts to challenge the CIA's data, the speech would become infamous for its dubious, and downright false, intelligence. "We have first-hand descriptions of biological weapons factories on wheels and on rails," Powell declared. "[Saddam] has the ability to dispense these lethal poisons and diseases in ways that can cause massive death and destruction." But the startling claim turned out to be based on a source known as "Curveball"— who some in the CIA knew was unreliable. George Tenet later admitted: "We let Powell down."

On March 19, 2003, George W. Bush ordered the invasion of Iraq. Then, as he wrote in his memoir, he took "a slow, silent lap around the South Lawn. I prayed for our troops, for the safety of the country, and for strength in the days ahead . . . there was one man who understood what I was feeling. I sat down at my desk in the Treaty Room and scrawled out a letter":

Dear Dad,

At around 9:30 am, I gave the order to SecDef to execute the war plan for Operation Iraqi Freedom. In spite of the fact that I had decided a few months ago to use force, if need be, to liberate Iraq and rid the country of WMD, the decision was an emotional one. . . .

I know I have taken the right action and do pray few will lose life. Iraq will be free, the world will be safer. The emotion of the moment has passed and now I wait word on the covert action that is taking place.

I know what you went through.

Love,
George

At that moment, whatever his private doubts, George H. W. Bush pushed them aside. A few hours later, he faxed a reply.

Dear George,

Your handwritten note, just received, touched my heart. You are doing the right thing. Your decision, just made, is the toughest decision you've had to make until now. But you made it with strength and with compassion. It is right to worry about the loss of innocent life be it Iraqi or American. But you have done that which you had to do. . . .

Devotedly,
Dad

The next day, "Operation Iraqi Freedom" began with a thunderous barrage of aerial bombardment, melodramatically dubbed "shock and awe" by the Pentagon. It was followed by a swift assault by coalition forces. Within days, the Iraqi army was routed; in Baghdad, an enormous iron statue of Saddam was toppled, symbolizing victory.

Removing Saddam's regime would be the easy part. What followed was a steady spiral downward into anarchy, chaos, and bloodshed. Rumsfeld, who during the Vietnam War had insisted on telling the truth about the U.S. Marines left behind during Saigon's final hours, stretched credulity during his frequent televised briefings, swatting at critics ("You go to war with the army you have") and shrugging off mayhem and the looting of national treasures: "Stuff happens!"

Card was more candid about the administration's blunders. "I would like to have had greater recognition of how hard it is to win the peace after you've won the hard part of a battle," he says. "First of all, there was intelligence that some of the Iraqi troops would wave the white flag and they would fall in behind the coalition forces and help direct traffic and meet the needs of the Military Police. But the white flags were never waved."

He continues: "There was also intelligence that the bureaucrats in Iraq would show up to work and make sure the sewer system worked, or the lights came on, or the traffic lights worked. And the bureaucrats didn't show up—so that intelligence was flawed. That was a great frustration."

Card also believed that American war planners were ignorant about Iraqi society. "There were factions and tribes, and I guess we in America didn't really understand the nature of the tribal community in Iraq to the extent that we should have," he says. "I wish that Lawrence Wright had written his book, **The Looming Tower**, before we went to war in Iraq. And yes, more troops. I wish there had been more troops on the ground. I think that would have made a difference."

The greatest intelligence failure, of course, was the erroneous prediction that Saddam had WMDs in the first place. "I think all of us thought, 'I'm sure they're still out there and I'm sure we'll still find them,'" says Card. "Hindsight is always better than foresight and we're now debating the hindsight."

But even those mistakes paled in comparison to what happened in May of 2003; in an effort to stabilize the country, Bush appointed Paul Bremer, a career ambassador, as head of the coalition authority. At the time the White House was debating what to do about Saddam's ruling Ba'ath Party. On the one hand, the party's ranks included thugs and murderers who needed to be weeded out. On the other, nearly all the people who make society function—bureaucrats, police, teachers, and others—were members; dissolving the party would mean cutting them off. Even worse, unpaid Iraqi soldiers would almost surely join the insurgency and start killing American soldiers.

"And then I remember being surprised," Card says, "when Paul Bremer announced from Baghdad what the policy would be. And that was a big decision. But it hadn't been decided inside the White House yet."

Powell vividly recalls "the horrible day when suddenly Bremer reversed everything that had been agreed to and disbanded the Iraqi army. And then threw out all the Ba'ath Party members, which went down to schoolteachers, nurses, you name it." The secretary of state was stunned and furious. "I immediately called Dr. Rice. 'Condi! Do you know about this?' Her answer was no. 'Did the president know this was going to happen?' The answer was no. I said, 'This is horrible!'"

It was, says Powell, "a catastrophic, catastrophic strategic decision. It was under the assumption that suddenly democracy and happiness would break out everywhere, and instead we got chaos." For being blindsided, Powell blamed not Bremer, but Bremer's superior, Rumsfeld.

"Interesting," says Rumsfeld, when I tell him what Powell said. "I mean, Colin Powell was a member of the National Security Council. He takes part in all our discussions of these things. He knows better, I think." Rumsfeld suppresses a smile. "Bremer obviously had a very long leash. He was on the ground. The president wasn't. Andy Card wasn't. Colin Powell wasn't. I wasn't. He was."

The former secretary of state still sounds incredulous about Bremer's decision, which typified the disconnect between Powell and the rest of Bush's national security team. "Here's the major problem I have, and it illustrates some of the issues we had," says Powell. "We never had a meeting. We never had a meeting that said we want to change the recommendation the president has accepted about keeping it [the Ba'ath Party]. The Pentagon never said, 'Let's have a meeting to discuss this.' It just happened."

The decision-making free-for-all was no way to run a White House, or a war. And yet Card seemed powerless to corral his feuding colleagues. Rumsfeld would never have tolerated such dysfunction as Gerald Ford's chief of staff. But he pleads ignorance about the role Card played for W. Did George W. Bush think he could be his own chief of staff? I ask him.

"I have no idea."

"But you were there. You were in and out of the Oval Office."

"It's a black box if you're not in the White House. You come in and you make your case and you leave. And then Bush goes up in the private quarters with Condi Rice, or out to Camp David with Condi."

Indeed, Dr. Rice was gaining the president's favor as his first term wore on and would eclipse Cheney as Bush's closest confidant in his second term, replacing Powell as secretary of state. Rumsfeld clearly had disdain for Rice—and resented her frequent weekend visits with Bush at Camp David.

I ask Rumsfeld: Didn't Bush also go with **him** to Camp David?

"Well, hell, no—not with **anybody else**! She was part of the family! And then the word would come down: He's decided to do this, that, or the other thing."

Could a more empowered chief of staff have tamped down these rivalries and vendettas? "I think the best answer for that very pressing question—and I think it's a real question—has to come from Andy Card or others who were in the

White House with him," says Powell. "The reality of it all is that there's only one president, and the president found it acceptable, I guess."

WHILE THE OUTCOME in Iraq was still uncertain, Bush was about to confront another vexing challenge at home. In late August 2005, a massive hurricane in the Gulf of Mexico bore down on New Orleans. It overwhelmed the levees, flooding 80 percent of the city, killing nearly thirteen hundred people and displacing hundreds of thousands more. Four days of nationally televised chaos ensued, with state and local authorities bickering—while Bush appeared helpless.

"That was probably the most challenging and frustrating time in the White House," says Card. "Because the public expected the president to be the only leader in the challenge. But the truth is, a governor plays a big role in a disaster relief effort." Ultimately Bush federalized the response, superseding the inept local authorities. But the damage had been done. The human toll was immense. And the political toll was compounded by a tone-deaf photo op of the president peering down from **Air Force One** while flying over the flood zone. The Katrina fiasco "eroded citizens' trust in their government," Bush wrote. "It exacerbated divisions in our society and our politics. And it cast a shadow over the rest of my presidency."

Meanwhile, in Iraq, Bush was learning first-hand what Powell had warned him about: If you break it, you own it. The occupation was much bloodier than anyone expected. Forming a workable government was a nightmare: The Sunni-Shia divide proved impossible to bridge. Not only was the country paralyzed and lacking basic services; a vicious insurgency had taken root. Coalition and Iraqi forces were being killed at an alarming rate. A new and insidious weapon, the IED, or improvised explosive device, made travel on roadways a mortal risk. The chaos would lead to full-scale sectarian war in 2006.

In his book **State of Denial**, Bob Woodward wrote: "Card [was] convinced that Iraq would be compared to Vietnam. And that history would record that no senior administration officials had raised their voices in opposition." Ever loyal to his commander in chief, Card pushes back on that assessment. "I thought the title of Bob Woodward's book should be **State of Resolve**, because it showed that the president had the resolve to follow through," he says.

But Card was troubled by the growing domestic opposition to the war. "I did not see it necessarily as Vietnam, but I could see that the climate in America would be more akin to the climate around Vietnam," he says. "I remember being concerned about how long the war was taking, both in Afghanistan and in Iraq. And I knew that America could become war weary very quickly."

In April 2004, a scandal had fanned the flames of antiwar sentiment. CBS News had broadcast graphic photographs taken at an Iraqi prison known as Abu Ghraib. They showed prisoners subjected to horrific abuses by their American captors: hung naked from the ceiling; hooded and attached to electric wires; menaced by snarling dogs. Though he had not known about the abuses beforehand, Rumsfeld went to Bush and offered his resignation.

Card and Bush had discussed firing Rumsfeld before. He'd become the scowling symbol of a divisive war. But the timing was wrong; they had no good candidate to replace him. And Cheney was vehemently opposed to making his mentor the scapegoat. Bush sent Cheney to tell Rumsfeld that his resignation letter had been rejected. "So I called Rummy and went over and spent about an hour with him and persuaded him that he couldn't leave us, not then," says Cheney. "We needed him too badly." Cheney had repaid the favor his mentor had done for him thirty years earlier, when Rumsfeld persuaded Ford to overlook Cheney's DWIs and hire him as his deputy.

As the 2004 election approached, Colin Powell had worn out his welcome. Bush had never been comfortable with his celebrated general and diplomat; to him, Powell was like the popular, know-it-all older brother who was always telling you what to do. Powell, for his part, insists he never intended to stay for a second term: He was just an old soldier doing a last tour of duty. But in truth he was pushed before he was ready to go. On November 10, Powell received a phone call from the White House. It was Card—who got right to the point. "The president would like to make a change," he told him. Two days later Powell delivered his resignation letter, though he stayed until January 2005. Powell's warnings about Guantánamo, the Geneva Convention, and military commissions had gone unheeded. His UN speech was a cross he would always carry. "I asked myself, 'Did I miss something? Should I have seen something I didn't? Did my instincts fail me?'" he says. "And maybe they did, I don't know. And it's just a burden I bear— and I get asked about it almost every day."

"If people tell you they want to leave the White House, they're probably lying," says Card. "Nobody really wants to leave the White House." But as his first term wound down, Card told the president he, too, was ready to step aside. Bush at first rejected Card's offer to resign. But in March 2006, the president changed his mind. He was hearing complaints about White House dysfunction. Over lunch in early 2006, an old Texas friend had pulled out a pen and a napkin and sketched the way he thought the White House was being run. "It was a tangled mess, with lines of authority crossing and blurred," Bush wrote in his memoir. "He told me that several people had spontaneously used the same unflattering term: It started with 'cluster' and ended with four more letters."

And so in late March, Bush invited Card and his wife to Camp David for the weekend. "My wife and I went up to the bowling alley, and President Bush came up, and I could tell it was not just to chitchat," recalls Card. "He was on a mission. And he said, 'You know, I think it might be time to make a change.' And I said, 'Well, you should feel comfortable about that. You don't have to even say it again. Thank you very much, Mr. President. It's been a great privilege.'"

Card had been in the job almost five years and three months, eclipsing Jim Baker's modern record. "The president knew I needed to go and he knew I needed to go for my own good," he says. "It was an emotional experience for me, but it wasn't necessarily sad. It was the end of a chapter and the president needed to make the change."

As Card's replacement, Bush chose his OMB director, Joshua Bolten. The son of a CIA officer, Bolten was a wonkish number cruncher, but also had a wilder side: An avid motorcycle buff, he had organized "Bikers for Bush" during the campaign. He was the second Jew, after Ken Duberstein, to hold the position; Karl Rove gave him the nickname "Bad Mitzvah." "Fortunately," says Bolten, "it never stuck."

Bolten thought the White House was still in denial about the Iraq War. "I had the feeling that the conflict was going worse than anybody was willing to acknowledge because everybody had been so invested in it," he says. "And I took it as one of my roles as chief of staff to say, 'I am the new guy here—but this looks very bad to me.'"

Bolten continues: "I told the president I thought his apparatus was not serving him as well as it should, because he wasn't being given alternatives. I rarely intervened in national security meetings, but I viewed it as my job as chief of staff to be the one to say, 'Why aren't you giving the president better options? Why aren't you letting him decide, other than having to go along with the military strategy as it's presented to him? The president was elected to make these decisions.' And the product of that work was the surge." In January 2007, a so-called surge of more than twenty thousand additional U.S. troops, commanded by General David Petraeus, succeeded in temporarily rolling back the insurgency, and bringing better security to Baghdad and Al Anbar Province.

But solving the Iraq quagmire would require more than just new strategies. It would require changes in command.

Bolten believed it was time for Rumsfeld to go,

and this time, in November 2006, Bush agreed. Cheney was opposed, but he could not change the president's mind. "In the end obviously it was the president's decision to make," says Cheney. "But he called me and asked me if I wanted to be the one who delivered the news to Don or should Bolten do it, and I said I'd take care of it. So I called Don." Rumsfeld was ready to go and offered no resistance to his old friend. "It was an amicable parting," says Cheney.

Years later, I asked Rumsfeld: "Was the aftermath of the invasion more difficult than you expected?"

"I guess there is no way you can anticipate what will actually happen. Was the degree of the insurgency predictable? I don't know. It wasn't predicted with the certainty that it later was manifested."

"Do you blame yourself for that?"

"Oh, goodness." He pauses to consider that. Then he says: "You know, one always wants things to work out better than they can work out."

A PRESIDENCY THAT had begun with a calamitous crisis, September 11, 2001, would end with another: the worldwide financial crisis that struck in the fall of 2008.

"For me it was a more dramatic moment than 9/11," says Bolten. "Obviously the financial crisis wasn't the personal and human tragedy that 9/11 was, but in terms of pulling the levers of governance, the financial crisis to me was bigger." The bursting of the U.S. housing bubble, a subprime mortgage debacle, and a failure to regulate Wall Street excesses led to disaster in August 2008. A few weeks later, Lehman Brothers, the nation's fourth-largest investment bank, declared bankruptcy. "I thought, 'This is a circumstance in which the actions that this president takes and the people around this table take, the decisions that are made in the next few days, may tell the course of the global economy for decades to come.'" Bolten continues: "The most gut-wrenching decision was in September of 2008, when the economic advisers came into the Roosevelt Room and told the president that the calamity that was over the cliff was as great, and possibly greater, than the Great Depression. And the medicine they were bringing was something that would have been anathema to any Republican president, including this one—which was, 'Go to the Congress and ask them to appropriate nearly a trillion dollars, to hand out to the Wall Street fat cats and banks that caused the problem in the first place.'"

Bush took the medicine, though it went against everything he believed. On October 3, 2008, he signed into law the Emergency Economic Stabilization Act, which authorized TARP (Troubled Asset Relief Program), allowing for $700 billion of toxic assets to be bought from financial institutions. "He said, 'Let's go for it,'" says Bolten. "And as shocking a decision as he had just made, he went around after that meeting and physically touched some of the key players, and I saw him giving them reassurance, saying, 'We're doing the right thing. We'll get through this.'" Bush's calm handling of the financial meltdown, with help from Bolten and his economic team, helped to avert catastrophe.

It was a considerable achievement, and George W. Bush could take credit for others on his watch: routing the Taliban in Afghanistan; decimating al-Qaeda in its lair; preventing another attack on the U.S. homeland; investing billions of dollars in the fight against AIDS in Africa. Unlike his father, he had the satisfaction of being reelected to a second term.

But in the end, the Iraq War would define Bush's place in history, just as the Gulf War had defined his father's. The son's war, Operation Iraqi Freedom, cost the lives of 4,491 Americans and hundreds of thousands of Iraqis; it left approximately 32,000 Americans wounded.

"You can say the chief should have been more powerful," says Powell, "Condi should have done it differently, Colin should have marched in and done this, Rumsfeld should have done whatever it is Rumsfeld should do. But the president was the president. And as he liked to say, he was the decider."

Why George W. Bush chose to launch an ill-fated war that would turn much of the world against America remains something of a mystery. CIA director Tenet argues that the decision to go to war is more complicated than one intelligence report. "Countries don't go to war just because of National Intelligence Estimates," he says. "Countries go to war because of geopolitical reasons, policy considerations, their own view of the world at the time. In this instance, perhaps: how to remake the Middle East. Policymakers need to be a little bit more forthcoming about what their own motivations were."

Brent Scowcroft believes the true motivations had little to do with WMDs. "After 9/11, I think they said, 'Look, this is a nasty world, we're the only superpower and while we've got that unprecedented power, we ought to use it to remake the world. And we're in this mess. Why don't we take this little jerk of a dictator, kick him out, make Iraq a democracy, it'll spread to the region, and we will have done something for the world.'" Colin Powell offers a view remarkably similar to Scowcroft's. "They had this thinking—I'll call it that, nothing more—that if only we could make a democracy out of Iraq, the whole Middle East would change. I have no idea how they came to that conclusion."

The Iraq War would indeed remake the Middle East—but not in the way Bush and his advisers intended. Amid the bloodshed and instability, the occupation also spawned al-Qaeda in Iraq. That terrorist group would in turn give birth to a much deadlier menace, a scourge to the region and the world: ISIS.

"I wanted the wars that were part of the war on terror to be conducted according to the president's expectation," says Card. "And that was a hard thing, because his expectations were always noble and expectations are seldom met in a war." Seldom were the expectations greater, and the results more disastrous, than in George W. Bush's Iraq War.

I ask James Baker what Bush 41 thinks about that war today. "I'm not going to characterize it," he says. "But surely that's going to be the test of 43's legacy."

It was a war that would also define an ambitious young senator from Illinois, who was running for president to succeed George Bush. Barack Hussein Obama said he wanted to be president so that he could end the kind of thinking that got America into Iraq. At his side was an intense, driven young aide for whom the war was personal. Denis McDonough, who would become Obama's longest-serving chief, had helped draft the Senate resolution authorizing the Iraq invasion. He'd been haunted by it ever since.

9

"Between Bad and Worse"

Rahm Emanuel, William Daley, Jacob Lew, Denis McDonough, and Barack Obama

I n a Reno, Nevada, hotel room, one month before the 2008 presidential election, Barack Obama had gathered together his closest advisers. With his Republican opponent John McCain sinking in the polls, and victory all but certain, the upstart senator from Illinois wanted to talk not about campaigning, but about governing. Obama could not afford to let anyone think he was measuring the White House drapes, so the meeting was not on his calendar, and the attendees were sworn to secrecy.

The assembled group was a **Who's Who** of the men and women who would follow Obama to the White House: David Axelrod, Valerie Jarrett, David Plouffe, Bill Daley, Peter Rouse. But they weren't the only ones: Also present were Erskine Bowles and John Podesta, who had flown in for the occasion, and on a speakerphone, Leon Panetta—all former chiefs of staff to President Bill Clinton. Now Obama posed the urgent question of his nascent administration: Who should be his White House chief of staff?

Bowles, courtly and owlish in his horn-rimmed glasses, seldom minced words. He spoke up immediately. "Leave your Chicago friends at home," he told Obama sharply. "They will only cause you grief." Jarrett and Axelrod—both Chicagoans— glared at him, evidently taken aback. Daley, son of a legendary Chicago mayor, had to stop himself from laughing out loud. But for Bowles, the pattern was self-evident: "If you look back over history, the people who got most presidents in trouble are their old pals from home," he says. "Look at Carter: Ham Jordan and Bert Lance. Nixon: Haldeman and Ehrlichman. Lyndon Johnson: Bobby Baker. Those people were way above their depth. And all of a sudden they become experts. That's just not good for the guy making the decisions. What you want are great people around you who are strong where you're not."

Next Panetta weighed in. "I said, 'Mr. President, you've got to have a chief of staff who can be your son of a bitch when tough decisions need to be made,'" he recalls. "'You've got to be the good guy. That person has to take the heat for it. And that should not be one of your pals—who might share the same concern that you have about getting rid of somebody.'"

Podesta stressed the interaction of the chief and staff. "These are the people you are going to spend all day with," he said. "These are the people who are going to guide your strategy, who are going to tell you when you're doing something right, tell you when you're doing something wrong. And you've got to have someone who manages that team, who has your respect and their respect. It has to go up and down."

Obama heard them out. Then he asked: Would Panetta or Bowles consider another tour of duty? "Mr. President, been there, done that," said Panetta. Bowles also politely but firmly declined. The conversation turned to other candidates. "Sounds like we're talking about Pete," said Obama, flashing a smile at Rouse, the chief of his Senate office. A Capitol Hill veteran, Rouse was so knowledgeable about Washington that he was dubbed "the 101st senator." A Japanese American bachelor, devoted to his cats, he was modest, indefatigable, and calm; as one staffer said, "He put the no-drama in Obama." Obama had once told **TIME**: "Pete Rouse is as well connected and as well known and as popular and as smart and as savvy a person as there is . . . and is completely ego-free." Bowles agreed. "I thought the guy was terrific in every way—knowledgeable, supportive, would speak truth to power."

There was just one problem: Rouse did not want the attention that goes with the job. Instead, he would take an office in the West Wing as a senior adviser and confidant (and would serve as interim chief on two occasions). Another close friend, former senator Tom Daschle, was also an early favorite to become chief. Daschle was much like Obama: thoughtful, grounded, and calm; but he had been a principal, a Senate majority leader. Nobody could quite picture him in the role of staff.

The conversation turned to Rahm Emanuel. At least one of the former chiefs thought the combative, hard-charging ex–Clinton aide was all wrong: He would stomp on too many toes, break too much china. As a political operative, Rahm was a force of nature, to be sure. But someone with the steady temperament and organizational skills to be chief of staff? Not so much.

But Axelrod was enthusiastic about his friend, and so were the other chiefs. "Obama quickly focused on Rahm," recalls Podesta. Although they were both from Chicago, Obama and Emanuel were not really close friends. No one doubted Rahm's ability to tell the president what he didn't want to hear. And Obama needed someone with Washington experience to turn his agenda into reality; Emanuel had fought on both sides of some of the bloodiest White House–Capitol Hill wars. "I think the reason he picked Rahm, and really wanted Rahm from the get-go," says Podesta, "is that he saw that moment as a time to expend all your energy passing stuff. Rahm had the experience under President Clinton but also had been elected to the House and moved up through the leadership." Faced with a global financial crisis—with credit frozen, banks failing, and the auto industry on the verge of collapse—Obama needed someone who could pass legislation on Capitol Hill. Fast.

Emanuel and Obama would be an odd couple: the brash, profane Washington insider and the cool, cerebral outsider who vowed to change the way the game is played. But Obama's willingness to consider Emanuel, like Reagan's courting of James Baker, showed he was serious about getting things done. The president-to-be was confident about his ability to govern, but he was also a student of history. "He wanted to do it right," says Bowles. "He didn't want to repeat the mistakes of the past. And he certainly wasn't afraid to surround himself with strong people. I left there more impressed than I was when I went in."

Rahm Emanuel was raised in Wilmette, Illinois, the middle son of a pediatrician and a psychiatric social worker; his father was a sabra, a native-born Israeli who had served with the Irgun, the Jewish underground resistance. (**Sabra** comes from the

Hebrew for prickly pear cactus, a desert plant with needles on the surface and sweet fruit within.) It was a family of high-octane strivers: Rahm's older brother, Ezekiel, a brilliant oncologist and bio-ethicist, would help devise Obama's health-care policy. His younger brother, Ari, inspired the high-powered Hollywood agent Ari Gold on the HBO series **Entourage**. Rahm had studied liberal arts—and ballet—at Sarah Lawrence, and then received a master's degree in communications from North-western before setting out on his political career. As a young Illinois senator, Obama had rubbed elbows with his congressional counterpart, and was amused by his persona. Introducing him at a charity event, Obama told the audience about the time Rahm, a teenager working at a deli, suf-fered a terrible accident with a meat grinder; part of his middle finger was sliced off—rendering him "practically mute." Later Obama would tease Rahm about a camel ride during a trip to Egypt. "This is a wild animal known to bite, kick, and spit," Obama said. "And who knows what the camel might do."

Though he was fond of Obama, Emanuel was reluctant to take the job. He was on track to be-come the first Jewish Speaker of the House, a long-held goal. "I loved being a congressman," he says. "I had just gotten reelected." Emanuel also had just refinished his Chicago house and would have to uproot his family. He'd been through the

White House wars before—so why would he once again "hit the chop button on the blender"? But Emanuel's upbringing had taught him that "when the president asks you to do something, you had two answers which are yes or yes sir. And I kept, for about twenty-four to forty-eight hours, trying to figure out if there was a 'none of the above' answer. And I knew there wasn't."

On January 20, 2009, he moved into the office just vacated by Josh Bolten, where a month earlier the former chiefs had come to give him their advice. Emanuel loved to show off the big outdoor patio commissioned by Don Regan (at taxpayer expense, and larger than the president's). He kept the old furniture, but added a modern touch: a GPS system that tracked the president's movements. On his desk was a nameplate, a present from his brother Ari: It read, "Undersecretary for Go F*ck Yourself."

The challenges were profound, but so was the opportunity. Obama had big majorities in the House and Senate. "Rahm really believed that a crisis is a terrible thing to waste, which was one of his famous lines early on," says Jonathan Alter, author of **The Promise: President Obama, Year One.** "Rahm is about points on the board and winning the news cycle. There weren't that many huge strategic differences of opinion between Rahm and others in the administration. But on specifics, there was a lot of friction."

In some ways, Emanuel was an outlier among the Obama loyalists. The campaign's true believers had signed on to change the way Washington worked. "You have to remember that the Obama world was conceived in opposition to the way things had been done in Washington," says a former White House staffer who worked on the campaign. "And that is not just the Republicans, but Democrats—specifically the Clintons. So the idea of overreacting to the news cycle, the idea of tough, hard-charging politics, Obama ran against a lot of that." As for Emanuel: "Rahm had a very Washington view of us: 'Yeah, they got this far. Hope and change and all that kind of stuff. But they're all young, they're all naive. There's too many kids running around—and we've got to be a little more serious.' "

Emanuel's focus was laser-like. With subordinates, the chief did not suffer fools and pounced when he sensed weakness. When one young aide stammered while giving an answer, Rahm snapped: "Take your f*cking tampon out of your mouth and tell me what you have to say." The "undersecretary for go f*ck yourself" lived up to his billing. "The Rahm freak-outs, the yelling—that stuff's all real," says a former senior adviser. But the act was so famous by now that it was almost like theater. "It was hard for anyone to be very afraid because they sort of knew that was his style. It was like, 'There's Rahm.' "

Like a schoolyard bully, Emanuel would retreat when his targets pushed back. "I don't work well with people who are, like, yellers," says Jon Favreau with a laugh. "Obama's never yelled at me," says the president's former chief speechwriter, twenty-seven at the time. "Axelrod has never yelled at me. Plouffe's never yelled at me. So I realized that when someone is like that, the way you work with them is to not show fear. Sometimes Rahm wanted to stick lines in speeches. And so he's sitting in my office, yelling at me: 'Put this in!' And I didn't think it was good. He goes, 'F*ck you!' And I go, 'No, f*ck **you**!' And we got along great after that."

Bowles, Emanuel's old boss in the Clinton White House, chalks up some of his legendary bluster to insecurity: "Rahm's a pussycat underneath it—he gets his feelings hurt like **poof**." Bowles snaps his fingers. "If Obama didn't go to his fiftieth birthday party, it'd **kill** him." The ruthless, take-the-hill persona also masked a true believer's passion for progressive policy. In that sense, the ultimate Clintonista was also an Obamian. "You wouldn't think this from his reputation but he believes deeply," says Favreau. "He's so passionate and angry sometimes because he believes in all of the issues. And he'll fight for the stuff—he'll get angry because none of it's bullshit to him."

As chief, Emanuel tried to emulate his other old boss Panetta. "I think he had a perfect balance of politics, humanity, and interest in public policy and giving the president unvarnished truth," he says. But matching Panetta's control of the White House would not be easy. Obama's administration was a hothouse of brains and egos: director of the National Economic Council Larry Summers; Treasury Secretary Tim Geithner; director of the Office of Management and Budget Peter Orszag; Secretary of State Hillary Clinton; Secretary of Defense Robert Gates. And then there were the friends from home. "Even if the president says there's going to be one funnel, there's never one funnel," says a senior adviser. "And Rahm handled that as well as I think anyone can. But it's just the reality of someone coming in with those kind of long-standing relationships. And someone who's known you for like twenty-five years is not going to then be funneling things through an intermediary."

Obama's closest advisers were known as the Chicago Mafia. David Axelrod and Valerie Jarrett, hometown friends of the president, were now senior advisers in the West Wing. Jarrett, who was close to both the president and the first lady, was portrayed by the press as a kind of Lady Macbeth: her nickname was "the Night Stalker"—because she visited the residence at all hours. During the transition, Emanuel was so bent on getting rid of "VJ," as she was known, that he tried—unsuccessfully—to talk Illinois governor Rod Blagojevich into appointing Jarrett to Obama's vacant senate seat.

But VJ's influence over Obama, and her involvement in decisions, was exaggerated. Though she was a close confidant, she rarely pushed her own views. "She's probably the most 'yes' person of all the advisers," says a former staffer who knows them well. "So nothing the Obamas do is ever wrong; everything you said in that speech is wonderful; every time you smile it's wonderful—everything is great! That's Valerie!" Still, the tension between Emanuel and Jarrett was palpable. "It's tough to have her around when you're trying to tell the president, 'Well, no, I think this is wrong.' Because she's always there saying, 'Oh, **yes**, it's fine.'"

Right out of the gate, Emanuel and Obama's true believers clashed over values. Obama had vowed to banish "earmarks," the pork-barrel goodies that Congress loves to stuff inside legislation. But in March, Congress sent up an appropriations bill that was full of them. Emanuel thought a veto would poison relations with Capitol Hill. "It's messy, but Rahm was like, we just have to get it done," recalls a senior official. Obama hated the bill, but ultimately saw it Rahm's way and agreed to sign it. "And the campaign people were aghast, because this was a guy who had campaigned on this purity and no earmarks and blah, blah, blah. And the first thing, literally, he does, is sign a bunch of messy appropriations bills. So there was that tension."

Emanuel knew he'd need the support of Congress if he wanted to stave off the next Great Depression. "The economy was in free-fall, past a recession, towards something much more severe," he says. "The financial world had frozen up to the point where nothing was moving. The economy was in a tailspin. The entire auto industry was flat on its back and people were openly talking about it collapsing. Any one of those would have been worth an entire term in the sense of a historical moment. We had three of them simultaneously— all to be dealt with immediately." In one respect, Obama was in a worse position than FDR: While Roosevelt could declare a bank holiday to prevent a panicked run on bank deposits, billions in assets could now vanish with the click of a keyboard mouse. And then there was the fear that they had not reached bottom yet. When Roosevelt took office, says Emanuel, the Depression "had already been two years into the process and you knew how bad it was. We were on the doorstep of how bad it was."

The first priority was to stimulate the cratering economy. Some members of the economic team thought the emergency called for a stimulus package exceeding a trillion dollars. When Emanuel heard that figure, he started screaming. "No way I'm going to the Hill with a package that begins with a 'T'!" he said. In the end, after Emanuel called in every favor he had on Capitol Hill, Congress in February passed a $787 billion economic stimulus bill.

But after the stimulus came a pivotal decision: What should come next? "The president had three major initiatives: health care, energy, financial regulation of Wall Street," says Emanuel. Obama would have to decide which was the most urgent priority and whether it was politically palatable on Capitol Hill.

Emanuel was convinced that health-care reform should wait; it was too heavy a lift after the big stimulus package. "It was my belief that we should go first with financial reform and get it done," he says. "I gave the reasons why politically and policy-wise." But Obama was unmoved. What was his political capital for, if not passing the most important part of his domestic agenda? "I didn't come here to put my popularity up on a shelf and admire it," the president said. And then he told them, "Come on, isn't anybody else feeling lucky? I'm feeling lucky." Emanuel got the message. "The president made his call, he went with health care first. And I made my argument why I would do it differently. I had been through some health-care battles of my own. And he listened to them, asked me again, and made his judgment." Emanuel still carried scars from the fiery crash of Hillary Clinton's bill twenty years earlier. But like a good soldier, he saluted—and prepared to carry out the president's agenda. "I executed his wishes because I even came in from my son's bar mitzvah to round up votes on that weekend."

Emanuel was struck by the fact that both presidents he'd served, Clinton and Obama, demanded honesty. "Look, they had different temperaments. President Clinton could blow up at you and the next minute put his arm around you and say, 'Let's go and play some cards.' That's not the way President Obama would react. But both wanted to get the straight scoop, unvarnished."

To avoid repeating Hillary's fate, Emanuel would need all the help he could get (and not just from his brother Zeke). To craft a plan, Obama and Emanuel decided to recruit a medical executive named Nancy-Ann DeParle. A former Rhodes scholar, who had run the Tennessee Department of Human Services when she was just thirty-one, DeParle remembered Emanuel from a brief stint in the Clinton White House. "I didn't like him," she recalls. "I thought he was rude." When Emanuel first telephoned her while she was driving her car, she blew him off and hung up. "My husband said, 'You were pretty nasty,'" she recalls. But Emanuel kept calling, and DeParle finally agreed to a meeting at the White House. Rahm worked her over, promising that health care was the president's holy grail, insisting that only they could do it. DeParle was won over. "He can be very persuasive and very charming," she says. "Rahm looked me in the eye and he said, 'We'll **do** this.' We did a pinky finger clasp on it. And we promised each other, 'Let's not come away with nothing.'"

Now that he had his marching orders, Emanuel was obsessed. "No distractions!" he would shout, when someone brought up another subject. "Come on, let's get going!" DeParle, now director of the White House Office of Health Reform, would walk into his office and find him lost in thought. "Rahm would be sitting at his desk, his fingers to his forehead, and you could just see this incredibly complicated diagram above his head. He was finding some way to the goal." His constant greeting to DeParle was, "Let's do this!"

Still, Emanuel argued for a limited, practical approach. "Rahm was so chastened and wounded by his experience with Hillarycare that he became a convert to the incremental approach," says Alter. He pushed for something similar to the plan Erskine Bowles had negotiated back in the '90s that provided coverage for impoverished children. Emanuel's idea became known as "The Titanic"— women and children first. Obama pushed back. "The president basically said, 'Look, if it costs three hundred billion or five hundred billion or seven hundred billion or a trillion dollars, they're still going to say it's massive,'" recalls Orszag. "'And by going with the 'mini-me' version, I'm not really solving the full problem I wanted to solve. I'm disappointing my political allies and they won't fight as hard. And I think I'd get creamed just as hard, so there's no upside either.'"

While DeParle and the health-care team wrestled with the details, Emanuel went to work twisting arms. "What Rahm did is he went and he cut deals with all the big interests that had stopped health care in previous years," says Alter. "He had to buy off the pharmaceutical industry, buy off the hospitals, one by one, buy off the AMA, one by one, security industries. And he broke a lot of china doing that." Emanuel jettisoned the so-called public option, angering liberals—even though Obama had not emphasized the public option during his campaign. And to avoid the fate of Hillary's bill, which was delivered "like a stone tablet," as Axelrod put it, and torn apart by special interests, Emanuel and his team decided to let Congress participate in the writing of the bill.

"Rahm called the Hill constantly," says DeParle. "He had lunches every day in his office with Congress people. He started every day in the congressional gym. Why? Not because he enjoyed driving a half hour out of his way. It was so that he could talk to them, take their temperature on things." Podesta was amazed by Emanuel's single-minded focus on the Hill. "They literally operated on a congressional calendar," he says. "They thought about their work in congressional work periods. Whereas that wouldn't cross my mind!" He laughs. "But that's because I lived on the other side of a hostile

Congress, and they were living with a very substantial Democratic majority."

For all of Emanuel's private wheeling and dealing, the writing of the Affordable Care Act was an ugly, public process. James Baker thought Obama's hands-off approach was a far cry from the way he and Reagan shaped legislation. Obama "didn't send up his own number one policy prescription," says Baker. "He subcontracted that out to the Congress to draft the stimulus bill and to draft the health-care legislation. I found it incomprehensible that a White House wouldn't put a bill up there." So did some key members of Obama's team. "I thought it was totally untenable for us not to have full legislation," says Orszag. "The president kept talking about his plan, but we didn't actually have a legislative proposal at that point that was fully fleshed out. I was like, we are going to get killed. We have a two-page agreement. We didn't get killed. No one cared." Indeed, in the end, on March 21, 2010, the Patient Protection and Affordable Care Act passed by 219 to 212 votes in the House; and 60 to 39 votes in the Senate. Not a single Republican in either chamber voted yes. And the Democratic majority that had passed the bill would vanish soon enough. Obama and Emanuel's successors would face an opposition obsessed with a single goal: ensuring that Obama would be a one-term president.

· · ·

EVERY AFTERNOON, at about five o'clock, Emanuel and the president would conduct "the Wrap"—a walk around the circular driveway on the South Lawn. "Sometimes we'd talk about the family but mainly we talked about the to-do list or particular projects or a particular challenge he was facing," says Emanuel. A tough day meant multiple laps. The first lady teased them about it: "Michelle used to say, 'Oh, **look**—the boys are on their walk!'" But it was on walks like these—just the president alone with his chief—that history would be made. "There are dark moments in that process of passing health care, while you're working through the Afghanistan strategy, your different departments are leaking, you're trying to make a coherent policy. The press is trying to decide it for you. You're trying to figure out what's best," says Emanuel. "There's a lot of moments where you're suspended in thin air, there's no net, there's no safety. There's nobody that's grabbing you and you're all out there."

In October of 2011, five months into his first term as mayor of Chicago, Emanuel talked with me about his stint as Obama's chief. As mayor of Chicago, he was battling a murder epidemic, a bitter teacher revolt, and a massive pension crisis. Yet that seemed almost tame compared to being in the vortex of the White House: "The rewards are few," he says of being chief of staff. "The pains are magnified. You get all the blame and never any of the credit. You are in the cockpit seat. And when anybody gives you advice about, 'Oh, you should do this. You should do that'—unless they've sat in that cockpit seat and been strafed by friendly fire as well as enemy fire, they don't know anything about the job. Is it miserable going through it? Are you getting wind shear, whiplash, can't tell vertical from horizontal—up from down? Yeah! But I guarantee you, if you ask every one of the chiefs, 'Would you have traded it to do something else?' to a person, they would say, 'I'm glad I did it.'"

Emanuel was sensitive about reports of battles over health care between the president and his advisers. But he insists the alternative would have been worse. "The notion that there were camps," he says, "white hats versus the black hats, people fighting for the president's soul—you give me a time when that didn't happen in a presidency, and I'll give you a presidency that didn't create any waves or make anything happen." What about the tension between Obama World and his realpolitik? "There was quote-unquote the true believers versus the pragmatists. You're **supposed** to have that. If you don't, you're not having the creative tension you need in a White House—that's how you get kind of the intellectual energy and the political energy to get things done. You also need it not to become acrimonious, personal, and then spill out. My point is, you need this, and a good president wants it."

But Emanuel would not be around to wage those battles much longer. On September 7, 2010, Richard M. Daley, the mayor of Chicago, announced that he would not run for reelection. It was a once-in-a lifetime opening for Emanuel, and he leaped at it. In two years as chief, Emanuel had a lot to be proud of: passing a massive economic stimulus; saving the auto industry; putting health-care reform on track to become law. Obama appreciated how much Emanuel had helped to make it all possible. But his high-wattage act was wearing thin, tiring people out. When Emanuel made it clear that he was serious about leaving, Obama did not offer much resistance.

At the East Wing ceremony announcing his departure, the president was generous in his praise, citing Emanuel's role in everything from "preventing a second Depression to passing historic health-care and financial-reform legislation to restoring America's leadership in the world." Emanuel was choked up. Obama gave him a going-away gift: a photograph of the president and his chief walking the South Lawn.

Austan Goolsbee, the White House economist, thought Rahm's departure called for something special. At his last daily staff meeting, the outgoing chief was presented with a gift-wrapped box.

"So he opens up the box, and Rahm goes, 'This is a f*cking dead fish!'" says Goolsbee. It was not just any dead fish, but an Asian carp. "It's a nasty, nasty fish. When they get scared they leap in the air; a woman got hit in the head and broke her neck." In a nod to Emanuel's famous Luca Brasi stunt, Goolsbee had scoured every Chicago-area seafood market to find it. Later he got a message from the chief's office: "'Rahm says that was the most thoughtful gift anyone's ever given him. He said it almost brought a tear to his eye.'"

To replace Emanuel, the president turned to another Chicagoan, Bill Daley. Daley, scion of the city's political dynasty, had been Bill Clinton's secretary of commerce and manager of Al Gore's 2000 campaign. The theory was that Daley, a former JPMorgan Chase executive, could build a bridge between the White House and the business world; many CEOs still loathed Obama for his fiery anti–Wall Street rhetoric, and for enacting the Dodd-Frank Act, regulating banking practices. "I think they had the sense Obama's some left-wing lunatic who can't understand them, never will, is out to destroy business," says Daley. "And I laughed when friends of mine in business said he's antibusiness. You **can't** be antibusiness if you're the president of the United States." Axelrod, Daley's good friend, pushed for him. "There was all this talk at the time that Obama needed more outreach to the business community; we needed sort of an 'adult in charge,'" says Orszag. "All of that was picture perfect for someone like Bill Daley to come in."

Daley had not even received his security clearances when his first crisis erupted, on January 8, 2011. "I wasn't supposed to start until the following Wednesday—and Congresswoman Gabby Giffords was shot on Saturday morning in Arizona," he recalls. Daley, who was still living out of a suitcase at a downtown hotel, rushed to the White House to deal with the attempted assassination. "I'm sitting in the Situation Room—and there was a question: Should I have been there? Because I didn't have the security approvals yet. There was great concern about the shooting, what was going on, what was behind it? Was it any sort of conspiracy? Was it a terrorist? Was it just one individual? The congressional leadership was suddenly under a lockdown. They were trying to find them all. So that was a concern; where were the other leaders of Congress? Do they have adequate security?"

The Giffords tragedy was just the first of a string of crises on Daley's watch—from the Japanese tsunami to the Arab Spring. And it wasn't long before the javelins began flying inside the West Wing.

Daley was a bad fit from the start; to the president's true believers, his arrival felt like a hostile takeover. The chief made it painfully clear that there was a new CEO in town. He canceled the traditional 8:30 a.m. staff meeting, leaving people out of the loop, and barred key aides from others. "The doors to the chief of staff office were shut all the time—that's never the way it was with Rahm," says a former senior staffer. "Daley looked at all of the young Obama people like we were part of the problem," says another former aide. "We were enablers—there were very few advisers that he found common cause with."

Then, too, Washington had changed since the Clinton years, and Daley was not up to speed. "It honestly seemed like someone held a nation-wide competition: 'Enter a drawing to become **White House chief of staff!**'" says a former aide. "Every day he was amazed by something new— like 'I didn't know the federal government worked like **this**! I didn't know **that**.' He was learning the whole thing as he went." If Emanuel struck some Obama faithful as old school, Daley was from the Pleistocene era. "He was the embodiment of the Washington view of what was wrong with Obama," says the aide. "'If only he had John Boehner over for more cocktail parties. If only he reached out more. If only he did X. If only he did Y. If only he listened to Simpson-Bowles'—all this centrist pundit, **Meet the Press**, **Sunday Morning** show bullshit. That was Bill Daley. All the way. Just bought it hook, line, and sinker."

Daley was annoyed that he couldn't appoint his own deputies; instead he inherited Alyssa Mastromonaco and DeParle, who was almost a de facto chief. And though his family was Chicago royalty, Daley also ran afoul of the president's hometown pals. "He got eaten alive by the Chicago crowd," says a senior aide. "Which is ironic since he's from Chicago." Erskine Bowles agrees: "Obama already had the Chicago Mafia. And Daley wasn't part of that little clique. And that little clique that is in every White House—if you try to mess with their relationship, they will **spit** your ass out."

Jarrett and Emanuel may not have been the best of friends, but Daley and Jarrett couldn't even stand to be in the same room together. More crucially, the president and Daley didn't really click. Obama liked brainy advisers who mastered the nitty-gritty of policy; that wasn't Daley's strong suit. He would much rather talk politics or Chicago sports. "In meetings, when Daley spoke," recalls a senior adviser, "Obama started to go, like, 'OK, next.' And I could notice it because I know Obama well. It wasn't so obvious to others because Obama didn't want to demean him in the eyes of everyone else."

This close Obama friend continues: "If you look at Rahm and Denis McDonough, the two attributes that they share that led them to be able to counterbalance the Chicago crowd is they delve deep into details. They get granular. And that makes it hard for someone who's kind of floating up here to compete. Rahm was an expert in policy and communications and strategy. And Bill Daley was an expert at none of those things."

Daley was keenly aware that he was a walking target. "There's not a part of your body that someone isn't shooting at," he says. "And sometimes they're your friends. You know, someone once said: 'In Chicago, if someone's going to stab you, they'll stab you in the stomach; in Washington, it's always in the back.'"

The knives were out, and not only in the West Wing. Daley would soon get an education in how much Washington had changed since the days when antagonists like Bill Clinton and Newt Gingrich could cut bipartisan deals. On Daley's watch, Obama would throw everything he had into obtaining a so-called grand bargain; it was an effort to cut a deal with the Republicans—to curb spending and reduce the national debt, while avoiding sequestration, and the fiscal cliff.

John Boehner, who'd become Speaker in January 2011, struck them as someone they could do business with. "After Boehner became Speaker, it's kind of like 1995 with Gingrich," says Alter of the White House thinking. "There's not going to be a big Obama bill, but what you might get is this grand bargain." Daley was optimistic. "The Speaker made it very clear. He said, 'I didn't come to Washington to get a big title, I came to Washington to get a big deal.' And we believed him. And the president and the Speaker kind of get along. So

I think there was a real sense that we could do a deal."

The round-the-clock negotiations ran from June until the end of July. "It was two months that were like one long day," recalls Jack Lew, the OMB director. "We were there on the Fourth of July working. And I think the president thought the Speaker really wanted to reach an agreement."

Obama and Daley had not bargained on the intransigence of the Tea Party Republican caucus; as Podesta put it, one house of Congress was now controlled by "a cult worthy of Jonestown." After taking the proposed deal to his caucus, Boehner came back and told Daley there was no deal. "There was a relatively small number in Congress who were willing to drive the economy over the cliff and default on the national debt," says Lew. Obama persisted—going back to Boehner repeatedly, to no avail. For Obama, the failure of the grand bargain was a heavy blow. Daley called it "the most gut-wrenching nonmilitary decision I saw him make: coming to the realization that the long-term fiscal situation of the country was not going to be addressed."

Daley took responsibility for the defeat. "I was chief of staff, so I have to take the blame," he says. "I think there were lots of reasons, but it was on my watch and I encouraged the president.

"We may have been naive as to the Speaker's ability to deliver a deal. But the reality is, I think we did it right. We tried. We went the extra mile. But as chief of staff, I think you have to say to yourself, 'This didn't happen on my watch.'"

"They had a whole frustrated year fighting about that," says Alter of the president and his chief. "In August, when Obama was turning fifty, they had this terrible low point—the absolute low point of the presidency." The Republican senate minority leader, Mitch McConnell, would not stand up to his radical caucus. Podesta agrees it was the nadir of the Obama presidency: "where he realized McConnell couldn't deliver anything. He'd wasted months and months trying to negotiate with him. His own people got dispirited. His supporters got dispirited and with little or nothing to show for it."

"The truth is you can go to war a lot easier than you can do things domestically," says Daley. "And that's an irony of the situation we're in. It is very easy to go to war. It is very difficult to affect things domestically because you must go to Congress." To get anywhere with his agenda, Obama realized, something would have to change. He plunged into his reelection battle, hoping to change Congress.

Domestic policy would be pushed to the back burner for a while. But in the meantime, Obama would notch his most spectacular overseas triumph—and he would do it by keeping Congress in the dark.

Daley's first inkling that something dramatic was afoot came on his first morning as chief. "In the PDB [the Presidential Daily Brief], which is the morning intelligence briefing, it was mentioned that there was this compound outside of Abbottabad that was being watched—with the hope that it could even be Osama bin Laden." The previous August, when Emanuel was still chief, the CIA had tracked a courier to the compound. A tall man in a white robe could be seen pacing on the top floor. "You have a house, with higher walls than normal, no Internet connection—and they burn their trash," Emanuel says. He pauses for dramatic effect. "Do you think a judge would give you a search warrant based on that data?"

As evidence mounted that "the pacer" might be bin Laden himself, CIA director Panetta and the national security team presented three options: a joint paramilitary raid with the Pakistanis; obliterating the compound with a three-thousand-pound bomb; or launching a unilateral commando raid into the sovereign territory of an ally. As the first two options were ruled out, the JSOC (Joint Special Operations Command) focused on sending members of SEAL Team Six, an elite commando unit, by helicopter from a U.S. base in Afghanistan. The commander, Admiral Bill McRaven, insisted, "We do this ten times a night—this isn't something we can't do." But Obama was concerned: What if the Pakistani military detects the mission and responds aggressively? "He wanted a more robust potential response if the Pakistani army for some reason came in force," recalls Daley, "because you had a very limited number of SEALs." Obama sent McRaven back to the drawing board.

Daley was shocked by the young president's audacity. "I must say, I sat there thinking, 'You know, you've been here two and a half years, you really don't have the history in these issues. This is pretty gutsy, to be pushing McRaven around on his plan!'" But shortly thereafter McRaven returned with a revised plan calling for doubling the number of helicopters and adding twenty-four more SEALs. And when the raid began, and the first helicopter on the scene crashed into the compound wall, those extra choppers would mean the difference between success and disaster.

Another disaster was narrowly averted during the planning for the mission. Unbeknownst to the president and Daley, Panetta had briefed Congress as part of a routine budget review. At the closed session, Panetta told members about the covert operation to get bin Laden. When they learned about Panetta's briefing, Obama and Daley were furious. "We were absolutely flabbergasted," says Daley. "I was livid that the CIA went ahead and did this." Daley was convinced a leak was inevitable and would torpedo the mission. "I figured any morning I'd get up and the **Washington Post** would be on the doorstep. And there'd be the headline: 'Osama's in Pakistan: U.S. Planning Attack.'"

But by pure luck, the secret held; on April 29,

2011, just before boarding **Marine One**, the president summoned Daley, along with national security aides Denis McDonough, John Brennan, and Tom Donilon to meet him in the East Wing. He then gave the go-ahead for Operation Neptune Spear. "He was rolling the dice on his presidency," recalls Daley. "He knew that. And off he went to the helicopter and we all went back to the West Wing. And I remember walking back down along the Rose Garden and thinking what a monumental decision that was: We were within forty-eight hours of the presidency being on the line."

Sixty-three hours later, Obama announced to the world that the United States had conducted a mission that resulted in the death of the world's most wanted terrorist.

For Daley, it was a rare moment of triumph in a terrible year: from the Giffords shooting to the dashed hopes of the Arab Spring to the failure of the grand bargain. Daley's authority was ebbing rapidly. "The key to success as chief of staff is being empowered by the president," says Daley's old friend Bowles. "When people saw that Bill Daley wasn't empowered, he was dead. You have zero power then, and you might as well just pick yourself up and go home."

In November 2011, the White House announced publicly that Daley would share some of his managerial responsibilities with Pete Rouse, Obama's old confidant, who continued to enjoy the president's trust. Panetta, by then Obama's secretary of defense, saw the writing on the wall. "I called Daley, and I said, 'Bill, the president just cut your legs out from under you.' He said, 'Well, I'm hoping that's not the case.' I said, 'Bill, let me tell you something. When the president goes public saying that the chief of staff is just going to be in charge of these elements, you are going to find your authority undermined. You're going to have to think long and hard about whether you want to stay in that position.'"

Daley would suffer a final indignity before his inevitable exit. In mid-November 2011, a White House worker discovered a bullet hole in one of the windows of the second-floor residence. "Somebody had pulled up on Constitution Avenue, rolled down his window, and took an AK-47 and hit the White House with, I think, four to six rounds," says Daley. "Well, you know that's just unbelievable." Equally unbelievable was the fact that no one had noticed, and when the bullets were discovered, no one told the president or first lady until four days later. "Obviously there was great concern around the shooting at the building," says Daley. "What did this mean? What did it mean for their lifestyle? What did it mean for their kids walking the dog and being out on the lawn or being out on the balcony?"

Daley got an earful from the president: The first

lady was "pretty ticked off, and rightfully so," says Daley. "She felt she had not been briefed, and that was my responsibility through her chief of staff. Mrs. Obama is extremely bright, has been through a lot. And you'd better, if you want to survive as chief of staff, make sure that the first lady—any first lady—doesn't get blindsided."

Daley, frustrated and bitter, let it all pour out in an interview with **Politico**—calling his time in the White House "brutal" and "ungodly." He also criticized Senator Harry Reid, with whom he had bickered over budget negotiations. Dissing the majority leader of his own party, like hanging up on the first lady, as Don Regan had done with Nancy Reagan, might not be a hanging offense—but it was close.

"It may have been just a bad day," says Daley. But the job had taken its toll. "I would take back the word 'ungodly.' But it can be brutal, no question about it. The partisanship, the anger, the bitterness—it was a very difficult year. You not only have the attacks from the outside coming. You also have an inside dynamic that becomes frustrating. And with our politics as they are today and our media as it is today . . ." He lets the sentence trail off.

On January 9, 2012, Daley went to the president and gave him his resignation letter. The president accepted it.

AMONG POSSIBLE CONTENDERS to re-
place Daley, one choice might have been historic:
Nancy-Ann DeParle. No woman had ever become
White House chief of staff. The reasons aren't hard
to fathom. "It may have something to do with the
fact that there hasn't been a female president," says
Robert Reich. "I think male presidents, particularly
male presidents who want or need strong chiefs of
staff, are prejudiced toward having men. And that
probably has to do with their own upbringing and
cultural prejudices: Women are always considered
to be bitches when they're tough and strong; men
are considered to be powerful and heroic."

Still, Obama was comfortable with strong
women—at home and in the West Wing. And
DeParle fit the bill: She was smart and organized
and had earned the president's complete trust.
But DeParle's background was policy, not politics,
and so she was ruled out. "She was the closest any
woman has come to being chief of staff, unless you
include Hillary Clinton," says Alter. "I think there
should be a woman as chief," says McDonough,
who adds: "I can tell you that Nancy would have
been excellent."

OBAMA'S BRAINY OMB director Jacob "Jack"
Lew would become his third chief of staff. With

the possible exception of Pete Rouse, no one was more compatible with the president. After Panetta and Josh Bolten, Lew would be the third budget director to become chief, a modern trend: "Budgets are not about numbers," says Lew. "They're about values. It's about what do you believe in, in a world of limited resources—what are the things you're going to double down on, and what are the things you're going to do less of." Grinding through the stimulus package, the grand bargain, and the debt ceiling, Lew and Obama had bonded. "You get to know people pretty well when you're making those decisions," says Lew. "He knows what I think about a pretty broad range of things. And I know pretty well what he thinks. And it probably shouldn't come up too often that we have big disagreements."

After Ken Duberstein, Bolten, and Emanuel, Lew was also the fourth Jewish chief, and he performed his White House duties around the Saturday Sabbath. "With the help of the people I work with, I drew some boundaries," he says. "People don't call me for trivial things on a Saturday. But they appreciated that I was fully prepared to be available 24/7—including Saturday, when there was a need."

Lew's tenure began on a high note. On June 28, 2012, the Supreme Court ruled on the Affordable Care Act. "I wasn't unhappy to be able to walk in and tell the president that the Affordable Care

Act was constitutional," says Lew. "At the moment when we walked in and told him that the Supreme Court had upheld the statute, the TV screens were still saying that it had been found unconstitutional. So it was a puzzling moment." For Obama, it was sweet vindication; there were high fives and hugs all around.

Darker days would soon follow. On July 20, a deranged gunman opened fire inside a movie theater in Aurora, Colorado, during a midnight screening of the film **The Dark Knight Rises.** When the shooting stopped, twelve people had been killed and seventy injured. It was unlike anything Lew had dealt with at OMB. "I think that the life-and-death issues have a special character," he says. "Getting that call in the middle of the night that a terrible act of violence occurred and having to immediately gear up the White House and notify the president—it has a somberness and a seriousness to it that's unlike any of the other things that you do."

There was even worse news to come. In December, at the Sandy Hook Elementary School in Newtown, Connecticut, a twenty-year-old man with a semi-automatic rifle murdered twenty first graders, as well as six adult staff members. It was the deadliest school shooting in history, and it deeply affected Obama; speaking about the massacre on TV that afternoon, he had to pause to wipe away tears. But his efforts to bring a gun control bill to Congress were blocked. Faced with a Republican House, thoroughly poisoned relations with the opposition party, and a slow economic recovery, the Obama presidency was stalled. Obama had plunged headlong into his reelection campaign, but all bets on the outcome were off. In late 2011, a Nate Silver cover story for **The New York Times Magazine** put the president's odds of being reelected at 17 percent.

While Obama continued to project confidence, there were private moments of doubt. DeParle became a confidant. "For a while, he thought he was going to lose," she says. One day, as the president and his health-care expert were walking through the West Wing, "he put his arm around me and said, 'Nance, let's just make sure we leave something behind.'" Even if the worst happened, at least they would have the Affordable Care Act.

Obama liked Lew, and hoped he would stay on as chief. But Lew was determined to become secretary of the treasury: if he couldn't get that job, he told Obama, he would return to New York and the business world. In December 2012 Tim Geithner announced that he would step down from his cabinet position. Obama agreed to nominate Lew as the 76th U.S. treasury secretary.

OBAMA'S FOURTH AND final chief would face a challenge common to every reelected modern president: the second-term curse. It might sound superstitious, but the wreckage of recent history was all too real: Richard Nixon and H. R. Haldeman had been destroyed by the rampant criminality of Watergate, and their ham-handed efforts to cover it up. Ronald Reagan and his chiefs had barely averted disaster in the Iran-Contra scandal. Bill Clinton and Podesta had narrowly survived impeachment over his affair with Monica Lewinsky.

Now, with his legacy on the line, Barack Obama turned to his deputy national security adviser Denis McDonough.

A native of Minnesota, Denis Richard McDonough was raised with eleven brothers and sisters in a high-achieving and devout Catholic family. Prematurely gray at forty-eight, he had, as one writer put it, "the rangy build of a defensive football back and the ashen asceticism of a 16th-century Vatican fixer." In truth, McDonough looks too skinny to tackle anyone; but he compensates with steely intensity. He played safety at St. John's University in Collegeville, Minnesota. In all things, but especially foreign affairs, he is a fanatical believer in process. It stems in no small part from his belief that **lack** of process led the United States into Iraq. "When I sat with the president to talk about the job, I told him, 'If you're looking for a domestic policy adviser like Jack or like Rahm, I'm not your guy,'" says McDonough. "'If you're looking for someone who will get you something square, honestly arrived at, transparently developed, then I'm your guy.' So the way I see it, I'm a keeper of a process that gets things to the president."

Square is a favorite McDonough word: it means "honest," but it also describes the man who would become Obama's alter ego for the next four years. If Emanuel, with his dramatic flair, was well suited to the crises of the first term, McDonough—wiry, intense, and a workaholic—seemed tailor-made for the heavy lifting of the next four years. But McDonough's "no-drama" discipline concealed a ferocious competitive drive.

"I don't golf with the president," he says. "I don't play basketball with him. It's reported I play basketball with him—I played with him once. Maybe twice." What Obama and his chief **did** play—with fierce intensity—was policy and politics, and increasingly, the art of governing by executive order.

McDonough talks about everything in football metaphors. When Congress obstructs a bill, he says: "You know, I'm always thinking about it in terms of blockers. Who's trying to stop me from getting the ball? All right?" He says the only person he knows who is more competitive is Barack Obama: "And he's like"—with his hands, McDonough pantomimes Obama hitting an imaginary blocker—" 'I've gotta get rid of **this**! I gotta get rid of **that**!' "

McDonough will never forget the look in the president's eyes after the first presidential debate in 2012, when he was outperformed by Mitt Romney. "He felt like he had let us down," he says. But then resolve kicked in. "He was, like—**I am determined as hell to get where I want to go.** And it's in a way that I've never seen—in sports, in life, in politics." He chuckles, in disbelief. "This guy is, like, he **knows** where he's going and he's going to get there! We've all played sports with these guys. They're not looking at the scoreboard, man. They're just going to pummel whoever the f*ck is in front of them. And then they'll figure out the score after that." Sure enough, Obama pummeled Romney in the next debate and went on to win reelection.

As deputy national security adviser, McDonough had been withering with people who screwed up: At a meeting after a national security leak, he shouted: "The president got rat-f*cked!" But as chief, his outbursts were fewer, and he became an inclusive manager. "The most important thing a chief can do, and I learned this from Jim Baker's book," he says, "is establish clear lines of responsibility. As a result, you get clear accountability. There's no accountability without clear responsibility."

The Chicago Mafia had disbanded—Axelrod had gone back to Chicago; but Jarrett remained, and McDonough knew how to play her. "Let's take Valerie," says McDonough. "She's part of the so-called Mafia. VJ makes my job easier, not harder. The fact that she's close to the president and to the first lady. That coupled with the fact that she is a consummate professional. So when we take 'do-outs' [assignments] out of a meeting, VJ takes her do-outs, she's the first one to have her do-outs back. She never forgets a do-out. And even if it's the shittiest do-out on the list, she'll take it."

Tom Daschle, a friend of both the president and McDonough for twenty years, believes they were a perfect fit. "I think Denis's style and approach is exactly what the president needed and wanted. Denis's style is really the president's style. They give each other strength. President Obama really benefited from Denis's common sense and judgment and ability to manage all the egos that exist in any administration."

By now, Obama also had on-the-job experience. "You could just see it—the president was more comfortable in his role," says Peter Orszag. "And the White House just seemed to be functioning better operationally. Now it's also the case that there was not as much big legislation going on."

To critics, that was the problem: The president seemed to have given up on getting anything done on Capitol Hill. His major second-term goals—immigration reform, climate change, gun control—had gone nowhere. Republicans and Democrats alike complained that Obama would not reach across the aisle; he detested all the schmoozing and glad-handing that was part of the job. Even some Democrats thought Obama had something in common with Jimmy Carter: They were the smartest guys in the room, but also the least social. Why couldn't Obama do what Ronald Reagan had done with Tip O'Neill—invite Republican leaders over to the White House residence for whiskey and get bipartisan deals done?

Panetta, recently retired as Obama's defense secretary, watched with growing concern. "I mean, look: As smart as Obama is, he doesn't like politics, he doesn't like the give-and-take that it takes to get things done," he says. "Therefore, you need to delegate that to a tough chief of staff or to somebody else who can get that done. Quite frankly, I don't understand this sense of giving up on key legislation on the Hill. I know they've had tough times, and it's tough politics. But the sense that somehow they're not going to push either a budget deal or immigration reform or infrastructure funding or trade legislation—because the politics are just too tough. I cannot accept that. You cannot give up."

On a bright weekday afternoon in October 2016, McDonough sat with me on the patio outside his West Wing office. He bristles when I bring up Panetta. Clinton's ex-chief, he says, just doesn't get the ugly new reality on Capitol Hill—where the political climate is so toxic that Republicans won't be **seen** with the president. "I can't tell you how many guys tell me, 'Look, it's great that we're talk-ing. Let's just not let anybody know,' " he says. "It's different than when Leon was here, and it's differ-ent than even when Podesta was here." Part of it, he says, is that Congress is never around. "These guys get here on Monday night or Tuesday night and they leave on Thursday night. Right? So that leaves you Tuesday nights and Wednesday nights for when the president presumably can schmooze with these guys. Why doesn't the president go golf-ing with these guys on the weekend? Well, because they're not **here**."

McDonough is just getting wound up. "I have a rule. Every day, I have to touch ten members of Congress. Phone call. Letter. E-mail. Text. And if people can't at the end of the day get to yes on something, and they need to blame it on us, so be it. That's what happens with presidents. John [Podesta] used to laugh in here all the time about this nostalgia for congressional relations under the Clinton administration. He said, 'These guys—they **hated** us!' Right? But this is just the way it works. And that's okay. Leon . . . I've got my views on Leon. So be it. I wish him well."

But McDonough can't stop: "I'm proud of the way we've done our business and I'm proud of the issues we've taken on, and most of all I'm proud of not being afraid of big problems. You know what I mean? Trying to run through those. And I real-ize now being in this job that everybody in Washington wants to be a White House staffer. They're experts—like, 'Well, you should have done the statement on the way to the chopper instead of the Roosevelt Room.' Who gives a shit? You know? And that's what the president would say: **Who gives a shit?** You know? I've got something I'm trying to do, and I'll explain it to the American people." McDonough reaches again for a football simile—citing a receiver for the New York Giants who is flashy but inconsistent. "All this stuff about style points and shit . . . if you've got the style points but you don't got the substance, you know? You'd be like Odell Beckham Jr. Right?"

Observers have said that McDonough is like a son to Obama. Podesta says he's more like a brother. When I ask McDonough, he says simply, "I'm his staff guy. That's the relationship." On their nightly walks around the South Lawn driveway, they talked mostly about the nation's business. "I walk with my cards and I inevitably end up with several cards full of do-outs. There's ideas that he'll want to bounce off me. There's ideas that I want to bounce off him." But some of the "do-outs" were personal. "Oftentimes it's also an opportunity for him to give me some parenting advice," says McDonough, who has three young daughters. "His youngest is the same age as my oldest. So he's given me a lot of good advice." McDonough tried to make sure the president was home on time for dinner with Sasha and Malia. "I get calls if he's not home at six thirty or so," he says with a laugh. "Among the many strengths of this president, he is very self-aware. And he is aware of the times when he is less sharp—and the times he is away from Mrs. Obama and the girls is one of those times. And so he's going to be very aggressive about protecting that. And it's my job to do that for him as well."

THE PRESIDENT AND McDonough would need to be at their sharpest in October 2013, as they faced the biggest test of Obama's domestic agenda. The government website healthcare.gov was at last about to be launched.

The much-anticipated rollout was a fiasco. The website crashed completely, leaving tens of thousands of frustrated insurance seekers unable to enroll. The debacle threatened the president's health-care program, severely damaged his credibility, and confirmed the widespread hunch that government could do nothing right. And it had all happened on McDonough's watch.

"I'm horrified that we screwed it up so bad, for the president and for the taxpayers," says McDonough. "What happened is, we just didn't test the system." The screwup itself was bad enough. Even worse, McDonough had failed to heed repeated warnings from the president before the launch. For months, Obama had attended weekly meetings on the implementation of the ACA. McDonough recalls: "He literally ended every meeting with, 'This is great, guys. But you know that if the website doesn't work, none of this works.' **Every** meeting. And I think he was right to expect that we were testing the website. Was it working? And obviously it wasn't."

The whole process was fundamentally flawed. "We just didn't test the system, right?" says McDonough. "That's management failure one. Management failure two is that the way the government procures technology is to say, 'This is what we need. Go build it.' They procure by piece. And each piece, or each step, has to prove itself; otherwise, it doesn't get paid. And so what we had in the Affordable Care Act was, there's no general contractor, there's nobody proofing the whole system. Everybody has their individual piece. The thing turns out to be a piece of shit. And everybody's saying, 'Well, what? **My** thing works.' Right? And then this guy says, "Well, **my** thing works—so it must be him or him.' Right?"

The sum of the parts was a disaster. "And I'll never forget that day, having to explain to the president that the problem is not because so many people want health care, it's because the site is fundamentally flawed," says McDonough. It was his lowest moment as chief. "Definitely. Walking down the hallway to tell the president, and not knowing whether I'd be coming back the next day. Yeah."

The president did a slow burn. He did not yell—which only made McDonough feel worse. "He didn't say much. That was the problem. If I could've had it out with him—that's better, you know? Finally, he said, 'Look, I asked you to put together a meeting a week. I said at the end of the meeting what I needed. And this is what I got. What the hell?'" Six months later, the director of Health and Human Services, Kathleen Sebelius, would resign under fire. But McDonough says the fault was his own: "The buck was with me. Implementation of major projects like that? Even if it's in one agency? It's on me."

Critics of both parties pounced, some saying the problem was not just the website, but the president's false promises. Terry O'Donnell, the veteran Republican White House aide, told me: "How this White House and the chief of staff could permit the president to go out and say publicly that if you like your policy, you can keep your policy, if you like your doctor you can keep your doctor, twenty-nine times, and be false, I mean that to me is an indictment of the staff system." "The chief of staff has got to say to the president of the United States, 'You cannot do that,'" says McDonough's old critic, Panetta. "Because you're going to put yourself in a hole and it's going to be embarrassing to you and could undermine the very plan that you're trying to put in place. The role of the chief of staff has to be the flashing red light when you anticipate that the president may be doing the wrong thing, or that he's not being well served. And you can't just kind of turn your head and cross your fingers and hope that everything's going to be okay."

Panetta isn't finished: "I cannot imagine as chief of staff not being damned sure that the Affordable Care Act is going to work. Because you bear a lot of that responsibility—to ensure that the staff has got their act together. I would have developed a task force and met with that task force in my office every damn day to make sure that the president's most important legacy was going to be working well."

Panetta raises one more concern: that Obama's chief might be unable to tell the president hard truths. "McDonough is very much an extension of the president. And I think in many ways you pay a price for that because sometimes you can have so much loyalty to the president that you don't want to confront him. And as chief of staff you've got to be the person who can tell the president what he may not want to hear."

McDonough says he'll take his cues from Obama, not Panetta: "I do see my job at certain points to be an extension of the president," he says. "As to whether I tell the president what he needs to hear, I'll let the president answer that question.

If he's ever going to give me a performance review, he can tell me whether I've done that." John Podesta, who watched Obama and his chief up close, says Panetta's worry was misplaced: McDonough never pulled his punches. "He does not sugarcoat anything. He's brutal, honest—in his face." As for the website failure, Podesta says: "A sort of technical rollout like that is very hard—maybe they should have had a red [troubleshooting] team on it. In retrospect they should have, but it's very hard to know. You say, 'Is it going to work?' And they say, 'Yes, it is.' And so what is going to probe the fact that this thing is actually kind of all f*cked up from the get-go?"

McDonough believes that out of the ashes of the rollout, progress was made. "I'm proud that we were able to make some lemonade out of those lemons. And that includes some institutions that we started—the U.S. digital service—and a much more aggressive chief technology office. We have a very aggressive set of reforms in procurement. I'm really proud of that."

IF THE FAILURE of the grand bargain marked a low point of the Obama presidency, the crash of the health-care website set off another bout of soul-searching. Two thousand thirteen was a pivotal year. The president's agenda was mired in partisan gridlock. On a Saturday afternoon in July, at an

East Wing reception, the president spotted three former chiefs across the room: Duberstein, Bolten, and Podesta. Obama approached them, looking frustrated. "No matter what I do in this town, all I get are singles and bunts," he complained. "Singles and bunts" would become a favorite metaphor: It was a lament he would repeat publicly almost a year later at a press conference during a visit to the Philippines.

It was not the first time Obama had reached out to the former chiefs. After losing sixty-three House seats to Republicans in the 2010 midterm elections, the president had invited Duberstein to the Oval Office for a private talk. Did Ronald Reagan ever doubt his own agenda? he asked him. How did Reagan deal with the crazies—the extremists on Capitol Hill? A few days later, as he boarded **Marine One**, Duberstein noticed that Obama was carrying a copy of Lou Cannon's book, **President Reagan: The Role of a Lifetime.**

Now, three years later, Duberstein advised Obama against trying to do too much at once. "Americans like their change in small sips," he told the president—as Podesta looked on. It was Podesta who had run Obama's transition team and brought the former Clinton chiefs to that secret meeting in Reno four years earlier. Obama had tremendous respect for his brains and strategic savvy.

McDonough was, if anything, an even bigger fan. He had known Podesta since they'd worked together in Daschle's office, where Clinton's former chief had become a mentor. They were both Catholics who shared the same parish, lean and competitive—and ran together almost every morning; though Podesta is almost twenty years older, McDonough concedes, "the f*cker still beats me sometimes." When McDonough became chief, he immediately reached out to his old friend, who started coming to his office on Saturdays. "I needed someone I could let my hair down with," says McDonough. "That's the thing with this job. There's no way to let your hair down. You don't let your hair down with the president. You don't let your hair down at home." With Podesta, McDonough could "close the door and say, 'Look, I don't know what to do with this.' Or 'This thing is really pissing me off.' You know? 'Do you have ideas?' And he had a lot of good ideas—from the very tactical to the quite strategic. There's no doubt that was vital for me."

At the same time, the president was mulling adding a new weapon to his arsenal: executive orders. The idea—the "aha!" moment—was Obama's. "The president was very explicit with me," says McDonough. "'I don't need new authority. I need to execute on the authority that I have.' And he just said, 'Let's not go through that maelstrom of Congress in the hope that we get something. If we've got what we need to get it done, let's execute smartly.'" By the summer of 2014, it was clear the

Democrats would get clobbered in the upcoming midterm elections. "And so we needed to have a plan for the day after we got our ass kicked," says McDonough. "As the president says, 'Plan beats no plan.' And so we got together—a small group. What were the weapons, and how would we deploy them? On immigration. Cuba. Iran. Climate. Clean Power Plan. Executive action. And we just said, 'This is going to be our plan.'" Podesta had pioneered the use of executive orders in the Clinton years and weighed in. "Not only does he know this stuff, he knows how to make a deal, and he knows how to make a deal with f*cking China, India," says McDonough. "So I needed his help. And I remember saying to the president, 'You know, we gotta get John in here.'" Obama required no convincing. "He said, 'Pfft. Good luck with that. I've been trying to get him in here for five years.'"

Obama called up Podesta. "His pitch to me was, 'I need you to come back here,'" he recalls. "Everyone else was trying to fix health care. 'So you need to come back here while everyone else is attending to the forest fire.'" Obama wanted Podesta to take charge of climate change. "He said, 'I want to make sure the stuff I promised gets done. And you can mess around in everything else too. But this is the thing I really need you to do.'"

Podesta came on board as a senior adviser—and immediately kick-started negotiations with the Chinese. President Xi was scheduled to meet with Obama at Sunnylands, California, on June 8. Podesta suggested that Obama take Xi aside and persuade him to agree to a provision in a previous treaty, the Montreal Protocol, regulating HFCs—hydrofluorocarbons, which are major contributors to the greenhouse effect. "And so we did it," says McDonough. "And that was the first step toward the Paris agreement. So this is a big deal. And it all comes from John and those Saturday afternoons we spent right here."

It was a path around gridlock, and a turning point for the administration. To execute the new strategy, McDonough formed small teams dedicated to big projects: the global climate accords; the Iran nuclear deal; the diplomatic opening to Cuba. McDonough's obsession with process paid off. "Denis was very clear about holding and then firing," says Podesta. "**Boom. Boom. Boom. Boom.** He's very good at that. He had lots of moving parts, lots of things getting f*cked up, a lot of stuff could leak. It all held, it was tight, and then it rolled out. And it changed Obama's fortunes; his job approval rating started drifting up after that."

Indeed, Obama's fortunes had improved. Obamacare was finally getting traction—despite a spike in premiums, and challenges from big insurers. The president's approval rating, fifty-five percent, was higher than Reagan's at the end of his second term. McDonough reels off their second-term achievements: "Twenty-two million people with health insurance who wouldn't have had it otherwise. Inflation at the lowest levels for the last four years running since the postwar years. The streak of job creation and growth coming out of the depths of that recession. The lowest incarceration rate and the highest graduation rate on record." Moreover, unless you counted the health-care rollout, there had been no second-term curse.

But perhaps McDonough's defining moment as chief of staff came in the late summer of 2013. The former deputy national security adviser had been at Obama's side as the president struggled to wind down two bloody wars in Afghanistan and Iraq. Now Obama and his chief of staff faced the risk of launching the country into another Middle Eastern war—this one in Syria.

Obama had firmly resisted getting the U.S. involved militarily, fearing a quagmire. But as the bloody conflict raged into its third year, the president and his advisers worried that Syrian dictator Bashar al-Assad might resort to using chemical weapons. In August 2012, the president issued a pointed, and public, warning. "We have been very clear to the Assad regime," Obama declared, "that a red line for us is we start seeing a whole bunch of chemical weapons moving around or being utilized. That would change my calculus. That would change my equation." A year later, in the Damascus suburb of Ghouta, the Assad regime brutally defied the president's warning: The Syrian army massacred fourteen hundred men, women, and children, using the deadly gas sarin.

The clamor for a military response was fierce—even from within the administration. On Friday, August 30, 2013, Secretary of State John Kerry delivered a thundering speech from the Treaty Room of the State Department—an impassioned case that the world could not stand by in the face of such atrocities. The president echoed Kerry's outrage: "It's important for us to recognize that when over a thousand people are killed, including hundreds of innocent children, through the use of a weapon that 98 or 99 percent of humanity says should not be used even in war, and there is no action, then we're sending a signal that the international norm doesn't mean much. And that is a danger to our national security."

Obama was under enormous pressure to enforce his "red line"—with a unilateral military strike against the Syrian regime. The president had the constitutional authority under Article 2 to order cruise missile strikes or other reprisals. The question confronting Obama and his advisers was: Should he?

The answer would define Obama's foreign policy legacy. After all, he had run for president in order to change the kind of unilateralist thinking that had led the United States into Iraq. Obama had opposed that war from the beginning. But as an aide to Majority Leader Daschle, McDonough had helped draft the resolution to invade. "It still bothers me a lot," he says. Daschle says it was a formative experience for his young adviser. "We talked about it a lot. Going to war is always one of the most troubling and momentous moments in anyone's official capacity, and you remember those instances very well. So we look back with a great deal of regret." For McDonough, the Syrian crisis brought those regrets back to the surface.

That afternoon, the president met with his National Security Council to hear final arguments. When they were done, Obama stepped outside to take a walk. He asked McDonough to join him. The president and his chief circled the South Lawn driveway for an hour. When they returned to the Oval Office, where his national security team was waiting, the president made a stunning announcement: Instead of launching an attack, he would stand down. The matter would go to Congress for a vote. Susan Rice, the national security adviser, was apoplectic; America's credibility, she argued, would be seriously damaged. But the president was unmoved. He was at ease with his decision.

News of the development set off a firestorm of criticism from Congress, the foreign policy establishment, and the media. Democrats and Republicans accused the president of abdicating American leadership, sending a dangerous signal of weakness to the world. Panetta and James Baker piled on. "Once everybody said that it was a red line that had been crossed, I just think the president's credibility was very much on the line," says Panetta. "And to suddenly back off and send it to the Hill was the wrong message to send to the world." "Anytime the president of the United States makes a threat, he'd better be damn well prepared to carry it out," says Baker. "You don't ever walk away from that."

McDonough has not talked about what he told the president during their walk. Was it the president's decision to call off a strike—or did McDonough talk him into it? I ask him. "No, if I'm going to make a policy argument with the president, I do that in the presence of my colleagues," he says. "I don't do that when I'm with him alone. It's not fair. I make it when somebody can rebut it—keep me honest. Hold me accountable." Their talk, he says, was "a continuation of a debate that had been going on throughout that day." Obama and his chief shared an almost visceral dislike of the foreign policy establishment. "Something that I've long believed," says McDonough, "is that foreign policy is undercut by a degree of 'me-tooism.' There's a conventional wisdom that the use of force is important for the use of force's sake— because it demonstrates our strength. Right? If we don't use force, somehow we've lost our credibility. Which obviously goes to the heart of why the president thought he should run for president. Right? That's the mind-set that got us into Iraq: We're going to do it even if the costs outweigh the benefits. And he refuses to do that. And the red line, the so-called red line debate, is a perfect example of that." As for the national security team being shocked, McDonough points out that three members had argued **for** going to Congress: Vice President Biden, Kerry, and Defense Secretary Chuck Hagel. And McDonough notes that the president's threat to use force brought Russia to the bargaining table, resulting in the removal and destruction of Syria's chemical arsenal. "That's what I've said so far, and the rest of whatever happened that day rests with Obama," he says.

It was a momentous day, wrote Jeffrey Goldberg in **The Atlantic**—one way or the other: "the day the feckless Barack Obama brought to a premature end America's reign as the world's sole indispensable superpower—or, alternatively, the day the sagacious Barack Obama peered into the Middle Eastern abyss and stepped back from the consuming void."

The decision had been made by Obama, alone with McDonough—one elected, the other appointed and unconfirmed—the latest in a long line of presidents and chiefs who made history together. "I think it captures the relationship of the two men," says Daschle. "The president had a lot of voices, but there was only one person who walked with him that day, and that was Denis. The last person the president spoke to about that decision was Denis. And arguably the most influential person he spoke to was Denis."

EARLIER THAT SUMMER, Barack Obama stood before a small audience in the White House theater. The occasion was a screening of **The Presidents' Gatekeepers**, a documentary about the White House chiefs. "There are a couple of things you learn when you get here," the president said. "Number one, the bubble is even worse than you thought. Number two, the Truman Balcony is pretty cool." Turning serious, Obama talked about the extraordinary sacrifices of soldiers in uniform and their families. And then he pivoted to the subject of the evening. "There are a lot of people here whose job is to make my life easy. I live above the store. But these guys go home every night. And they are up before dawn doing the nation's business and then they have to come and deal with me. And they are humble. I see two of them right now," the president added, flashing a grin, pointing to Duberstein and Bolten in the last row. "They're hiding all the way in the back. That's **typical**." The president said he'd like to stay, but he had unfinished business. "I'm sorry," he said. "But my chief has other plans for me." And with that, the leader of the free world went off in search of Denis McDonough.

Epilogue

Donald Trump's stunning election victory over Hillary Clinton poses the unsettling question: What kind of president will he be? Will he run the White House the way he campaigned: demonizing opponents and making seat-of-the-pants decisions, with no regard for facts or nuance? Or will the burden of the office put a brake on Trump's worst instincts—and enable him to govern effectively?

The answer will depend in no small part on whether he empowers his chief of staff. Trump is no Ronald Reagan, but they have some things in common: almost no one thought the ex–Hollywood actor had the knowledge or bandwidth to be president. "We thought he was terrible," recalls James Baker. "Reagan was a grade B movie actor—**Bedtime for Bonzo**. He was going to get us in a nuclear war; he was dangerous." The former California governor knew nothing about the federal budget or the throw weight of nuclear missiles (incredibly, candidate Trump had never heard of the nuclear triad).

But if he had a second-class intellect, as Oliver Wendell Holmes once said of Franklin Roosevelt, Reagan had a first-class temperament; he listened to informed people around him—particularly Baker, his consummate chief of staff.

Trump is likely to have several chiefs; Bill Clinton and Barack Obama each churned through four. But his presidency cannot succeed unless Trump gives them the authority to do the job. As we have seen in the experience of every president since Eisenhower, the White House staff, the Executive Office of the President, and the administration itself cannot function effectively without a strong chief. (Jimmy Carter and Bill Clinton learned this lesson the hard way during their first two years.) Although the Reagan White House was run by a "troika," Baker controlled the levers of power—and at pivotal moments, he saved Reagan from himself and his hardline advisers. That duty—telling the president what he does not want to hear—will prove all the more important for Trump's chief, who will be advising a man who has shown no evidence that he has the focus, knowledge, or discipline required to be commander in chief. Never has a president been more in need of a "reality therapist," as Ken Duberstein calls the chief's position.

"Power in Washington really does reside in the White House," says Erskine Bowles. "And the little cabal that surrounds the president controls the flow of information to him. And information is power." Trump's chief must control that flow of information to the president and be his honest broker when decisions are made. This will be especially challenging with a national security adviser who is prone to cockeyed conspiracy theories. (And yes, he must shut down Trump's Twitter account when necessary.) The chief must be the gatekeeper who decides who sees the president. He must almost always be in the room to prevent end runs by people pushing their own agendas. Baker was vilified by Reagan's hardliners as a "pragmatist." But he prevailed because Reagan was interested in results, not conservative orthodoxy. Trump's chief will come under fire from the administration's ideologues. That's okay: Trump has no fixed ideology.

"A great president can get away with a mediocre chief; a mediocre president can't possibly," says Robert Reich. "If you have a good White House staff—not just the chief, but the complete staff—it can mean the difference between success and failure," says Baker. "You can't have a White House staff that is dysfunctional. You can't have a White House staff that can't implement. And we've seen some of those White House staffs—and that's a tragedy for the president and the nation."

As we've seen in cycles from H. R. Haldeman through Denis McDonough, the right chief can help a president govern effectively; the wrong chief can spell calamity. When, after four years, Baker swapped jobs with Treasury secretary Donald Regan, the ill-fated handoff led to the Iran-Contra scandal. Regan failed to grasp the danger of a harebrained, off-the-books scheme to trade arms for hostages that was being hatched in the White House basement. George W. Bush's Iraq War was enabled by a White House so dysfunctional that there was never even a meeting of principals to debate the decision to go to war.

Javelin catcher, confidant, consigliere, battlefield commander. Donald Trump's chief will be all of those things, but above all, as Clinton's Leon Panetta puts it, he must be the son of a bitch who can speak truth to power. Richard Nixon, who shared Trump's obsession with enemies, turned the White House into a criminal enterprise. But it could have been even worse: Haldeman ignored many orders that were illegal or beyond the pale—such as Nixon's demands to firebomb the Brookings Institute and give lie detector tests to **everyone** in the State

Department. Angered by a leak, Reagan wanted to strap up every cabinet officer to a polygraph machine. When Baker heard about the plan, he charged into the Oval Office and persuaded the president to rescind the order.

Donald Trump's chief is going to have a lot of days like that. And the stakes could not be higher. Watergate. Iran-Contra. The Iraq War. The Obamacare rollout. Every one of those debacles might have been avoided if the White House chief of staff had been more vigilant, subjecting those decisions to a rigorous process designed to avoid catastrophe.

"It's a crucially important position," says Jack Watson, Carter's final chief. "It affects everything. It affects the president's relationships with Congress and the cabinet. It affects the integrity and effectiveness of the decision-making process. It affects the way presidential decisions are explained and implemented. Do I believe the modern presidency requires that kind of chief of staff in order for a president to be successful? I emphatically do."

Given his lifelong inclinations, President Trump may try to run the White House himself—his gut instincts unchecked, his decisions uninformed, his Twitter account unfiltered. Or he may empower his chief of staff to implement his agenda, advise honestly on difficult choices, and tell him what he does not want to hear.

Working next to the most powerful person in

the world is an extraordinary privilege. For Trump's chief, the job also carries a profound responsibility: He may well represent the thin line between the president and disaster.

Chris Whipple
December 6, 2016
New York City

Notes

Introduction: "I Brought My Pillow and My Blankie"

2 **"Black Man Given Nation's Worst Job"** The Onion, November 4, 2008, vol. 44.

3 **But to his amazement** W. Marvin Watson and James Jones, sometimes considered chiefs under Lyndon Johnson, held the title appointments secretary; they were not invited by Bolten.

3 **"It really was an amazing day"** Interview with John Podesta, November 9, 2012.

3 **"It's a space where you feel the presence of history"** Interview with Joshua Bolten, September 26, 2011.

4 **"This was unique"** Interview with Dick Cheney, July 15, 2011.

5 **a bygone era of civility** In December 2016, following Joshua Bolten's precedent with Rahm Emanuel, Denis McDonough invited all the living chiefs to the White House to meet with Donald Trump's incoming gatekeeper, Reince Priebus. Ten ex-chiefs were present; James Baker, Leon Panetta, and Erskine Bowles did not attend. "Several of us made the point that he has to be first among equals," recalls one chief of their advice to Priebus. "If there is power sharing in the White House, you can't get things done." Few came away confident that Priebus was up to the challenge of corralling Trump or his headstrong advisers.

7 **"Always remember"** Interview with Ken Duberstein, August 10, 2011.

8 **"Never forget the extraordinary opportunity"** Interview with Jack Watson, August 11, 2011.

9 **"Try to keep some perspective"** Interview with Mack McLarty, September 22, 2011.

10 **"I was very good"** Interview with John Sununu, August 11, 2011.

11 **"Always, always be straight"** Interview with Leon Panetta, November 9, 2012.

11 **"These are truly historic people"** Interview with Andy Card, October 12, 2011.

13 **"Immediately pick your successor"** Interview with Donald Rumsfeld, June 14, 2011.

14 **"somewhere to the right of Genghis Khan"** Robert Hartmann, **Palace Politics** (New York: McGraw-Hill, 1980), 283.

14 **"control your vice president"** Interview with Dick Cheney, July 15, 2011.

15 **"Every president reveals himself"** Interview with Richard Norton Smith, November 7, 2013.

17 **"One of the things I've learned"** Barack Obama, interview with Charlie Rose. **Charlie Rose**, PBS, April 19, 2016.

17 **"But every president knows"** Samuel Kernell and Samuel K. Popkin, eds. **Chief of Staff: Twenty-Five Years of Managing the Presidency** (New York: University of California Press, 1988), 189.

17 **"People ask me"** Interview with Erskine Bowles, December 16, 2011.

18 **'Thank God—only two more . . .'** The chief's job may be more grueling than its television version, but it pays considerably less. George W. Bush's Andrew Card was once introduced to the actor John Spencer, who portrayed chief of staff Leo McGarry in **The West Wing**. "How much do you make?" Spencer asked him. "$145,000," replied Card. Mystified, Spencer responded: "Is that per episode?"

18 **Bill Daley came down with shingles** Interview with Bill Daley, May 3, 2012.

1 "The Lord High Executioner"

23 "the largest corporation in the world." Samuel Kernell and Samuel L. Popkin, eds. **Chief of Staff**, 184.

24 **the second-closest popular vote margin in history** Recently discovered notes by Haldeman seem to confirm the decades-old charge that Nixon sought to ensure his 1968 election by sabotaging peace talks between the Johnson administration and South Vietnam. Haldeman's notes record Nixon's order, made during a telephone call, to throw a "monkey wrench" into the talks. LBJ was livid about Nixon's interference, and privately accused him of treason. But it is not clear that Haldeman himself did anything to follow up on Nixon's commands.

24 "a crisis equal in magnitude to Lincoln's" Theodore P. White, **The Making of the President: 1968** (New York: Antheneum, 1969), 485.

24 "Poor Ike" James B. Chapin, UPI, April 16, 2002.

25 **Brownlow Committee** President's Committee on Administrative Management. **Report of the Committee** (Washington, DC: Government Printing Office, 1937).

25 **first White House chief of staff** John Steelman, who served President Harry Truman for six years, is sometimes referred to as the first White

House chief. But Steelman, a trusted confidant, did not exercise the wide-ranging powers of Sherman Adams.

25 **"Possessed of the disposition of a grizzly"** TIME, January 8, 1956, vol. 67, issue 2, 20.

27 **"Eisenhower had told Nixon that every president has to have his own 'SOB.'"** H. R. Haldeman with Joseph DiMona, **The Ends of Power** (New York: Dell, 1978), 86.

28 **"Bob Haldeman would have been a superstar"** Interview with Larry Higby, February 21, 2012.

29 **"Nixon was envious"** Interview with Evan Thomas, March 18, 2016.

29 **"Ivy League suits, a straight arrow"** Interview with Tom Brokaw, March 15, 2016.

30 **"There was no real close personal bond"** Interview with John Dean, April 3, 2016.

30 **"... Nixon's politics appealed to Haldeman."** "One of the great mysteries about Haldeman is, what drives him?" says Nixon biographer Thomas. "One of his clients was Walt Disney, who was an awful man. And so Haldeman thinks, 'I'm used to dealing with weirdos and geniuses. And if I could do it for Walt Disney, I could do it for Richard Nixon.'"

31 **"He has no time to think"** Memo, H. R. Haldeman to Richard Nixon; June 20, 1967; Folder 12, Box 33, White House Special Files; Richard Nixon Presidential Library and Museum, Yorba Linda, California.

31 **"There has to be a staff system."** Interview with Donald Rumsfeld, May 6, 2014.

32 **"Our job is not to do the work of government"** William Safire, **Before the Fall: An Inside View of the Pre-Watergate White House** (Garden City: Doubleday, 1975), 116.

34 **"similar in a way to Cathy and Heathcliff"** Ibid., 11.

35 **image making escaped Haldeman's attention** A history of UCLA alumni recounted the staging of the 1947 homecoming parade: "The student chairman, Bob Haldeman '48, suggested a change in the format. Instead of the queen and her court riding unceremoniously in convertible automobiles, he proposed that a special float be built to transport them in style. Alumni volunteers accepted the challenge, producing a beautiful conveyance in record time."

35 **"Harry Robbins Haldeman is Richard Nixon's son of a bitch"** Newsweek, May 7, 1973.

36 **"Haldeman absolutely reamed both of them"** Interview with John Dean, April 3, 2016.

36 **"when in fact, it hasn't"** Memorandum for Mr. Magruder, July 7, 1970. Reproduced at the Richard Nixon Presidential Library.

37 **"He expected perfection"** Interview with Terry O'Donnell, February 5, 2014.

37 **annual Gridiron dinner.** The volume of these memos is staggering: Over two days at Yorba Linda's Richard Nixon Library, the author and

his wife could barely scratch the surface of these Nixon-Haldeman exchanges.

37 **A single day, March 16, 1970** Richard Nixon Presidential Library and Museum, Yorba Linda, California.

39 **"The most important thing"** Interview with Stephen Bull, February 25, 2016.

39 **State, Defense, Commerce, Treasury, HEW, Labor** The Department of Health, Education and Welfare (HEW) was renamed the U.S. Department of Health and Human Services in 1979.

40 **". . . they've got to get Haldeman to fire me . . ."** John Dean's role in Nixon's Watergate crimes remains controversial; the president's loyalists still regard him as a villain who was up to his neck in the "White House horrors." But Dean says he tried to strangle the so-called enemies program at birth: "They first of all had to push me and push me and push me to write a memo to design this program and I finally did. I thought I wrote a memo that Haldeman would find so obnoxious—the 'screw your enemies' document—that he would say, 'We're not gonna do this, obviously!' And when that memo came back and he said, 'Great! Go!' I almost shat! I realized I don't know these people at all!"

40 **Nixon called a cabinet meeting** H. R. Haldeman, **The Haldeman Diaries: Inside the Nixon White House** (New York: Berkeley Books, 1994), 375.

42 **"Haldeman's anti-Semitism is one of his fatal flaws."** Interview with Evan Thomas, March 18, 2016.

42 **A presidential memo, casually dictated to aide Peter Flanigan** Richard Nixon Library.

42 **"'I think there's a cabal of Democrats'"** Interview with Fred Malek, March 11, 2016.

43 **"this commissioner who was Jewish!"** It is not quite true that "nothing happened." Four people on Malek's list of Jewish employees got demoted, with Malek's active involvement.

44 **"I was ordered by the president"** Samuel Kernell and Samuel L. Popkin, eds., **Chief of Staff**, 22.

45 **spirited out of the State Department** There are several theories about what Nixon was after when he demanded a break-in at the Brookings Institution: (1) classified documents related to the **Pentagon Papers**; (2) information showing that LBJ had ordered a bombing halt in Vietnam for partisan political purposes; and (3) information LBJ had obtained from wiretaps implicating Nixon in a plot to sabotage the Paris Peace Talks during the 1968 campaign.

45 **"Just go in and take it. Go in around 8:00 or 9 o'clock."** OVAL 533-1: June 30, 1971; White House Tapes; Richard Nixon Presidential Library and Museum, Yorba Linda, California.

46 **"Those sons of bitches are killing me"** OVAL 534-2(3); July 1, 1971; White House Tapes;

Richard Nixon Presidential Library and Museum, Yorba Linda, California.

46 **the harebrained plot would come to life again.**
Nixon's edicts ranged from the illegal to the inane.
Enraged by a statement made by his Interior secretary, Walter Hickel, an avid tennis player, Nixon ordered Haldeman to have the White House tennis court paved over. He ignored the demand.
"There was an unspoken understanding between them," explains historian Richard Norton Smith.
"The old man could be bombastic or illegal or whatever—and Haldeman would protect him from himself." (Until he didn't.)

47 **that would end his presidency.** There are also those who argue that Nixon wanted to keep the war going until he could not be blamed for losing it. According to this school of thought, any peace settlement agreeable to North Vietnam would have doomed his reelection chances.

47 **"I call it the Madman Theory"** H. R. Haldeman with Joseph DiMona, **The Ends of Power**, 122.

48 **"had an eye for history"** Safire, **Before the Fall**, 117.

49 **". . . the system that later became the tapes."**
The taping system was known only to the president; Haldeman; aides Alexander Butterfield, Larry Higby, and Stephen Bull; and a handful of Secret Service technicians. It was sound activated—except in the Cabinet Room: "Alex

Butterfield always wanted to know instantly when the president went in the Cabinet Room," recalls Bull. "And I wondered: 'What's the big deal?'" The big deal was that tapes in the Cabinet Room had to be switched on manually each time.

49   **"For want of a toggle switch, the presidency was lost."** H. R. Haldeman with Joseph DiMona, **The Ends of Power**, 120.

50   **The sensational leak . . . enraged Nixon.** Oddly, Nixon at first seemed unconcerned about the **Pentagon Papers:** the secret history was mostly about the misdeeds of his predecessors JFK and LBJ. But Kissinger was apoplectic and fanned the flames of the president's ire. "Henry is the one who told Nixon that if you don't go after Ellsberg you'll be considered a weakling," recalls John Dean. "It'll damage our back channel with the North Vietnamese in Paris; it'll result in the Chinese being unwilling to deal with us—and the world will see you as a weakling."

50   **"He feels strongly that we've got to get Ellsberg nailed hard."** H. R. Haldeman, **The Haldeman Diaries**, 368.

50   **But other Nixon confidants** Haldeman describes Colson as "the President's personal hit man; the impresario of hard-ball politics. I had been caught in the middle as complaints thundered in about 'Wildman' Colson either crashing arrogantly, or sneaking silently, through political em-

pires supposedly controlled by top White House staffers. . . . Colson cared not who complained; Nixon, he said, was his only boss. And Nixon was behind him all the way on projects ranging from his long-dreamed-of hope of catching Senator Ted Kennedy in bed with a woman not his wife, to more serious struggles."

50 **". . . salute, and go do it!"** Interview with John Dean, April 3, 2016.

52 **"If done under your assurance that"** Egil Krogh and David Young, Memorandum, August 11, 1971. SSE Exhibit # 9.0, 6SSE 2644-45, the Richard Nixon Presidential Library.

52 **the White House gave the green light** What was the reason for the Watergate break-in? Theories range from gathering intelligence on the Democratic presidential campaign, to getting dirt on DNC chairman Larry O'Brien and the billionaire Howard Hughes, to proving that lower-level DNC officials were involved in a prostitution ring.

53 **"phenomenal, out-of-sight . . ."** Interview with John Dean, April 3, 2016.

54 **"The news item was jarring . . ."** H. R. Haldeman with Joseph DiMona, **The Ends of Power**, 26.

55 **". . . I had felt no instinctive aversion . . ."** FBI director Hoover's boast to Nixon that LBJ had ordered the bugging of Nixon's campaign plane was just bluster. Cartha "Deke" DeLoach, the

FBI agent who supposedly carried out the bugging, confirmed that it never happened.

55 "... **Pentagon Papers and other research-type stuff.**" Hunt's "research-type stuff" included the bungled break-in at Daniel Ellsberg's psychiatrist's office.

57 **"Haldeman is more important to me than Adams was to Ike"** Stephen E. Ambrose, **Nixon: Ruin and Recovery, 1973–1990** (New York: Simon & Schuster, 1991), 99.

57 **As he recalled in his diary** H. R. Haldeman with Joseph DiMona, **The Ends of Power**, 368.

58 **"I knew I needed to talk to Ehrlichman ..."** Ibid., 371.

59 **"... I just couldn't face going on ..."** Ibid., 374.

59 **"two of the finest public servants it has been my privilege to know."** Richard Nixon speech announcing resignations of H. R. Haldeman and John Ehrlichman, April 30, 1973.

60 **"Cap Weinberger, bless his soul"** Caspar W. "Cap" Weinberger was Nixon's secretary of health and human services.

61 **"I love you, as you know."** TELEPHONE 45-41; April 30, 1973: White House Tapes; Richard Nixon Presidential Library and Museum, Yorba Linda, California.

61 **"a cancer growing on the presidency."** OVAL 886-6; March 21, 1973; White House Tapes; Richard Nixon Presidential Library and Museum, Yorba Linda, California.

62 "... it would be a highly controversial move to destroy them." Richard Nixon, **RN: The Memoirs of Richard Nixon** (New York: Simon & Schuster, 1978), 901. Nixon later regretted his decision, writing: "In the early morning of July 19 I had made a note on my bedside pad: 'Should have destroyed the tapes after April 30, 1973.'"

63 **Haldeman would defend Richard Nixon** He did so even when the disgraced president later threw his ex-chief under the bus, telling David Frost, in a paid television appearance, that his mistake was not firing Haldeman and Ehrlichman sooner.

64 **"Son of Nixonstein"** Paul Conrad, **Los Angeles Times**, August 3, 1973, 33.

65 **"Had we dealt with [Watergate] ..."** Samuel Kernell and Samuel L. Popkin, eds., **Chief of Staff**, 67.

2 "Beware the Spokes of the Wheel"

68 **"ruthless little bastard."** OVAL 464-12; March 9, 1971; White House Tapes; Richard Nixon Presidential Library and Museum, Yorba Linda, California.

69 **"... Washington in the summertime."** I looked back on that day many, many years later," Cheney recalls, "when I was riding to Capitol Hill in a limousine as the newly elected vice president to-

gether with George Bush to get sworn in as the Bush-Cheney administration. I couldn't help but be amazed at all that had transpired since."

69 **"Our high school and college circumstances . . ."** Actually, Rumsfeld had graduated from Princeton; Cheney had flunked out of Yale not once, but twice.

71 **and Ford his understudy** Years later, as Ronald Reagan recovered from a would-be assassin's bullet, Haig, his secretary of state, would famously mangle the succession of power, declaring: "I am in control here."

72 **his belongings into a cubbyhole** "Bob [Hartmann] moved into the office that Rose Mary Woods used to have, which is right next door," recalls Dick Cheney. "It had a back door entrance to the Oval Office. And he just moved in and took over. Squatters' rights." Rose Mary Woods, Richard Nixon's longtime secretary, jealously guarded her direct access to her boss—and never forgave H. R. Haldeman, when he forced her to report through him.

73 **"Soon I began to depend [on] . . ."** Gerald R. Ford, **A Time to Heal** (New York: Berkley Books, 1979), 183.

73 **Kennerly had carte blanche** Kennerly was one of Ford's first official appointments. Sitting in the living room of Ford's house in Alexandria, Virginia, Kennerly told the new president he had

two conditions for becoming his White House photographer: "One was that I would report directly to the president. The second was that I would have total access. Ford took a drag on his pipe and said: 'I suppose you want **Air Force One** on weekends too?'"

73 **"I was every political adviser's worst nightmare."** Interview with David Hume Kennerly, December 3, 2012.

73 **Hartmann called Haig and his staff "the Praetorians"** Robert Hartmann, **Palace Politics**, 35.

73 **and proceeded to end-run them.** Hartmann did not like Cheney either. "He said I had 'the snake-cold eyes of a riverboat gambler,'" says Cheney. "I took it as a compliment."

74 **personified by the glowering Haldeman** Ford shared the popular belief that Haldeman had helped cause Watergate by isolating the president. And he disliked Nixon's chief personally; in their encounters on Capitol Hill, Ford had bristled at Haldeman's arrogance.

75 **"Americans weren't just dumbstruck . . ."** David Gergen, **Eyewitness to Power: The Essence of Leadership Nixon to Clinton** (New York: Simon & Schuster, 2000), 117.

75 **Ford had cut a secret deal** In fact, Ford had made no backroom deal; he simply concluded that his presidency would be paralyzed by the prospect of a Nixon prosecution. A pardon, he was con-

vinced, was his only chance to put Watergate behind him. (A quarter century later, Ford's decision would be vindicated by a Profile in Courage Award from the Kennedy Library.)

77 **"I concluded he was right . . ."** Gerald R. Ford, **A Time to Heal**, 182.

77 **". . . Rumsfeld feels is appealing"** Rumsfeld granted the author exclusive access to this and other private memoranda from his tenure as chief of staff. In a September 22, 1974, memo, also previously unpublished, Rumsfeld dictated: "I did appreciate [the president's] comment that a position of substance and importance in the Cabinet would be available in the coming months, and he agreed. He said, 'Don, you have a commitment on that.'"

78 **Rumsfeld would return from Europe** Because Ford was still sensitive about flip-flopping on his vow to have a "spokes of the wheel" model, Rumsfeld's title would be "staff coordinator" instead of chief.

78 **permitted to see Ford alone** Kennerly also had access to Ford, and unusual privileges. A notorious bachelor, he would often bring his dates along on **Air Force One**. (A conservative Ford opponent threatened an investigation into "transporting minors across state lines for immoral purposes.") But Ford enjoyed the company, and Rumsfeld knew better than to object.

79 **the secretary of state would come on time** After

meeting with Ford in the Oval Office, Rumsfeld noted in a memo: "By 9:15, when I had finished, and Kissinger still had not arrived for the third day in a row, the President said, 'Maybe we ought to change Kissinger's time.' . . . I said, 'Frankly, the fact of the matter is you're the President of the United States and he is one of your Cabinet officers and it is a very bad signal in the White House and in the Department of State and elsewhere in this town for him to be 15 and 20 and 30 minutes late for meetings with you three days in a row. It positions you in the wrong place.'"

79 **called "yellow perils"** "I'd go out and dictate a note: the president wants this that and the other thing and I told him this this and this," recalls Rumsfeld. "My secretary would type them up and then we would start doing those things." Whether or not Rumsfeld knew that "yellow perils" was an offensive stereotype about Asians is unclear.

79 **". . . you don't have a lot of leisure time . . ."** Years later, as George W. Bush's defense secretary, reviewing a memo on interrogation techniques for military detainees at Guantánamo, Rumsfeld would reject waterboarding and some of the harsher techniques approved by the CIA. "However," he wrote in the margin, "I stand for 8-10 hours a day. Why is standing limited to four hours?"

80 **he was told to leave Yale for good** A good student

and star football player in high school, Cheney had been awarded a fully paid scholarship to Yale. He squandered it: "I needed a purpose to be there, and I didn't have one. It was a great place to party. We had a couple of guys there that were really good students. And they managed to do that by not spending too much time hanging out with the rest of us."

80 **facedown on the floor of a jail cell** "It was a wake-up call," Cheney told me. "I had a hell of a hangover. And I realized that if I stayed on the road that I was on I was going to come to a bad end." Cheney had another incentive to get sober. His girlfriend, Lynne Ann Vincent, threatened to leave him: "She was going to dump me. That would be a fair statement."

81 **". . . and go with someone less controversial . . ."** Cheney could scarcely believe that he and Rumsfeld were running the White House. "Don and I were taking on the job because Nixon left and Ford took over and we were young enough and foolish enough to think we could do it. It was maybe not an insurmountable task, but a tough set of propositions."

85 **"Standup desk, navy guy."** Interview with Brent Scowcroft, May 7, 2014.

86 **"Rockefeller was a Roosevelt Republican."** Interview with Richard Norton Smith, November 7, 2013.

86 **"Rummy, you're never going to be president!"**
Rumsfeld insists the encounter never took place.

87 **". . . people who disagreed with him."** Speaking
to me forty years later, Rumsfeld said of Rockefeller: "He wasn't qualified to be vice president
of **anything.** I don't think he was at the top of his
game when he was vice president to Gerald Ford.
Undoubtedly, in his earlier career, when he was
younger, he probably handled things in a different way that made him more successful."

87 **"Rumsfeld did not take advice . . ."** Gail Raiman
interview with Richard Norton Smith, Gerald R.
Ford Oral History Project, May 6, 2011.

88 **. . . his Secret Service name was "Backseat."** Of
his code name, Cheney says, "I thought it was
appropriate because it was a staff job. You're not
supposed to be out there making public policy
pronouncements. If the chief of staff is out there
pontificating on the size of the budget, you are
going to begin to create doubt in the minds of
your colleagues or the cabinet about your ability
to be an honest broker."

89 **". . . He knew he had been had."** On another
occasion, Cheney conspired with the press corps
to spring an elaborate trap on **Newsweek** correspondent Tom DeFrank. While DeFrank was out
reporting, live sheep were herded into his hotel
room, where they defecated all over everything.

90 **a subject so arcane** Says Cheney: "He was the

first president since Harry Truman, in 1948, who briefed his own budget. He had the whole cabinet lined up. . . . Anybody who was there that day never forgot. . . . He handled every question beautifully and it was a performance that [showed] the true breadth and capabilities of the man."

90 **"I told him that in talking about his relationship . . ."** Donald Rumsfeld memo shared with author.

91 **Congress rejected his plea** "He made a plea personally for the funds," recalls Rumsfeld. "And when it was turned down he was furious. I heard him as angry with the Congress as I've ever seen him."

92 **"The situation is dire but salvageable."** Donald Rumsfeld memo shared with author.

92 **"Kissinger said the Vietnam situation was hopeless . . ."** Donald Rumsfeld memo shared with author.

93 **"the war has been marked by so many lies . . . end with one last lie."** Donald Rumsfeld, **Known and Unknown: A Memoir** (New York: Penguin, 2011), 209.

94 **"He had climbed out of the debris left by Nixon . . ."** James Cannon, **Gerald R. Ford: An Honorable Life** (Ann Arbor: The University of Michigan, 2013), 283.

95 **"We gotta change our strategy."** Interview with Stuart Spencer, March 21, 2016.

95 "... very dull, terrible speeches." Lou Cannon interview with Richard Norton Smith, Gerald R. Ford Oral History Project, November 16, 2009.

96 "... long national nightmare ..." Gerald Ford (August 9, 1974), "Swearing-In Ceremony," President's Speeches and Statements, Gerald R. Ford Presidential Library.

96 "This has got to be the dummest..." Memo shared with author by Donald Rumsfeld. It wasn't just Hartmann's work habits that bothered Rumsfeld. In this post–**Mad Men** era, liquor flowed freely at the White House, but Hartmann took his drinking to another level. "Bob imbibed heavily," says Cheney. After one trip on **Air Force One**, the presidential motorcade was forced to wait, idling on the tarmac—until Hartmann could be carried off the plane.

97 FUNDAMENTAL PROBLEMS The Rumsfeld Archives, Memorandum for the President, October 24, 1975.

101 "leaving the spot open for others" George Bush with Victor Gold, **Looking Forward: An Autobiography** (New York: Bantam Books, 1987), 155.

102 Bush was a last-minute substitute. Rumsfeld remains furious that George H. W. Bush peddled the rumor in his book. Forty years later, in an interview at College Station, Texas, I asked the forty-first president if he believed Rumsfeld had conspired to send him to the CIA. "That was

kind of the common wisdom," Bush replied. "But he denied it, and I accept his word. I have no reason to doubt him, to doubt his word of honor on that." If that was intended as an olive branch to his old rival, Rumsfeld, in a subsequent interview with me, swatted it away. "That's a clever answer," he snapped. "But you know what he wrote in his book. What I could never understand was why George Herbert Walker Bush didn't accept President Ford's version."

102 **Scowcroft, who would become** Decades later, Scowcroft and Cheney would stop speaking to each other over the Iraq War, when Scowcroft opposed the impending U.S. invasion in an essay for the **Wall Street Journal**. Scowcroft said of his former friend Cheney: "I've known him for thirty years. But Dick Cheney I don't know anymore."

102 **"a very regular, down-to-earth guy"** Interview with Bob Schieffer, March 9, 2016.

103 **depended in no small part** "For a long time, I don't think Jerry Ford knew that I was only thirty-three when I went to work for him, and then thirty-four when I took over," Cheney told me. "I remember the day I took my parents in to see him in the Oval Office. We had a very nice time, took pictures, had my kids there, my mom, my dad, my wife. And then they left and the president kept going on about what a remarkably young man my father appeared—he's

in tremendous shape, he just looks so good. The fact was my dad was younger than he was."

103 **"Once Reagan got his voice and started whipping us . . ."** David Gergen, **Eyewitness to Power,** 135.

104 **repudiate his own foreign policy** To appease his conservative delegates, Ford agreed not to fight language in the party platform condemning détente with the Soviet Union. This made Henry Kissinger, détente's architect, apoplectic. But Ford, backed by Cheney and Stu Spencer, argued: " 'Look here, we don't have the votes to stop it. Do you want to win this vote and lose the nomination?' "

105 **Ford corrected his gaffe** Cheney recalls, "We had to clean it up. And we sat Ford down and said, 'Mr. President, you gotta go out there and say you understand that the Soviets still do dominate Eastern Europe.' And he said, 'Oh, all right, I'll do it.' So we got the press all around, and as we walked out, he spun around on his heel and jabbed me in the chest and said, 'Poland is not dominated by the Soviet Union!' " Cheney turned pale. But Ford went out and dutifully corrected his error.

105 **he began to hit his stride** Jimmy Carter had committed a few blunders of his own. The Baptist nominee confessed to **Playboy:** "I've looked on a lot of women with lust—I've committed adultery in my heart."

106 "It was still close enough . . ." James Cannon, **Gerald R. Ford: An Honorable Life**, 440.

106 "I'll never forget the look on his face." Interview with Ron Nessen, February 27, 2015.

106 "I didn't care for the task." Dick Cheney with Liz Cheney, **In My Time: A Personal Political Memoir** (New York: Threshold Editions, 2011), 107.

3 "The Smartest Man in the Room"

110–111 ". . . I am not saying that lightly" Interview with Jack Watson, August 11, 2011. Thomas P. "Tip" O' Neill, the Democratic Speaker of the House, wrote: "When it came to understanding the issues of the day, Jimmy Carter was the smartest public official I've ever known." Katharine Graham, publisher of the **Washington Post**, agreed, saying: "Carter is by far the most intelligent president of my lifetime."

115 **Jordan gave up his summer job spraying mosquitos** Peter G. Bourne, **Jimmy Carter: A Comprehensive Biography from Plains to Postpresidency** (New York: Scribner, 1997), 155.

115 **an unabashedly good old Georgia boy.** Jody Powell had actually grown up on a cotton and peanut farm just a few miles down the road from Carter's. But in style and demeanor he was more worldly than Ham Jordan.

115 **"He not only lacked the polish"** Peter G. Bourne, **Jimmy Carter**, 185.

116 **a fifty-nine-page memo.** 1976 Presidential Campaign Director's Office, Campaign Director—Hamilton Jordan, "Memorandum—Hamilton Jordan to Jimmy Carter, 11/4/72, Box 199.

116 **"He had the most brilliant . . ."** Interview with Gerald Rafshoon, September 23, 2013.

116 **". . . sort of the Burt Reynolds or Dogpatch figure."** Interview with James Fallows, November 19, 2014.

117 **from energy policy to foreign affairs.** Watson and Novak assigned teams to produce twenty-four folders of exhaustive research on subjects from economics to foreign policy.

118 **"We were all slogging away . . ."** Interview with Stu Eizenstat, May 15, 2015.

118 **"Carter had these true believers . . ."** Interview with David Rubenstein, May 14, 2015.

118 **"I'm in charge . . ."** Interview with Alan Novak, February 8, 2014.

119 **" 'I want Ham to take the lead on this.' "** Interview with Jack Watson, February 17, 2015.

119 **"It was two months into the transition . . ."** Samuel Kernell and Samuel Popkin, eds., **Chief of Staff**, 189.

120 **"But that's not going to happen."** Marilyn Berger, "Cyrus R. Vance, a Confidant of Presidents Is Dead at 84," **New York Times**, February 3, 2002.

121 **Dick Cheney met regularly with Carter's transition team** Interview with Dick Cheney, July 15, 2011.

121 **Giving advisers equal access** Recalling the transition meetings with Cheney four decades later, James Fallows was struck by his charm and cooperative spirit: "He was an unrecognizably different figure from the malign being we know now. He was humorous and bipartisan. What happened to **him**?"

123 **Charles Kirbo had urged the nominee** Peter G. Bourne, **Jimmy Carter: A Comprehensive Biography**, 359.

123 **"Some Thoughts on Organizing the Executive Office of the President."** Memo from Carter library dated November 3, 1976.

124 **He hated administrative duties** "I would be out there playing tennis with Ham on the White House court," recalls Fallows. "That was in the days of cellphones that were the size of toaster ovens—and he would get some call from the prime minister of England. And he would fumble for some slip of paper in his tennis shorts."

124 **head of intergovernmental affairs** In his memoir, Carter wrote of Watson's role: "His responsibilities were to see that the various leaders of government agencies worked in harmony and that governors and other state and local officials had an effective representative in Washington.

He also arranged cabinet meetings, prepared the minutes and insured [sic] that when new laws were passed, they were implemented properly and without delay." But however important these duties might be, Watson had been removed from Carter's inner circle.

126 **"Instead Ham would give them to me."** Interview with Landon Butler, April 13, 2015. Jordan argued that returning phone calls would somehow undercut his congressional liaison, Frank Moore, who had played the same role for Carter with the Georgia legislature. But Moore was a stranger to Washington, and many believed he was in over his head.

127 **"Hannibal Jerkin"** Tip O'Neill with William Novak, **Man of the House: The Life and Political Memoirs of Speaker Tip O'Neill** (New York: Random House, 1987), 311.

127 **the thirty-ninth president spoke with me** Interview with Jimmy Carter, September 14, 2011.

128 **". . . without adequate thought . . ."** Other than Jordan's, the smartest political mind in the White House might have been the first lady's. "Rosalynn's political judgment was sometimes better than Jimmy's—**frequently** better than Jimmy's," says Watson. "I don't deny that," Carter told me. "In fact, Rosalynn was much more sensitive to the political aspects of the presidency than I was."

129 **Carter was forced to accept** Of that plan for

"those worthless dam projects," he later wrote: "I regretted it as much as any budget decision I made as president."

129 **"I can give him 150 pages to read . . ."** Interview with Brent Scowcroft, May 7, 2014.

129 **"'Thank you for empowering us . . .'"** Interview with Arnie Miller, February 5, 2014.

129 **requests to play on the White House tennis court.** Memo from Carter Library dated May 26, 1977. Although some Carter loyalists have questioned whether the president actually scheduled play on the White House tennis court, he did—as a memo from the Carter Library attests.

132 **"We failed to appreciate until too late the repercussions . . ."** Jody Powell, **The Other Side of the Story: Why the News Is Often Wrong, Unsupportable and Unfair—an Insider's View by the Former Presidential Press Secretary** (New York: William Morrow and Company, Inc., 1984), 111.

134 **"1979. A good year to pronounce the American century dead . . ."** Kevin Mattson, **"What the Heck Are You Up To, Mr. President?": Jimmy Carter, America's "Malaise," and the Speech That Should Have Changed the Country** (New York: Bloomsbury, 2009), 13.

135 **the only way to reach them** In his diary entry for July 4, 1978, Carter wrote: "I got up early and read Pat Caddell's memorandum—one of the most brilliant analyses of sociological and politi-

cal interrelationships I have ever seen. The more I read it along with Rosalynn, the more I became excited."

136 **"expectations akin to Moses's descent from Mt. Sinai."** Peter G. Bourne, **Jimmy Carter**, 445.

137 **so-called malaise speech** Carter never actually used the word **malaise** in the famous speech.

138 **The move was meant to be pro forma** The entire cabinet submitted their resignations, but only three members were replaced: HEW secretary Joseph Califano, Treasury secretary Michael Blumenthal, and Energy secretary James Schlesinger. As the president recalled in his diaries: "I accepted the recommendation of the attorney general that all cabinet members submit resignations so that I might accept those that should leave. This announcement to the press created an impression of crisis and sent the wrong message about my confidence in the remaining cabinet members."

142 **"Obviously, I regret . . ."** In his interview with me in 2011, Jimmy Carter reflected on Operation Neptune Spear, the mission that succeeded in killing Osama bin Laden: "It brought back vivid memories to me. As you know, one of the helicopters crashed in that attempt to get Osama bin Laden and I'm sure that because of my experience [the ill-fated 1980 mission to rescue the American hostages] they probably doubled up on the margin of error so that they wouldn't make the same mistake that I made."

142 **was now in charge of preparing Reagan** James Baker had been given the assignment of preparing Reagan by campaign manager Stuart Spencer: "I trusted Jimmy, I knew he had good judgment. He was well prepared. But the most important thing he did—and that was his lawyering—was the ground rules. So they can't get an advantage. The podium sizes, the distances, the subject matter. Those negotiations where being a lawyer came in, he just did a great job."

143 **"My standing in the public opinion polls fell."** Jimmy Carter, **Keeping Faith: Memoirs of a President** (Fayetteville: The University of Arkansas Press, 1995), 542.

144 **"made her the most famous antinuclear advocate in America . . ."** Ibid., 574.

144 **"It was out of my hands . . ."** Ibid., 575.

145 **inflation, unemployment** Carter describes his predicament this way: "The crisis that affected the global economic system when I was in office was caused by Iraq's invasion of Iran.

"And it cut off all the oil supply from those two countries abruptly so there was an oil shortage, which resulted in skyrocketing inflation in this country and even worse in England and France and Europe and Japan. I think that was something that would have been overcome and it was not a permanent and deeply entrenched economic problem."

147 **"Unfair Battering Taken by Hamilton Jordan"** Richard Cohen, **Washington Post**, December 7, 1980; C1.

150 **"I have great respect for President Carter . . ."** Interview with John Podesta, November 9, 2012.

4 "One Hell of a Chief of Staff"

152 **"That was a traumatic thing for me . . ."** Interview with James Baker, May 24, 2016.

155 **it was the beginning of a close friendship** Baker describes his friendship with George H. W. Bush as "absolutely deeply personal. And still is—he and Barbara were the last nonfamily to see my first wife before she died. We were not only friends; we were tennis partners, we won doubles championships together before he ever went into politics. We've been political partners. He's my daughter's godfather. And we're extraordinarily close."

155 **"Ed couldn't organize a two-car funeral."** Interview with Stu Spencer, March 21, 2016.

156 **". . . Number two, he's upwardly mobile . . ."** Spencer says of his friend Baker. "The fact that Jimmy was so protective of his image was a joke between us. I did an interview on him one time, and they said, 'What is the biggest problem Jimmy has?' I said, 'He chews Red Man

tobacco.'" Spencer laughs. "Baker goes, 'Jesus Christ, you **said** that!'"

157 **". . . Nancy thought he was good-looking."** Interview with Lesley Stahl, June 14, 2011.

157 **"'We're gonna go with Jimmy Baker.'"** Interview with Margaret Tutwiler, May 2, 2016. Dick Cheney also thought Baker was an inspired choice: "I always admired Reagan for being willing to take on somebody like Jim who worked so hard to beat Reagan. That was a classic move on Reagan's part and Jim was exactly what Reagan needed."

157–158 **whereas Reagan had once been called** The unflattering description came from Clark Clifford, the eminence grise of the Democratic Party. James Baker was not amused. "How ridiculous, how off base Clark Clifford was! He may have served the country well during his time but he was one of these eastern elite guys who couldn't accept the fact that this man of the people had been elected president."

158 **"He did not know one missile system . . ."** Lou Cannon, **President Reagan: The Role of a Lifetime** (New York: PublicAffairs, 1991), 78.

158 **he "went ape shit."** Ed Meese insists that he did not expect Reagan to name him White House chief: "Not necessarily. A lot of people thought that would happen. But when he laid out his plan for the White House it made a lot of sense to me."

159 **"Baker had a memo typed up for their sig-**

natures." James A. Baker III with Steve Fiffer, **"Work Hard, Study . . . and Keep Out of Politics!": Adventures and Lessons from the Unexpected Public Life** (New York: Penguin, 2006), 112.

159 **". . . and I was still in a position . . ."** Again, Ed Meese insists he was happy with the division of labor carved out with Baker: "The things I was most interested in were the policy and then dealing with the executive branch and the heads of the executive branch, and being the White House member of the cabinet."

159 **"Baker knew it immediately."** Interview with Richard Norton Smith, November 7, 2013.

160 **"About to inherit worst economic mess of any Pres."** The private papers of James A. Baker III, Sealy Mudd Library, Princeton University.

163 **"Reagan really needed a chief of staff."** Interview with Brent Scowcroft, May 7, 2014.

164 **". . . focus is essential for a new president."** David Gergen, **Eyewitness to Power**, 166.

166 **Meese bitterly accused Baker** "There was a considerable amount of leaking, negative to me, at various times," says Meese. "And where that came from and whether that was Darman—I doubt Jim personally did it, he's not that kind of a guy. But whether Darman did or not—there was a certain 'us' and 'them' attitude between my office and my cabal and Jim's cabal, our groups."

167 **"He had this zen quality"** Interview with Susan

Zirinsky, April 25, 2016. Powerful as he was, Baker was down-to-earth with the press corps, as Zirinsky found out during an early morning jog: "A jeep pulls out of the vice president's house, the Naval Observatory—and somebody rolls down the window and shouts: 'Want a ride, little girl?' So I look, and it's Jim Baker. So I laugh and say yes. And I jump in the car." Zirinsky suspected that Baker's early morning visit with the VP meant something was up; sure enough, with Baker's help she was able to put together a scoop soon thereafter: George H. W. Bush was running for president.

167 **"if they start shooting at you, just duck . . ."** Peggy Noonan, **What I Saw at the Revolution: A Political Life in the Reagan Era** (New York: Random House, 1990), 50.

168 **"Reagan was very secure in his own skin."** Interview with Peggy Noonan, May 14, 2016.

170 **"I dismissed Haig's statement as utterly absurd."** Richard Darman, **Who's in Control?: Polar Politics and the Sensible Center** (New York: Simon & Schuster, 1996), 49.

171 **"As of now, I am in control . . ."** "Al Haig ended up imploding, in my view," says Jim Baker. "Whenever things weren't going his way, he might suggest that he might leave or resign. And with Reagan, you didn't do that. And Al did that numerous times and I'll never forget the time the president picked up on the offer. He said, 'Well,

I'm sorry you feel that way, Al, but let me have the letter.' And that was it. It ultimately cost him his job. He was only there for a little over a year, maybe sixteen months." Haig resigned as secretary of state on July 7, 1982, after seventeen months.

173 ". . . the effective removal of the president of the United States" Richard Darman, **Who's in Control?**, 53.

174 "**A calmer reality returned.**" Ibid., 58.

176 "**. . . with new material, a new joke**" Cheney remembers Baker's supply of jokes coming in handy on a hunting trip. "He and I were on a duck hunt in Louisiana a couple of years ago, we were down in Cajun country. And you're hanging out with a bunch of characters. And Jim sat there and listened—and then he just cut loose. Joke after joke after joke, had everybody rolling in the aisles. And I said, 'Jim, where the hell did you come up with all that material?' He said, 'It was Reagan.' He said when they went in every morning, the president would not start the meeting until they'd given him a joke. And he acquired this fantastic store of humor."

177 **called it a "riverboat gamble."** Howard Baker, **Face the Nation**, CBS, August 3, 1981.

179 **In December 1981, The Atlantic published . . .** William Greider, "The Education of David Stockman," **The Atlantic**, December, 1981. Stockman elaborated on his loss of faith in supply-side eco-

nomics in his 1986 book, **The Triumph of Politics: Why the Reagan Revolution Failed.**

180 **"I want to see that sorry ass of yours dragging on the carpet."** James A. Baker III with Fiffer, **"Work Hard, Study . . . and Keep Out of Politics!,"** 166.

183 **"biggest leaker in Washington"** Ed Meese III, **With Reagan: The Inside Story** (Washington, DC: Regnery Gateway, 1992), 114. Meese, one of the "four horsemen of [Baker's] apocalypse," still insists Baker would not have worked out in the NSC job: "I can't imagine him having been successful in that role—because of the clash there would have been with Cap Weinberger, Jeane Kirkpatrick, and Bill Casey."

183 **"My decision not to appoint Jim Baker . . ."** Ronald Reagan, **An American Life** (New York: Threshold Editions, 1990), 448.

185 **"smothered by facts and figures."** Paul Laxalt, press conference on October 11, 1984.

186 **"less of a hard-bitten person than he pretends to be."** Lou Cannon, **President Reagan: The Role of a Lifetime,** 482.

187 **". . . they never sent out . . ."** Nancy Reagan had enormous respect for Baker, and even chose him to give her eulogy. But her admiration wasn't unconditional. In her memoir **My Turn,** she wrote: "Although Jim did a lot for Ronnie, I always felt that his main interest was Jim Baker. He was an

ambitious man, and when he was worn out after four years as chief of staff, he made it clear to Ronnie he wanted to be Secretary of State. Ronnie stuck with George Shultz, but when Bush became President, he got his wish."

187 **"F*ck yourself and the horse you rode in on!"** Lou Cannon, **President Reagan: The Role of a Lifetime,** 489.

188 **made a list of pluses and minuses** The private papers of James A. Baker III, Sealy Mudd Library, Princeton University.

190 **" 'Do things the way James Baker III did them.' "** Interview with Mary Matalin, April 2, 2014.

191 **". . . James Baker would be on everyone's list."** Interview with John Podesta, November 9, 2012.

191 **"In governing, you make love to your opponent."** Interview with Ken Duberstein, August 10, 2011.

192 **Baker submitted a letter** The private papers of James A. Baker III, Sealy Mudd Library, Princeton University, February 3, 1985.

5 "Don't Hang Up on the First Lady"

194 **"Mr. President, I've finally brought you someone your own age to play with."** Lou Cannon, **President Reagan: The Role of a Lifetime,** 493.

194 **"Don has something he wants to discuss with**

you . . ." Donald T. Regan, **For the Record: From Wall Street to Washington** (San Diego: Harcourt Brace Jovanovich, 1988), 227.

197 **"If by some miracle I could take back one decision . . ."** Nancy Reagan with William Novak, **My Turn: The Memoirs of Nancy Reagan** (New York: Random House, 1989), 312. Nancy's personnel radar was more perceptive when it came to Bill Clark, who had a short-lived run as national security adviser. "I didn't think he was qualified for the job," she wrote. "Clark had been in Ronnie's administration in Sacramento, but even then I had never really gotten along with him. He struck me as a user. . . . I spoke to Ronnie about him, but Ronnie liked him, so he stayed around longer than I would have liked."

197 **"He looked like George Raft . . ."** Interview with Peggy Noonan, May 14, 2016.

199 **"Don Regan knew none of this . . ."** Lesley Stahl, **Reporting Live** (New York: Touchstone, 1999), 222.

199 **"Regan thought he was the CEO . . ."** Interview with Ken Duberstein, September 23, 2014.

200 **". . . I said, 'Screw him.'"** Interview with Stuart Spencer, March 21, 2016.

201 **"The cemetery I reviewed was ideal . . ."** Michael K. Deaver, **A Different Drummer: My Thirty Years with Ronald Reagan** (New York: HarperCollins, 2001), 104.

202 **". . . a callous offense to the Jewish commu-**

nity." H. W. Brands, **Reagan: The Life** (New York: Anchor Books, 2016), 479.

202 **"My life became a living hell . . ."** Michael K. Deaver, **A Different Drummer**, 104.

203 **"How the hell did that happen?"** Donald T. Regan, **For the Record**, 260.

203 **"She blamed Don Regan . . ."** H. W. Brands, **Reagan: The Life**, 485.

203–204 **"Nancy Reagan stammers slightly when she is upset"** Regan, **For the Record**, 3.

204 **started leaning more heavily** Explaining why she consulted Quigley, Nancy wrote, "Very few people can understand what it's like to have your husband shot at and almost die, and then have him exposed all the time to enormous crowds, tens of thousands of people, any one of whom might be a lunatic with a gun. . . . I was doing everything I could think of to protect my husband and keep him alive."

205 **"I must have had some inkling . . ."** Nancy Reagan with William Novak, **My Turn**, 313.

207 **"Our message will be that we can't and won't answer any Q's . . ."** Douglas Brinkley, ed., **The Reagan Diaries** (New York: HarperCollins, 2007), 448.

209 **the verge of impeachment.** Stuart Spencer, the president's old friend, has his own theory about how Reagan might have unwittingly approved the Iran-Contra operation: "Ollie North is certifiable, nuts. McFarlane is a smart guy but

emotionally unstable. Casey—'Mumbles'—you couldn't understand him, he couldn't talk. I can see those three guys, they knew that Reagan was in favor of the Contras; he was really upset about the American hostages; and they said, 'We'll take advantage of that.' And they sent 'Mumbles' over to tell him about it. And Reagan didn't have his hearing aid on! I believe all of this could have happened."

210 **"Open it up."** Lou Cannon, **President Reagan: The Role of a Lifetime**, 544.

210 **"That Reagan approved the arms sales is not a matter of dispute."** Ibid., 524.

212 **". . . opposing the Sandinista government there"** Meese describes Reagan's motivations in shipping arms to Iran: "He agreed to small quantities—the objectives were, number one, to develop some sort of communication with moderate elements within the Iranian government. Second, to try to influence the Iranian government not to support terrorism. Third, to end the Iraq-Iran war before it became more of a deal, preferably with nobody winning. And fourth, getting Iran to use their influence to get the hostages from Hezbollah back." As for the illegal diversion of money to the Contras, Meese says: "He knew nothing about that."

213 **"If anything devious had been going on . . ."** Nancy Reagan with William Novak, **My Turn**, 318.

214 **"Iran-Contra never would have happened on James Baker's watch."** Interview with Dick Cheney, April 30, 2015. As Treasury secretary, Baker says he was kept in the dark about the Iran-Contra affair. "The national security adviser at the time was John Poindexter," he says. "He saw to it that I was not invited to the National Security Council meetings that had to do with Iran-Contra.

"And after it all blew up, I'll never forget I ran into him in the West Wing lobby, and he said, 'You know, Jim, I'm sorry I didn't invite you.' I said, 'Are you kidding? You did me the biggest favor that anybody could ever do for anybody by not inviting me to those meetings. But I'll tell you this, John, if I'd been invited, I would've objected.'"

215 **". . . That may be a hanging offense!"** According to Stu Spencer, Regan's trouble began when he hung up on the president's daughter Maureen: "When I heard he'd hung up on Maureen Reagan, I said, 'Well, that's the beginning.' Maureen liked to give all of us advice and counsel, and you had to listen to her. She was a good gal, smart. Well, he dumps on her. And Maureen's the kind of girl, she's up at the residence—'that son of a bitch, blah, blah, blah!' for everybody to hear up there. And one thing about Reagan, you did not do these things to his women. And then when he did it to Nancy, I just said, 'It's over.'"

217 "The first part of next week." Donald T. Regan, **For the Record**, 97.

217 "It's not a bad idea." Douglas Brinkley, ed., **The Reagan Diaries**, 478.

218 " 'Well, wait until he sees the zoo I have in mind.' " Interview with Howard H. Baker Jr., August 16, 2011.

220 "It was a bunch of cowboys out there." Interview with Ken Duberstein, September 23, 2014.

223 "You can survive it." Interview with Stuart Spencer, March 21, 2016.

224 "Howard was a complete change from what we had . . ." Nancy Reagan with William Novak, **My Turn**, 331.

226–227 "A nuclear war cannot be won and must never be fought." Lou Cannon, **President Reagan: The Role of a Lifetime**, 149.

229 . . . wrote some of his best material. "It's interesting now to see that historians have concluded that President Reagan wrote a lot of his own speeches," says James Baker. "He wrote letters in longhand to people. We had this post office box where anyone could communicate with the president around the staff. And he would spend a lot of time responding to letters that he would receive."

229 "No chest-thumping. No Soviet-bashing." Peter Robinson, "Tear Down This Wall: How Top Advisors Opposed Reagan's Challenge to

Gorbachev—But Lost," **Prologue**, vol. 39, issue 2, 2007.

232 "... **Reagan and America would prevail.**" Of Reagan's iconic line, Duberstein says: "The State Department was concerned that it would undercut Gorbachev's efforts with **glasnost** and **perestroika.** It was too strong. The NSC weighed in on behalf of the State Department, but not as strongly. But it was the right thing to do. It was as Reagan as it comes: defining and bold primary colors."

232 "**The record will show ...**" David A. Stockman, **The Triumph of Politics**, 447.

6 "The Prime Minister"

236 "**I do.**" Interview with Craig Fuller, August 6, 2016.

236 "**I had a reaction, ...**" Comparing Fuller and Sununu as possible White House chiefs of staff, George H. W. Bush told me: "Of course, I love Fuller. In a way it was a tough call. But Sununu just seemed to fit the bill for what I was looking for." Barbara Bush says, "I liked Craig Fuller too, very much. Nobody asked me, but I sort of thought he should be [chief] too. But John Sununu is a great friend of ours."

236 **an obscure high-IQ organization.** It's a dis-

tinction Sununu does not take overly seriously. "They drafted me," he says. "I made the mistake of responding to a mail-it-in test that was in a magazine once—and I guess I did quite well and that society decided I qualified and told me I was now a member. It has no meetings, I've never met anybody in it, and it is one of these odd facets of public life that I've had to live with."

237 **"It's sometimes nice to be right!"** Interview with John Sununu, August 11, 2011.

237 **"John greeted us . . ."** Interview with Barbara Bush, October 24, 2011.

239 **". . . looking for someone who had been an elected official."** Interview with Tim McBride, February 8, 2014.

239 **"He would be a good complement to him."** Interview with David Bates, February 11, 2014.

239 **"Outstanding in every way."** Interview with George H. W. Bush, October 24, 2011.

240 **George Will dubbed him Reagan's "lap dog"** George Will, "George Bush: The Sound of a Lapdog," **Washington Post,** January 30, 1986.

240 **Garry Trudeau eviscerated him . . . Doonesbury,** November 3, 1984.

240 **"Fighting the 'Wimp Factor.'"** **Newsweek,** October 19, 1987.

240 **(and enraged his son George W.)** In his book about his father, **41,** George W. wrote of the **Newsweek** story: "I was shocked to see the cover of the magazine scheduled to hit the newsstands

that week: **George Bush: Fighting the 'Wimp Factor.'** The thrust of the story was that Dad was not tough enough to be President. I was amazed that anyone who knew his life story—the Navy pilot who fought in World War II, the Congressman who endured death threats to vote for the open-housing bill—could even suggest that he was a wimp."

242 **"'That Sununu is a f*cking asshole!'"** Interview with Andy Card, October 12, 2011.

242 **"I think somebody told him he should do it."** Interview with Dick Cheney, April 30, 2015.

243 **"'I will keep you informed as to what I'm doing.'"** Interview with Brent Scowcroft, May 7, 2014.

243 **". . . we operated that way."** Interview with James Baker, November 20, 2013.

244 **Soviet Union would end with a whimper** Sununu was a fan of Bush 41's national security team: "I hope the American people understand how lucky they were having George Herbert Walker Bush, Brent Scowcroft, and Jimmy Baker as the foreign policy team in those difficult, difficult times—with the collapse of the Soviet Union going on and the first post-Soviet, serious foreign policy issues facing the country. I can't think of three people, frankly in that century, who could have handled the complexity of that situation any better."

247 **". . . So I took a big hit on it . . ."** George H. W.

Bush told me that if he could do it all over again, he would not have declared, "Read my lips, no new taxes." "I think I wouldn't have done that—'cause that highlighted any increase in revenue, and that ended up haunting me. I mean, if I hadn't used that strong rhetoric there at the convention, it might've been a little different. But maybe I still would've caught hell for it."

247 **". . . it's an invasion."** Interview with Colin Powell, June 27, 2014.

247 **caught both the CIA and the Soviet KGB** Secretary of State James Baker was on a trip to Siberia with his counterpart, Soviet foreign minister Eduard Shevardnadze, when Saddam's surprise attack on Kuwait began. As a result, Baker was able to persuade the Soviets to denounce Saddam's aggression. "For the first time," Baker wrote, "the Soviet Union was actively engaged in joining the United States in condemning one of its staunchest allies . . . the world as I had known it for my entire adult life would no longer exist."

250 **Times editorial page, New York Times**, March 1, 1991.

252 **"It is all designed for a purpose."** National Press Club speech, December 11, 1990.

252 **"It is rude. It is intolerable."** James P. Pfiffner, "The President's Chief of Staff: Lessons Learned," **Presidential Studies Quarterly**, vol. 23, no. 1 (1993): 94.

253 "**Sununu just didn't know how to play the role.**" Interview with Stuart Spencer, March 21, 2016.

255 "**That is unadulterated bullshit.**" Interview with Ken Duberstein, September 23, 2014.

258 "**. . . after a long pause, he said, 'Fine.'**" George W. Bush, **41: A Portrait of My Father** (New York: Crown, 2014), 226.

258 "**He submitted his resignation shortly thereafter.**" George W. Bush, **Decision Points** (New York: Crown, 2010), 82.

258 "**why don't you tell him?**" Interview with Andy Card, February 28, 2015.

259 **George H. W. Bush's chief finally submitted his handwritten resignation letter.** Letter, John Sununu to George Bush, December 3, 1991. Presidential Daily Files, George Bush Presidential Library.

260 **Bush penned a reply.** George H. W. Bush, **All the Best: My Life in Letters and Other Writings** (New York: Touchstone, 199), 541.

261 **a gesture that touched** In the letters to his children, Sununu says, the president "was very specific and direct, going out of his way to emphasize the contributions I had made. And that they should understand that what I did as chief of staff was a reflection of his agenda. So, as always, George Bush writes a fantastic letter."

262 "**. . . reminded of the Agatha Christie novel . . .**"

James P. Pfiffner, "The President's Chief of Staff: Lessons Learned," 97.

264 "... nobody thinks we're doing a damn thing about the economy." Jon Meacham, **Destiny and Power: The American Odyssey of George Herbert Walker Bush** (New York: Random House, 2015), 496.

265 " 'we are going to do something different.' " Interview with Samuel Skinner, August 10, 2011.

266 **the eccentric billionaire Ross Perot.** Bush believes that Perot ran against him in 1992 because of personal pique. It stemmed from the time Vice President Bush told Perot that Reagan did not want him to be their point man on POW issues. "I said, 'Look, the president doesn't want you to go to Vietnam anymore—'cause we've got new leaders on this thing.' And I think he took it very personal. We had a friendship. He visited Barbara and me in Maine and all that. And then it got ugly and mean, and I didn't like it at all. I think he was driven by a personal dislike, a personal resentment of me, you might say, and that inured to Clinton's benefit."

266 **Bush was disillusioned with Skinner.** Jon Meacham, **Destiny and Power**, 505.

267 **"I never really hesitated to say yes."** Interview with James Baker, November 20, 2013.

268 **the president sent his new chief a note** George H. W. Bush, **All the Best**, 565.

269 "This is the last day of campaigning . . ." Ibid., 571.

7 "An Iron Fist in a Velvet Glove"

273 "He'll become unfocused . . ." Robert B. Reich, **Locked in the Cabinet** (New York: Alfred A. Knopf, 1997), 7.

274 **and Bill rarely showed up.** Interview with Robert Reich, May 8, 2014. On the Yale campus in the early '70s, Bob Reich was an enormously popular "teaching assistant" for a lecture course on "civil liberties and civil rights"; the author, a Yale undergraduate, was one of his students. Many of us pegged Reich, not Clarence Thomas, as a future Supreme Court justice.

274 **"Clinton spent an enormous amount of time picking his cabinet . . ."** Interview with John Podesta, August 17, 2016.

275 **Harry and Linda Bloodworth-Thomason.** The Bloodworth-Thomasons, creators of the hit television show **Designing Women**, were close friends and informal advisers to the Clintons.

275 **" 'It could make it stronger, you know.' "** Interview with Mack McLarty, September 22, 2011.

276 **"People would wander in and out . . ."** Interview with Erskine Bowles, December 16, 2011.

277 **"It drove the first lady crazy . . ."** Interview with

Leon Panetta, November 9, 2012. Bob McNeely, the White House photographer, knew that meetings were out of control when the president started asking his opinions: "Clinton wanted to hear everyone. Clinton asked me about stuff—on stuff that I'd have to say, 'Sir, if Tony Lake hears I'm giving you foreign policy advice, he'll cut my nuts off! Really, don't!'"

277 **"The fact that on the campaign trail he would linger . . ."** Interview with Mack McLarty, September 22, 2011.

277 **"Every fifteen minutes of every day was scheduled."** Interview with Erskine Bowles, February 25, 2014.

279 **"He twisted arms."** Interview with Bob McNeely, April 24, 2014.

281 **"Over the last months she had reached some conclusions."** Bob Woodward, **The Agenda: Inside the Clinton White House** (New York: Simon & Schuster, 1994), 254.

285 **the powerful insurance lobby.** A particularly devastating commercial against health-care reform featured a couple sitting at their kitchen table. As they pored over insurance plans, Harry and Louise complained to each other: "Having choices we don't like is no choice at all."

287 **"I handed him the book I was reading . . ."** George Stephanopoulos, **All Too Human: A Political Education** (New York: Back Bay, 2000), 285.

289 "**. . . and what we're thinking.**" Panetta elaborates on the responsibilities of the chief of staff: "He's not chief of the White House. He's not chief of the country. He's chief of staff, which means that your responsibility is to work with the president's staff to tee up the decisions that the president has to make. Secondly, you have got to be someone who can deal with Capitol Hill because so much of what the president has to get through in terms of legislation involves the Hill. And lastly you have to be the person that says no. In the end you've got to be the son of a bitch who basically tells somebody what the president can't tell him. And that's the only way you maintain the kind of discipline that you have to maintain on behalf of the president."

293 "**. . . when discipline is necessary.**" Bowles says of Panetta: "Leon was so good at making sure the president was prepared. And people like George [Stephanopoulos] were much more disciplined under Leon than they had been before. Of course George was cut out by the president. But he became Leon's primary adviser, and that was very helpful to Leon because he knew how the president would feel—even if he was no longer talking to the president."

294–295 "**The president wanted to get rid of Stephanopoulos . . .**" Interview with Leon Panetta, May 20, 2014.

295 **"I give it to Rahm."** Interview with Erskine Bowles, February 25, 2014.

297 **"The president is relevant . . ."** East Room Press Conference, April 18, 1995.

300 **depicted the House Speaker as a crybaby . . . New York Daily News,** November 16, 1995.

303 **". . . he is the boss."** Dick Morris's White House career came to a dramatic end one night during the 1996 Democratic Convention—when it was revealed that he was cavorting with a prostitute at the Jefferson Hotel, and letting her listen in on his calls with the president. Clinton sent Bowles to the hotel to fire him.

305 **grandson of FDR's secretary of the interior.** The president's eleventh-hour decision to pass over Ickes as chief was vintage Bill Clinton. As John Podesta recalls: "The way Harold found out that he wasn't going to be the chief of staff was when the 'Washington Wire' ran in the **Wall Street Journal**—it's a column on the front page on Fridays. And in that column was that Erskine was coming back as chief. That's how Harold found out!"

310 **"You better come down here right away."** Lanny J. Davis, **Truth to Tell: Notes from My White House Education** (New York: The Free Press, 1999), 23.

310 **"He was so disturbed . . ."** Interview with Peter Baker, September 2, 2016.

310 **"I was compelled as never before to live parallel**

lives." Bill Clinton, **My Life** (New York: Alfred A. Knopf, 2004), 771.

316 **". . . what he thought was his friendship . . ."** Photographer McNeely wonders if Clinton might have been more truthful about Lewinsky if Panetta had still been in charge: "I always felt that had Leon been the chief of staff when that whole story broke with Lewinsky, he would have gone in and demanded the truth, and said, 'If I've found you're lying to me, I'm going to walk out on the South Lawn and resign. You are not going to keep us in the dark.'"

317 **". . . he was a better hearts player than Erskine Bowles"** Bill Clinton, **My Life**, 821.

321 **". . . exhausted to the point of foolishness . . ."** Joe Klein, **The Natural: The Misunderstood Presidency of Bill Clinton** (New York: Doubleday: 2002), 203.

322 **". . . Bill Clinton would challenge the cynicism."** Joe Klein, **The Natural**, 216.

323 **". . . I couldn't help but be amazed at all that had transpired since."** Interview with Dick Cheney, July 15, 2011.

8 "The Decider"

324 **Not since John Quincy Adams's administration** Not long after Adams's presidency, Blair House

became famous as the meeting place for President Andrew Jackson's "Kitchen Cabinet," an unofficial group of trusted friends and advisers. As the Blair House website states: Jackson's "official cabinet was fractured by factional disputes, largely resulting from the fierce rivalry between Vice President John C. Calhoun and Secretary of State Martin Van Buren. The infighting was so pronounced that the Cabinet became virtually ineffectual, and Jackson stopped holding Cabinet meetings." It wouldn't be the last time a presidency was riven by a rivalry between the vice president and secretary of state. The feud between Dick Cheney and Colin Powell contributed to the dysfunction of Bush's first term. Martin Van Buren ended up resigning—and so did Colin Powell.

324 **"I admired his abolitionist principles . . ."** George W. Bush, **Decision Points**, 86.

326 **"I folded up the easel . . ."** Interview with Andy Card, October 12, 2011.

328 **Bush wanted him to be** In his memoir, Bush writes: "Andy was humble, loyal, and hardworking. He had served under every chief of staff during both the Reagan and Bush presidencies. He had the sound judgment and steady temperament I needed, along with a caring heart and a good sense of humor."

329 **"I think that Andy probably gave George W. Bush great comfort . . ."** Interview with Peter Baker, September 2, 2016.

330 "'**You're the solution to my problem.**'" Interview with Dick Cheney, April 30, 2015.

330–331 **all the fund-raising and glad-handing.** According to Stu Spencer, Rumsfeld had also considered running for president—before George W. Bush entered the race in 2000. "I got a phone call from Rummy and he said, 'I'm going to run for president and I want you to run the campaign,'" recalls Spencer. Spencer did not leap at the offer. "Rummy liked power and was a smart guy. But he was abrasive—like sandpaper to deal with. Nothing came of it, thank God."

332 "... **anything I wanted** ..." Cheney's counselor, Mary Matalin, describes the understanding between her boss and Bush: "They cut a deal. It was explicit going into it. Cheney didn't want to come and do education policy or 'No Child Left Behind' or all that kind of jazz—so it was absolutely clear. He didn't want to be the vice president. He had to divest of millions and millions of dollars and uproot his family and his grandkids—and he didn't go in there to just be a veep. He had certain issues that Bush wanted him to focus on: They were the 'honest broker/ liaison' and 'deal fixer on the Hill.' Cheney never big-footed anybody. He was straightforward with everybody. He never snuck around. And everybody there loved him."

332 "**Cheney was the chief of staff.**" Interview with Erskine Bowles, February 25, 2014.

333 "... the job he really wanted: CIA director." Interview with Brent Scowcroft, May 7, 2014. Scowcroft remembers advising Cheney when he was vetting people for jobs in W's administration: "I talked to Dick almost every day about different people who would be good for here or there. I remember him talking about Rumsfeld. Rumsfeld wanted to be DCI [Director of Central Intelligence]. It was just two friends talking about personalities, and which personalities worked where." Cheney says that making Rumsfeld DCI "wasn't a done deal." The issue became moot when Bush's first choice for defense secretary was unavailable, and they turned to Rumsfeld to run the Pentagon.

334 "... I was never blindsided ..." The vice president's counselor, Mary Matalin, says Cheney and Rumsfeld did not game the system; they won their battles on the merits: "The context was not that Rummy and Cheney had been chiefs of staff, but that they had defense and intelligence history. They had the subject area expertise on the priority issues of the president's. So it wasn't that Andy was rolled because they knew where the levers were; they had expertise and he had to defer."

335 "The president wanted a guy who could deal ..." Interview with Mary Matalin, April 2, 2014.

336 "'Too late. The president signed it.'" Interview with Colin Powell, June 27, 2014.

337 "Guess what? We got a nuclear agreement . . ." Interview with Colin Powell, August 25, 2016.

339 "'We don't want the clock to start ticking.'" Interview with George Tenet, August 8, 2015. Tenet says the "Blue-sky memo," as the paramilitary plan against al-Qaeda was called, was originally created at the request of Clinton's national security adviser, Sandy Berger. But neither administration gave a green light for the plan. "There's no doubt that policymakers across two administrations understood—from me and all of our analysts and people who briefed them—the magnitude of the threat in front of them," says Tenet.

339 "The sky's falling." Interview with Cofer Black, April 17, 2015.

340 "I do not recall George coming in with his hair on fire . . ." Interview with Dick Cheney, April 30, 2015.

344 the order he had just given. Cheney describes what the Secret Service agent told him just before he gave the order to shoot down approaching airliners: "He explained to me that he received a message over his radio that there was a plane, an unidentified aircraft, headed for 'Crown'—which was the code name for the White House—coming in from the west, from Dulles Airport at

a very high rate of speed. And we got down to a place that's sort of a room. And you got a secure phone and a small black-and-white television set on a shelf. We got on the telephone. At that point, they told me that the plane that had been headed for the White House had gone into the Pentagon. It was American Flight 77."

345 **"We pushed the limits . . ."** Interview with Dick Cheney, April 30, 2015.

346 **"That was decided, and the decision was handed down."** Interview with Colin Powell, August 25, 2016.

347 **"But after 9/11 he just really turned."** Interview with Brent Scowcroft, May 7, 2014.

347 **"He was different"** Interview with Colin Powell, June 27, 2013.

348 **Schieffer, too, thought Cheney's heart problems . . .** Interview with Bob Schieffer, March 9, 2016.

348 **the vice president's dark new outlook.** Some of Cheney's friends, including Mary Matalin and Don Rumsfeld, insist Cheney hasn't changed a bit. "It's total bullshit," says Matalin. "He is the same guy he was in college. The reason I love him so much is because he doesn't change. He is so dependable. I was kind of shocked at some of the guys of his age group, if you will, who took out after him because they didn't like the aggressiveness of the policy—but that wasn't him, that was Bush." Rumsfeld is also unequivocal about

his protégé: "He is basically the same person today that he was when I first met him in 1969. He's intelligent. He's a serious person. He's not a showboat. He's a workhorse. The idea that he changed from a good person to a bad person or to Darth Vader—that's press talk. That's nonsense."

350 **"I want you to develop a plan to invade Iraq."** Peter Baker, **Days of Fire: Bush and Cheney in the White House** (New York: Anchor, 2013), 160.

351 **" 'Look, this has gotta stop. . . .' "** Cheney insists that it was CIA director Tenet who drew a connection between Iraq and the 9/11 plotters. "I was asked by Tim Russert, this was the Sunday after 9/11 in that interview, if there was any evidence of Iraqi involvement, and I said no, that I hadn't seen anything. Within a matter of days, I was presented by George Tenet with the photograph of Mohammad Atta [a 9/11 hijacker] supposedly taken in Prague, Czechoslovakia. So there's a 70 percent chance that he was in Prague to meet with senior Iraqi intelligence officials. It was the first hard evidence: The meeting took place in April, five months before 9/11. George Tenet gave that to me." Tenet says the photograph was discredited shortly thereafter, and that he repeatedly told Bush administration officials there was no link.

353 **"Scowcroft gets it right."** Interview with Dick Cheney, April 30, 2015.

355 **"Of all people, Dad understood the stakes."** George W. Bush, **Decision Points**, 238.

356 **"iron-ass" adviser** Jon Meacham, **Destiny and Power**, 588.

357 **"We went hunting . . ."** Interviews with Stuart Spencer, April 24, 2016, and James Baker, May 24, 2016.

357 **that Bush seek a UN resolution** In his op-ed for the **New York Times**, Baker did not argue against using force against Saddam. But he insisted there was "a right way" to go about regime change, and he took an implicit shot at the president's hawkish advisers: "We should try our best not to have to go it alone, and the president should reject the advice of those who counsel doing so. [He meant Cheney.] . . . The president should do his best to stop his advisers and their surrogates from playing out their differences publicly and try to get everybody on the same page. The United States should advocate the adoption by the United Nations Security Council of a simple and straightforward resolution requiring that Iraq submit to intrusive inspections anytime, anywhere, with no exceptions, and authorizing all necessary means to enforce it."

358 **Colin Powell was not happy . . .** Interview with Colin Powell, August 25, 2016.

360 **"We let Powell down."** Interview with George Tenet, August 18, 2015.

361 "... scrawled out a letter ..." George W. Bush, **Decision Points**, 224.

361 ... he faxed a reply. Ibid., 225.

364 "... and we're now debating ..." Bush described his reaction to learning that there were no WMDs. "I had sent American troops into combat based in large part on intelligence that proved false. That was a massive blow to our credibility—my credibility—that would shake the confidence of the American people. No one was more shocked or angry than I was ... I had a sickening feeling every time I thought about it. I still do."

364 "'Condi! Do you know about this?'" Interview with Colin Powell, June 27, 2014.

365 "Interesting ..." Interview with Donald Rumsfeld, May 6, 2014. Rumsfeld elaborates on Bremer's decision to disband the Ba'ath Party: "There was full awareness in Washington that there was going to be a de-Ba'athification process of some kind. What does that mean? How deep does it go? And if I go back to Germany after World War II, the damage and the carnage and the disorder and the looting and the things that happened in Germany were unbelievable ... and you don't go from that order and discipline without a gap in the middle. So it's easy to say, 'Bremer this and Bremer that. He should have done this. He should have done that.'"

366 "**the best answer for that very pressing question . . .**" Interview with Colin Powell, August 25, 2016.

367 "**It exacerbated divisions in our society . . .**" George W. Bush, **Decision Points**, 310.

369 **overlook Cheney's DWIs** Cheney says that he and his mentor Rumsfeld had an understanding: "Don told me, 'You know, at the end of the day, we're even up. You work your butt off for me and I appreciate that. I'm loyal to you and you appreciate that. But you don't need to go away thinking that I owe you something or you owe me something.'" When I asked Rumsfeld about this, he was flummoxed. "I have no recollection of saying anything like that, nor can I imagine why I would have said that," he told me. "But I am eighty years old, and my memory is not perfect."

370 "**'Did my instincts fail me?'**" Interview with Colin Powell, June 27, 2014.

371 "**. . . and the president needed . . .**" As reelection approached, Cheney told the president that he too would step aside if Bush thought he was a drag on the ticket. "I did consider his offer," wrote Bush. "I talked to Andy, Karl [Rove], and a few others about the possibility of asking Bill Frist, the impressive Tennessee senator. . . . The more I thought about it, the more I thought Dick should stay. I hadn't picked him to be a political asset; I had chosen him to help me do the job."

372 **"Fortunately . . . it never stuck."** Interview with Joshua Bolten, September 26, 2011.

372 **better security to Baghdad** In March 2006, Bush appointed a ten-person bipartisan panel, the Iraq Study Group, in an effort to find a way out of the quagmire. James Baker, one of the members, recalls a memorable interview they did with Bush and Cheney: "We went into the White House and met them in the Roosevelt Room. And we're talking to the president about the way forward in Iraq. And [former senator] Alan Simpson's there. And at one point he looked at Cheney and said, 'Now **Bruce**—'cause his name is Richard Bruce—**Bruce**, you **have** to be willing to sit down with people! And **talk** to people! And **compromise!**'" Baker lets out a laugh. "Right there in the Roosevelt Room! And W was like this!" Baker mimicks the annoyed expression on Bush's face.

373 **"It was an amicable parting"** Cheney, well aware of his Darth Vader reputation, had offered Bush **his** resignation several times, but the president turned him down. "The third time I went in, I said, 'Look, you really need to think about this. You know, I'm not without controversy. And if you want to get somebody else in here, all you've got to do is say the word.'" Cheney says Rumsfeld took the news of his firing in the same spirit. "That's the way Don handled it," he says.

373 **"Oh, goodness."** Interview with Don Rumsfeld, May 17, 2012.

375 **"And as he liked to say, he was the decider."** Interview with Colin Powell, August 25, 2016.

376 **"Policymakers need to be a little bit more forthcoming . . ."** Interview with George Tenet, August 18, 2015.

376 **"After 9/11, I think they said"** Interview with Brent Scowcroft, May 7, 2014.

376 **"I have no idea how they came to that conclusion."** Interview with Colin Powell, August 25, 2016.

377 **"I'm not going to characterize it . . ."** Interview with James Baker, May 24, 2016.

9 "Between Bad and Worse"

379 **"Leave your Chicago friends at home"** Interview with Erskine Bowles, December 16, 2011.

379 **stop himself from laughing out loud.** Bill Daley was amused by Bowles's chutzpah: "Erskine's advice was gutsy considering three of us were from Chicago sitting in the room. I thought, 'That's typical Erskine, just throw it out there!'"

379 **Lyndon Johnson: Bobby Baker** The political career of LBJ's close friend and adviser Bobby Baker was ended by a salacious scandal: He was accused of using federal money to provide bribes and sexual favors from prostitutes in return for

business contracts. Facing an investigation, he resigned as secretary to the majority leader on October 7, 1963.

379 " 'You've got to be the good guy.' " Interview with Leon Panetta, November 9, 2012.

380 "These are the people you are going to spend all day with." Interview with John Podesta, November 9, 2012.

380 "the 101st senator" Jeff Zeleny, New York Times, November 5, 2008.

382 his father was a sabra Jonathan Alter, The Promise: President Obama, Year One (New York: Simon & Schuster, 2010), 162.

386 "Obama's never yelled at me" Interview with Jon Favreau, March 28, 2016.

386 "Rahm's a pussycat underneath it" Interview with Erskine Bowles, February 25, 2014.

391 "I thought he was rude." Interview with Nancy-Ann DeParle, September 25, 2014.

392 "Rahm was so chastened and wounded" Interview with Jonathan Alter, September 23, 2016.

394 "He subcontracted that out to the Congress" Interview with James Baker, May 24, 2016.

398 " 'This is a f*cking dead fish!' " Sam Whipple, "Austan Goolsbee: D.C.'s Funniest Celebrity on Capital, College, and . . . Carp?" The Kenyon Observer, April 16, 2014.

398 "You can't be antibusiness if you're the president of the United States." Interview with Bill Daley, May 3, 2012.

401 "**Obama already had the Chicago Mafia.**" Interview with Erskine Bowles, February 25, 2014.

403 "**a cult worthy of Jonestown.**" Glenn Thrush, "The Reboot," **Politico**, December 17, 2013.

408 "**'the president just cut your legs out from under you.'**" Interview with Leon Panetta, May 20, 2014.

410 "**I can tell you that Nancy would have been excellent.**" Interview with Denis McDonough, October 5, 2016.

411 "**And I know pretty well what he thinks.**" Interview with Jack Lew, August 9, 2012.

414 **McDonough looks too skinny to tackle anyone** Glenn Thrush, "Obama's Obama," **Politico**, January/February 2016.

414 "**'I'm not your guy.'**" Interview with Denis McDonough, October 5, 2016.

417 "**Denis's style is really the president's style.**" Interview with Tom Daschle, October 5, 2016.

417 "**the president was more comfortable in his role.**" Interview with Peter Orszag, August 10, 2016.

418 "**As smart as Obama is, he doesn't like politics.**" Interview with Leon Panetta, May 20, 2014.

423 "**if you like your doctor you can keep your doctor**" Interview with Terry O'Donnell, February 5, 2014.

426 "**all I get are singles and bunts**" Screening of **The Presidents' Gatekeepers** at the White House, June 11, 2013.

426 **How did Reagan deal with the crazies** Interview with Ken Duberstein, September 23, 2014.

428 **" 'I need you to come back here.' "** Interview with John Podesta, August 17, 2016.

430 **"That would change my equation."** McDonough says that despite widespread speculation on Capitol Hill and in the media, Obama's "red line" declaration had not been made inadvertently, or off-the-cuff; he and the president discussed the warning beforehand.

433 **"You don't ever walk away from that."** Interview with James Baker, May 24, 2016.

434 **It was a momentous day** Jeffrey Goldberg, "The Obama Doctrine," **The Atlantic**, April 2016.

435 **"my chief has other plans for me."** Screening of **The Presidents' Gatekeepers** at the White House, June 11, 2013.

Bibliography

Adams, Sherman. **Firsthand Report: The Story of the Eisenhower Administration**. Santa Barbara: Greenwood, 1961.

Aitken, Jonathan. **Nixon: A Life**. Washington, D.C.: Regnery, 1994.

Allen, Jonathan and Amie Parnes. **HRC: State Secrets and the Rebirth of Hillary Clinton**. New York: Broadway Books, 2014.

Alter, Jonathan. **The Promise: President Obama, Year One**. New York: Simon & Schuster, 2010.

———. **The Center Holds: Obama and His Enemies**. New York: Simon & Schuster, 2013.

Ambrose, Stephen E. **Nixon: Volume 1—The Education of a Politician 1913–1962**. New York: Simon & Schuster, 1987.

———. **Nixon: Ruin and Recovery 1973–1990.** New York: Simon & Schuster, 2014.

Anderson, Martin and Annelise Anderson. **Reagan's Secret War: The Untold Story of His Fight to Save the World from Nuclear Disaster.** New York: Crown, 2009.

Annis, Lee Jr. **Howard Baker: Conciliator in an Age of Crisis.** New York: Madison, 1994.

Anson, Robert Sam. **Exile: The Unquiet Oblivion of Richard M. Nixon.** New York: Simon & Schuster, 1984.

Axelrod, David. **Believer: My Forty Years in Politics.** New York: Penguin, 2015.

Baker, James A. III with Thomas M. DeFrank. **The Politics of Diplomacy: Revolution, War & Peace, 1989–1992.** New York: Putnam Adult, 1995.

Baker, James A. III with Steven Fiffer. **"Work Hard, Study . . . and Keep Out of Politics!": Adventures and Lessons from an Unexpected Public Life.** New York: Penguin, 2006.

Baker, Peter. **The Breach: Inside the Impeachment and Trial of William Jefferson Clinton.** New York: Scribner, 2001.

———. **Days of Fire: Bush and Cheney in the White House.** New York: Anchor, 2013.

Bernstein, Carl. **A Woman in Charge.** New York: Vintage, 2007.

Beschloss, Michael R. and Strobe Talbott. **At the Highest Levels: The Inside Story of the End of** the Cold War. New York: Open Road Media, 2016.

Blumenthal, Sidney. The Clinton Wars. New York: Farrar, Straus and Giroux, 2003.

Bohn, Michael K. Nerve Center: Inside the White House Situation Room. Lincoln: Potomac, 2004.

Bourne, Peter G. Jimmy Carter: A Comprehensive Biography from Plains to Post-presidency. New York: Scribner, 1997.

Bowden, Mark. Black Hawk Down: A Story of Modern War. New York: Grove Atlantic Press, 1999.

Branch, Taylor. The Clinton Tapes: Wrestling History with the President. New York: Simon & Schuster, 2009.

Brands, H. W. Reagan: The Life. New York: Anchor, 2016.

Brill, Steven. America's Bitter Pill: Money, Politics, Backroom Deals, and the Fight to Fix Our Broken Healthcare System. New York: Random House, 2014.

Brinkley, Alan and Davis Dyer, eds. The American Presidency: The Authoritative Reference. New York: Houghton Mifflin, 2004.

Brinkley, Douglas. The Boys of Pointe Du Hoc: Ronald Reagan, D-Day, and the U.S. Army 2nd Ranger Battalion. New York: William Morrow, 2005.

Brinkley, Douglas, ed. The Reagan Diaries by Ronald Reagan. New York: Harper Collins, 2007.

————. **The Notes: Ronald Reagan's Private Collection of Stories and Wisdom.** New York: Harper-Collins, 2011.

Brinkley, Douglas and Luke A. Nichter, eds. **The Nixon Tapes: 1973.** Boston: Mariner, 2015.

Broadwell, Paula and Vernon Loeb. **All In: The Education of General David Petraeus.** New York: Penguin, 2012.

Buchanan, Patrick J. **The Greatest Comeback: How Richard Nixon Rose from Defeat to Create the New Majority.** New York: Crown Forum, 2014.

Bumiller, Elisabeth. **Condoleezza Rice: An American Life.** New York: Random House, 2009.

Bush, Barbara. **Barbara Bush: A Memoir.** New York: Scribner, 2010.

Bush, George H. W. **All the Best: My Life in Letters and Other Writings.** New York: Scribner, 2013.

Bush, George H. W, with Victor Gold. **Looking Forward: An Autobiography.** New York: Doubleday, 1987.

Bush, George H. W. and Brent Scowcroft. **A World Transformed.** New York: Vintage, 2011.

Bush, George W. **Decision Points.** New York: Crown, 2010.

————. **41: A Portrait of My Father.** New York: Crown, 2014.

Califano, Joseph A., Jr. **The Triumph and Tragedy of Lyndon Johnson, The White House Years: A Personal Memoir by President Johnson's Top**

Democratic Adviser. New York: Touchstone, 2014.

Cannon, James. **Gerald R. Ford: An Honorable Life.** Ann Arbor: The University of Michigan Press, 2013.

Cannon, Lou: **President Reagan: The Role of a Lifetime.** New York: PublicAffairs, 1991.

Carter, Jimmy. **Keeping Faith: Memoirs of a President.** Fayetteville, University of Arkansas Press, 1995.

————. **Living Faith.** New York: Random House, 2001.

————. **White House Diary.** New York: Farrar, Straus and Giroux, 2010.

Chafe, William H. **Bill and Hillary: The Politics of the Personal.** Durham: Duke University Press Books, 2016.

Cheney, Dick with Liz Cheney. **In My Time: A Personal and Political Memoir.** New York: Threshold, 2011.

Cheney, Richard B. and Lynne V. Cheney. **Kings of the Hill: How Nine Powerful Men Changed the Course of American History.** New York: Touchstone, 1996.

Christopher, Warren. **Chances of a Lifetime: A Memoir.** New York: Scribner, 2001.

Clarke, Richard A. **Against All Enemies: Inside America's War on Terror.** New York: Free Press, 2004.

————. **Your Government Failed You**. New York: Ecco, 2008.

Clifford, Clark with Richard Holbrooke. **Counsel to the President: A Memoir**. New York: Random House, 1991.

Clinton, Bill. **My Life**. New York: Alfred A. Knopf, 2004.

Clinton, Hillary Rodham. **Living History**. New York: Simon & Schuster, 2003.

————. **Hard Choices**. New York: Simon & Schuster, 2014.

Cockburn, Andrew. **Rumsfeld: His Rise, Fall, and Catastrophic Legacy**. New York: Scribner, 2007.

Colodny, Len and Tom Schachtman. **The Forty Years War: The Rise and Fall of the Neocons from Nixon to Obama**. New York: HarperCollins, 2009.

Daalder, Ivo H. and I. M. Destler. **In the Shadow of the Oval Office: Profiles of the National Security Advisers and the Presidents They Served—From JFK to George W. Bush**. New York: Simon & Schuster, 2009.

Darman, Richard. **Who's in Control: Polar Politics and the Sensible Center**. New York: Simon & Schuster, 1996.

Davis, Lanny J. **Truth to Tell: Notes from My White House Education**. New York: Free Press, 1999.

Dean, John W. **Blind Ambition Updated Edition: The End of the Story**. New York: Polimedia, 2009.

————. **The Nixon Defense: What He Knew and When He Knew It.** New York: Penguin, 2015.

Deaver, Michael K. **A Different Drummer: My Thirty Years with Ronald Reagan.** New York: HarperCollins, 2001.

Donaldson, Sam. **Hold On, Mr. President!** New York: Random House, 1987.

Doyle, William. **Inside the Oval Office: The White House Tapes from FDR to Clinton.** New York: Kodansha America, 1999.

Draper, Robert. **Dead Certain: The Presidency of George W. Bush.** New York: Free Press, 2007.

Ehrlichman, John. **Witness to Power: The Nixon Years.** New York: Simon and Schuster, 1982.

Emanuel, Ezekiel J. **Brothers Emanuel: A Memoir of an American Family.** New York: Random House, 2013.

Farrell, John A. **Tip O'Neill and the Democratic Century.** New York: Little, Brown, 2011.

Fink, Gary M. and Hugh Davis Graham, eds. **The Carter Presidency: Policy Choices in the Post– New Deal.** Kansas: University Press of Kansas, 1998.

Fleischer, Ari. **Taking Heat: The President, the Press, and My Years in the White House.** New York: William Morrow, 2005.

Ford, Betty with Chris Chase. **The Times of My Life.** New York: Harper Collins, 1978.

Ford, Gerald R. **A Time to Heal: The Former Pres-**

ident Speaks Out. New York: Harper & Row, 1979.

Frank, Justin A., M.D. **Bush on the Couch: Inside the Mind of the President.** New York: Free Press, 2011.

Gates, Robert M. **From the Shadows: The Ultimate Insider's Story of Five Presidents and How They Won the Cold War.** New York: Simon & Schuster, 2011.

————. **Duty: Memories of a Secretary at War.** New York: Knopf, 2014.

Gelman, Barton. **Angler: The Cheney Vice Presidency.** New York: Penguin, 2009.

Gergen, David. **Eyewitness to Power: The Essence of Leadership Nixon to Clinton.** New York: Simon & Schuster, 2001.

Ghattas, Kim. **The Secretary: A Journey with Hillary Clinton from Beirut to the Heart of American Power.** New York: Times, 2013.

Gibbs, Nancy and Michael Duffy. **The Presidents Club: Inside the World's Most Exclusive Fraternity.** New York: Simon & Schuster, 2012.

Glad, Betty. **An Outsider in the White House: Jimmy Carter, His Advisors, and the Making of American Foreign Policy.** Ithaca: Cornell University, 2009.

Goodwin, Richard N. **Remembering America: A Voice from the Sixties.** New York: Open Road Media, 2014.

BIBLIOGRAPHY

Greene, John Robert. **The Presidency of Gerald R. Ford**. Kansas: University Press of Kansas, 1995.

Haig, Alexander M., Jr. **Caveat: Realism, Reagan, and Foreign Policy**. New York: Scribner, 1984.

Haig, Alexander M., Jr. with Charles McCarry. **Inner Circles: How America Changed the World**. New York: Warner Books, 1992.

Haldeman, H. R. **The Haldeman Diaries: Inside the Nixon White House**. New York: Berkley Books, 1995.

Haldeman, H. R. with Joseph DiMona. **The Ends of Power**. New York: Dell, 1978.

Hartmann, Robert T. **Palace Politics: An Inside Account of the Ford Years**. New York: McGraw-Hill, 1980.

Harwood, John and Gerald F. Seib. **Pennsylvania Avenue: Profiles in Backroom Power**. New York: Random House, 2009.

Hayden, Michael. **Playing to the Edge: American Intelligence in the Age of Terror**. New York: Penguin, 2016.

Hayes, Stephen F. **Cheney: The Untold Story of America's Most Powerful and Controversial Vice President**. New York: HarperCollins, 2007.

———. **The Age of Reagan: The Conservative Counterrevolution 1980–1989**. New York: Crown Forum, 2009.

Heilemann, John and Mark Halperin. **Game Change: Obama and the Clintons, McCain and Palin,** and the Race of a Lifetime. New York: Harper-Collins, 2010.

Hersey, John. The President. New York: Knopf, 1975.

Hersh, Seymour M. Chain of Command: The Road from 9/11 to Abu Ghraib. New York: Harper, 2004.

Hess, Stephen. Organizing the Presidency. Washington, D.C.: Brookings Institution Press, 2012.

Holbrooke, Richard. To End a War. New York: Modern Library, 2011.

Isikoff, Michael. Uncovering Clinton: A Reporter's Story. New York: Three Rivers Press, 2011.

Johnson, Richard Tanner. Managing the White House: An Intimate Study of the Presidency. New York: Harper & Row, 1975.

Jordan, Hamilton. No Such Thing as a Bad Day: A Memoir. New York: Pocket, 2000.

————. A Boy from Georgia: Coming of Age in the Segregated South. Athens: University of Georgia Press, 2015.

Kantor, Jodi. The Obamas. New York: Little, Brown and Company, 2012.

Kaplan, Fred. The Insurgents: David Petraeus and the Plot to Change the American Way of War. New York: Simon & Schuster, 2013.

Kaufman, Scott. Rosalynn Carter: Equal Partner in the White House. Kansas: University Press of Kansas, 2007.

Kengor, Paul. The Crusader: Ronald Reagan and the

Fall of Communism. New York: Harper Perennial, 2007.

Kernell, Samuel and Samuel L. Popkin, eds. **Chief of Staff: Twenty-Five Years of Managing the Presidency.** Oakland: University of California Press, 1986.

Kessler, Glenn. **The Confidante: Condoleezza Rice and the Creation of the Bush Legacy.** New York: St. Martin's Press, 2007.

Kessler, Ronald. **A Matter of Character: Inside the White House of George W. Bush.** New York: Sentinel, 2004.

Klein, Edward. **The Amateur: Barack Obama in the White House.** Washington, D.C.: Regnery, 2012.

Klein, Joe. **The Natural: The Misunderstood Presidency of Bill Clinton.** New York: Doubleday, 2002.

Koch, Doro Bush. **My Father, My President: A Personal Account of the Life of George H. W. Bush.** New York: Grand Central, 2006.

Kutler, Stanley L. **Abuse of Power: The New Nixon Tapes.** New York: The Free Press, 1997.

Lewis, Charles. **935 Lies: The Future of Truth and the Decline of America's Moral Integrity.** New York: PublicAffairs, 2014.

Magruder, Jeb. **An American Life: One Man's Road to Watergate.** New York: Atheneum, 1974.

Mann, James. **The Rebellion of Ronald Reagan: A History of the End of the Cold War.** New York: Penguin, 2009.

————. **The Obamians: The Struggle Inside the White House to Redefine American Power.** New York: Penguin, 2012.

Mattson, Kevin. **"What the Heck Are You Up To, Mr. President?": Jimmy Carter, America's "Malaise," and the Speech That Should Have Changed the Country.** New York: Bloomsbury, 2009.

Mayer, Jane. **The Dark Side: The Inside Story of How the War on Terror Turned into a War on American Ideals.** New York: Anchor, 2009.

McClellan, Scott. **What Happened: Inside the Bush White House and Washington's Culture of Deception.** New York: PublicAffairs, 2009.

McCullough, David. **Truman.** New York: Simon & Schuster, 2003.

McGinniss, Joe. **The Selling of the President 1968.** San Francisco: Byliner, 2012.

Meacham, Jon. **Destiny and Power: The American Odyssey of George Herbert Walker Bush.** New York: Random House, 2015.

Medved, Michael. **The Shadow Presidents: The Secret History of the Chief Executives and Their Top Aides.** New York: Times Books, 1979.

Meese, Edwin III. **With Reagan: The Inside Story.** Washington, D.C., Regnery Gateway, 1992.

Mollenhoff, Clark R. **The President Who Failed: Carter Out of Control.** New York: Free Press, 1980.

Mondale, Walter with David Hage. **The Good Fight:**

A Life in Liberal Politics. New York: Scribner, 2010.

Morell, Michael. **The Great War of Our Time: The C.I.A.'s Fight Against Terrorism—from Al Qa'ida to ISIS**. New York: Twelve, 2015.

Morris, Dick. **Behind the Oval Office: Getting Re-elected Against All Odds**. New York: Renaissance, 1998.

Morris, Dick and Eileen McGann. **Because He Could**. New York: Harper, 2004.

Morris, Edmund. **Dutch: A Memoir of Ronald Reagan**. New York: Modern Library, 2011.

Mudd, Roger. **The Place to Be: Washington, CBS, and the Glory Days of Television News**. New York: PublicAffairs, 2009.

National Commission on Terrorist Attacks Upon the United States. **The 9/11 Commission Report: Final Report of the National Commission on Terrorist Attacks upon the United States (Authorized Edition)**. New York: W. W. Norton & Company, 2004.

Nessen, Ron. **It Sure Looks Different from the Inside**. New York: Simon & Schuster, 1978.

Newton, Jim. **Eisenhower: The White House Years**. New York: Anchor, 2011.

Nixon, Richard. **RN: The Memoirs of Richard Nixon**. New York: Touchstone, 1978.

Noonan, Peggy. **What I Saw at the Revolution: A Political Life in the Reagan Era**. New York: Random House, 1990.

————. **The Time of Our Lives.** New York: Twelve, 2015.

Nye, Joseph S., Jr. **Presidential Leadership and the Creation of the American Era.** Princeton: Princeton University Press, 2013.

Obama, Barack. **The Audacity of Hope: Thoughts on Reclaiming the American Dream.** New York: Crown, 2006.

————. **Dreams from My Father: A Story of Race and Inheritance.** New York: Broadway, 2007.

O'Neill, Thomas P. and William Novak. **Man of the House: The Life and Political Memoirs of Speaker Tip O'Neill.** New York: Random House, 1987.

O'Reilly, Bill and Martin Dugard. **Killing Reagan: The Violent Assault That Changed a Presidency.** New York: Henry Holt & Company, 2015.

Panetta, Leon and Jim Newton. **Worthy Fights: A Memoir of Leadership in War & Peace.** New York: Penguin, 2014.

Perlstein, Rick. **Nixonland: The Rise of a President and the Fracturing of America.** New York: Scribner, 2008.

————. **The Invisible Bridge: The Fall of Nixon and the Rise of Reagan.** New York: Simon & Schuster, 2014.

Plame, Valerie. **Fair Game: My Life as a Spy, My Betrayal by the White House.** New York: Simon & Schuster, 2007.

Podesta, John. **The Power of Progress: How America's Progressives Can (Once Again) Save Our Economy, Our Climate, and Our Country. New York: Crown, 2008.

Popadiuk, Roman. **The Leadership of George Bush: An Insider's View of the Forty-First President.** College Station, Texas: A&M University Press, 2009.

Powell, Colin with Joseph E. Persico. **My American Journey.** New York: Ballantine, 2010.

Powell, Colin with Tony Koltz. **It Worked for Me: In Life and Leadership.** New York: Harper Perennial, 2014.

Powell, Jody. **The Other Side of the Story: Why the News Is Often Wrong, Unsupportable and Unfair—an Insider's View by a Former Press Secretary.** New York: William Morrow & Co., 1984.

Prados, John, ed. **The White House Tapes: Eavesdropping on the President.** New York: New Press, 2003.

Quigley, Joan. **"What Does Joan Say?": My Seven Years as White House Astrologer to Nancy and Ronald Reagan.** New York: Birch Lane Press, 1990.

Rather, Dan. **Rather Outspoken: My Life in the News.** New York: Grand Central, 2012.

Reagan, Nancy with William Novak. **My Turn: The Memoirs of Nancy Reagan.** New York: Random House, 1989.

Reagan, Ron. **My Father at 100: A Memoir.** New York: Plume, 2011.

Reagan, Ronald. **An American Life**. New York: Threshold, 2011.

Reeves, Richard: **President Nixon: Alone in the White House**. New York: Simon & Schuster, 2001.

Regan, Donald T. **For the Record: From Wall Street to Washington**. New York: Harcourt Brace Jovanovich, 1988.

Reich, Robert R. **Locked in the Cabinet**. New York: Random House, 1997.

Remnick, David. **The Bridge: The Life and Rise of Barack Obama**. New York: Vintage, 2010.

Rice, Condoleezza. **No Higher Honor: My Memoir of My Years in Washington**. New York: Broadway Books, 2011.

Risen, James. **State of War: The Secret History of the C.I.A. and the Bush Administration**. New York: Free Press, 2006.

————. **Pay Any Price: Greed, Power and Endless War**. New York: Mariner, 2014.

Rodman, Peter W. **Presidential Command: Power, Leadership, and the Making of Foreign Policy from Richard Nixon to George W. Bush**. New York: Knopf, 1994.

Rollins, Ed with Tom DeFrank. **Bare Knuckles and Back Rooms: My Life in American Politics**. New York: Broadway, 1996.

Rosen, James. **Cheney One on One: A Candid Conversation with America's Most Controversial Statesman**. Washington, D.C.: Regnery, 2015.

Rove, Karl. **Courage and Consequence: My Life as a Conservative in the Fight.** New York: Threshold Editions, 2010.

Rowan, Roy. **The Four Days of Mayaguez.** New York: W. W. Norton & Company, 1975.

Rumsfeld, Donald. **Known and Unknown: A Memoir.** New York: Sentinel, 2011.

———. **Rumsfeld's Rules: Leadership Lessons in Business, Politics, War, and Life.** New York: Broadside, 2013.

Safire, William. **Before the Fall: An Inside View of the Pre-Watergate White House.** New York: Doubleday, 1975.

Savage, Charlie. **Power Wars: Inside Obama's Post-9/11 Presidency.** New York: Little, Brown and Company, 2015.

Scheiber, Noam. **The Escape Artists: How Obama's Team Fumbled the Recovery.** New York: Simon & Schuster, 2012.

Schieffer, Bob. **This Just In: What I Couldn't Tell You on TV.** New York: Berkley, 2003.

Sick, Gary. **October Surprise: America's Hostages in Iran and the Election of Ronald Reagan.** New York: I. B. Tauris & Co., 1991.

Smith, Jean Edward. **Eisenhower: In War and Peace.** New York: Random House, 2012.

———. **Bush.** New York: Simon & Schuster, 2016.

Smith, Richard Norton. **On His Own Terms: A Life of Nelson Rockefeller.** New York: Random House, 2014.

Sparrow, Bartholomew. **The Strategist: Brent Scowcroft and the Call of National Security**. New York: PublicAffairs, 2015.

Speakes, Larry. **Speaking Out: Inside the Reagan White House**. New York: Scribner, 1988.

Stahl, Lesley. **Reporting Live**. New York: Simon & Schuster, 1999.

Stephanopoulos, George. **All Too Human: A Political Education**. New York: Back Bay, 2000.

Stockman, David A. **The Triumph of Politics: The Inside Story of the Reagan Revolution**. New York: PublicAffairs, 2013.

Sullivan, Terry, ed. **The Nerve Center: Lessons in Governing from the White House Chiefs of Staff**. College Station: Texas A&M University Press, 2004.

Suskind, Ron. **The Price of Loyalty: George W. Bush, the White House, and the Education of Paul O'Neill**. New York: Simon & Schuster, 2004.

———. **Confidence Men: Wall Street, Washington, and the Education of a President**. New York: HarperCollins, 2011.

Tenet, George with Bill Harlow. **At the Center of the Storm: My Years at the CIA**. New York: Harper Perennial, 2007.

terHorst, J. F. **Gerald Ford and the Future of the Presidency**. New York, W. H. Allen, 1975.

Thomas, Evan. **Being Nixon: A Man Divided**. New York: Random House, 2015.

Todd, Chuck. **The Stranger: Barack Obama in the White House.** New York, Little, Brown and Company, 2014.

Toobin, Jeffrey. **The Oath: The Obama White House and the Supreme Court.** New York: Anchor, 2012.

Vance, Cyrus. **Hard Choices: Critical Years in America's Foreign Policy.** New York: Simon & Schuster, 1983.

Warrick, Joby. **Black Flags: The Rise of ISIS.** New York: Anchor, 2015.

The White House Transcripts: The Full Text of the Submission of Recorded Presidential Conversations to the Committee on the Judiciary of the House of Representatives by President Richard Nixon. New York: Bantam, 1974.

Wilber, Del Quintin. **Rawhide Down: The Near Assassination of Ronald Reagan.** New York: Henry Holt and Co., 2011.

Williams, Marjorie. **Reputation: Portraits in Power.** New York: PublicAffairs, 2009.

Wolffe, Richard. **Revival: The Struggle for Survival Inside the Obama White House.** New York: Broadway, 2010.

Woodward, Bob. **The Agenda: Inside the Clinton White House.** New York: Simon & Schuster, 1994.

———. **Plan of Attack.** New York: Simon & Schuster, 2004.

———. **The War Within: A Secret White House History 2006–2008**. New York: Simon & Schuster, 2008.

———. **Obama's Wars**. New York: Simon & Schuster, 2010.

———. **The Price of Politics**. New York: Simon & Schuster, 2012.

———. **The Last of the President's Men**. New York: Simon & Schuster, 2015.

Woodward, Bob and Carl Bernstein. **All the President's Men**. New York: Simon & Schuster, 2007.

———. **The Final Days**. New York: Simon & Schuster, 2013.

Author's Note and Acknowledgments

The journey that led to this book began more than six years ago, with a phone call out of the blue from a stranger. Jules Naudet, the brilliant filmmaker who, with his equally talented brother Gedeon, made the iconic documentary **9/11**, wanted to know if I would partner with them on their next film. The result was **The Presidents' Gatekeepers**, a four-hour documentary on the White House chiefs of staff, which aired on the Discovery Channel in September 2013. It was the beginning of a beautiful friendship, and a splendid collaboration (our most recent film, **The Spymasters: CIA in the Crosshairs**, aired on Showtime). Along the way, David Hume Kennerly, the Pulitzer Prize–

winning former White House photographer, also became a filmmaking partner and friend.

The interviews I conducted for **The Presidents' Gatekeepers** were the springboard for this book. But those interviews were just the beginning of the journey—spanning five years, and five decades of presidential history—an effort to understand the men who have been the presidents' closest confidants and have helped them shape the world. My goals were to frame modern presidential history through the eyes of the chiefs of staff and to make their stories as intimate and granular as I could.

I went back to most of the chiefs for in-depth interviews, often for multiple sessions. I interviewed two presidents, Jimmy Carter and George H. W. Bush (twice), four secretaries of state, and many of their colleagues and deputies. General Colin Powell kindly sat with me for two revealing interviews; Brent Scowcroft was wise and honest about the chiefs he has known and observed. Stuart Spencer, the veteran Republican campaign maestro, was an invaluable source, and a terrific storyteller. Robert Reich, my favorite teaching assistant when I was a Yale undergraduate (he was Bill and Hillary Clinton's Yale Law School classmate), gave me a crash course on Clinton's chiefs of staff. Thanks to **The Spymasters**, I was able to draw on interviews I had done recently with every living CIA director, from George H. W. Bush to John Brennan.

For a project this ambitious, I needed a writer's

equivalent of a chief of staff; I found one in Caroline Borge Keenan. A former ABC News friend and colleague, Caroline not only fact-checked the manuscript, she also was a brilliant collaborator, honest broker, and speaker of truth to power. John Sugden was a marvelous researcher in the early stages of the book and contributed insightful original reporting on the Iran-Contra affair. Nick Kachiroubas shared his excellent doctoral dissertation on the chiefs and helped track down Carter's staffers. Carolyn Lipka, a Yale undergraduate when this all began, also contributed research.

My good friend and literary agent Lisa Queen had the temerity to believe that I could make the leap from writing for the screen to writing for the page. I am grateful for her confidence. David Chidekel, our entertainment attorney, deftly negotiated our film deals. Judy Twersky and Sarah Breivogel are the best publicists anybody could ask for. Chatwalee Phoungbut is the gifted graphic designer who built my website chriswhipple.net.

At the Discovery Channel, David Zaslav, Eileen O'Neill, Nancy Daniels, and the talented team at Peacock Productions made our documentary **The Presidents' Gatekeepers** possible. Igor Kropotov was our skilled cinematographer.

At Crown, I went through editors the way Obama churned through chiefs of staff: I had four of them, each brilliant in his or her own way. Rick Horgan was enthusiastic and encouraging from the outset.

AUTHOR'S NOTE AND ACKNOWLEDGMENTS

Zack Wagman was a fellow political junkie. And then there were the editors who brought the book to fruition: Domenica Alioto and Emma Berry. No first-time author has ever had better editors: smart, savvy, patient—and kind. Cliché or not, this book would not exist without them. Thanks also to Claire Potter and Courtney Snyder for their support.

Few authors have had help from a more talented group of journalists and writers. Peter Baker, author of the brilliant **Days of Fire: Bush and Cheney in the White House**, shared his expertise and encouragement; how he found time for that while taking command of the Jerusalem bureau of the **New York Times** is beyond me. Jonathan Alter, who wrote the excellent Obama biographies **The Promise: President Obama, Year One** and **The Center Holds: Obama and His Enemies**, helped steer me to sources and gave me great notes on chapters-in-progress. Evan Thomas, author of the terrific **Being Nixon**, read my Haldeman chapter. Thomas Powers, Jonathan Larsen, and Lynn Langway all read portions of the book and were kind in their assessments. Anne Fadiman, my friend from the old monthly **LIFE**, made me believe I could do this. Susan Zirinsky, the CBS News legend (and my friend and partner on **The Spymasters**), shared her amazing knowledge of the chiefs and cheered me on. Greg Zorthian, my college roommate, gave terrific notes. My sister, Ann

Marr, read the manuscript from start to finish and gave brilliant editorial suggestions, and support. David Sleeper, my first editor when we were undergrads at Yale's **New Journal**, offered encouragement every step of the way.

Tom Brokaw, Bob Schieffer, Sam Donaldson, Dan Rather, Lesley Stahl, and Bill Plante shared their unrivaled expertise on the White House chiefs from Haldeman to McDonough.

Talking to the chiefs gave me a view from thirty thousand feet; to get a look from the ground up, I sought out many of the chiefs' colleagues and staffers. Jean Becker, George H. W. Bush's chief of staff, Sandy Hatcher, James A. Baker III's executive assistant, and Remley Johnson, Donald Rumsfeld's assistant, were incredibly helpful. A few sources chose to remain anonymous, but many shared their insights on the record: Stephen Bull, John Dean, Larry Higby, and Terry O'Donnell educated me about Nixon's H. R. Haldeman; David Kennerly and Ron Nessen told terrific stories about Ford's Donald Rumsfeld and Dick Cheney; Jay Beck, Landon Butler, Stuart Eizenstat, Alan Novak, and David Rubenstein were fascinating on Carter's Hamilton Jordan and Jack Watson; Margaret Tutwiler and Craig Fuller helped me understand Reagan's James Baker; Tim McBride shared his thoughts on Bush 41's John Sununu; Mary Matalin gave me an insider's view of Bush 43's Andy Card; and Jon Favreau, Peter Orszag, and Norm

Eisen were brilliant on Obama's Rahm Emanuel, Bill Daley, Jack Lew, and Denis McDonough.

The historian Richard Norton Smith gave me a tutorial on the evolution of the White House chief's role. I pored through the chiefs' memoranda in the presidential libraries, their personal papers in university archives, and oral histories, memoirs, and biographies of key players of their time.

But the heart of this book is the collection of extended conversations I had with the chiefs themselves. They are fierce partisans but bonded by the shared experience of having endured the toughest job in Washington. Donald Rumsfeld generously sat with me for multiple interviews and gave me exclusive access to previously unpublished memos he dictated after meetings with Gerald Ford. Dick Cheney fondly recalled his days as Ford's thirty-five-year-old chief of staff, when he was "young enough and foolish enough" to think he could run the White House. We also talked about his experience a quarter century later as George W. Bush's powerful vice president. Cheney spent hours with me—at his home in McLean, Virginia, and his house in Jackson Hole, Wyoming. (We did one four-hour session just a few days before he underwent his heart transplant.)

Jimmy Carter's final chief, Jack Watson, generously shared his time and wisdom; his enthusiasm for public service, and for life, is infectious. James A. Baker III gave me a master class on how the chief of staff should operate and shared his insights into Ronald Reagan. He also regaled me with the Gipper's jokes. Howard H. Baker Jr., Reagan's third chief, participated despite his failing health; he gave me a remarkably insightful interview two years before his death in 2014. Nobody knows the history of the job, or its subtleties, better than Reagan's final chief, Ken Duberstein. A gifted storyteller, Duberstein not only taught me that the chief is the president's "reality therapist," he also helped me with important sources, and even suggested the introduction.

George H. W. Bush's John Sununu was quick-witted and entertaining—even when he was denouncing our film for failing, in his view, to make enough of George H. W. Bush's Gulf War leadership. (I look forward to more frank exchanges with Bush 41's controversial former chief.) Samuel Skinner was thoughtful and candid about the challenges he faced as Sununu's successor during a difficult period of the Bush presidency.

Thomas F. "Mack" McLarty, Bill Clinton's first chief, may be the most decent man in Washington: smart, charming—and refreshingly honest about how difficult it was to keep the forty-second president on track. Leon Panetta, who succeeded McLarty, was eloquent about the job's requirements—and blunt in his assessments of his successors. Erskine Bowles is an interviewer's delight: articulate, humorous—and candid: as when he told Barack Obama, in a room full of his home-town pals, "Leave your Chicago friends at home." Clinton's final chief, John Podesta, was wise, insightful, and generous with his time; even at the height of Hillary Clinton's presidential campaign, he gave me a lengthy interview at his Brooklyn office in the fall of 2016.

Andy Card, George Bush's long-serving chief, may be the most humble and dedicated public servant I have ever met. He was extraordinarily helpful and great company. Josh Bolten, Card's successor, has a keen appreciation of White House history and a wry sense of humor; he was fascinating on how he coped with the financial crisis of 2008.

Rahm Emanuel brought his colorful vocabulary, and energy: At our first sit-down, he gave "a three-hour interview in an hour and a half," as my partner David Kennerly observed. Emanuel also shared the notes he saved from the day thirteen former chiefs gathered at the White House to give him advice. Emanuel's successor, Bill Daley, was candid about his tough year as Obama's second chief and about their failure to reach a grand bargain. Obama's third chief, Jack Lew, was gracious and articulate about his brief tenure. Finally, Denis McDonough, Obama's last chief, kindly agreed to sit with me for a memorable and insightful interview on the patio outside his West Wing office in October 2016.

In my career as a journalist, I have had extraordinary teachers, mentors, and colleagues: Bryce Lambert, Roy Rowan, Bill Zinsser, Tom Powers, David B. Davis, John Morton Blum, Paul Trachtman, Bruce McIntosh, Jonathan Larsen, Philip Kunhardt, Dick Stolley, Judy Daniels, Loudon Wainwright, Jeff Wheelwright, John Neary, Jed Horne, Steve Robinson, Ed Barnes, Cheryl McCall, John Loengard, Bobbi Baker Burrows, Ann Morrell, Grey Villet, David Turnley, Eugene Richards, Michael O'Brien, Heinz Kluetmeier, Harald Sund, Ross Baughman, David Burnett, Don Hewitt, Mike Wallace, Ed Bradley, Steve Kroft, George Crile, Chuck Lewis, Rich Bonin, Josh Howard, Dave Rummel, Phil Scheffler, Rick Kaplan, Phyllis McGrady, Betsy West, Ira Rosen, Shelley Ross, David Tabacoff, Meredith White, Sylvia Chase, Jay Schadler, Cynthia McFadden, Nancy Collins, Chris Wallace, and John Quinones. Joe Hartman made me believe I could do anything when I grew up. Joe Duffey, whose thrilling 1970 Senate campaign was my first exposure to national politics (and who launched the careers of Bill Clinton, John Podesta, Gary Hart, and John Kerry), still inspires me over lunches at the Cosmos Club. My first boss at **Foreign Policy** magazine, Richard Holbrooke, became a lifelong friend and mentor. My great friend Harry Benson taught me how to get a story. Diane Sawyer taught me the art of the interview. Charlie Gibson showed me how to be a class act. Jeff Sagansky encouraged me, after decades at the networks, to go out on my own as an independent producer.

I was blessed with generous friends. David Friend, editor of creative development at **Vanity Fair**, recommended me to the Naudet brothers. Dick Swanson, the celebrated former **LIFE** photographer, shared his great pictorial archive; his beautiful wife, Germaine, the renowned Vietnamese chef and restaurateur, treated my wife, Cary, and me to glorious feasts at their home in Maryland. Jim Rosenthal vouched for me with his colleague Erskine Bowles. Milt Kass was my confidant on and off the tennis court. Daniel Fass introduced me to his Obamacare friends, and kept me laughing. Best friends Ward and Susan Pennebaker put me up in Houston when I came for interviews with Jim Baker and George H. W. Bush. When it was time to start writing, Trip McCrossin let us move into his beautiful place on Shelter Island. Donna, Jim, and Janet Caulkins offered unflagging encouragement, as did Verne and Lee Westerberg. Jennifer Whipple gave her constant support.

This book hasn't been easy on my family. My son, Sam Whipple, put up with a sleep-deprived, disheveled father and tiptoed around stacks of books piled to the rafters. Instead of complaining, he contributed his own original reporting; the story of Rahm Emanuel and the Asian carp came from his excellent interview with Austan Goolsbee. Sam will make a terrific chief of staff, speechwriter—or president—someday.

My wife, Cary Whipple, transcribed endless interviews; spent hours with me in musty presidential libraries from Atlanta to Yorba Linda; compiled endnotes; tracked down photographs of the chiefs—and did a thousand other things to make this book possible. More important, she gave me her love and support. She was, to use her favorite superlative, **ridiculous**. I love her more than ever.

Finally, this one's also for you, Dad.

If **The Gatekeepers** sheds any light on the role of the White House chief of staff in every presidency, the credit goes to the chiefs themselves. Any mistakes are on me. And of course, the conclusions are mine alone.

Index

INDEX

ABOUT THE AUTHOR

Chris Whipple is an acclaimed documentary film-maker, writer, journalist, and speaker. A multiple Peabody and Emmy Award–winning producer at CBS's **60 Minutes** and ABC's **Primetime**, he is the chief executive officer of CCWHIP Productions. Most recently, he was the executive producer and writer of Showtime's **The Spymasters: CIA in the Crosshairs.**